Mi≷
of the
Galactic Salesman

written by
Robert S. Sanders, Jr.

Illustrations by
Jason Daniel Fisher

color cover drawing by
Jason Daniel Fisher

Robert S. Sanders, Jr.

Edited by:
Becky Menn-Hamblin and Laurelyn Douglas

Front and rear cover illustrations by:
Jason Daniel Fisher

Design, typography, and text production:
TypeByte Graphix

Library of Congress Catalog Card Number: 96–84828

ISBN: 1-886371-35-0

Armstrong Valley Publishing Company
P.O. Box 1275
Murfreesboro, TN 37133
PHONE: 1-615-895-5445
FAX: 1-615-893-2688

Table of Contents

A Message From the Author

I began to write this novel MISSION OF THE GALACTIC SALESMAN in January 1995, and my purpose for writing it is to give the readers a sense of wonder about other planets and star systems throughout the galaxy and also about how important communication is. The origin of life has always been of interest to me, and I have presented several ideas and speculation about how some of it came to be on Earth.

This novel's main theme is not about wars or battles between different galactic races. There is already far too much of that on the shelves of bookstores. Mine is a wholesome novel about setting up communication with other star systems and what they have to offer us on that level. Also, I have written this novel to bring an awareness to the reader about other sentient lifeforms throughout the galaxy and on Earth as well.

Further, I have written this novel to present an example of true friendship. During my life so far, I have noticed that friendships are not always valued, and they are too easily tossed aside over small reasons or sometimes for no reason at all. Some of the characters in my novel are takeoffs of real people, and their names have been altered to protect their true identities. In real life, most of them are friends of mine, but not all. With two of them, through unfortunate circumstances, our friendships have come to an end. With some of the others, we have merely drifted apart, which, of course, is understandable, and I still consider them to be friends. I have always valued the friendships that I have, and I can only hope that others do also.

As we reach the end of the millennium, all of us need to realize that Earth's population is increasing at an accelerating and alarming rate to a, no doubt, crowded future. It is therefore becoming increasingly important to preserve as much of our national heritage as possible, namely the national forests and national parks. Unfortunately, many of our national forests have already been severely damaged by clear-cutting and exploitation. So far, our national parks have been entirely protected, but that may change in the future.

Our national forests and parks were set aside to be enjoyed, and all Americans deserve to have their national forests *and* their national parks in perfect, pristine condition. They are *not* to be mowed down, mined, and exploited. I urge every reader of my novel to take measures to preserve our national heritage before it may be too late. For some of our national forests, it already is. We have our future generations to consider.

Trees have the right to inhabit this Earth in the form of old-growth forests. Out of my respect for the forests and trees of Earth and elsewhere, I have decided to capitalize the names of all trees referred to throughout my story.

Introduction
& Character Sketch

This story takes place in 1985 in Middle Tennessee and is mainly about a group of eight teenage fellows who are in their junior year in high school. They are all great friends of one another, are morally straight, open-minded, smart, enthusiastic, and interesting. All of them have a real quest for adventure, exploration, and travel.

The main character is Robert Joslin who lives on a farm southwest of Murfreesboro. The story opens in the winter with Robert and some of his friends sledding down the slopes of a nearby hill. Later, there is a visit to the high school where they attend. One March weekend they all meet on Robert's farm to camp out and make plans for a summer road trip and hiking adventure.

Robert has an amazing dream that night of being able to travel to other planets in other star systems, and when he wakes up, he realizes that he has retained this ability in real life. He is able to pass this ability on to his friends, and they alter their plans and have a great summer adventure travelling to and from places on Earth and other planets. They learn many things about the galaxy and about life on other planets and also learn about some of the past history of Earth and how it came to be. Through their experiences, they come to realize that they know many things that few, if any people on Earth know.

Robert has lived on his parents' farm all of his life, and his father, Bob, is a full-time farmer of crops and cattle along with being a part-time lobbyist. His mother, Pat, is a former school teacher. Robert has a keen interest in travelling and exploring, bicycling, plantlife, and the sciences. He grew up being a believer in conventional evolution of life on Earth and leaned toward believing only what there was convincing evidence for. However, his mind became more open to new ideas, and he's always listened to what others have to say. During their adventures, he and his friends learn a lot and alter their belief systems accordingly.

Chris Chanford is interested in philosophy and lives in the south part of Murfreesboro. He and Robert have known each other since 7th grade, and he sometimes helps the others in understanding the philosophies and differences in the foreign cultures of the civilizations that they visit.

Morris England is a very intuitive person, to say the least, even though he doesn't like to call himself psychic, and he lives a few miles east of

Murfreesboro. He is able to sense many answers and explanations from the spirit world, both in dreams and in real life. Through his intuitive abilities, he carries a great deal of knowledge about Earth and other star systems. Like Chris, he understands and explains the philosophies about the reasons that people and things are the way that they are.

On the same night that Robert has his dream, Morris also has a dream in which he meets Tom, who is both a galactic salesman and a communications engineer from the planet around Sirius B in the Sirius binary star system. Tom informs Morris that the Sirians have lost contact with their fellow Sirians now residing on Earth as human beings and proposes his mission to have Robert and his friends build a galactic communications device to link Earth's telephone network to them and also to other star systems. In the dream, he makes a deal with Morris. Can Tom fulfill his mission and re-establish contact with their fellow Earth-incarnated Sirians?

William Johns is a friend and distant cousin of Robert, and he lives near Rockvale, which is five miles from Robert's place. He has an interest in old cars and, like Robert, is a firm believer in only the basics when it comes to cars. He is the primary helper on Robert's car project at the beginning of the story.

William's father works for the phone company and knows a lot about telephone equipment. He is very essential in helping them build the required switching equipment for use in the galactic communications device and is able to obtain surplus central office equipment for that purpose.

Steven Price is a good friend of Robert's, having known him since middle school, and he has lived in the southeast of Murfreesboro all of his life. His parents are teachers. Steven also has an interest in old cars but is more interested in auto body than mechanics, and he owns an immaculate 6-cylinder 3-speed Chevrolet Bel Air. In addition to his interest in cars, he also loves to tinker with electronic circuitry and proves very useful in modifying some of the electronic components used in the galactic communications device that they build.

Steven at first hesitates about travelling and having adventures, but soon comes to love it as he has a taste of it. As a result of his participation in their adventures and also in the construction of the galactic communications device, he comes to realize how important communication is and how it far exceeds and surpasses useless weaponry and war.

Andrew Tremain moved into Tennessee in 1979. His parents are missionaries, and as a result of that, he has lived in other parts of the world. Andrew lives in Murfreesboro and is very knowledgeable on the transmission and reception of communications equipment. He is always interested in what is happening and has some helpful suggestions in the method of construction of the sending-receiving towers that are built in conjunction with the galactic communications device.

James Westfield is new to Tennessee, having moved from Devonport,

Tasmania, Australia in December 1984. His father is a builder and is as strong as an ox, and they live on a farm around six miles east of Robert's place. They quickly become great friends since both of them have a real interest in plantlife and travel. James is very straightforward or concrete as far as not believing in anything psychic or paranormal. In addition to passing on his knowledge of Australian plantlife to the others, he has a burning desire to travel and experiences enough surprises during their adventures to really astound him.

Paul Wilson is an old-time friend of Robert's, having known him since early childhood. He has lived near Murfreesboro all of his life, and his father runs an aluminum fabrication plant making mostly utility boxes. Paul has a keen sense of business and is musically talented and enjoys the outdoor adventures of their summer travels.

Greg Nelson and Eric Smotherman are two more friends who do not participate in the whole adventure because of their busy schedules. Greg eventually wants to be a dentist, and Eric wants to work in the pottery business, which is what his father does. Both of them live in Murfreesboro.

There are additional characters.

Mr. Gordon Mayfield is their high school science teacher, and he is interested in extraterrestrial life. His discussions in class contribute somewhat to Robert's having his amazing dream.

Mr. Michael Vance is their American history professor and causes the class to have original thoughts and to speculate and give their opinions on certain events and alternative scenarios.

Read through the adventures of Robert and his friends as they help fulfill Tom's mission, travel to many places, including other star systems, and meet alien lifeforms, both male and female.

Other characters are described as they are brought up throughout the story. At the end of the book in the Appendix is a technical description of the main characters.

1 The Meeting of the Sirian Council

It was late January 1985, and this winter had been severe. Nearly a foot of snow lay on the ground, and it had accumulated from two recent snowfalls. Robert Joslin and two friends of his were having fun in the snow, sledding down the open slopes of the Pinnacle of the Versailles Hills, which were 15 miles southwest of Murfreesboro, Tennessee. Most of the hills in the area were forested, but the Pinnacle was mostly bald, with its summit being one of the highest points in the county at over 1,200 feet. The summit afforded some excellent views of the surrounding fields and countryside. Murfreesboro could be seen in the distance.

William Johns and Morris England had just sledded to the bottom of the slope and were walking back up. Robert was waiting at the top for them, and they reached him after a couple of minutes of climbing.

"Let's all three sled down at the same time," Robert suggested, "and see which one of us goes the fastest and the furthest."

"All right," said William.

Morris went along with it, and they took their positions.

"Ready? Set? Go!" shouted Robert.

All three of them leaped on their sleds and took off down the hill, engulfed in a spray of powdered snow as they went. Morris went the furthest with Robert and William not far behind. They dismounted their sleds and began walking up to the top again.

"Whew-wee!" shouted William. "This is great fun sledding up here!"

"Yeah, I do like it up here," said Morris.

"This is the best sledding I've ever seen," said Robert.

"Thank goodness it's warmer than last week," said Morris.

"I'm telling you what," William declared, "last week was about the coldest weather I believe I've ever seen!"

"I hope it *never* gets that cold again," Robert added.

"Me neither," said Morris. "I'd say that all of our outdoor shrubs got killed last week."

"I don't doubt it," said William.

"At least that cold's behind us," assured Robert. "February is soon to come, and it's always warmer than January."

By this time, they had reached the top again. Down they went again, racing each other to see who could go the fastest and furthest. This time, Robert pushed barely ahead of the other two. Again, they dismounted their sleds and returned to the top of the slope.

"What do you say we walk on up to the summit," offered Robert, "and see the view of the countryside covered in snow."

Morris and William agreed, and they continued up the steep hillside which proved to be difficult to climb due to the snow.

"Robert," William asked, "did you say you just purchased a Ford LTD wagon?"

"Yes, I just bought it last week. It's a white 1979 Ford LTD full-size station wagon."

"Are you going to do some work on it?" William wanted to know.

"Yes, I'm going to make it a basic workhorse of a car and put a 6-cylinder manual in the place of the V-8 automatic," Robert answered.

"Boy, that's going to be a *job*!" exclaimed William. "Would you like some help with it?"

"Yeah, I sure would," said Robert. "Thanks for offering. Once all of this ice melts, I'll give you a call, and we can start on it."

"Okay, that sounds good," William agreed.

The three of them were now near the summit. It was an overcast day, and the views of the nearly pure white landscape stretching to the horizon were just incredible. They reached the summit which had a small survey marker in the form of a small concrete pillar.

"This is my first time up here with snow on the ground," Robert announced. "The surrounding countryside really looks different, doesn't it?"

"Almost enchanted," said Morris.

"This blanket of snow really makes it seem quiet," said William.

"Yes, I agree," said Robert. "Look at all of those snow-covered fields stretching to the horizon way off in the distance."

At this moment, Morris began to feel something a little strange.

"Robert, William," Morris announced. "Some strange thoughts are going through my head."

"Tell us, Morris, what is it?" Robert wanted to know.

Robert and William stood perfectly still and silent in the cold air so as not to disturb Morris' thoughts.

"I'm not really sure what it is, but it's strange. I get the feeling that a group of people in another star system are meeting at this moment to have a discussion about the people of Earth. It seems they need around 10 people to help them on a project of some sort, and they're not giving any details. It's something about that they've lost contact with some of their people on Earth, and they need some help. Yes, they need 10 people. I'm sure of that. There's something about travel by thought, whatever that means. It's fading. I'm losing it. It's gone now."

"What was all that about?" Robert asked.

"How do you do that?" William added.

"You know how your ear sort of rings at times?" said Morris.

"Yes," Robert answered.

"Well, it's sort of like that," Morris went on, "except that a faint voice comes through, and I can listen to it. Just as the ringing in the ear fades after a minute or so, so does this voice."

"Where do you think they were?" William asked.

"It was another star system. I'm sure of that much."

"Could you see anything?" Robert asked.

"No, I only heard it, and faintly at that," Morris answered. "I suppose being on this summit made it easier for me to receive that message. Plus, the snow on the ground makes it quiet."

"Do you think you have mental telepathy?" William wanted to know.

"Yes, I suppose that's what it could be," Morris answered. "It surprises me that hardly anyone else can hear things like I just heard."

"I know," said William. "I wish we all had that ability."

"Let's go on down and do some more sledding," said Robert. "I'm getting cold standing still up here."

"Okay," they said.

★ ★ ★

It was a warm, sunny day, and the Sirian Council of the planet around Sirius B had decided to have a meeting. Twelve members had gathered, and the meeting was outdoors in a grove of Tamarisk shrubs on this mostly dry planet of shrubs, cactus-like plants, and reddish-colored soil. Wasser, as his name would best be known in the English language, was the chief of the council members and opened the meeting. They communicated mostly by transmitting thoughts and visual images to and from one another and sometimes spoke in their native Sirian language.

"As you know," Wasser announced, "we 12 are gathered here to represent the 20 million human beings presently residing here on this planet around Sirius B. I'm sure you are aware of the reason for this meeting. It concerns our people who have gone on to be incarnated and born on planet Earth in the Sol System. Certainly, you already know that Earth is the third planet out from that star which they call the Sun.

"Our problem is that we have lost contact with the humans that we intended to communicate with on Earth, and that is because most Earthlings are not fully conscious human beings like we are here on Sirius B. There's a long story about the reason for that which we won't discuss today. Does anyone have any ideas on how we can re-establish contact with those now living on Earth who have gone to sleep on us?"

A council member, Tom, who was an engineer, decided to answer that question and spoke out:

"My theory is that since Earth humans are not fully conscious like we are here, most of them have lost the ability to use mental telepathy. To make up for that, ingenious as they still are, they now have the ability to communicate to and from nearly any location on Earth through the use of radio, tele-

phone, and television. Nearly every resident on Earth has a telephone, and I propose that we tap into their telephone network."

"That is an excellent idea, Tom," said Wasser, as he expressed his thoughts of approval. "Do you have any ideas on how we may be able to physically tap into these telephones?"

"Well," Tom explained, "all telephones are connected to and routed through one of the many local switching offices called exchanges, which work in conjunction with long distance switching offices that connect telephones across vast distances on Earth. I propose that we find some Earthlings who are willing and ask them to help us by building one of those exchanges. Afterwards, and I'll round up a crew for this, we could build the sending and receiving station using gravity waves to link us up to Earth."

"A splendid idea indeed!" Wasser remarked.

A woman, whose English name was Manta, spoke to Tom.

"Tom, I'm sure you're aware that for whatever group of Earthlings that you choose, you will need to offer them something of value so that it will be worth their while in helping you with your project."

"Oh yes, Manta, I'm fully aware of the sense of fairness that most Earthlings possess, and I fully agree with that philosophy. Presently, I'm in contact with a male who is 17 Earth years of age, and he lives in what the Earthlings call 'Tennessee.' I communicate with him when he dreams, and he can even receive messages by thought when he is in the waking state. He associates with several other people near his age, and they are all very intelligent. I believe they may be just the group of people we are looking for, especially since they have not yet settled down to the Earth customs of dating and marriage. Let's see. Do you have any ideas of what I could offer them?"

One of the younger members in the group, whose name was Caymar, spoke out:

"I believe a gift that would certainly make it worth their while would be to grant them the ability to transport themselves by thought."

"Why, *yes*, of course!" Tom exclaimed. "That would be an excellent trade-off."

"Also, Tom," Caymar continued, "you've been wanting for some time for someone on Earth to have that crystal ball of yours. Why don't you give it to one of the members in that group?"

"Yes, I believe I will," Tom answered, pleased with Caymar's suggestion. "In fact, I have already informed the male who is 17 about the crystal ball in a dream, only I told him that he would have to buy it later. I'll give it some thought and will see what I can do. Meanwhile, I'll round up a crew of engineers, and we'll draw up a proposal and present it for approval."

"That sounds like a very good plan, Tom," said Wasser. "Their ability to travel by thought would give them a chance to visit other worlds like this one. Plus, they would be able to see parts of Earth they otherwise would never see. With an offer from you like that, they will almost certainly help you on your project. Anyway, you give it some thought, as you told Caymar you would, and we'll hear back from you fairly soon with your proposal."

"Right. I will do everything possible to make it a success," Tom assured the council.

"Very fine, Tom," said Wasser. "Now, does anyone else have any ideas to bring up during this meeting?"

The meeting continued for some time as they discussed other ideas on Earth and ideas on other star systems as well. During the next month, Tom rounded up a crew of engineers, and they immediately went to work making plans and drawing up a proposal.

2 The Car Project

A month had passed, and it was a nice, warm sunny Saturday in late February. Robert Joslin and his friend and distant cousin, William Johns, had been working for several hours on Robert's 1979 white Ford LTD station wagon that he had purchased at the first of the year with, of course, the V-8 automatic that was in it. Since 1971, all full-size Fords were made with an automatic transmission, and all of them from 1979 to the present came with a V-8 engine, neither of which was Robert's preference.

So, since January, he had been converting it to a 6-cylinder manual, and William had come over several times to help him since he also had an interest in cars. Robert recently purchased a 6-cylinder 240 engine out of a 1969 Ford Econoline van and a 3-speed w/OD (4-speed) manual transmission out of a 1980 Ford F-100 pickup truck.

He had already successfully installed the engine and transmission, which was done with great difficulty and included the help of an expert welder friend on the other side of town who helped him fabricate the homemade motor mounts. There were additional complications that had been met and overcome along the way. Robert certainly was glad to have this difficult part of the project behind him. Fortunately, the bolt pattern for mounting the manual transmission matched the automatic one, so that step had been easy.

Today, Robert and William were figuring out how to mount the clutch and brake pedal assembly, which came out of a 1973 Ford Maverick. How were they going to mechanically connect the clutch pedal through linkages and shafts to the lever arm on the side of the bell housing?

"How in the world am I going to hang this clutch and brake pedal set to give it enough travel distance to disengage that clutch?" Robert asked William.

"It looks like to me you're going to have to reshape that firewall," suggested William. "I don't see how you're going to get anything by that brake power boost."

"Well, let's take it out," said Robert, "and I'll go with manual brakes. I prefer manual brakes anyway. After all, power brakes are too sensitive. Tell you what, go and fetch my sledge hammer out of the garage while I remove this junk." William went to fetch it and returned to the concrete pad where they were working just outside the yard.

"Thanks, William. I've got the booster off. Here, hold that sledge hammer against the firewall while I go inside and hit it with my hammer until I reshape it to the contour and angle I need." He started tapping and, in just a few minutes, reshaped it to where he wanted it. "Perfect!" Robert declared, feeling triumphant as he held the clutch and brake pedal assembly against the firewall to check for clearances and travel distances.

"William, I'm going to mark and drill the holes to mount this thing. I need a thick piece of sheet metal to reinforce this thin firewall. There are some pieces in the garage just this side of the metal cabinet. Could you fetch them?"

"Sure, I'll be right back."

William soon returned with some eighth-inch galvanized pieces, and Robert went to work cutting the metal to the proper size with his jigsaw. After drilling some holes, he placed the pieces on the firewall and successfully mounted the clutch and brake pedal. They continued working on his car until nearly dark.

"Well, it's getting dark," said William. "That's quite a project you have there. I'm hoping to do something similar to my old Chevrolet someday."

"Whenever you're ready to start, let me know. I'll be glad to help out," Robert offered.

"Okay, thanks."

"And thank you for your help too. Stay and have supper with us."

"Sure, I'll be glad to. I always like home-cooked meals. I'll just call my parents and tell them I'm staying a while longer."

"Great!" said Robert. "I really look forward to having this car on the road soon, and I'm really proud that this full-size Ford will have a 6-cylinder manual."

They walked inside, now that it was nearly dark.

Robert lived on a farm around 10 miles out of Murfreesboro, and William lived further out near Rockvale. While Robert lived close enough to be on the Murfreesboro telephone exchange, William was on the Eagle-ville-Rockvale exchange, which was not long distance.

As they walked inside the house, Robert called out, "Mother, William's going to stay for supper. He's going to call his parents and tell them."

"That's fine," she said.

William picked up the handset of the black Western Electric rotary dial desk phone to call his parents. After dialling the Eagleville number, the ringing could be heard over the line.

"click...pop...BBBBBB...BBBBBB...BBBBBB...Hello?"

"Hello, Dad?" -pause- "I'm going to stay over and eat supper at Robert's. I'll be home in a couple of hours." -pause- "Okay, thanks. Bye."

They sat down to supper. Robert's father, Bob, said, "Robert, that's a mighty big job you're doing on that LTD wagon of yours, but we have a bunch of fencerow cleaning that needs to be done before spring comes with poison ivy and bugs. You *are* going to do some of that, aren't you?"

"Oh, yes. Of course," Robert reassured him.

"Mighty fine, son. What are you planning to do this summer, possibly with your modified station wagon?"

"I'm not sure yet. I may go on a road trip out West or somewhere like that."

"Well, Robert, you're certainly welcome to take the summer off from here so long as you can complete the fencerow cleaning and do some barn siding repairs."

"Oh, yes. I'll have that done in plenty of time," declared Robert, quite sure of himself.

"That's good. I'm sure that you will too," his father said.

"William," Robert asked, "do you and some others want to go travel-ling with me this summer?"

"Yeah, sure! I'd be glad to. I really like hiking and travelling. How soon after school's out are you thinking of leaving?"

"Pretty much right away. Maybe a few days?"

"That soon? Great! Let's a bunch of us go for the whole summer. We'll have a great time!" exclaimed William in an excited manner.

"Yes, certainly! Who do you think we can invite to come with us?"

"Well, let's see. What about Steven Price?" William suggested. "You know that he likes to work on cars also."

"Yeah, that's true. He'd be a great companion to have with us! Since he knows so much about cars, he'd be another one who could help if my LTD wagon happens to break down."

"That's true," William agreed.

"Let's call him and see if he wants to join us." They got up from the table, having finished supper. "Thanks for supper, Mother and Daddy."

"You're welcome, son," they both said.

As Robert went to dial Steven's number, he said to William, "See if you can think of anyone else while I call Steven."

After dialling Steven's number, the ringing could be heard over the line.

"click...PRRRRRRR...PRRRRRRR...PRRRRRRR...Hello?"

"Steven?"

"Yes. Oh, hey Robert! How's it going?"

"Great! How are you?"

"Fine."

"Listen. William and I were wondering if you would like to join us on a road trip and hiking adventure this summer starting just a few days after school gets out?" Robert offered.

"Hmm . . . tempting. Yeah, that sounds inviting. I'd be glad to. Actually, that sounds fantastic!" Steven came around to exclaim.

"Great! We'll discuss the details later. I'll let you go for now."

"Okay thanks, Robert. I'll see you later."

"Okay, see you later."

"Bye."

Robert hung up and said, "So, William, who else do you think would like to join us?"

"Let's see. Your car's a nine-passenger station wagon, right?"

"Right. It is for now, until we put the stickshift on the floor," Robert added.

"And I guess we can pull a trailer behind us to hold our camping gear and backpacks since you don't have a luggage rack, right?"

"Right, we can."

"What about Chris Chanford, Greg Nelson, and Eric Smotherman?" William suggested.

"Those sound fine to me. I'm not sure if Greg and Eric will have the time, but I'm sure Chris will. Let me also check with Morris England, Andrew Tremain, James Westfield, and Paul Wilson."

"Isn't James that new guy from Australia?"

"Right," said Robert, "and let me tell you, he knows an incredible amount about trees in Australia."

"That's good. That's just like you isn't it?"

"Yes," Robert admitted. "As you probably know, he just came in December and is half a school year out of phase with us since the seasons are inverted in Australia. But he won't have to attend summer school. All he has to do is take a proficiency test, and then he will fit right in."

"That's good. Tell you what, I'll call Chris, Greg, and Eric, and you call Morris, Andrew, James, and Paul."

"Sounds good. Why don't I just call Morris now. I've got something to tell him, anyway."

Robert went over and dialled his number.

"click, buzz ^ buzz ^ buzz ^ buzz ^ buzz ^ buzz ^ buzz ^ buzz"

"The line's busy. William, do you want to call anyone from here or wait till you get home?"

"That's okay. I'll wait until I get home."

"All right."

"Well, I guess I better head home now. I've enjoyed working with you on that car."

"Me too," said Robert. "Thanks again for your help. When can you return?"

"I'd say next Saturday, March 2nd."

"Okay, great! I'll see you later."

William walked out, got into his car, and drove away.

The next day, Robert decided to clean fencerows for the morning and work on his car during the afternoon. He was connecting the clutch pedal to the engine through linkages, and he cut some more pieces of metal with pieces coming from thick pipe, flat bar stock, and fairly thick sheet metal. All of this was done using a hacksaw and a jigsaw. At times, careful measurements had to be made. After several more hours, he believed he had it all figured out and ready to take to his welder friend this coming week.

He called his four friends and found out that they all could take him up on his trip offer to go travelling and hiking this coming summer. This really pleased him that they would not have to work, and he looked forward to their adventures together.

The upcoming week at Riverdale High School would prove to be busy for everyone. Riverdale was built in 1971 on the southwest side of Murfreesboro, and it opened in the Fall of the following year. Its sister high school was Oakland High School, built at the same time on the northeast side of the town. Both schools were the same size and were identical twins. Riverdale was built on a low, round hill in the middle of a field near the Stones River, and a new road was built to access it from both Salem Pike and Shelbyville Pike. Riverdale's capacity was around 1,500 students, and it included grades 9 through 12. It was large, and all classrooms had at least six wonderful, transparent, clear glass windows in the outside walls to allow the natural light to come in and save on the cost of electric lighting.

Robert Joslin and his closest friends: Chris Chanford, Morris England, William Johns, Greg Nelson, Steven Price, Eric Smotherman, Andrew Tremain, James Westfield, and Paul Wilson were juniors in high school and attended Riverdale. All of them were very smart with various interests and were in the upper-level classes. All 10 of them had U.S. history and chemistry classes together, and most of them had other classes like unified geometry, English, and other electives.

This particular day was Wednesday, February 27, and, of course, Robert wasn't yet driving his newly acquired Ford LTD wagon. Normally, he drove his parents' 1970 red Volvo wagon which had over 200,000 miles on it and still ran very well.

It was nearly second period, and U.S. history class with Mr. Michael Vance was about to begin. The seven-second beep sounded, and he greeted his class.

"Good morning students. How are you today? Today we are going to discuss some possible alternative scenarios to World War I considering what would have happened if the Germans had won. What I'd like each of you to do is to write a five-page report on what you think would have happened after their victory. Now, let's get some ideas or topics from the class. Starting with you, Mr. Westfield, what do you think?"

"Well, coming from an Australian viewpoint, I think the German forces would have been so confident, following their victory in Europe, that they would have attempted taking us over, and that's quite right. That's all they would have done, for they would have had a terrible struggle crossing the hot, swampy, Northern Territory. Those that would have survived crocodile attacks would have surely died of thirst in our hot central deserts with temperatures in excess of 50° Celsius. Australia's certainly no picnic to invaders."

"Very well thought out, Mr. Westfield. Who else would like to comment?"

Morris raised his hand.

"Okay, Mr. England, let's hear what you think."

"Actually, I think the Germans, sly as they are, would have done some investigating about the underground civilizations that exist at Agartha and Shamballa under what is Tibet. The Germans would have led these underground inhabitants to believe that a Lemurian type of government was going to be returned to the surface of Earth, thereby fooling them and using their underground tunnels, which connect all over the world by the way, and taking the world over."

"Very interesting and far out," commented Mr. Vance. "Now, what about your view, Mr. Joslin?"

"Oh, let's see here. I think the Germans would have met up with a lot of opposition by the countries taken over and that there would have been an uproar that would have led to a revolution around five years later."

"Yes, Mr. Joslin, that is definitely a possibility."

Class continued as they further discussed the outcome of World War I and the possible alternative scenarios. During the last 10 minutes of class, Mr. Vance decided to bring up a different subject.

"Now class, during our final 10 minutes, I'd like to find out your different viewpoints on the concept of war in general. Yes, Mr. Nelson, I see your hand is up. We'll start with you first."

"It seems to me that history books are written around major wars, and,

of course, major turning points come about as a result of wars. Actually, I think history dwells too much on war and that history books need to dwell on more positive aspects that were important."

"Very interesting point, Mr. Nelson. Mr. Tomlin, what do you think?"

"I think war carries with it fame and glory, and that it is an honor to serve your country and die for your country, if that be the case. War is an amazingly effective means for a country to get its point across and have its way. Look how famous some American generals became defending our soil. Some of them became president."

"Yes, most of that is true, Mr. Tomlin. Mr. Price, tell us what you have to say about this."

"I think any man does well to serve his country by defending it from invaders. I agree that giving your life while serving your country is a high honor. I love my country, and we wouldn't be here enjoying our freedoms today if it hadn't been for our forefathers' fighting and bloodshed."

"Yes, that's very much on track and well stated, Mr. Price. Mr. Joslin, I see your hand is up. Tell us what you think."

"I'm glad to be a citizen of this country, but I'm not proud of the fact that wars were fought for it to exist as it does today. I wish more peaceful means through communication had been implemented and that reason would have prevailed over wars. Actually, I think we would be enjoying at least as many, if not more freedoms, if the Revolutionary War had never been fought in the first place. Look at England today. They have as many freedoms as we have, and there is far less crime there than here."

"Very informative and well thought out Mr. Joslin. Mr. England, what would you like to say about this?"

"For several thousand years, the dark forces have been in control of Earth, and they feed off of the turmoil and the wars waged by its inhabitants. I view Earth as a planet and not from the standpoint of any particular country. Viewing it on a global level, I think war is absurd, to say the least! Making weapons means nothing more than feeding the war industry and means that there will certainly be more wars. Look at the nuclear arms race. At present, it is flying away at an alarming rate, and the majority of Americans think it's wonderful. We'd be a lot better off spending all of our defense money on peace and communication and on establishing contact with those on other star systems."

"I know your viewpoint is sometimes far-fetched, Mr. England, and I think your views on a would-be peaceful planet are excellent, but remember," Mr. Vance reminded, "that man forfeited that chance for a utopian society when Adam was banished from the Garden of Eden some 6,000 years ago."

"Actually," Morris went on, "that was more like 300,000 years ago. Read Zecharia Sitchin's book titled: *The 12th Planet*, written in 1976. Really, that's just an excuse that man uses today to give him reason to keep on fighting. Just because the text of the *Holy Bible* says that wars were fought to serve what it calls 'God' with a big 'G' doesn't justify our having wars today. If nothing else, we can observe the barbaric ways that they fought and then decide to use peace and negotiations today."

"How in the world is *that* procedure ever going to stop a potential enemy from striking? We'd be goners if we laid our weapons to rest!" Mr. Tomlin suddenly barked out.

"You see," Morris pointed out, "that is exactly the mindlock that the dark forces have instilled into our minds from the etheric level. 'We must fear our enemy,' they want us to think. It looks like they've done a good job of it as most Earthlings do fear the enemy, and the dark forces have had a good feed off of the turmoil and wars that have resulted from such thinking.

"Many star systems have overcome the days of physical war, and they fight with each other using only their minds and with *no* physical violence. At least they have a sense of concern and protection for their environment, and they certainly don't destroy it with physical warfare.

"Other groups have raised themselves to such a spiritually evolved state that they can simply change the minds, as you might say, of would-be enemies by transmitting and radiating thoughts of peace and love. Before you know it, the enemies are so overwhelmed by friendship and love that they forget all about attacking what would have been their victims."

"Who are the dark forces, Mr. England?" Mr. Vance wanted to know.

"They are a collection of entities operating on the etheric level or a higher plane of existence, and like I said earlier, they feed off of the turmoil and wars on Earth. Their headquarters is underground in the Middle East. Those of the dark forces are removed from knowledge, and since they are uninformed, they therefore create systems that are also uninformed because that is how they believe they must operate. They are not of the light, which represents those of peace, friendship, and love. The lifestyle of the dark forces is one based on fear and control, not honoring other lives, and exploiting them for their own selfish gain as well.

"Several million years ago, the light forces arrived to this galaxy to overcome the dark forces since light brings with it information and knowledge. The *Holy Bible* labels the collective group of dark forces as 'Satan' or 'The Devil.' You can read all about it in Genesis I."

"How do you know about all of this, Mr. England?"

"I have fantastic and vivid dreams, and I do a lot of research during my dreams as well."

"That is a most interesting explanation you have just given us," Mr. Vance declared. "Who else would like to add comment?" James Westfield raised his hand. "Okay, Mr. Westfield, how would a view from Tasmania tie into this?"

"The Aborigines have been inhabitants of Australia for some 40,000 years or more, living a wonderful life of harmony with no wars. Just in the last few hundred years, white man and other recent settlers to Australia have wreaked havoc on them. The worst of it occurred in Tasmania because there are no longer any Aborigines left in the whole state. Back 50 years ago, it was great sport and recreation to go out and hunt Aborigines. It was a most horrible thing that the new settlers of Tasmania did to the now extinct Aboriginal tribes of Tasmania."

"That was very moving, Mr. Westfield."

-Beeeeeeeeep- The seven-second beep sounded, and class was over.

"We'll see you tomorrow, class," Mr. Vance concluded.

Most people who left U.S. history class went on to chemistry with Mr. Gordon Mayfield as the teacher. Everyone had already arrived and was seated. They were talking and visiting with each other until the five-minute class change was ended by the seven-second beep.

Mr. Mayfield was a unique and interesting science teacher. Most of the students had had him for general science their freshman year, a course that he did not enjoy teaching, by the way, and they would probably also have him for physics the next year. He knew his chemistry and lectured very well on its technical content. Lab experiments were conducted at the end of each chapter, and their lengths ranged from 20 minutes to as long as a solid week, depending on what type of experiment was done. Robert Joslin and Andrew Tremain were lab partners.

What made Mr. Mayfield most interesting was his viewpoint about possible life on other planets in other star systems. Every three weeks or so, he would be lecturing and would somehow get off of the subject for the last 10 to 15 minutes of class. He would theorize on time travel possibilities, black holes, and what intelligent beings would be like on other worlds. Today was one of those lucky days, and he went into a 10-minute discussion about extraterrestrials and possible UFO's.

"You know, I believe there are plenty of extraterrestrials throughout the cosmos. One day I was at a lake, and I watched one of these odd-looking saucers flying over the lake, coming from its other side, oh, I'd say 500 feet above the ground. A fighter plane was chasing it, and about when they got overhead, man I tell you, it lowered the boom and took off, leaving that fighter jet like he was standing still!"

At this moment, Robert raised his hand to ask a question.

"Yes," Mr. Mayfield said.

"How long ago did you see this?"

"Oh, I'd say it was 10 to 15 years ago," he replied. "Yeah, that was quite a sight to see! Another time, I watched one of these saucers just floating and gliding in front of some hills. After a while, it just went on over to the other side of the hills and disappeared behind them."

Paul Wilson asked a question, "Do you think these inhabitants of other worlds look like us or look quite different, and do they breathe the same type of atmosphere as we do here on Earth?"

"Oh, I'd say most or all of them look like us, breathing the same type of atmosphere."

Paul was confused and asked, "But how can that be? The chances of the same types of lifeforms evolving on other planets and looking like us seem almost impossible."

"There's more out there in the way of forces and life forces than we know, and as you know, the laws of chemistry and physics are the same throughout the whole cosmos," he explained. "There may be some sort of universal intervention that we are far from understanding at this time, and it may operate on the molecular level. Or think about it, as life evolves on each planet into the millions of different lifeforms, there will almost always be some of them that will look most like us out of the whole lot. That's just probability, and that's why I think the way I do. If there is evolution, I believe it's been tampered with on a galactic level, or it may be controlled or predetermined by unknown forces on a higher level."

This was all very interesting to most of the class and caused Robert to wonder more about how mankind got here in the first place. He had always believed in evolution in a very conventional way, that it occurred by natural selection over a course of 4 billion years or so and with no intervention. Suddenly it dawned on him that extraterrestrials could have visited Earth and could have taken and distributed Earth's life to many other planets, and vice versa.

"Mr. Mayfield," Robert asked, "what do you think of the possibilities that beings of some sort could have visited Earth long ago and could have taken life from here to other planets and stars?"

"I think that's very possible and probably happened. I mean, even in more recent times, we've probably been visited. The pyramids in Egypt and the landing strips in Peru, as examples, are evidence, I think, of visits from outer space beings."

"Then why are they so subtle, not making themselves known?" Robert wanted to know. "They seem to be so secretive."

"I think they may be working in secret with the government. Or I'm not even sure they may *be* extraterrestrials. They may be our own people visiting from the future in their flying saucers or what we call UFO's.

"You see, I think time travel is very possible," he continued, now adding a new subject to the conversation, "and I think that through wormholes or even black holes one can travel back in time or even forward and that there are many other shortcuts to and from other planets and stars. Why, some of these extraterrestrials may raise themselves to other vibratory levels in other dimensions above and beyond our 3-D world, possibly giving them enormous shortcuts to other stars, while if they had to travel in a linear fashion, . . ."

-Beeeeeeeeep-

". . . it would take millions of years to get there. Okay, we'll see you tomorrow."

Robert and his friends and the rest of the class left to go on to fourth period. James Westfield walked up to Robert and spoke to him.

"That sure was some off-the-wall stuff! None of my teachers back in Devonport, Tasmania ever spoke about such things. Is he *on* something?"

"Oh, no. Of course not! Mr. Mayfield is one of the straightest people you'll ever meet. He just has an amazing imagination, as I think most scientists do. Scientists have to be able to think, and they have to be inquisitive to learn more. I'm quite glad he talks about off-the-wall subjects like that. By doing so, he causes us all to think beyond our normal monotony of everyday life on Earth. I enjoy listening to him when he gets off the subject of class like that, and I'm always sorry when the bell rings to end it."

"Yeah, you're right," James admitted. "Each person is different, and some have vivid imaginations. They all have their place here on this world. I would love to visit some other planets if it were only possible."

"Maybe it is," Robert speculated.

"I've always had a burning desire to travel," James added. "There is so much I want to see. I can't wait until school's out in May so we can take that road trip out West or wherever."

"Less than three months to go."

"True," James agreed. "I must make a mad dash to my next class. Mine's on the other end of the building. See you later."

"Okay, see you later, James."

While James rushed off to his next class, Robert walked to his. Little did Robert know that this lecture that Mr. Mayfield gave would spur him on to have an incredible dream a few days later. In the meantime, he pondered more about other planets and what sort of life could be on them, and these thoughts soon imbedded themselves into his subconscious mind.

School was out at 2:45 p.m., and Robert had his clutch linkage pieces and air cleaner pieces cut, bent into shape, and ready for welding. He drove over to his welder friend and was right there in on it while he welded each piece together exactly as Robert wanted it. After three hours of electric stick welding and some torch welding, especially on the thin metal of the air cleaner pieces, he had done a fine job, and Robert was pleased with the work.

Robert took his welded parts home and bolted them onto his car this afternoon, and they fit very well. He was able to push in the clutch pedal and disengage the clutch between the engine and the transmission. After fitting the modified air cleaner on top of the carburetor with the remote filter down off to the side, the hood would not close down because the frame structure on the underside of the hood itself was in the way. So, he used a skillsaw with an abrasive rotating disk and carefully sawed away at the frame in the areas that prevented the hood from being closed. It worked, and the hood closed with only ¼ inch clearance over the air cleaner. It was very close, but it was enough.

By now, it was well into the evening, and he went inside the house to call William on the phone and tell him the good news.

"William?"

"Yes. Oh, how's it going, Robert?"

"Just fine. Guess what! I just finished installing all of the clutch linkage this evening and also installed the air cleaner," Robert proudly stated.

"Really? That's great!"

"And the welder did a great job, too!"

"Good! Now I know who I can use when I'm ready to do some converting on my car. Did he charge you a lot?"

"No, he only charged $8, and that was to cover the cost of the welding rods and the gas for the torch; very nice of him."

"Well, good. So, when I come Saturday, we're going to need to wire up the engine and cut a hole in the floor, right?"

"Right," said Robert. "I'm not going to have time to work on it anymore this week. I was lucky not to have any homework tonight, but I'm sure I'll have some tomorrow night. Whatever homework I have this weekend, I'll do it Friday afternoon to get that worry out of my way."

"Okay, so will I. Tell you what, why don't we have a bunch of us come over this Saturday evening and have a cookout? We can stay up in your cabin, too."

"Yeah, sure! That sounds like a great idea," Robert approved. "Let's invite the same people that we want to have join us this summer on our road trip. That way, we'll have a chance to make plans."

"Okay, sure. We can both ask them at school tomorrow."

"Okay, see you tomorrow."

"Okay, bye."

-click-

The rest of the week at school went fine without an overload of homework, and the weather was excellent for the weekend. William came over to Robert's on Saturday morning, and they did some more work on his car. They installed a longer accelerator cable and connected the wiring harness to the engine to make it start, run, and charge.

"Boy, I'm telling you what!" William remarked. "That sure is a mess of wires under this hood."

"I know," agreed Robert, "and look at that bundle of wires that used to feed and control that old variable venturi carburetor. It must be an inch thick! This single barrel carburetor uses no wires at all, and the whole engine with its point-type ignition runs off of one hot wire to the spark coil."

"Cars used to be more simple," said William. "I think it's a good idea to go back to the basics, like you're doing here. They're a heap easier to work on."

"I agree. Let's see. This voltage regulator needs to be replaced. You know, speaking of basics, I'm going to get rid of this power steering, too."

"Good idea!" William agreed. "You'll have a better feel of the road, and you won't lose your steering if your engine stalls out."

While William worked on the wiring, Robert took a manual-steering box which he had earlier purchased from a salvage yard. It had come out of an older Ford station wagon. As he modified the steering box to fit his car, he discovered that there were complications in mounting it. Using a grinding wheel and other tools, he overcame them and successfully installed it.

Meanwhile, William had completed the wiring and said, "Well, Robert. I guess we're ready to cut a hole in the floor and install your modified stick and hope it will actually clear under the dashboard as you go through each gear."

"I hope it works too. We'll need to drill holes in the floor after cutting and peeling back the carpet. Then we'll cut from hole to hole using a jigsaw."

After they successfully installed the stick according to Robert's instructions and found that it just cleared the dashboard panel in reverse, first, and third gears, William asked, "Ready to start it?"

"Yes, but it's going to be loud with no exhaust system on it yet. Let's start it and take it for a short test-run."

Robert checked the wiring connections and got in the car and started it.

It sputtered loudly at an idle. William got in, and Robert said, "Well, here goes."

He pushed the clutch pedal to the floor and moved the stick into first gear and slowly engaged the clutch. The car rolled away from a stop, going faster than expected. Robert soon realized that he was going to need a rear end with a lower gear ratio. This meant more work, but he was glad to finally drive his car for the very first time. He declared:

"This is a day of history, March 2, 1985: the first day that a full-size Ford LTD drove under its own power with a clutch and a manual transmission."

"This thing's geared way too high, isn't it," William commented.

"Yes, it definitely needs a rear end swap and an exhaust system." Robert agreed.

They took it out on the road for a few miles, and it drove well, but it was somewhat loud. So, they didn't go over 40 mph. After returning and parking it on the concrete pad again, William said:

"Well, I guess our friends will be arriving pretty soon."

"Yeah, we got this car running just in time," said Robert, as they were both getting out of the car. Steven Price just arrived and was walking around the outside of the yard toward them to see how they were doing on the project.

"Hello, Steven. How are you?" called out Robert.

"Fine. How are you? How are you coming on your car project?"

"Just fine. We just took this car out for its first run."

"Is that right? Too bad I missed it," said Steven. "That's great that you already have it running."

"I know it. What a feeling of triumph it is to finally have it on the road!"

"I'll bet," Steven agreed.

"Here come some more guests, Robert," said William.

"Okay, I guess we're done here."

Robert, William, and Steven picked up all of the tools and stashed them in the car and walked out front to greet the others.

3 The Amazing Dream

It was now 5 p.m., and in addition to Steven; Chris Chanford, Morris England, Andrew Tremain, James Westfield, and Paul Wilson had arrived. Greg Nelson and Eric Smotherman couldn't come. William had something to tell Robert about Greg and Eric.

"Robert, between Chris, Greg, and Eric, only Chris has the summer free to join us. Greg has to go to summer school out of state for a preliminary training course that will introduce him to dentistry, and Eric has to work for his father making pottery. They might have a few weeks off later in the summer and could possibly join us wherever we are then."

"I'm sorry Greg and Eric can't join us for all of it," said Robert, regrettably. "Actually, I didn't see how 10 of us could have piled into my car. I'd say eight of us will be plenty, even that I would like to have had Greg and Eric come along also. You know, that means all eight of us are presently here, and we can therefore make plans."

After visiting, exploring, and looking around for a while, they got some firewood and built a bonfire out in the field between the house and the woods. All eight of them were the best of friends and got along well with each other, having a lot in common. They trusted each other, never betrayed one another, and considered themselves very fortunate to have each other for friends. Each of them had a mind of his own and took time to think about different things. Even though most of them liked music and would sometimes listen to it, none of them were the type that drove sports cars and blasted their stereos. Further, none of them passed away all of their free time watching lots of television. Even though James Westfield was a newcomer, he fit right in immediately, and it soon seemed as though they had always known him.

They roasted hot dogs and marshmallows over the fire, got their sleeping bags and pads, and went up into the woods to sleep in the cabin. After entering the woods, they walked the several hundred yards slightly uphill on a trail that Robert had made seven years earlier. It was a fairly cold night, but it didn't frost.

Morris England brought up the subject about Mr. Mayfield's discussion from this past Wednesday.

"You know, Mr. Mayfield brings up some interesting topics, like that discussion he had with us in class this past Wednesday."

"Yeah, I believe there's no reason to think there's no life out there," said Paul. "Actually, it would be arrogant to think that Earth would be the only planet in the universe with life on it."

"Oh, yes. There's plenty of life out there and a lot of intelligent beings at that," Morris told them. "I've had plenty of dreams of going to other star systems and visiting all sorts of lifeforms, including people."

"People?! Is that right?" exclaimed Robert.

"Yes, indeed," Morris confirmed. "That extraterrestrials transferred life to and from other planets and star systems is very true."

"I thought it could be true. Tell us some of what you've seen in some of your dreams," Robert requested.

"Well, one time I made a visit to a place, Sirius B, I think, and there were these creatures that looked sort of like flying dragons with these sorts of scales on them; weird creatures they were. What I noticed was that they were having a war, but they fought with their minds; no physical violence."

"So, that's where you found out what you told all of us in history class the other day," Paul remarked.

"Right. That's part of it," confirmed Morris.

"What else have you dreamed of?" Robert further asked.

"Not too long ago, I had a dream that I was out on another planet and this galactic salesman approached me and started to tell me all about a

crystal ball about the size of a fist and how useful it would be to me in my life. He went on to tell me that I would find it in the future and said, 'Oh, you'll have to buy it.' Anyway, he carried on and on about this ball, telling me about all of the cracks in it and everything, and he showed it to me. I soon had enough of hearing him go on about this bloomin' ball and eventually told him, 'I'm going to wake up now.' And I did. I haven't seen the ball yet."

"Wow! That's an interesting dream!" Robert remarked. "Where do you think this galactic salesman was from?"

"I'm not sure, but I'd say that he may have been a member of the Galactic Federation."

"What did he look like, a person or some other sort of creature?" Chris wanted to know.

"He was definitely a human being, and he carried a walking staff with a glowing iron ball on top of it."

"I don't know about you all," spoke up James, "but I just don't think that dreams relate to real life. I don't ever get anything from them."

"Oh, dreams mean a lot," Morris insisted. "Even though my dreams are more vivid than most people's, I believe that everyone needs to pay attention to his dreams and see if there is any connection with real life."

"Yes, I agree," Steven commented and now spoke to Robert. "I've had lots of dreams of my past lives, and for that, I believe in reincarnation. In one lifetime, Robert, you and I were brothers in Russia in the early 1700's. Travel was forbidden. I was okay with it, but you were just about fit to be tied, not being allowed to travel. You swore that if you ever lived another lifetime on Earth, you would travel and explore as much as possible to make up for it."

"Isn't that something!" said Robert. "I just don't have any memory of any past lives, but it is true that I really have a desire to travel and explore."

"Based on a philosophical viewpoint," Chris spoke out, "I certainly would need to see some proof or case studies on reincarnation before I could believe in it."

"Oh, it's very true," Morris insisted. "That's for sure. It's just that since very few people remember their past lives, they naturally don't believe in it. I remember several of my past lives even though I haven't had a past life on Earth in a long time."

By now, they had all arrived at Robert's cabin that he had built out of Cedar logs, Oak and Hickory sawmill lumber, and tin roofing two years earlier. It was a nice get-away place and was great for group campouts like this one.

William made a comment in the continuing conversation. "I'm not sure what to think about life elsewhere in other star systems. It's very interesting, but I certainly haven't ever had any dreams about being on other planets."

"I have before," said Robert. "Once I dreamed back in 1978 that I travelled as a passenger in a spaceship to Mars and back. It was a fantastic dream, and I remember it very well. I even walked into a store in the town where we landed so I could buy some camera film to fit my camera. None of the sizes were familiar to me, so I had to buy both camera and film to take pictures. On the way back, I actually remember seeing the sky turn from black to blue upon re-entry into Earth's atmosphere."

"Wow! That's amazing!" William exclaimed. "I wish I could have dreams like that."

"Oh, I'd say you will some day."

"Look at what we've been talking about," Steven pointed out, "and it all stems from Mr. Mayfield's class discussion. It's amazing how one thing leads to another."

"I know, and I do find it very interesting," Robert added.

They continued talking about this subject for some time, and they completely forgot to discuss their plans for the summer road trip and hiking adventure. That worked out fine because the dream Robert was going to have tonight was going to change all of that. Finally, around 11 p.m., they had talked enough and went on to sleep in Robert's cabin.

All of these subjects they discussed plus Mr. Mayfield's discussion the other day must have gone into Robert's subconscious mind. He dreamed that he and his friends were on another planet. It was a planet with a bluish color just like Earth, but he knew it was another planet. In the dream, he associated most closely with James Westfield while the other six were also there.

In the dream, they had the ability to transport themselves. There was a silver platter that they used. They proceeded to transport objects to and from Earth. Certain materials could not be transported. They would put the object on the platter and would sometimes wave the platter sort of under it. Next, they would place one hand on each side of the object, not touching it, and would move their hands up and down very slowly, keeping a hand's thickness distance away from the object.

As they would concentrate and think a certain way, supplying energy to the object through their hands, a pink glow would overcome the object, and a sound of whirring wind with varying notes would be heard. Within five seconds, the object would disappear. It was very important not to touch the object during the transporting procedure, because part of the hands supplying the energy might have disappeared with it.

They transported several objects. Next, they transported themselves to different places including other planets and then returned to where they had initially been transporting objects. Robert went ahead and transported himself home to Earth, having made arrangements for his friends to come a little later and meet him. He arrived at the end of his driveway and looked upward into the northwest sky, wondering when they would come. They didn't arrive before his dream ended.

Robert woke up in his cabin with all of his friends there, and all of them had been in the dream. He wondered if he had the ability in real life because the dream seemed so real, and he was in a state of shock and surprise because he remembered this dream with perfectly clarity. Everyone else was still asleep, so he stayed quiet and just made a mental note of it, intending to tell them all of the details later.

It was just getting light outside, so Robert decided not to go back to sleep. Besides, he was too excited to go back to sleep after that amazing dream. So he lay there pondering the possibilities of doing such transporting of objects and of people in real life. *How nice it would be to travel to planets like that, if only it were possible*, he thought.

Around 20 minutes after waking up, Robert suddenly felt a jolt go through his whole body, which really surprised him. Everyone else started waking up now, and Morris quickly got up and came over to Robert saying, "Robert, you and I need to go outside and talk by ourselves."

"About what?"

"I'll tell you when we're alone. Let's go." Morris now called out to all of them. "We'll be back in a few minutes, everyone."

Robert knew that Morris was the first person he was going to tell about the dream, but he couldn't imagine that there would be anything so urgent from Morris that couldn't wait. They walked down the trail around 100 yards, and Morris started talking.

"You had that dream that we were all transporting objects, right?"

"Uh . . . yeah! I sure did!" Robert replied, no doubt absolutely amazed that anyone else actually had the same dream. "You mean you had that dream, too?"

"Yes, and as you know, you transported yourself home and were waiting for us to come later."

"That's right. So, what happened? What kept you all?" Robert eagerly asked.

"After you transported yourself home, the galactic salesman came."

"You mean the same one you told us about last night?"

"Yes, exactly," Morris verified. "He came with that same crystal ball in his hand, doing his best to convince me how important it was and how useful it would be to me in my life. I told him that I just wasn't that interested in buying it.

"Suddenly, the salesman told me, 'Wait! Don't wake up yet. Let me make a deal with you. I'll arrange for this ball to be given to you tomorrow. Tomorrow, someone will happen to find the ball in your presence and will then just give it to you. Furthermore, I will grant Robert Joslin the power to transport objects, including himself, and he may grant this gift to as many as nine people of his choosing, thereby making a total of 10 people, including himself, with this special gift.'

"I said to him, 'Now what if Robert doesn't choose to give me this gift?'

"He replied, 'Oh, he will because I'm also going to grant you the gift of transmitting to anyone you wish at will, clear visual images of what you see in your mind. When Robert knows that you have this ability, he will certainly choose to grant you the gift of transporting yourself and objects because your ability to transmit visual images of places will make travel to those places possible, especially to other planets.'

"I said, 'But I haven't been to other planets in real life.'

"He said, 'That's true, but you *have* been to other planets in your dreams, and those places are very real, whether you believe them to be or not.'

"I told him I was very glad to know that, and he continued, 'Now, Morris, I need your help on a project, and I think that Robert's farm would be a suitable place to put it. Oh, don't worry. It won't take up the whole farm. It's only the size of a house. What I need to do is to set up a galactic communications device to link Earth's telephone network to my home planet, Sirius B, and to other star systems as well. You see, we have lost contact with many of our fellow Sirians now residing on Earth as human beings, and through this device, we will be able to re-establish contact with them. I'll be supplying the towers with the electromagnetic rings and crystals, and they will be teleported by my crew to the site at a later time. Meanwhile, and I wish Robert hadn't rushed off back to Earth so soon, I want you all to see about obtaining some surplus telephone central office equipment to build a central office, possibly in the corner of Robert's woods. Can we make a deal?'

"Anyway, I thought about it a few minutes and said to him, 'Let me get this straight. You want me to have the ball, and it will be given to me tomorrow. Robert receives the gift of transporting himself and other objects, and he may grant this gift to as many as nine others of his choosing. I receive the gift of transmitting visual images to other people. You get to have a galactic communications device installed to link Earth to other planets and star systems with you and your crew supplying the towers you mentioned and with our supplying the central office equipment. Am I right?'

"He told me, 'That's correct. This device will use gravity waves which travel instantaneously, but I'll give you further instructions on all of that later.'

"I told him, 'One more thing. I don't think we're going to want to be carrying silver platters everywhere we go to be able to transport ourselves. Can that part of it be deleted?'

"He told me, 'No, it cannot, but I can arrange for it to be as if it isn't physically there. I'll send down 10 platters, and they will be on the etheric level. In other words, they will be in another plane of existence and will not be detected by anyone on a physical level. They will be attached permanently once they are assigned, and they won't be felt. Plus, they will be burden-free and maintenance-free. Upon installation, he and the others of his choosing will feel a sudden jolt, and that is all. Are there any other points we need to cover?'

"I told him, 'No, that's all.'

"He said, 'Deal?'

" 'Deal,' I told him.

"He said, 'Great! I'll talk to you later.'

"With that, we all came home. I don't believe any of the others will remember the dream, but I knew that you would. It's just a sense I have," Morris finished.

"That's absolutely amazing!" exclaimed Robert. "So that's what it was that I felt 20 minutes after waking up. Yes, of course, Morris. I grant you the gift."

Morris suddenly felt a jolt and calmly said, "Thank you very much. Now, let's go tell the others."

They walked back to the cabin, walked inside, and both said, "Get up! We've got something to tell you. Everyone come outside now."

Once they all got up and gathered outside, Robert announced:

"I have just been granted the gift of transporting myself and other objects, and I have the right to grant this unique and wonderful gift to nine other people of my choosing. I have already chosen Morris, and I'm choosing the rest of you here. I grant you the gift."

At that moment, they all felt a sudden jolt which was quite surprising to them. Robert continued.

"I grant both Greg Nelson and Eric Smotherman in the northwest of Murfreesboro the gift."

At that moment, they, in their separate places and still asleep, suddenly felt the jolt and were awakened. Of course, at the time, they didn't know what they had just felt and figured maybe it was an earthquake or something like that.

"This wonderful gift will stay with all of you for the rest of your lives," Robert went on, "and since we here are the best of friends, I couldn't think of more appropriate people to whom I could grant this gift. You have something that few, if any people on Earth, have. We are to use this gift in a responsible manner, and it would be a good idea if we all kept it a secret among ourselves, at least for now."

Morris asked, "Did any of you have any dreams last night?"

"I did," James spoke out. "I remember something . . . like us . . . doing something, but I just can't place my finger on it."

"Anyone else?"

No one else answered.

"Okay then," Robert proposed, "let's see if this gift really works. Does anyone have any suggestions on where to go?"

"How about another planet?" suggested Steven.

"Let's not do that just yet in case we get stuck and can't return," Robert advised. "Let's choose some place on Earth. That way, if we get stuck, we can at least return home the hard way."

"Good point," Steven agreed.

"Let's get on with it before any of us get cold feet and chicken out," James impatiently said.

"Okay, but let's not all go this first round," Robert advised them. "How about if three of us go right now?"

"I'll come," James volunteered.

"Me too," said Morris.

"Let's go to Tasmania," James suggested.

"Okay, that sounds good. The rest of you five stay here," Robert directed. "We'll be back in five minutes. Okay, James and Morris, let's see. We'll have to stand in a triangle, each of us facing the one in front of us, and we'll put our hands on either side of that person, not touching him." They took their positions according to Robert's instructions, and he continued, "Now, James, think very clearly of a place in Tasmania where you want to go, and I will supply the force through my hands as I think the certain way like I did in my dream. This force will go through each of you and will affect me as it goes around, full circle. Are you ready, James and Morris?"

"Yes," they answered.

"Okay, here goes."

Robert felt nervous and anxious as he began to supply the energy and think the certain way as he remembered doing in his dream. A pink glow actually started to overcome them, and a whirring wind of varying notes or pitches started to sound. They faded in a period of five seconds along with the pink glow and the sound of the wind that was produced by the phenomenon. Needless to say, the five remaining by Robert's cabin just couldn't believe their eyes and stared at the place where they had just disappeared, wide-eyed in amazement and with their mouths dropped open!

Meanwhile, James had thought of a nice open area in a Buttongrass plain with small lakes and Pencil Pines growing along their shores. In seconds, they arrived. It was the middle of the night, for in Tasmania, the time was 17 hours ahead, or 7 hours behind plus a day.

"Wow!" James remarked. "That's the most incredible experience I've ever had!"

"You're not kidding!" Morris agreed.

"I . . . I can't believe it worked!" gasped Robert. "It actually worked! What do you know about that! But it's dark."

"That's right. That would make sense," said James. "Tasmania's on a different time zone."

"This seems too good to be true, but it's really happening, isn't it. We're not dreaming, are we?" Robert asked.

"No, this is for real," Morris assured them. "I know the difference. Believe me. Besides, it's dark, isn't it?"

"Yes," answered Robert.

"Then that's proof enough," said Morris.

"Let's really prove it," James suggested. "Come over here to this tree." As they followed him over to it, he continued, "This is a Pencil Pine, *Athrotaxis cupressoides*, and it grows only in selected wetter areas at higher altitudes in Tasmania. Let's take a small twig back with us, and if I still have it when we get back to your cabin, then we'll know that we were really here."

"Good idea," said Robert.

"Oh, it's great to be back here, brief as it is!" declared James. "Now I can come back any time I like."

"That's right," Robert confirmed. "Each of you now knows what if feels like to transport yourselves. So, put your hands on each side of you and think yourselves back to my cabin, transmitting the energy through your hands and thinking of the same feeling that you felt when we came here. I'll see you there."

Robert transported himself back, and Morris and James soon followed. Whirring wind began to sound, and three separate pink glows began to rapidly appear near Robert's cabin, and the other five watched the three of them materialize as the pink glows faded and the whirring wind died down again.

"You're back!" all five of them exclaimed in unison.

"What was it like?" Andrew eagerly asked.

"Absolutely amazing!" shouted James. "Wait. Let's see here." James reached into his pocket for the Pencil Pine twig and pulled it out. "Yes! It's here! We actually *did* go! We were there!"

"What's that?" Paul asked.

"That's a Pencil Pine twig, and it is found only in Tasmania in wetter areas at higher altitudes."

William looked at the twig in James' hand and said, "Maybe you really *did* go."

"Of course, we went!" James insisted. "Come on. Let's go, all of us."

"Okay, sure," said Andrew, speaking for the five of them. "You three look like you survived it fine. Let's go for the adventure!"

"Okay," Robert directed, "all eight of us will need to get in a large circle. James, you get one third of the way around from me. Morris, place yourself another third of the way around from James. All of us will need to place our hands on either side of the person in front of us, not touching

him. Morris, James, and I will think of the same place in Tasmania and will supply the energy through our hands. Are we ready?''

"Yes," everyone answered.

All of them took their positions, and Robert said, "Well, here goes." A pink glow overcame all of them, and the whirring wind of varying notes sounded, and they disappeared in five seconds.

Now they were back in the Buttongrass plain in Tasmania, all eight of them.

Upon arriving, Steven said, "Huh! It's dark!"

"I'm not believing this!" Paul exclaimed.

"That's amazing! I don't know what to say," said Chris.

"I'm telling you what. That's incredible!" William remarked.

"How can this be happening?" Andrew asked. "This just doesn't seem possible."

"Oh, but it is, and we're back," James assured them.

"Look at those stars," said Paul, as he looked up into the night sky. "That is some incredible Milky Way Galaxy!"

"That's right, and it really shows up well, here in the Southern Hemisphere," James added.

"Okay, if everyone has seen enough for right now, let's go ahead and return while it's still fresh on everyone's mind on how to transport oneself," Morris suggested.

"Good idea," agreed Robert. "None of us want to be stuck here, do we?"

"No," they answered.

"Okay, all of you now have the ability to transport yourselves," Robert told them. "We don't need to get in that circle anymore. That was just to show you how it felt. Place your hands on each side of you, and think about returning to my cabin, transmitting the energy through your hands and thinking of the same feeling that you felt when you came here."

All of them followed Robert's instructions and quickly arrived back at Robert's cabin, except for Chris. He arrived around 15 seconds later saying, "I had some trouble transmitting the energy, at first, but I believe I've got the hang of it now."

"Thank goodness you're back!" said Robert, quite relieved to see him. "We were beginning to worry about you."

"Oh, I'm okay. No, really, I've got the hang of it now," Chris assured them.

"Okay, good. Come on. Let's go down to the house and eat breakfast," Robert suggested to everyone. "I'm really hungry by now. As soon as we get there, I'll call Greg and Eric and tell them to come here immediately."

They packed up their sleeping bags and roll pads and walked down to Robert's house for breakfast. After all of the excitement this morning, they were definitely hungry.

As soon as they got to his house, Robert went straight to the phone to call Greg first. He dialled his number.

"...tttttttt"

"What?!" Robert exclaimed, and he immediately hung up the phone. "How can that be? It rang like Nashville rings. Here, I'll dial a number in Eagleville. He randomly dialled a number and listened.

"...ttttttttttttttt...ttttttttttttttt...Hello?"

"Is this 274-6259?" Robert asked.

"Yes, it is," the called party answered.

"Well, your phone rings like Nashville now. It doesn't have that loud, clanky ring anymore."

-no response-

"I was just checking. Sorry to bother you. Bye."

"Okay, bye," the called party said.

-click-

"Here, I'll call Greg again," said Robert in a state of shock. He had already had enough surprises for one day. He dialled his number.

"pheep ^ pheep ^ pheep ^ pheep ^ pheep"

"Now it's busy. That's the Nashville busy signal too. I'll just call later. Let's eat."

As they helped themselves to different cereals, Robert asked William, "William, your father works for the phone company. Do you know anything about this?"

"Yes, Dad's been very busy this weekend. He told me that he would be up until after midnight last night because they cut Murfreesboro over from a crossbar exchange to a digital exchange at midnight last night."

"It looks like Eagleville changed, too," Robert added.

"Yes, Eagleville is now an extension of Murfreesboro. So, it got changed out, too."

"So, that's what happened," Robert realized. "We got a new exchange. The phone company didn't bother telling anyone. They just *did* it!"

"Yeah, that's usually how they work," William agreed.

"You know, we never did have International Direct Distance Dialling out of Murfreesboro. Eagleville and Smyrna *did* have it. I'll call the operator and ask her if we do now."

Robert got her on the line and asked, "Yes, do I have International Direct Distance Dialling?"

"Yes, you do, starting today," she answered.

"Okay, thanks," said Robert.

As he hung up, he said, "She said, 'Yes, you do, starting today.'"

By now, everyone was already seated at the tables and sofas, eating cereal. While they were eating, Robert's mother looked at them and said:

"What happened to you all? You look like the cat that swallowed the canary."

"We do have something to tell you," Robert answered. "It's something that happened to us this morning, but we're not sure how to tell you. It's so unbelievable, but true, and we don't want it going public."

"I see. Well, you don't need to tell me right now. I'm sure you will when the time is right. It's nothing bad, is it?"

"Oh, no. Certainly not," Robert assured her. "It's very good indeed, as you can tell by the looks on our faces. I'll explain it all later."

"Okay, fair enough," she said.

As soon as they finished breakfast, Robert called and reached both Greg and Eric and told them that he had something very important to tell them and for them to drop whatever they were doing and come out immediately. They did just that and were at Robert's in half an hour.

Meanwhile, as they were all waiting for Greg and Eric to arrive, they went outside into the field between the house and the woods and had a discussion. Robert started the conversation.

"Morris, weren't you telling me that the galactic salesman wanted some sort of communications device to link Earth with his home planet and other planets?"

"That's right."

"How useful would some of that equipment in Eagleville and Murfreesboro be, since they just cut over and may not be using some of it anymore?"

"I'd say that's exactly what we need," said Morris.

"I thought so. Hey, William," Robert called out.

"Yes."

"What's going to become of all of that central office equipment out of Murfreesboro and Eagleville?"

"I'd say they'll probably just junk it," William answered.

"Junk it?!" exclaimed Robert, no doubt surprised.

"That's right. They don't care. They've gotta get that stuff off the books *real fast.*"

"That's terrible! How wasteful!"

"I know," William agreed. "If you want some of that stuff, Dad will probably just give it to you."

"Really? Well, that's better than just junking it. Here, let's go call him and see. Will you call him? Tell him it's important and that we need to build a communications device."

"Okay, I'll see what I can do," said William. "I'll go call him right now."

"I'll come in with you and help you explain."

"Good. I'll need it."

The others had been listening to the conversation without any input, but they began wondering of possible ways to set up such equipment. Most of them had no idea what a central office even looked like on the inside.

Robert and William walked inside, and William reached his father, Mr. Johns. He had only recently awakened after staying up past midnight, dealing with the cutover. Mr. Johns recommended that step-by-step equipment would be more suitable for their purpose than crossbar equipment, and he offered to give them a tour of the Eagleville exchange as it would be completely torn out, starting tomorrow.

As they walked back outside where the others had been waiting, Robert announced:

"William just reached his father, and he's offered to show us the Eagleville exchange, which was on step-by-step until last night. They're going to tear it out tomorrow, so today's our last chance, if we ever want to see it."

While they had been waiting, Morris had told them about his dream, and they were definitely curious enough to see this step office. This would give them a better idea on how to construct the proposed galactic communications device. Since they were smart and enthusiastic people, they never missed a chance at seeing something that would broaden their knowledge.

Greg and Eric arrived. It was now late morning. As they stepped out of the car, they asked:

"What's this all about? What's the hurry?"

Robert asked them, "Did you both feel sort of a sudden jolt this morning when you woke up?"

"Yes! How did you know? Was that an earthquake?" they wanted to know.

"No, it wasn't. I granted you a gift," Robert answered.

"You granted us . . . *what*?!" they both asked, very confused.

"I granted both of you the ability to transport both objects and your-selves."

"You did?"

"Right," Robert answered. "You've arrived just in time. We're on our way to Eagleville to meet William's father. He's going to show us the Eagle-ville exchange. Here, four of you get in my car. Morris, you get in the other car. Both of us will explain everything on the way."

They were off to Eagleville!

4 The Tour of the Step Office

Eagleville was a small crossroads of a town 15 miles west of Robert's place, and it had a population of approximately 400 people. The road going to it was State Highway 99, which was a narrow road with plenty of curves, humps, and dips. It had no shoulders but instead had ditches on either side. The short bridges crossing creeks were sometimes bumpy and were never wider than they had to be, barely wide enough to allow two trucks to squeeze by each other. Certainly, their mirrors would have clashed. Some of these bridges had concrete walls on each side, and needless to say, large chunks had been broken off due to being hit.

One stretch of highway just before Rockvale was almost like a roller coaster with a whole series of humps and dips, and it was actually a thrill to drive it at 55 to 60 mph. Robert took great delight in taking out-of-state guests along this stretch of highway when he would give them a tour of the area. In actual fact, nearer to Eagleville, there were places on the highway that contained a bridge on a hump on a curve. James made a comment about how this highway reminded him of the road from Don to Forth near Devonport, Tasmania.

By the time they arrived in Eagleville, Greg and Eric had been told everything, and everyone else also knew the details of Robert's dream and of Morris' deal with the galactic salesman about the galactic communications device. As they entered Eagleville, they pulled over on the right side of the highway just before the crossroads and parked in front of the exchange, which was a square brick building. Mr. Johns was already there waiting for them.

He greeted them. "How are you all doing? Come on in, and I'll show you what a step office looks like." He unlocked the door and led everyone inside. "It's awful quiet in here now since the cutover. It used to be that you'd walk in here and hear all sorts of clicking and clacking sounds."

"Why would there have been all that clicking?" Andrew wanted to know.

"That's how the step switches work," he answered. "Come on over here. This step-by-step exchange has 1,000 lines. Each of these shelves that you see here contains 20 Strowger switches. As you see, there are five rows of them, one on top of the other. This makes up a row, or what we call a rank, and there are several of these rows or ranks in this step office. This rank on the far right contains the line-finder groups of switches. The next rank over contains the switches that take care of the last two digits of a phone number, and those switches are called the connectors. Further over are the ranks of 1st selector switches and 5th selector switches, and they take care of the prefix, which is 274, as well as the 4th and 5th digits of any local phone number.

"When a subscriber on this exchange picks up the handset of his phone, a Strowger switch in the rank of line-finder switches steps up and over to his phone number and connects him to a dial tone. Each switch is capable of connecting to any line out of a group of 100 different lines, and there is a line-finder group of switches assigned to every 100 lines. Also, each group of 100 lines out of the 1,000 lines is assigned to a different line-finder group.

"Anyway, when a subscriber dials the prefix 274, a Strowger switch in the rank of 1st selector switches steps up 2 positions, drops off; 7 positions, drops off; and then 4 positions and drops off. This is known as digit absorption. Now, the switch unlocks for the 4th digit dialled. Let's take 6474, for example. This same 1st selector switch steps up 6 positions, holding that vertical level, and quickly scoots horizontally across the contacts until it finds one out of a choice of 10 available 5th selector switches, which are in the next rank. When it finds one, it stops on that contact and connects to it. Next, the 5th selector switch steps up 4 positions, holding that vertical position, and also quickly scoots horizontally until it finds and connects to an available connector switch. The connector switch steps up 7 positions and over 4 positions. At that exact moment, the phone call is connected to the dialled number, and the ringing begins. The caller is connected to a ring back tone source and hears the ringing over the line.

"As you can see, no Strowger switch can handle more than two digits of a phone number, except for digit absorbing 1st selector switches. That's how they're made. Here, I'll pull one of these covers off and show you inside the switch." He pulled off the cylindrical mailbox-shaped metal cover and revealed the vertical shaft. "You can see how the vertical shaft is made with the gears in it, both in the horizontal and vertical dimension. These relays behind it serve to step the shaft up and then over, giving it a choice of 100 positions to travel to. Below the shaft, you will see the semicircular array or group of metal contacts. This is known as the bank, and every Strowger switch has a bank mounted underneath it. Therefore, each shelf has 20 banks as it does 20 Strowger switches."

Robert had a question. "Why does the switch in the 1st selector group just fall off when 274 is dialled?"

"Those first three digits of the phone number are the same for everyone on this exchange. So, they are not really needed. It's just that every number has seven digits, and even though you have the same prefix as the person you are calling, that prefix still has to be dialled. It used to be that you could just dial the last four digits, but when automatic equipment was installed to dial direct to Murfreesboro and Smyrna from here, it made it where the prefix always had to be dialled."

"How does touch tone work here?" Andrew wanted to know.

"It doesn't in a direct sense," Mr. Johns answered. "See, these switches are built to work off of the pulses of a rotary dial phone. However, a person could use a touch-tone phone because we had installed equipment to convert tone to pulse. You can see the converter boxes up there, hanging off the back of those line-finder switches."

"How do you dial out of the exchange?" Steven asked.

"As soon as a subscriber dials a '4' for Smyrna's 459 or an '8' for Murfreesboro's prefixes, that 1st selector group connected him to an outgoing line instead of absorbing the digit. The same applies for 1-plus and 0-plus dialling."

"How can it connect it to an outgoing line if the switch just falls off?" Steven further asked.

"It only falls off for numbers starting with a '2'."

"Oh, I see."

"What produces the ringing, dial tone, ring, and busy signals?" Paul asked.

"Come on further back, and I'll show you. Here you'll see a stack of square metal boxes. One produces the dial tone. Another produces the ring back tone which was that loud clanky ring you heard through the phone receiver or handset. This one below it produces the busy signal. As you can see, they are all labeled.

"Further over to the right, you will see two larger square metal boxes. Each of these has a ringing generator or ringing machine within it. We only used one. The other was a backup or spare. This gave out a ringing voltage of 105 volts AC with a frequency of normally 20 cycles per second, except for party lines. The normal talking voltage of a telephone line is 48 volts DC."

"What would happen for party lines?" Chris asked.

"They would use different ringing frequencies. We used five different ones: 20, 25, 30, 40, and 50 cycles per second. This box above the ringing generator shows a selection of the five different ringing frequencies that were used at this exchange. Each subscriber's telephone instrument on a party line had a frequency ringer or cycle ringer inside of it, and it was made to ring only at that certain frequency for that particular party."

"Mr. Johns?" Robert asked.

"Yes, Robert."

"I was counting the number of Strowger switches in this rank of line-finder switches, and I only see 100. Didn't you say this was a thousand-line exchange?"

"Yes. You're very observant to notice that," he said, walking back over to the rank of line-finder switches. "We utilize line finders that work on ten-to-one trunking. In other words, every set of 10 phone lines is sort of assigned to one switch, even though any subscriber in a certain 100's group may be using any one of the 10 switches designated to his group depending on which switch in the line-finder group is available at that time. To put it another way, for a group of 100 phone lines, any one of a group of 10 line-finder switches may connect him to a dial tone when he picks up the handset of the phone."

"Does that mean that no more than 100 of the 1,000 lines can be used at the same time?" Robert asked.

"That's correct. The 101st user would pick up the receiver and would not be able to get a dial tone."

"When a call comes in from Murfreesboro or Smyrna or even from out of state, for that matter, how does that call reach the right number here since the dialling is done remotely?" William asked his father.

"Well, from Murfreesboro, for example, as soon as a subscriber on that exchange dials 274, the exchange stores the digits and routes them here to Eagleville. For long distance calls and out-of-state calls, the number is routed to the nearest toll office, which is in Nashville. The digits are stored there and are sent here to Eagleville again. That stored number comes in here on an incoming line as a digit train of pulses and operates the ranks of Strowger switches the same as if it were a local phone call, and the call is connected. That's why there is an 8 to 10 second delay before the ringing begins after the number is dialled from out of town."

"What supplies 48 volts DC to the telephones?" James asked.

"That battery bank on the back wall supplies it to all of the lines," Mr. Johns answered as he walked toward the back of the building again. "Come on back here and take a look."

"Boy, those batteries are huge!" exclaimed Eric. "They must be three times larger than a car battery, and there are so many."

"That's right, and they're connected in series. They've gotta be that big to supply the necessary voltage and current to feed 1,000 lines. Actually, we have a different 48 volt power supply, and these batteries are just back-ups and also serve to filter out noise to some degree."

Mr. Johns suddenly noticed something. "Hey, what's this thing sitting on this middle battery? It looks like a crystal ball or something. I don't remember seeing this here last night. I wonder who left it here?" He reached over and picked it up.

Morris was in a different part of the room looking at some other equipment and suddenly perked up at what he thought he heard.

"Did I hear you say *crystal ball*?" Morris asked.

"Yes," Mr. Johns answered. "There's a crystal ball over here. I just found it sitting here on top of this battery bank."

"Did you *really*?! Let's see it," said Morris enthusiastically, as he walked over to him.

Mr. Johns handed it to him.

"My goodness! It looks just like the one in the dream!" Morris exclaimed. "It's even got the same cracks running through it and everything. That's amazing!"

"I don't know how it got here," said Mr. Johns. "It wasn't here when the last of us left after midnight last night, so it can't belong to any of us working for the phone company. If you want it, you can have it."

"Oh, thank you! Thank you very much."

"You're welcome," said Mr. Johns.

Morris was beside himself in disbelief that what the galactic salesman from Sirius B had told him was true. He marveled over it and stared at it like it was the only thing on Earth at the moment.

Mr. Johns continued, "Now, you all need some equipment for a communications device of some sort, right?"

"Yes," Robert answered. "To be straightforward about it, we're planning to build a galactic communications device to link Earth's telephone network with planets in other star systems. So, I guess what we need is a telephone central office."

"With planets in other star systems?!" Mr. Johns asked, no doubt surprised.

"That's right, but we want it to be a secret," Robert added.

"You got *that* right!" Mr. Johns agreed. "Don't worry. I won't tell anybody. I'll be glad to help in any way I can. This has really got my curiosity up. This I've gotta see when it's in working order."

"Actually, we were wondering if you could help us set it up and be the chief technician and maintain it," Robert requested.

"For a galactic communications device? I wouldn't miss this chance for anything. I'd love to!"

"That's great! Thank you," said Robert.

"You mean there's life out there on other stars?" Mr. Johns asked.

"There sure is," Robert confirmed. "Morris, here, can tell you a lot more about that than I can, based on his dreams. I mean, look at the coincidence about that crystal ball and Morris' having already known about it from a dream."

"Oh yeah. That's true," he recalled. "Say, how many lines will this office need to have?"

"How many do you think, Morris?" Robert called over to him.

". . . Huh?" Morris said, having been giving his undivided attention to his newly acquired ball.

"How many lines do you think this central office for our galactic communications device needs to have?"

"Oh, I'd say 10 to 15 lines will be sufficient."

"Let's go ahead and make that 20," Mr. Johns offered, "since 20 Strowger switches come on a shelf."

"Okay. That sounds good," said Robert.

"Okay, I'll tell you what you'll need," he explained. "After all, they're just going to junk this step office equipment. You'll need a shelf of 20 line-finder switches. We're not going to worry about ten-to-one trunking for such a small office as you'll need. It will be one to one. You'll need three more shelves of 20 switches each: a shelf of 1st selector switches, a shelf of 5th selector switches, and a shelf of connector switches.

"Also, you'll need the equipment for handling incoming and outgoing calls. Of course, you'll need the boxes for producing the dial tone, ring back tone, busy signal, and ringing voltage. The batteries are still being used here, so I'll have to work something out about getting some of them later from elsewhere.

"I'll get you what you need when they tear it all out of here tomorrow, and I'll bring it over to your place tomorrow, Robert, with my truck and trailer. Oh, yeah. You'll need some of these metal racks for mounting it all, and you'll need some wire. Where can I deliver this, Robert?"

"You can place it all inside of the tenant house. It hasn't been lived in for several years now. I really do thank you for your kindness and help."

"Oh, no problem. I'm glad to do it," said Mr. Johns. "What are you going to do about the transmitting and receiving equipment to link up to the other star systems?"

"The galactic salesman that Morris is communicating with is supposed to take care of that," answered Robert. "All we know is that they will be towers with metal rings and crystals."

"Oh, I see. I'm interested to see what that will look like. Well, I guess that about wraps it up. Like I said, I'll get this stuff for you tomorrow and will set it inside your tenant house when I bring it over. If there's anything else I can do to help, don't hesitate to call."

"Thank you very much, Mr. Johns," said Robert.

"You're welcome. I'm glad to find a use for this stuff instead of just junking it. I'll go ahead and lock up here. We'll see you later."

"Okay, see you later."

The rest of them also thanked Mr. Johns as he saw everyone out of the building and locked up to go home. They got in their cars and returned to Robert's house. Upon arriving there, some of them went on home. Morris and William stayed a while longer and discussed with Robert the particulars of where the central office needed to be put. Greg and Eric also stayed because they had not yet had a chance to use their new gift. They started walking toward the woods.

By now, it was early afternoon. Things were happening so fast. Greg and Eric just could not wait any longer to find out what it would be like to transport themselves.

"Before you all do anything else," said Greg, "would you show Eric and me how to transport ourselves?"

"Yes, certainly," replied Robert. "Morris, William, let's go ahead and show them how it works. After that, we'll choose the central office location."

They agreed.

"Okay, let's go to Tasmania," Robert suggested. "All of us need to get in a circle, standing one in front of the other. Place your hands on each side of the person in front of you, not touching him, but keeping a hand's thickness distance away from him. Morris, William, and I will think of the scene in Tasmania and will supply the energy through our hands. A pink glow will overcome us, and we will arrive a few seconds later."

They took their positions and disappeared in five seconds.

Upon arriving, Eric exclaimed, "Wow! Incredible!"

"Amazing!" exclaimed Greg, quite astonished. "This seems like something out of a science fiction novel. Why is it dark?"

"Tasmania's 17 hours ahead, or 7 hours behind plus a day," Robert answered. "It's early Monday morning, and sunrise will be in about an hour."

"Oh, I see," said Greg.

"We are in the middle of a Buttongrass plain with small lakes and Pencil Pines, *Athrotaxis cupressoides*, according to what James told us earlier," Robert informed them. "They grow only in selected wetter areas at higher altitudes in these grassy plains. James already brought back a twig to prove that we had earlier been here. Here are some dead twigs on the ground. Pick one of them up, and we'll bring it back with us."

"Okay, good idea," said Eric, as he reached down and picked up a twig and put it in his pocket.

"Notice the night sky and how vividly the Milky Way Galaxy stands out, here in the Southern Hemisphere," Robert pointed out.

"Oh, wow! That's really something!" Eric remarked.

"Truly far out!" Greg added.

"It's too bad Greg and I don't have the whole summer off to join you all on your adventures," said Eric.

"Yes, it is," Robert admitted, "but maybe you both can join us at times here and there for shorter trips. The only thing is that we may be staging a normal road trip out West to all of our parents, except mine and William's, because we're not sure if we want to tell them this far-out truth. So, we may just drive my car somewhere, park and hide it, and disappear to travel wherever we desire. There are endless possibilities. We'll work something out."

"That sounds fair enough," said Greg.

"Good. Are we ready to return home?" Robert asked.

"Yes," said everyone.

"Okay, each of you now knows what it's like to transport yourselves," Robert explained. "Just put your hands on each side of you, not touching, however. Think of the place we just came from while transmitting the energy through your hands and thinking of the same feeling you felt when you came here.''

They proceeded to transport themselves back to Tennessee. Morris, William, and Robert returned right away, already familiar with the procedure. Greg and Eric arrived a few seconds later.

"Are you familiar with it now?" asked Robert, as soon as they had arrived.

"Yeah, I believe I've got the hang of it," said Eric.

"Me too," said Greg, "but I don't believe I want to attempt it by myself. If I were to get stuck somewhere else, no one would know where to find me."

"Yes, that would be right," Robert agreed. "It would be wise for us to transport ourselves only in groups, at least for now."

Eric reached into his pocket and found the Pencil Pine twig still there and took it out saying:

"Yep. I've got the twig. We really *did* go."

"Well, I guess we better go on home now," Greg suggested.

"Okay, we'll see you later," Robert, Morris, and William said.

"See you later," they said back.

They walked back to their car that was parked down in front of the house and drove away. Now Morris, Robert, and William began to discuss the central office.

"Where do you want to put the central office, Robert?" William asked.

"I think the corner of the woods would be a good spot for it, and it would be sort of hidden. What do you think, Morris?"

"That looks like a very good spot," Morris approved, as they were presently in that section of the woods. They began looking it over, pacing it off, and deciding how many trees would have to be removed.

"I'd say the building would need to be 20 by 20 feet and made out of concrete blocks," Robert suggested. "William, you said your father is going to supply the equipment. Morris, you said the galactic salesman is going to supply the receiver-transmitter apparatus. I guess that means that we are going to have to build a building to house it all. If all 10 of us chip in, say $100, I believe that we could pay for the whole building. We could meet out here one Saturday and could probably build it all in one day. How does that sound to both of you?"

"That sounds like a good plan," replied William. "I was thinking the materials would cost in the neighborhood of $1,000. So, with each of us chipping in $100, I believe that will cover it pretty well."

"Good. That's what I thought," said Robert. "Okay, let's tell the others what we need to do. I'm sure each of us can come up with $100.

After all, the gift from the galactic salesman of our being able to transport ourselves will save each of us thousands of dollars during our lifetimes."

"Morris," Robert asked, "did you say that gravity waves would be used and that they would be installing crystals and electromagnetic rings?"

"Yes, that's about it," he replied. "As you know, the galactic salesman didn't give me any details."

"Right, that's what I thought," said Robert. "I'd say that this crystal and large metal ring serving as an electromagnet will be supported by their own stand or tower and will probably be separate from the building?"

"I'd say so, yes," Morris replied.

"Okay," said Robert, "then we won't need any fancy roof support structure. We'll just make a roof from wooden rafters, plywood, and roofing shingles."

"Of course, we'll need a concrete floor," William added.

"Yes, that too. We'll need the following list of materials," Robert told them. "We'll need a concrete floor, a bunch of concrete blocks, mortar mix, and let's make the dimensions 20 by 15 feet. That way, we can use 16-foot 2-by-6's for the rafters. So, let's see. I suppose we'll need 15 of the 16-foot 2-by-6's, 10 pieces of 4-by-8-foot plywood, and probably 10 bundles of roofing shingles. We'll need plenty of nails. That's about all I can think of. Can you think of anything else?"

"Yes, we'll need a metal door and frame," William added.

"Oh yes, of course! I can't believe I left that out. We might be able to find one of those at a wrecking site where they're knocking down an old building. In fact, we may find our concrete blocks there also. Let's all be on the lookout and plan on having everything we need gathered and brought here by two weeks from now. William, I'll leave you in charge of raising the money from all of us, and I'll do what I can to get the materials. Morris, I'll let you take care of the plans of the sending and receiving equipment with the galactic salesman."

"Okay, that sounds like a good plan to me," said William. "I'll take care of raising the money, and I'll bring it to you as soon as possible."

"Great," said Robert. "I think next weekend, we all need to get away from it all. We could go hiking in Savage Gulf State Natural Area, if you like. This will give us all a chance to discuss our new gift and to go hiking at the same time. Plus, we can camp way up off the trail and practice transporting ourselves to and from places and therefore fine-tune our new ability."

"Yes, I absolutely agree," said Morris, "and we can meet here two weeks from now and build this building. Before then, it is imperative that we practice our new gift and ability so that we don't forget how to use it."

"True. I'd hate for some of us to forget how to use it," said Robert.

"Well, even if some of us did," explained Morris, "you know that you and I, Robert, will not forget, and that we can just retrain them if *they* do."

"Good. Then we're safe," said Robert. "Okay, so next weekend, all of us, if possible, will go hiking in Savage Gulf, and two weeks from now, Saturday, March 16, we'll meet here and build the central office building. Meanwhile, and I've got a terribly busy week, I'll cut these Cedar trees on the site and order a concrete truck to come out here and pour a 15-by-20-foot pad, 6 inches thick. Plus, I need to have an exhaust system put on my car and swap out the rear end."

"I can come over and help you several afternoons," offered William. "I believe that there's an in-service training this Wednesday, so we'll have the whole day off from school."

"Really? Thank goodness!" said Robert. "We'll need it, and we'll certainly use it. See if Steven can come over and help. We'll need three of us to swap that rear end out, I'm sure."

"Okay, I'll call him," said William.

"Great! Then are we all set for the next two weeks?"

"Yes," both William and Morris replied.

"Good. Then we'll let the others know the plans and go from there," Robert concluded.

"Well, I guess I'll head on home," said William.

"Okay, let's walk back to your car in front of the house. Tell your father I said thanks again."

The three of them returned to Robert's house from the woods. William got in his car and left, and Morris stayed.

"Morris, I believe it's time we explained everything to my parents," Robert brought up. "Let's go inside and tell them and hope they understand."

They entered and began the conversation. Robert's parents were surprisingly understanding and quite interested, as a matter of fact. They consented quite easily to the telephone central office and were very interested in seeing it operational when it would be connecting phone calls to and from Earth and other star systems. After they finished the conversation, Morris left, and Robert took a 20-mile bicycle ride on some nearby back roads.

The next day after school, Robert made some phone calls to salvage yards, searching for a suitable rear end for his Ford LTD wagon. He found out that the salvage yard east of Murfreesboro had one in a junk Ford LTD, and he made arrangements for them to unbolt it and remove it from the car and that he would be out there the next day to buy it and pick it up.

Not long after Robert had arrived home from school today, Mr. Johns pulled in with his truck and trailer, full of the step office equipment from Eagleville. Robert saw him coming and went outside to greet him and to show him where to unload it.

"How are you doing, Mr. Johns?"

"Fine, Robert. How are you?"

"Just fine. I'll ride with you to the tenant house, and I'll clear a space for the equipment."

"Okay, hop in."

They rode up to the tenant house, which was in the direction of the woods from the main house and off to the right.

"Man, I tell you what," said Mr. Johns, "those boys had the whole step office ripped out in a heartbeat! I couldn't believe it! I got over there at 8 o'clock this morning with my truck and trailer and directed the show. They were finished by 1 o'clock!"

"They didn't tear any of the stuff up, did they?" asked Robert, concerned.

"Oh no! I made sure of that, but man they were quick! I tell you!"

"That *is* awfully fast, to have it all taken down and out of there in five hours," Robert admitted.

By this time, they had pulled up in front of the tenant house, and they began unloading the equipment. They moved a few pieces of stored furniture aside to make room, and then they began bringing it in: racks, switches, boxes, and all.

"I went ahead and got all of the Strowger switches so there would be some extra ones for future use in case some of them go bad," said Mr. Johns. "I made sure and got enough of the racks to mount everything too."

"That's great. You say you'll get the batteries later, right?"

"Right."

"By the way," Robert asked, "are we going to have to have a power supply to supply the 105 volts AC ringing voltage?"

"Yes, we sure are. I hadn't even thought of that. I'll see about getting an old used one. By the way, you'll have to run wires from the utility pole to the site of the central office to feed it with the electricity it needs."

"The pole is here by the tenant house," said Robert. "I'd prefer to bury the wires. Do you have access to a backhoe or a front-end loader or something like that?"

"Yeah, I've got one at home. If you like, I'll come out and dig the ditch from the pole to the site and prepare the site for the concrete pad. How about this Sunday?"

"That's fine, Mr. Johns. I'll go ahead and cut the trees right on the site and have them cleared out of the way for you to come next Sunday."

"Okay, and it looks like you'll need a couple hundred feet of #4 gauge wire," said Mr. Johns. "You'll need three strands. So, that will be a total of 600 feet."

"Tell you what," Robert suggested, "why don't we run the wires from the switchbox in the barn? It's a lot closer to the site."

"Yeah, that's a good idea. That will save a lot of wire. I didn't realize you had a switchbox in the barn. Okay, I'd say you'll need three strands, each 100 feet long."

"Good, I'll get that when I buy the building materials next week," said Robert. "Thanks very much for everything."

"No problem, Robert. I'm glad to help out."

"By the way, Mr. Johns, since your flatbed trailer is here, could we load my Ford LTD wagon onto it and take it to the muffler shop? It doesn't have an exhaust system, and I didn't want to drive it 10 miles into town without it. I didn't know how I was going to get it there, but seeing your trailer there made me think of it."

"Hmm . . . You are caught in a bind there, aren't you. Let's see. Yeah, I've got time. Come on, let's load it up, and we'll take it in for you."

"Thanks. Oh, wait," as Robert suddenly remembered something else. "I need to show you the site so you'll know where to dig."

"Oh, yeah. That's right."

They walked into the corner of the woods and marked the area for the concrete pad to be poured. Then they took the truck and trailer to the concrete pad where the Ford LTD wagon was parked and loaded it up onto the trailer and took it to the muffler shop. Robert went in and ordered an exhaust system consisting of one pipe, a muffler, and a tailpipe. He left the car with them overnight.

Mr. Johns took Robert back home and then returned to his home in Rockvale. Thanks to his kind and sincere help, the step office was soon to become a reality on Robert's farm.

It was now Wednesday, March 6, and everyone had the day off due to teacher in-service training. Robert had found a rear end out of a junk Ford LTD in the salvage yard east of Murfreesboro. It had a 3.55 ratio and was a locking type differential. They were not cheap at $200, but Robert had been saving for quite a while to purchase his car and pay for the parts necessary for the conversion. Besides, this rear end had the perfect ratio for his car, and he wouldn't pass it up. He had picked it up with the farm truck and had brought it home yesterday. Also, he had brought his car home from the muffler shop with the help of his father.

William and Steven came over around 8 a.m., and the three of them started taking out the 2.26 ratio rear end.

"I can't believe that Ford ever installed 2.26 ratio rear ends!" Robert remarked. "I just have no power to accelerate."

"That *is* a ridiculous ratio," agreed William. "They're just useless for 6-cylinders, but then they never did put a 6-cylinder motor in one of these models."

"That's right," said Robert. "I noticed that this 3.55 ratio rear end came out of a Ford LTD with overdrive. This car didn't come with overdrive, of course, but it has it now with this 3 O/D 4-speed manual."

"So, you got your exhaust system yesterday?" Steven asked, changing the subject.

"Yep. I got it yesterday."

"Well, it looks really good," Steven complimented. "I believe they did a good job for you."

"Good. I'm glad you think so."

It took the three of them four hours to swap out the rear end. Some of the bolts had been really difficult to break loose, but using a breaker bar and placing a long pipe over that, gave them enough leverage. Robert had to go to town to buy some new sockets because some of them, some cheap ones, had split apart under the stress. This time he bought Sears Craftsman sockets, and they worked fine. After bolting the new rear end into place and checking all of the connections, the car was ready to drive.

"It looks like it's ready to roll," said William.

"Okay, hop in. Let's go for a drive," offered Robert.

Robert, William, and Steven got in. Robert started it, put the transmission in first gear, and engaged the clutch. The car crawled.

"Oh, that's *much* better!" Robert announced. "I'm glad to take care of that problem."

They took it out on the road and drove it at highway speeds, and it drove very well. After returning, William and Steven both commented to Robert that he had a good running car.

Robert asked them, "Since we still have time this afternoon after lunch, would you help me clear the site for the telephone central office building? You both can have the trees for firewood."

"Yeah sure. We'll be glad to," answered Steven, speaking for William too.

"Great, thanks," said Robert. "Come on inside. Let's eat lunch."

After lunch, Robert got the chainsaw and went to work clearing a site large enough to accommodate a 15-by-20-foot concrete pad. William and Steven drug out the trees as Robert cut them down. Robert never did like cutting trees and cut no more than absolutely necessary. Afterwards, he went into the barnyard where the trees now lay and cut them up into logs for fenceposts and firewood. When they finished three hours later, it was late afternoon, and everyone was ready to call it a day.

"I really do thank you for you help today, William and Steven."

"No problem, Robert," said William. "Now we have us a road-trip car large enough to hold eight of us, even nine, if necessary."

"Let's make arrangements for everyone to meet out here early Saturday morning with backpacks and camping gear," Robert suggested.

"Okay, that sounds good," said William.

"Were you able to round up $100 from everyone, William?"

"Not yet, Robert. I spoke to them all about it. I'll see to it that everyone brings the $100 with him when we all come on Saturday."

"Okay, fine," said Robert. "That way, I'll be able to go ahead and buy the materials the first of next week."

"Okay, I guess I'll head on home," said William. "I'll see you tomorrow at school."

"Okay, see you tomorrow," said Robert, speaking to both William and Steven.

William and Steven walked back to their cars in front of Robert's house and left. Robert stayed a while longer looking over the site and making sure everything was ready for Mr. Johns to come with his backhoe this coming Sunday.

5 The Trip to Savage Gulf

Saturday morning, March 9, arrived. All nine of them, including Greg and Eric, arrived around 8 a.m. Each of them brought Robert $100 to pay for the materials for the central office building. It was nice, warm, and sunny, a perfect day for hiking. All of them left their cars, except for Robert and Paul. Morris, James, Steven, and William rode with Robert in his LTD wagon. The others rode with Paul.

It was a two-hour drive to Savage Gulf State Natural Area via Woodbury and McMinnville, and Robert's Ford LTD wagon drove very well.

"These 6-cylinders are really smooth running engines, aren't they?" Steven commented.

"Oh yes. They're much smoother than the V-8's, especially when it's cold," Robert agreed.

"I know mine is in my Chevrolet Bel Air," said Steven.

"Down in Australia," James brought up, "most larger cars come equipped with a 6-cylinder manual."

"Is that right?" Robert asked. "You know, why couldn't this country have made more cars with a 6-cylinder manual? Nearly every one has a V-8 automatic."

"I think it's because Americans like their luxuries and like for their cars to be loaded with all the bells and whistles," Steven answered.

"I reckon he's right," said James. "Aussies like having a dependable workhorse of a car. They just don't care for luxury models."

"I wish Americans were more like that," said William.

"Me too," Robert agreed. "What types of cars does Australia have that are equipped with a 6-cylinder manual?"

"Mainly, they are the GMH Holden Kingswood which they only stopped making last year," James answered. "The Ford Falcon is still being made along with the Fairmont and the Fairlane, but the Fairlanes went all automatic 10 years ago. Also, you see the odd Chrysler Valiant with a 6-cylinder manual."

"Do they change gears on the column or on the floor?" William wanted to know.

"Most of them are on the column with the left hand. As you remember, all cars are right-hand drive in Australia."

"Oh, yeah. They drive on the left, don't they?" Robert asked.

"That's right," James answered.

"Are the clutch, brake, and accelerator pedals arranged the same as here?" William asked.

"Yes, they are."

"How similar to American models are the Holden Kingswood, Ford Falcon, and the Chrysler Valiant?" Steven asked.

"They're almost the same," James replied, "since they're built in Australia based on American design. The Holden Kingswood looks like a Chevrolet Chevelle. The Ford Falcon looks most like a Fairlane or Torino. And the Chrysler Valiant looks very similar to a Plymouth Satellite."

"Isn't that interesting," commented Morris, speaking for the first time since they had left Robert's house. "What does Australia have in the way of English and Japanese cars?"

"They have heaps of them," James answered. "The Japanese cars are identical to the ones here, and the English cars most commonly seen are the Ford Escort and the Ford Cortina."

"So, it's not all that much different from this country, except that more Aussie cars are equipped with a stickshift, right?" William asked.

"What's a stickshift?" James wanted to know.

"You know, manual gearbox," William clarified.

"Oh, right. Yeah, right," said James. "Most of them are manual. That's right."

James now changed the subject. "Robert, tell me about Savage Gulf and what it's like."

"Savage Gulf is a protected state natural area. We'll enter it on the Stone Door side near Beersheba Springs, which is south of McMinnville a good ways. The trail descends through Stone Door between two tall rock faces or cliffs, and then it goes through the canyon for nearly 10 miles and then nine more miles along the rim of the plateau to the ranger station on the other side.

"We'll go as far as Savage Creek, which is some seven miles from

Stone Door, and we'll leave the trail to go upstream alongside the creek. We'll be away from anyone else up there, and the scenery is beautiful with a virgin forest of Hemlocks, Yellow Poplars, Oaks, Hickories, and other trees. I'm sure you'll love it up there."

"I can't wait till the trees come out with their leaves so I can identify them," said James.

"That will be another month," said Robert, "but I can still identify them by the bark and tell you what they are."

"Oh okay, good."

They talked about various subjects the whole way to Savage Gulf, including possible places that they could transport themselves. They went through Woodbury and then climbed the three-lane hill that put them up on the Highland Rim. Next, they went through Centertown on the way to McMinnville.

"James, did you know that the McMinnville area is one of the largest in the country in growing and selling trees and having nurseries?" Robert mentioned.

"No, I didn't. Dad and I may want to come down here and buy a bunch of trees, then."

"Yeah, if you want trees, they sell for a lot less here than they do anywhere else because the nurseries in this area supply all of the nurseries in the surrounding towns."

"Okay, I'll keep that in mind," said James. "Thanks for telling me."

Most of the highway from Murfreesboro to McMinnville was a decent two-lane road with shoulders, and it had been improved and widened from long ago. However, there was a two-mile stretch several miles before McMinnville that had never ever been rerouted nor widened from the stagecoach days of the 1800's. It had been paved, of course, but it was not at all built up.

The highway narrowed considerably and plunged right through a thick forest with a mixture of Hemlocks and hardwoods. Brownish colored moss covered most of the forest floor. Tree limbs reached over from each side, making it seem as though one were driving through a tunnel. There were no ditches on either side, and a thin layer of dirt or dust sat on the pavement, having been washed onto it by previous rains. There were also some curves, and one place was particularly hazardous due to a rock outcropping which protruded about one-third of the way into the eastbound lane. This rock was imbedded in the ground and had always been there. Robert had to slow down to let oncoming cars pass by, so he could safely drive around the rock without running over it. For some reason, the highway department had never bothered to remove it.

"Good gracious!" James exclaimed, quite surprised at this stretch of road. "Is this the highway?"

"Yes. This is it," said Robert.

"You're joking!" James carried on. "Are you sure you haven't missed a turn and gotten onto some back road?"

"Positive," Robert answered. "You see, this two-mile stretch of highway is still on the original roadbed of the stagecoach days. It's the last of it left, and I'm quite glad it's still here because it's quite scenic."

"Why has it never been widened like the rest of the highway?" James wanted to know.

"I believe the local landowners were against it. They refused to give up their land for this stretch of highway to be bypassed, and I believe this stretch also has some historical heritage. You'll see just up the road, right after we emerge from this forest, where the four-lane highway just stops where they attempted bypassing this stretch. At present, that four-lane highway only bypasses McMinnville."

"Will they eventually bypass this stretch?" James further asked.

"Oh, one day they might. I know for now that they couldn't get it passed through the budget, so it wasn't funded. Plus, I believe the landowners are against the bypass since it would wreck their property."

They emerged from the forest and came to a crossroads. To the left was a bridge overpass that was part of the four-lane highway. They crossed a four-way intersection and soon merged onto the four-lane McMinnville bypass going further east. Sure enough, behind them they could see how the divided highway dead-ended on the other side of the bridge.

"That was really scenic and unique!" James suddenly spoke out.

"I fully agree as many others do," said Robert. "That's probably most of the reason why it's still there." Needless to say, William, Steven, and Morris already knew about this stretch of highway and therefore had no comment, seeing that Robert was doing well enough in answering James' questions.

Soon, they turned right, leaving the McMinnville bypass, and drove through downtown McMinnville to take the road to Beersheba Springs. After climbing up the steep, winding road that took them up onto the Cumberland Plateau, they entered Beersheba Springs where they turned left to take the small road to Stone Door.

They arrived around 10 a.m., obtained overnight permits, put on their backpacks, and set out hiking the easy trail for the first mile to Stone Door. This first mile was dominated by Shortleaf Pines (*Pinus echinata*) and plenty of hardwood trees. They soon arrived at Stone Door and went to the cliff's edge to see the fantastic views of the canyon below.

"Wow! That's some view!" James exclaimed. "And it's all forested."

"Yes, most of it has already been logged long ago, and it's grown back now," said Robert. "In fact, the only virgin forest left is in areas that they just could not get to."

"This sure is a tall cliff," said Chris.

"Yes, and the canyon is large too," said Robert. "This is one of my favorite places to visit."

They looked around for a few more minutes and then descended the steep trail between the tall rock faces of Stone Door until they reached the bottom of the cliff. Then they descended until they reached a trail intersection near the canyon floor. From there, the trail had its ups and downs, sometimes following old logging roads and crossing rivers and streams.

"Morris," said Greg, "tell us more about your new ability to transmit visual images with your mind."

"Yes, I've been working on it. I haven't really used it with anyone yet to see how well I can do it, but let's wait until we get to where we camp this afternoon. When we settle down and rest this evening, I'll transmit some visual images to all of you, and we'll see how well it actually works."

"Yeah, okay. I look forward to that," said Greg.

"What types of trees grow down here?" James asked Robert.

"Well, as you look around you, you'll see one type of tree still holding on to its brown leaves. Those are Beech trees, *Fagus grandifolia*," Robert explained. "They are one of the closest relatives to the American Chestnut, which as you may know, got wiped out by a blight brought over from Europe in the early part of this century. Chestnuts still remain, but they usually get knocked off at sapling size as they relentlessly sprout from old roots.

"Also, there are several types of Oak and Maple trees. They are under the genus of *Quercus* and *Acer* respectively. Plenty of Hickories, which are under the *Carya* genus, grow here along with several types of Ash, which are classified under the *Fraxinus* genus. Yellow Poplar, *Liriodendron tulipfera*, is also common and is Tennessee's state tree. Also, you will see plenty of Flowering Dogwoods, *Cornus florida*, and they bloom with large white flowers.

"In wetter areas, you'll find Yellow Birch, *Betula alleghaniensis*; Sycamore, *Platanus occidentalis*; Buckeyes, *Aesculus* genus; and Eastern Hemlock, *Tsuga canadensis*. A rarer tree is the American Hornbeam, *Carpinus caroliniana*.

"In more open areas, you'll find the Eastern Red Cedar, *Juniperus virginiana*. I'm sure there are other types I haven't mentioned. Tennessee is known for its variety of trees, especially in the Appalachian Mountains east of here."

"What types of wildflowers grow here?" James wanted to know.

"The most common ones are the Trillium, Jack-in-the-Pulpit, Bloodroot, Dutchman's Breeches, Hepatica, Mayapple, and Anemone. Phlox grows here too, but it's more of a weed. Probably the only ones you'll see today are the Hepaticas and the Trilliums since it is still early in the season."

"You know a lot about plants," said Eric.

"Yes, it's a hobby for me, and I think it's important to know as much as you can about trees, plants, wildlife, and that type of thing," said Robert.

"James," said Paul, "did you know that the Firs and Spruces are suffering from acid rain on Mt. Mitchell in North Carolina?"

"No, I didn't," he replied, quite surprised to find this out. "You mean it's happening in this country too? I thought it was only in Europe."

"It's here in this country too," Robert answered, speaking for Paul. "I went up Mt. Mitchell last summer, and they had the EPA up there studying it. I went to ask them a question, and they wouldn't even answer."

"It's as if they're *hiding* something from us or at least acting that way," Chris suggested.

"I thought the trees were dying only from the effects of the wooly aphid," said Steven.

"That's true," Robert partially agreed, "but I believe the trees have been weakened by the acid rain, and therefore the wooly aphid has set in. I'll bet the EPA will tell you that it's purely the fault of the wooly aphid in selected areas and that other mountain tops are unaffected. Well, the fact is that all other mountain tops are also affected, and in every case, the Firs and Spruces at lower altitudes are doing just fine. Why would a wooly aphid go only for the tops of the mountains? Mt. LeConte in the Great

Smoky Mountains, for example, is also losing its trees on its top. It's happening all through the Appalachians, even in Vermont."

"What do you think is causing it?" James asked.

"Mainly," Robert answered, "it's air pollution from factories and industries in the southeast United States. The prevailing winds blow from there over the mountains, and their tops act as a comb as the clouds pass over them. Mt. Mitchell's soil has as much lead in it as does the side of a freeway in Los Angeles."

"That's terrible!" Paul exclaimed. "And I'd say that what the EPA will do is study the site, pack up, go home, and file the report."

"That's right," Robert agreed, "and they probably won't do anything about it either. Oh, they may make some factories install scrubbers on their smoke stacks or pass some more emissions laws, but the fact is that fossil fuels will still be used."

They continued discussing this issue for some time as they made their way through the canyon, stopping for lunch along the way, and then continuing until they made a last short descent to Savage Creek.

Robert announced, "Here we are at Savage Creek. We get off the trail here and turn right and follow that logging road upstream until it dead ends. Then we push further through the forest itself. There's a really nice area up there way on top of a steep bank up from the creek, and it's nice and flat and under a bunch of Hemlocks. We can set up camp there if you like."

All of them agreed, turned right, and started upstream. The logging road climbed steeply in places and ended after about a mile. From there they pushed through forest, and the going was not easy as they had to step and sometimes jump from boulder to boulder. Many of the boulders were loose and would wobble under their feet, making it difficult to keep their balance. Despite the difficulty of the terrain, it was worth the trouble to see this magnificent forest, which had never been logged. Only Robert had been in this area before when he had hiked through here a year and a half earlier.

"Wow! Look at the size of these trees!" Andrew exclaimed.

"Aren't they huge!" said Morris.

"Yes, they certainly are," Robert agreed.

"I've never seen trees this big before," said William.

"Me neither," Chris added.

"Look at that big Oak tree," Paul pointed out. "It must be 75 feet to the first limb and straight as an arrow!"

"I'm glad this stand was never subjected to the sawmills," said James.

"Me too," Morris agreed. "It's nice that some of this was untouched and therefore preserved."

"This is really beautiful back in here," said Steven. "Listen to the creek below us."

"I've never seen Hemlocks and Poplars so huge," said Eric. "Some of them must be five feet in diameter."

"I know," said Greg. "Some of these Hickories are large too."

"You can see how difficult it would have been for the early loggers to have come back in here," Robert pointed out. "I think this bunch of boulders prevented them from coming and logging it."

"I reckon so," said James.

After an hour of pushing through the treacherous terrain, they arrived at the spot Robert recommended and set up their bedrolls under the grove of Hemlocks.

"This is incredible!" shouted James. "I'm so glad you brought us all here. Let's go down to the creek and see what's there."

They made their way down the steep 50-foot bank to the creek's edge. There on the other side of the creek was a waterfall, and it dropped into a beautiful crystal-clear pool. Some of them decided to take a quick swim in the cold water. Also, there were some stacks of logs bunched up together, having been washed down by previous floods. Some of them climbed around on them for a while.

It was now late afternoon, and after they had looked around enough, they returned to the top of the bank and ate supper. They decided not to have a campfire because it would not be good for the environment, and there was not an already existing fire ring. All of them were environmentally conscious enough to realize that campfires were unnecessary unless someone was really cold and needed to warm up. Shortly after 6 p.m., it got dark, and they began talking while they were resting and sitting in a circle.

"Okay, Morris," Greg brought up, "tell us more about transmitting visual images."

"Okay," he answered, "as you know, the galactic salesman arranged for me to have this gift in exchange for our making arrangements to have a galactic communications device installed for the purpose of connecting Earth's telephone network to other planets and star systems."

"Right," said Greg.

"What I'm going to do now," he continued, "is to transmit a scene from another planet."

After a few seconds, Robert said, "I see a mountainside."

"So do I," said Steven.

"Me too," said Andrew.

As Morris looked at every one of them, they all saw the same mountainside, and they therefore agreed that Morris' transmission of visual images really worked.

"This scene is on a planet in a star system in another galaxy," explained Morris, "and I've dreamed of being there before. There's supposed to be a stone hut not too far from the summit, and a lady who gives psychic readings lives there."

"Oh really? Let's go there," Steven suggested.

"Okay then," said Morris, "do all of you remember how to use your gift of transporting yourselves?"

Everyone answered that they did.

"Is everyone up to it?" Robert checked.

All of them answered yes, regardless of how they felt.

"Okay, let's go for it," said Robert, and he began giving the instructions. "This will be good practice for all of us. Everyone stand up and place your hands on either side of you, not quite touching, and think of that place you just saw in your mind. Transmit the energy through your hands, and remember how it felt last time you transported yourselves. As you remember, we all have an etheric silver platter under each of us, and it's not detectable on the physical level."

All of them stood up from the circle in which they had been sitting. As they took their positions and placed their hands on their sides, 10 separate sounds of whirring wind could be heard, and pink glows overcame them, causing them to disappear. In five seconds, they materialized on the side of the mountain on that planet in a faraway galaxy. It was broad daylight.

"My goodness!" Robert exclaimed. "We're actually on the side of the mountain, and this really *is* another planet!"

"Look at the sun here," Andrew remarked. "It's more of a bluish color than our yellow-white sun back on Earth."

"Look at these trees," said James. "Most of them seem coniferous. In fact, many of them look like trees back on Earth." As James pointed up the slope which contained grassy meadows dotted with more of these trees and shrubs, he added, "Look how many there are up the mountainside."

"Yeah, the trees and plants here look very similar to the ones back on Earth," Robert agreed, "but they are also different from the ones back in Tennessee."

"Come on," said Greg. "Let's go on up the mountain and see if the stone hut is really there."

For the next hour, they climbed the mountain slope, passing through lots of beautiful mountain meadows surrounded by mostly coniferous type trees. There were several streams and small lakes the size of ponds throughout most of these meadows. Views of the valley behind them were magnificent, and there was no sign of civilization anywhere. It looked totally pristine with nothing man-made until they would see the hut later on. There were no signs of any logging operations anywhere, not even on the distant forests seen on the other mountain slopes near the horizon.

"I don't believe any people live on this planet," said Chris.

"Or if they do, they really care for it well," Eric added.

"This is really wonderful how pristine this planet is," James commented. "Earthlings need to take lessons from the ones that may be living here."

"We hiked all day in Savage Gulf, and here we are hiking again," said Steven. "Boy are we going to sleep well tonight!"

"I'll say!" William agreed. "This planet seems so Earth-like. Can you believe we are actually probably over a million light years from home right now?"

"I don't know," said Greg. "I feel like we are just somewhere else on Earth."

"Oh, believe me," said Morris. "we are actually on another planet in another galaxy."

They finally came out onto a fairly level grassy meadow with the summit up the ridge to the right. Sure enough, right there in the meadow was the small stone hut that Morris had said would be there. It was 10 by 15 feet and had stone shingles. From the direction that they had come, the door was on the other side of the hut.

As they came around the side of the hut, a lady stepped outside to greet them. She was the psychic that Morris had told them about.

"Hello Morris," she said. "I see you brought your body with you this time. It looks like your friends did too. How do you like your new gift that Robert Joslin received and granted to all of you?"

The whole group was shocked that she could know these things. They had never seen her before in their life. For the next hour, she proceeded to give all of them psychic readings.

"That's amazing that you would know that," said Morris. "This gift of transporting myself is the most fantastic thing that's ever happened to me!"

"Oh, I know a lot," she went on. "I could see it in your auras as you all were coming up the mountain. As you know, Morris, you've visited me here in your dreams. I don't believe I've ever told you my name before, have I?"

"No, you haven't," he answered.

"My name is Virginia, and I live in the western part of your country. You see, I have the same ability that you all have recently acquired. It is a precious and rare gift that you have been granted. Very few Earthlings have this gift, but you 10 were determined to be the best choice because you all are of sound mind and body, and you care for your own planet. I'm sure you know that most Earthlings don't care and are quite physically destructive to the flora and fauna.

"Anyway, welcome to my mountain. The natives of this planet have designated me to be guardian of this mountain and to take care of the life forces and energies for all living things in this area. When I need to recharge myself, I just take my body and transport myself here to spend a few days several times a year. This wonderful place serves me well, and I serve it well."

"Who are the natives that live here?" Andrew wanted to know.

"Actually, they are people in a sense, but they don't look exactly like human beings," she answered. "The natives here live more on a semi-etheric level, and they spend a lot of time thinking. At present, they are in the process of converting from the etheric level to the physical level."

"When you say semi-etheric," Robert asked, "does that mean they look like ghosts?"

"No, I wouldn't say ghosts," she answered. "It's just that they are not yet totally existent on a physical level. They don't yet have physical bodies, so they can just travel anywhere they desire. All they have to do is to think of where they want to be, and they can be there instantaneously."

"That seems impossible," said Greg.

"Oh, it's possible, and it really happens," she confirmed. "Being from Earth, I have to transport myself like you 10 do, using the etheric silver platter, the pink glow, and the whirring wind. However, since the natives here do not yet have physical bodies, they don't require all of that."

"Where are we?" Morris asked. "That is, what is the name of this star system?"

"This planet is in a star system in another galaxy, but I believe you already know that, Morris. As far as the name of it is concerned, I'm not sure exactly how it would be pronounced in our language, that is, in English. It would be something like Lopeia, spelled L-O-P-E-I-A."

"Anyway," she went on, "the purpose of our meeting today is to give each one of you a reading and tell you some things about yourselves. Robert, I'll begin with you." She revealed a white piece of 8½-by-11-inch paper. "Here's a piece of paper. I need you to write 'SHS' on it."

Robert wrote "SHS" in huge letters large enough to cover the whole page.

Virginia commented, "You may have thought this stood for Spanish. Actually, it stands for this evaluation of you, taking you deeper into the spiritual. Come on in, and I'll give you a reading."

Robert followed her into the small stone hut and sat across the table from her. The appearance of the room was very simple. It showed no signs of being a typical setting of a fortune teller. Virginia didn't use any material items like a crystal ball or playing cards. Instead, she just gave the reading by looking mostly around his head. The other nine waited outside for their turn, and they rested and talked among themselves.

"Okay, Robert," she began. "You have very good grades in high school, and you have plenty of friends as I can see. Looking into the future, I see that two will remain true, true, true friends. That's not to say that the others won't be friends. They will all remain good friends. See, you 10 connect very well on all levels, and you've been together over many, many lifetimes in various star systems. All of you go way back.

"I can see that all 10 of you, especially you, Robert, maintain very high moral standards of never drinking, never smoking, and never doing drugs. That's one of the reasons that you 10 were chosen and bestowed the gift of transporting yourselves."

"That is absolutely correct," Robert verified. "All of us maintain very high moral standards."

"You see," she explained, "this is just part of your puritanical aspect of your belief system in being right, and it works very well for you."

"That's true," Robert confirmed. "Most Earthlings who maintain these high moral standards do it because their religion dictates it, but that's not why I do it."

"That's *right*," she commented. "Religion has nothing to do with it." She revealed a small photograph. "Now, look at this photo of these people standing on the mountaintop. Behind the fellow on the right is a man with a black robe and a roped belt much like a man dressed for a masonic meeting. You may not be able to see him, but he's there. He's your guide."

"I don't see him," said Robert.

"Oh, he's there," she insisted. "It's just that he exists in a different plane and is therefore invisible. Hold it a certain way, and you'll see him. It's sort of like a concealed holographic image."

Robert moved the photo through different angles. "Oh yeah!" he exclaimed. "Now I see him. Oh my goodness! Virginia, he's my great-grandfather! I recognize him from old family pictures that my parents have. He was a grand mason and died in 1953 at age 90."

"That's correct," she confirmed.

"Wait. If he's my guide, why is it that I'm not a devout religious man like he was?"

"Because," she explained, "once he passed on, he immediately realized that he had narrowed his belief system down to a final answer. When he passed over to the other side, he came to realize that his belief was not the final say and that there was more out there than anyone knows. He learned what it was like to live a life belonging to one religious denomination and that a true belief system requires an open mind containing knowledge that is subject to revision as one learns more about how things really are."

"I see," said Robert. "It is true that I always keep an open mind so that I can learn more."

"That's good," she finished. "Now, come on outside and I'll choose the next one for a reading."

They got up from the table and walked outside. Immediately, she chose another one.

"Greg Nelson, you're next. Come on inside and have a seat."

Greg entered, and as he was sitting down, he asked, "How do you already know our names?"

"When I look at a person, I can hear it," she answered. "My guide speaks to me regularly and gives me much of my detailed knowledge. Also, I am very experienced at reading the many light colors of a person's aura. Very few people read auras as well as I do.

"From what I see, Greg, it looks like you have a great life ahead of you. You will remain single for some time yet, having no great interest in marriage for that time. I'm looking at your colors here, and it looks like you will be a guardian of people's teeth, helping them in that aspect."

"That sounds about right," Greg confirmed.

"I can see that you and William have been good friends before," she went on, "more so than with the other eight, even that you've also been friends with all of them. As I was telling Robert, the 10 of you connect very well and go way back over many past lives in various star systems."

"That's very interesting," said Greg.

"Also, I see that you have an interest in dreams and how they work, as do Robert and Morris. Keep that interest. Those who pay attention to their dreams are very wise."

"I will," he said.

"All right, let's go outside now, and I'll give the rest of the readings out there."

They stepped outside the hut, and as Greg joined the others, Virginia stood just outside the doorway and looked from one person to another. After half a minute, she started.

"James Westfield, looking at you, I can see that your most recent past life was on this very planet. You were an excellent guardian of the flora and fauna here, and you channeled the life-giving energies to them very well. You have a keen interest in trees and plants as does Robert, and you believe that everything has its place in the world.

"You see, you're not really an Earth person. Your present life is new to you since it is your first incarnation on Earth. Even though you've been friends in past lives with your friends here, you've always known them on other planets in other star systems. You chose to incarnate on Earth this time because Earth is in a crisis and needs caring guardianship like yours. Remain a purist and you will have a very successful and fulfilling life."

James was stunned at how she could have known that he had a keen interest in trees and plants. He said, "I don't know how much I believe in reincarnation, but you *are* right that I care a great deal about Earth and that everything has its place in the world. Some of the trees here look like the trees of planet Earth. How can that be possible?"

"Oh, you must keep in mind that Earth's flora and fauna have been nearly wiped out by awful cataclysms over the last several hundred million years," she explained, "and that Earth has had to be restocked. Many of

the tree species on Earth, for example, also grow here. Everything on this planet is endemic to here, and whatever you see on Earth that is the same as here means that they were transported from here to Earth at some time in the past. What I'm saying is that extraterrestrials have visited many planets in many star systems since the Earth began over 4 billion years ago, and flora and fauna have been transferred to and from many star systems over that time period, and that's why a lot of it looks the same and is the same, to some extent. Not all planets have had to be restocked like Earth has, and these unaffected planets still have their endemic flora and fauna.

"As a comparison to extraterrestrials transferring flora and fauna to and from many star systems, think about what's happened on Earth in just the last 300 years," she explained, "with people and settlers bringing plants with them. I'm sure you're aware of the North American and European trees growing in Australia, especially the Monterey Pine and Monterey Cypress."

"Oh yes, very much so," James confirmed.

"Paul Wilson, looking at you, I can see that you have a great interest in music and a keen sense of business as well. I don't know if you'll get rich with a music career, but your business knowledge will carry you far.

"I can see that you'll be married before 10 years from now," she continued. "When you meet your future wife for the first time, you will immediately recognize her on a soul level, and you will instantly know that she will be the one to be your wife."

"How could I possibly know that?" Paul wanted to know.

"Oh, you will," she assured him. "Believe me. You will know. See, you and she had a great past life together, and you both made a pact that you would return again for another life together. Even though you may presently live far from one another, which I think you do right now, you two will find each other. Now, don't make an effort to find a wife. It will just happen for you."

"That's interesting," said Paul. "We'll just wait and see. What will her name be?"

"I can hear it," she answered, "but the voices are telling me that her name is not to be revealed to you until the time is near for you to meet her."

"Typical! Just typical!" Paul remarked.

"Paul," she explained, "if I were to give you her name, you would know too much, and it could very well block you from letting the natural course of events happen. You might possibly end up with someone else with the same first name, and that someone else would not be the one with whom you made the pact. Later, you would still meet the right one and would then realize that you had made a serious mistake."

"Oh, well if it's that serious," said Paul, "I guess I'd better not find out her name until the time is right."

"That would be very wise," said Virginia. "Now, Steven Price, I can see that you and Robert Joslin were brothers in Russia some 250 years ago. It looks like you both got along fine, but travel was forbidden. That didn't make any difference to you, but Robert was just about fit to be tied over not being allowed to travel. That's why he likes to travel and explore so much this time."

"Huh! You must have read my mind!" exclaimed Steven. "I believe in reincarnation, and I remember a lot about my past lives."

"You see, being brothers in a past life is why you two struck it off immediately and became fast friends this time," she explained. "You're a really fine person, and your life's purpose is to overcome your not having a desire to travel. Don't limit yourself, and don't feel guilty about travelling with your friends here. Travelling is a fantastic way to learn about the diversity of life and how all types are important, how they all have their place in the world, and how they all need to be cared for. Have a great time this summer on your travels. You'll learn more than you can ever imagine."

"Thank you," said Steven. "How did you know that I felt a tinge of guilt about travelling?"

"That's a carryover from your life in Russia, and that's what you're tuning in to," she answered.

"Morris England," she went on, "we've already had discussions in your dreams. I will tell you that your newly acquired crystal ball is very important to you in your life. It will help you connect things from the past with the present."

"It was really weird," Morris commented, "how it was just sitting on top of a battery bank over at the Eagleville telephone exchange."

"That's *right*," Virginia told him in a confident manner. "See, it needed to be charged up for use after that galactic salesman teleported himself to Earth with it and delivered it to that location."

"That's brilliant!" exclaimed Morris.

At this time, Morris was taking a leather pouch out of his daypack. He turned the pouch upside down into the palm of his hand, revealing the crystal ball so that Virginia could see it.

"Morris, that crystal ball in your hand is just *incredible!*" she remarked. "It's so powerful, and it's sending out the most beautiful rays of mostly white light. That really is a *gem!*"

"Thank you," Morris told her. "I really am glad to have it."

"Okay, Andrew Tremain," she chose next, "I'm looking at the colors around your head and see that you are very engineering oriented. You have a fantastic ability to create objects based on theoretical data in books. I'm sure you'll have some input on the sending and receiving equipment for that galactic communications device that you all are building on Robert Joslin's farm.

"Also, you and Robert have known each other mostly in the Pleiades, and you were both engineers there. There was a lot of competition between you two, and on one project a large bonus went to the one that got the first thing accomplished. Of course, there's no competition this time. Enjoy the project of building the galactic communications device."

"That's pretty good. You're fairly accurate," Andrew commented.

"Okay, Chris Chanford," she went on, "I'll choose you next. Your main interest is in philosophy. See, you've been one of the great prophets on Earth before, and your wisdom has affected and helped many people. Your travelling this summer with your friends will offer you great opportunities to broaden your knowledge and understand how beings of all types interrelate with one another."

"That *is* pretty good," said Chris. "Philosophy is my main interest."

"Now William Johns, looking at you, I can see that you have a great interest in working on cars and also a keen interest in airplanes. You were a chief technician for much of the equipment in use in the Pleiades thousands of years ago, and some of that has carried over to now. Enjoy your travels and learn as much as you can in life."

William stood there and made no comment.

"Eric Smotherman, you're right on track, this lifetime," she said. "You've been one of the great pottery makers of the old world, and continuing that this lifetime will help you relate to and understand the differences between then and now. For example, you'll relate to people far and wide because you'll have orders for your work from all parts of the world."

"Yeah, that's about right," he said. "I hope I can sell my pottery to all sorts of people far and wide."

"Well, that's about our time," she concluded. "I'm sure you'll return to this planet on your travels. Take care and have a great summer. Learn as much as you can."

Everyone thanked her, and she went back inside the hut. It had been nearly an hour since they had arrived at this hut, and the sun was now low on the horizon.

"Let's go up that ridge to the summit and see the sunset," James suggested.

All of them left the hut and made the final climb along the ridge in 10 minutes by which time the colors of the sunset were incredible with the most vivid colors of orange and red as they had ever seen.

"I've never seen such a vivid, colorful sunset before," said Greg.

"Absolutely spectacular!" exclaimed Robert.

"Fantastic!" Steven remarked.

They watched the sunset and took in the spectacular views of the surrounding mountains and valleys seen from this summit. What a great time they were having, seeing this other world for a brief time.

"Well, I guess we had better return to our campsite under the Hemlocks and hit the sack," Morris suggested.

"Yes, I guess it's time to go back," said Robert, looking at his watch. "It's getting pretty late for us, Earth time."

They placed their hands on their sides, and supplying the energy through their hands, they transported themselves back to their campsite on Earth in the grove of Hemlocks.

Upon arriving, James made the first comment. "I'll tell you, I never thought psychics amounted to very much, but *that* one was amazing! She hardly missed a lick!"

"I'll say!" Robert remarked. "If I have any more questions, I'll just go back to her. Forget any *other* psychics!"

"She *was* pretty good," said Chris.

"Yes, she was the very same one I had dreamed about," said Morris. "This proves to me that a lot of the places I've dreamed about are very real and that we can travel to them this summer."

"I can't wait!" shouted Paul. "I'm really looking forward to it. It will be fun."

"I'm telling you what," said William, "that was *some* psychic! I was too surprised to make a comment at the time."

"And she knew all about my pottery," said Eric.

"And about my future wife," Paul added. "We'll just see about that one."

They continued talking about their evening journey and about their visit with the psychic for another half hour before their excitement died down enough for them to go to sleep for the night. It was a peaceful night, and the creek could be heard way below at the foot of the bank. No sound of civilization could be heard this far into Tennessee's wilderness.

Sunrise was around 6 a.m., and they woke up soon after that to a beautiful, clear, sunny morning.

"I still can't believe we actually went to another planet last night," said Steven.

"Oh, we certainly did, and this is only the beginning," said Morris.

"I also can't get over her accuracy for details," Steven went on.

"You see," Morris explained, "she hears voices, those of her own spiritual guides. All of us have guides of some sort, and some of them are always with us. All our guides have to do is to communicate with her guides, and suddenly, she has all of the answers for whomever she's talking to. That's my theory."

"Yeah, that makes sense," said Steven.

Robert was just now waking up and said, "I'd say that most of the psychics on Earth aren't really able to hear those voices, and they just make stuff up."

James joined in and said, "I reckon that's right. I used to think that psychic stuff was all hogwash, but she made a believer out of me!"

"Yeah, you and all of us," Paul declared. "I'm never going to discredit psychic ability again."

"Me neither," said Robert, "at least for the ones who are authentic, which she certainly is."

By now, they had all awakened. After eating some breakfast, they decided to take a morning day hike further upstream along Savage Creek to explore more of this virgin forest. All 10 of them left their backpacks at the campsite and set out across the treacherous, rocky terrain, which was full of loose boulders, many of them covered with moss. Still, the sight of some of the large trees made the rough going worthwhile.

After making their way upstream, somewhat alongside and up from Savage Creek for about an hour, they came upon a huge tree, much larger than the others.

"My goodness! Look at that one!" exclaimed Robert.

"I'm telling you what," said William, "that's the largest tree I've ever seen!"

"Same here," Paul agreed.

All of them stood gazing up at it in amazement, not believing that something this big could be here.

"Here," said James, "let's see how many of us it takes to reach all the way around it."

James, Greg, and Robert were the first ones to it and took their positions.

"Can you reach my hand, Robert?" James asked.

Robert reached and said, "Barely," as he was just able to reach far enough to touch his hand.

"Three people can barely reach around this tree!" Greg declared.

"That means it's about 18 feet in circumference or roughly 6 feet in diameter," said Eric.

"Yes, this is a *very* large tree!" said Greg, emphatically.

"What type of tree is this, Robert?" James wanted to know.

"Let's see, James. The bark looks like a Buckeye, but it couldn't be." Robert looked around on the ground for seeds for the answer and found Buckeye seeds all over the ground. "It actually *is* a Buckeye tree! I had no idea they grew so large, and it's amazing that this type of tree would be the largest of any tree in here."

"What is a Buckeye tree?" James asked.

"It's a tree with clusters of five leaves and is just like a Horsechestnut, except for *that* one has seven," Robert answered. "Buckeyes are sort of a link between the Hickories, Chestnuts, and Beech trees. All trees are related if you go back far enough."

"I see," said James. "Yes, I've seen plenty of Horsechestnuts planted in gardens in Tasmania."

"Well, I guess we had better head back to our campsite and go on out of here so we can get back to our cars before dark," Steven suggested.

"Yeah, I guess we'll have to," said James. "I wish we could stay longer. I love it back here."

They decided to turn around here and make the long, treacherous walk out the same way they had come in, picking up their backpacks at the campsite on the way out.

"Of course, you know," Morris reminded, "we can come back any time we like with our new gift of transport."

"Oh, yeah. That's right," said Robert. "I didn't even think about it. I'm still not used to the idea."

They continued downstream alongside Savage Creek, arriving once again at the logging road, which they followed downhill until they reached the trail crossing. As they hiked the seven miles back to Stone Door, they didn't see anyone else, nor had they seen anyone the day before. Most people generally waited until later in the spring to go hiking.

Approximately two miles before they reached Stone Door, a thunderstorm moved in, and it began to rain. They soon crossed a creek with huge, overhanging boulders imbedded in its banks, and they quickly took shelter under two of them. Lightning came and sometimes struck nearby.

CRACK! POW!

"Golly, that was a close one!" yelled Andrew.

"I know," said Robert. "I hope we don't get struck."

"Look at it. What a downpour!" shouted James.

They remained under the large overhanging rocks until the storm passed

over. Twenty minutes later, the rain quit. The skies soon cleared, and they went on. In less than an hour, they were climbing up through Stone Door back onto the plateau.

After an easy last mile back to the parking lot, they got into their two cars and drove back to Murfreesboro. It was 7 p.m. by the time they arrived back at Robert Joslin's farm, where they each got into their own cars, commenting on what a great time they had, and drove home.

Robert went inside the house and proceeded to tell his parents all about their adventures in Savage Gulf, including their evening excursion to a planet in the Lopeia star system in a faraway galaxy. They were also impressed to hear about the large Buckeye tree that Robert and his friends had seen along Savage Creek.

After this discussion, his father, Bob, said, "Mr. Johns came over today and prepared the site for the concrete pad and dug a ditch from the barn to bury the electrical cables. You might go up and have a look at it."

"Okay," said Robert, glad to hear that this part of the project was finished. "I'll get a flashlight and go up there right now." He went up and saw that Mr. Johns had done a fine job, and he made plans to have a concrete truck come later in the week.

6 The Galactic Communications Device

Monday afternoon after school, Robert and Morris met and drove to different places around town, stopping first at Murfreesboro Ready Mix where they ordered a load of concrete to be brought by truck and poured the same time the next day. Next, they went to Autumn Electric and bought three 100-foot segments of #4 AWG wire suitable for burying.

They also stopped by Haynes Brothers Lumber Company to order the 2-by-6 rafters, half-inch plywood, 10 bundles of roofing shingles, and nails. Haynes Brothers didn't have concrete blocks, so they sent them to James Block and Brick Company for these and for the mortar mix. Robert and Morris made arrangements to have that delivered also. Robert had decided to go ahead and buy the concrete blocks new, since blocks from a wrecked building might have been stressed or cracked. After all, they were fairly inexpensive.

Last, they made a stop at Clark Iron and Metal to pick through their scrap to see what they could find. Sure enough, they found a metal door in good condition complete with the frame. They bought that on the spot. After these stops, Robert had spent around $600 and believed he had just enough left to pay for the concrete.

"Well, I guess that's about all I can think of, Morris," said Robert. "Can you think of anything else?"

"Nope. I believe we've got everything we need," said Morris. "Let's go back to my car at the parking lot at Riverdale, and I'll go home."

Robert returned to Riverdale and delivered Morris and went on home, glad to have all of the building materials rounded up and ready. He finished some homework, studied, ate supper, and eventually went to bed.

When Robert got home Tuesday afternoon, William came over and helped him build a sort of a mold for the concrete to be poured. Around the edges to be poured, Mr. Johns had dug deeper, forming a ditch, so that the building would have a foundation strong enough to support the walls. They also put layers of old woven wire fencing on the ground to make the concrete pad stronger, and they placed a piece of curved metal pipe under the mold to house and bring in the wires.

The concrete blocks and mortar mix had already been delivered along with the rafters, plywood, and roofing shingles, and they were covered with plastic. It was all there, ready to be used, and Robert's father had moved the cattle to the lower barnyard so they would be out of the way until this building project was completed.

Around 4:30 p.m., the concrete truck arrived and poured several cubic yards of concrete into the mold that Robert and William had just completed. They watched them rake and brush the concrete to a smooth surface over the next half hour, and they were impressed with their fine work. Robert paid them, and they left.

"That really looks good," Robert commented.

"Yes, it does," William agreed. "We'll all come out here Saturday and go to it. I don't see it taking us more than a day."

"Me neither, and I'm looking forward to it being built," said Robert.

They admired what had been done so far and called it a day. William got into his car and went back home.

The rest of the week went well at school, and Robert and the rest of them made plans to be at his place early Saturday morning to help him build the step office building.

Saturday, March 16, came soon enough, and the weather was beautiful and warm. The concrete pad had completely dried and was now ready for the concrete blocks to be laid on top of it. All nine of them arrived, ready to go to work while Robert directed the show and joined in with them on building it.

"Okay, I need someone to constantly mix mortar mix in this wheelbarrow using this hoe. There's plenty of water in that watering trough that the cattle use. Here's a bucket to use to collect and pour water into the wheelbarrow, and the mix needs to be of a thick, plastic-like consistency."

Paul took that job, and Robert continued giving directions. "I need four of you to lay blocks while the other four of you lay mortar using the triangular and rectangular trowels and scrapers I've supplied. I'll join in when I can and will make sure that the walls are going up straight and that the mortar joints are good.''

Things went very well, and they had all four walls and the door up and installed by noon. It had taken only five hours, and nearly all of the concrete blocks and mortar mix had been used.

All 10 of them really could hustle, and none of them had to play a radio to accompany them while they worked. They didn't need or want such things. Besides, they needed to talk to each other to keep things straight as they built the walls, and they enjoyed talking to each other and not having the radio's music imposed upon them.

When the walls were finished, they stopped for lunch and went down to the house to eat. Robert's mother served them sandwiches and pieces of fruit with a choice of various fruit juices, milk, or water to drink, and they ate on the front porch. After lunch and a short rest, they returned to the site and continued working on the building.

The weather remained nice and sunny all day, and they placed 16 of the 20 rafters on the building. The remaining four were cut up for spacers to tie the rafters together. Next, they nailed the 10 pieces of plywood in place and got ready to put on the roof.

"I forgot all about tar paper!" Robert suddenly realized. "Hold on a minute, and let me check to see if there's any in the barn." He went to check and was relieved to find two rolls of it. This saved him a trip all the way to town to purchase forgotten materials.

"Okay, I found some," said Robert, as he returned. "Each layer of tar paper needs to be tacked on the plywood horizontally with the first run along the bottom and the next run overlapping the previous layer just a little bit. You'll see the lines drawn on the tar paper. Those are used to line up the rows of shingles. The first row goes on turned around 180 degrees, and the next row goes directly on top of it facing the normal direction. Place each successive row of shingles offset from the previous row.''

With the 10 of them working, it took them only a few hours to totally finish building the roof and nailing on the shingles.

"I'm telling you what," William declared. "We made short order of that job!"

"We surely did," agreed Robert. "Thank you all very much for your help.''

"We're glad to," said Andrew. "I'm looking forward to seeing this thing in operation.''

"Me too," said Robert. "William's father said he will be coming to install the step office. I'm sure he's going to need some help to get it all finished in one day. Who can come tomorrow?''

"I can," said Morris.

"I wouldn't miss seeing this," Steven added.

"Me neither," joined in Andrew. "Count me in too."

"Dad wants me to help him with this tomorrow, so I'll be here too," said William.

"Okay, so that's five of us," said Robert. "I guess the rest of you have other plans?"

They confirmed that they had plans of various things to do for the next day and that they would have come if they could have. With that, they all called it a day, got into their cars, and drove home. The step office building was successfully built, and it looked really good. Robert's parents walked up from the house and were astounded to find it already standing and complete.

Mr. Johns and his son, William, arrived early Sunday morning in the phone company van. They were pulling a trailer with his backhoe on top of it. He would use the backhoe's front-end loader to cover over the electrical lines in the ditch from the barn to the new building.

"How are you doing?" Mr. Johns asked as he arrived and stepped out of his van.

"I'm doing fine. How are you?" Robert answered.

"Fine. William here says that you all built that building all in one day. Let's go and get all that step office equipment out of your tenant house, and I'll install it."

"Okay, let's go on up there," said Robert.

Andrew, Morris, and Steven now arrived, and they all went into the tenant house and carried the racks, switches, and boxes over to the new building, setting them inside on one side against the wall.

Mr. Johns began by laying the electrical wires in the ditch and connecting them to the panel box. Next, he buried them with his backhoe. Then he drilled a series of holes in the concrete floor, and Robert and the others helped him install the racks, the shelves of Strowger switches, and other boxes into place.

All of the bundles of wires had been cut at the back of each Strowger switch, and Mr. Johns had to start all over by first desoldering the hundreds of metal contacts. He had brought several soldering guns and plenty of braided metal to help soak up the solder. All of them went to work desoldering contacts, which took them some time.

Next, he got his roll of red, white, and blue wire out of his van and said, "Since this step office will have only 20 lines, it's going to be simpler to wire it up. Every switch has to connect to all 20 lines. Come on, and I'll show you how to wire it up."

They watched as he showed them the wiring arrangement required. He had also brought a main frame or terminal board over and told them that this was where all 20 lines would come into the step office. From this terminal board, he ran wires to all of the switches. The others soon got the idea on how it was done and went to work soldering the wires to the terminals.

Luckily, the rafters had not yet been boxed in with the trim, and the building had plenty of ventilation. However, Mr. Johns mentioned that it would need to be boxed in very soon to keep out rodents and birds so that they wouldn't be destructive to the equipment. 1 by 6 lumber would serve that purpose very well, and he recommended using hardwood instead of Pine so that squirrels wouldn't chew their way in so easily.

"Okay, that completes the wiring of your step office," said Mr. Johns triumphantly, as he soldered the last terminal and looked it over for accuracy. "You need a battery bank, and those huge batteries are not cheap. However, there is a surplus of them presently because a lot of large cities are demolishing their suburb exchanges and moving everything to one location as they convert to digital. So, I'll get you those batteries and bring them over next week."

"That's brilliant!" said Morris, glad to hear that.

"Oh yeah," Mr. Johns agreed. "There are many ways to get things done, especially when you know the right avenues."

At this moment, Morris got a strange or unusual feeling and started to hear someone speak. No one else could hear the voice. "Wait. I'm hearing something. Yes, it's a person. It's the galactic salesman!" Morris stepped outside of the building, and the others followed. "He says he's coming here right now to view our progress on the galactic communications device."

"Is that right?" said Mr. Johns. "How's he . . ."

Suddenly, the salesman appeared in an instant, startling everyone. He evidently had teleported himself silently without the pink glow and without the sound of whirring wind.

"Uh, how did you . . .?" gasped Mr. Johns, unable to complete his sentence.

"How did I get here?" said the galactic salesman. "Is that what you wanted to know?"

"Uh . . . yeah," he hesitatingly answered.

"Oh, I can teleport myself by just thinking myself wherever I want to go. I just take my body and leave and then arrive elsewhere."

"How is that physically possible?" Mr. Johns wanted to know.

"I just change the molecules in my body and dissolve them into an etheric form on another vibratory level, or a higher plane as you might say. Next, I just think of the location in which I want to materialize. Then, using my mind, I just sort of jump back into the physical 3-D plane."

"That really is amazing!" Mr. Johns exclaimed.

The galactic salesman was a tall man, nearly 6½ feet, and was slender with dark, straight hair of longer length. He wore a white robe and carried that same walking staff with a glowing iron ball on its top, just as Morris had previously mentioned. He was a fully grown man but had an almost boyish appearance.

"Yes, to the people of Earth, it is amazing," he explained. "You see, I live in the Sirius star system, and being a salesman for the Galactic Federation, I travel around a lot, which is how I know English along with many other languages, in case you were wondering."

"Yeah, I was wondering about that one," Mr. Johns admitted.

While everyone was standing just outside the step office building, the galactic salesman went into a lengthy explanation.

"Most Earth people are not fully conscious beings like their cousins living in other star systems, and that's because a lot of their abilities were disconnected many thousands of years ago during genetic experiments conducted by unscrupulous, uncaring beings. That's a long story that I won't go into right now, but I will say that the repercussions of those experiments are still existent on Earth today. The Galactic Federation intends to rectify that situation soon.

"For now, since most humans are unable to communicate on a spiritual level, the Galactic Federation needed to figure out a way to set up a physical communication link with their representatives and our fellow Sirians who are presently human beings on Earth.

"The problem that arose was that many of our fellow Sirians that went on to be incarnated as human beings on Earth forgot everything as they passed through the 'window of forgetfulness,' as you might call it. They therefore forgot their purpose and lost their ability to communicate on the spiritual or etheric level with us.

"Once this galactic communications device is in operation, we are going to dial them direct through Earth's telephone network, using this device as the link to our planet and other star systems."

"That's really something!" Mr. Johns remarked. "I'm glad to be a part of this."

"We thought we would be able to wake these people up," the galactic salesman went on, "by going into their dreams and things of that sort. That worked fine for you, Morris, but for so many others, it just didn't work. Since time is now of the essence, we had to think of a better way to communicate with them, and this galactic communications device will be our solution to the problem."

"Where do you actually live?" Robert asked.

"I'm from the planet around Sirius B," he answered, "and the Sirius star system is a binary star system with Sirius A, which is a large bright star and Sirius B, which is a small white dwarf star. Our planet is also called Sirius B, and the Sirians use some of our planet for storage, as they do a lot of buying and selling and trading of goods. It is there that I spend most of my time."

"You never did tell me your name," Morris brought up.

"For those who speak English, my name is Tom. The Galactic Federation and the Sirian Council chose me for this job because not only am I a salesman, but I am also a communications engineer."

"I see," said Mr. Johns. "Well, I'm Mr. Johns, William's father. I'm pleased to meet you. I believe you already know the other 10. Come on in, and I'll show you the step office that we've just finished building."

Tom followed him inside the building, and the others also followed. Mr. Johns proceeded to explain to Tom exactly how a step office works and connects phone calls. After around 10 minutes of explanation, which really fascinated Tom, they began to discuss the particulars of how they were going to link up this office with other planets. Robert and his friends also had some input.

"This is really a fascinating piece of electro-mechanical hardware!" Tom commented. "You really know what you're doing and what you're talking about. Let's discuss what we need to connect my planet and other star systems to this central office."

"Speaking of connecting this central office," said Mr. Johns, "I have yet to connect it to Murfreesboro. Golly! It's amazing what a person forgets. When I order those batteries, I'll place a work order with the phone company to run a trunk cable of 10 lines from Murfreesboro to here."

"Okay, that's fine," said Tom, "but I believe you'll want it to be fiberoptic because that's what will be required to make the link possible to other star systems."

"Why's that?" Mr. Johns wanted to know.

"Because what the Galactic Federation intends for me to install is a large, pyramidal-shaped, clear quartz crystal to do the transmitting and receiving, and a fiberoptic means of communication would be compatible with that, as it could transmit the light signals through the crystal, which would then oscillate the gravity waves activated or created by the metal electromagnetic ring."

"I see," said Mr. Johns. "Remember, Tom, that the lines going to the other planets and star systems will come into this exchange on the subscriber side, and that the trunk cable of 10 lines is just an incoming and outgoing cable of 10 pairs of wires. They do not need to be fiberoptic. Now, we can arrange for your subscriber lines to be fiberoptic. That's no problem. It's just that fiberoptic hardware is so expensive and so new in technology, that the phone company would never fill my work order for a fiberoptic 10-line trunk cable to be hung from here to Murfreesboro. In a few years, that may be different."

"Oh, okay," said Tom. "I see your point."

"I'll go ahead and get a converter box to convert hardwire signals into fiberoptic signals, and it will handle up to 20 lines. We'll attach this to your subscriber lines."

Andrew had a question. "Tom, why is it that they don't utilize a miniature black hole and produce focused gravity waves by oscillating the black hole and channeling it through some sort of wave guide?''

"That is far too dangerous and is against Galactic Federation code. That sort of method was used by the federation more than a million years ago, and an accident happened. Power was lost, and the black hole supports failed as a result. You can imagine the rest. The whole planet was swallowed up. It was an awful disaster, and many lives were lost. They had a terrible struggle directing that black hole away to eventually collide with another naturally existing black hole far away so that it could be swallowed up by it. They had to use multidimensional forces and a lot of energy in force fields. It cost a lot of time and effort, and it really was a mess for a while before the problem was finally resolved.''

"Wow! I never thought about that!" Andrew exclaimed.

"One always has to think about and weigh the possibilities of disasters when anything that poses potential danger is being implemented and built. Here on Earth, nuclear fission power is an example. There have already been accidents, and there will certainly be more. Earthlings have not considered how serious nuclear accidents can be, and the whole nuclear power program needs to be discontinued.''

"Will you explain to us how, from your planet, you will be able to get a dial tone and place a call through this step office?" Robert asked.

The question was intended for Tom, but Mr. Johns answered for him. "I believe we will need some equipment for, say, five of the 20 lines to receive the signals from space. There is such equipment presently in use for car telephones, and by modifying it to some degree, it could receive fiberoptic signals instead. I'll get some of this equipment. There's a surplus of it also, due to the fact that cellular telephones are replacing the old-fashioned car phones. Does anyone here want to attempt to modify this equipment once I get it in?''

"I can do it," Steven volunteered.

"Okay Steven. You're pretty good at electronics, aren't you?"

"Oh yeah. I quite enjoy it."

"Okay, it's yours to work with and modify for us," said Mr. Johns.

"Good. That will be a challenge for me," said Steven, glad to be of use.

"Once I get it, I'll bring it over to your house, and you can go to it."

"Fantastic!" Steven remarked.

"By the way," Tom brought up, "Mr. Johns is right that the car telephone equipment is necessary to link our method of transmitting and receiving to this step office. To answer your question, Robert, I will explain the parts used and how they work as best as I can.

"From Sirius, for example, we will have our own equipment that will produce a gravity wave signal, and it will be received by the metal electromagnetic ring to be installed here. It will convert the gravity wave signal to an electric field signal. Within that ring will be the large crystal which will receive the electric field signal from the metal electromagnetic ring that basically, in conjunction with the crystal, converts oscillating gravity waves into oscillating electric fields, and vice versa. The crystal has to be within the ring for this to occur, or no gravity waves will be produced.

"Imbedded within the large crystal will be a light sensitive receiver/ transmitter similar to Earth's fiberoptic converter box that can convert oscillating electric fields, coming off of the large metal electromagnetic ring, into light, and vice versa. Through the bottom of this crystal, light will be beamed into a receiving fiberoptic cable and directed into your step office by means of the car telephone equipment that Steven is going to modify."

"That's very impressive!" declared Mr. Johns. "Tom, how many lines are you going to want designated for the links to other star systems?"

"I believe five, as you were saying earlier, would be enough."

"Okay then," Mr. Johns informed him, "I believe you are going to need five units of your proposed electromagnetic ring and crystal apparatus, that is, if you would like for as many as five phone calls from other star systems to be connected to Earth's telephone network at the same time."

"Yes, that's a good idea," Tom realized. "I initially thought of just one, but five would really alleviate the possibilities of busy phone lines. So, I'm going to need to teleport five of these apparatuses down here and have them erected on towers by my team of workers from Sirius B."

Andrew had a question. "What about making each of these units directional and having line finders from each star system using this network? You might also mount tracking devices and servo motors on your units installed here so that any one of them can be aimed at your planet after you transmit a call command. This way, you can have telephone communication from more than five extraterrestrial locations."

"That is an absolutely brilliant idea!" Tom remarked. "I will inform the Galactic Federation of your suggestion, and we will certainly set up the equipment accordingly. I'm very glad you thought of that."

"Whatever type of equipment that you use on your star system," Mr. Johns brought up, "you are going to need some sort of telephone instrument that produces pulses that are necessary to operate these Strowger switches."

"That's true," said Tom, "but why don't I just transmit musical tones to go through your touch-tone converter boxes?"

"After going through all of that various equipment and apparatuses from your planet to this one, it's likely that the musical tones may lose their required pitch, and if that happens, the converter box won't recognize the notes and won't convert to pulse. The tone or pitch doesn't matter with a pulse. It will be recognized by the step office here, and your call will go through. I strongly recommend dialling from your planet using pulse signals instead of touch tone."

"That's a good point, Mr. Johns," Tom admitted. "Okay, pulse it is."

"Good. That will make it a lot simpler here at this step office."

"All right then," said Tom, checking to see if he had it straight, "you're going to place a work order for the phone company to run a 10-line trunk cable from Murfreesboro to here. You'll get the fiberoptic converter box and the car telephone equipment as well. Steven's going to modify the car telephone equipment to recognize light. Do I have this straight?"

"That's correct," Mr. Johns confirmed. "I'll also get the battery bank."

"Good. Then I'm going to have my crew teleport, from Sirius B, the five electromagnetic ring and crystal apparatuses including tracking devices and servo motors along with the metal stands to erect them. The crew will come with the equipment and will install it here next Saturday morning. Does that sound okay?"

"That sounds fine," said Mr. Johns.

"Okay, I'll be here next Saturday," said Tom. "In the meantime, you will have a chance to gather your equipment and have the 10-line trunk cable installed from Murfreesboro to here, right?"

"Right. Tell you what, Tom, we'll just meet you here next Saturday morning and we'll go from there. I will have the equipment gathered by then."

"That will be fine," agreed Tom.

"Okay, see you next week."

"See you then."

With everything arranged, Tom walked out of the step office and suddenly vanished, silently.

"That's really amazing how he can just vanish like that!" Mr. Johns remarked. "Okay, Steven, I reckon I'll bring that car telephone equipment to you on Tuesday or Wednesday."

"That's fine," said Steven. "Just leave it by the back door."

"Okay. Well, that's about it for today as far as I know," said Mr. Johns. "I'll see you here next week. Oh, Robert. I'll bring over the battery bank and the fiberoptic converter box next Saturday when we all meet here, and the phone company will come this week and hang the 10-line trunk cable."

"That will be fine," said Robert. "Now, remember that I want it buried from the tenant house to here."

"Right. I'll include that in the work order."

"Okay, good."

Everyone called it a day, went to their cars, and drove home. Robert, however, wasn't finished yet. He decided that he was going to box in the eaves with some 1 by 6 Oak lumber that was stored in the barn. It took him a couple of hours to cut the boards to the required length and nail them to the ends of the Pine rafters. The Oak lumber was cured and was so hard that he had to drill holes before nailing each board. With the eaves now boxed in, no one had to worry about rodents coming in and making nests in the Strowger switches.

Two days later on Tuesday, March 19, the phone company came and hung the 10-line trunk cable from Murfreesboro. As Robert had requested, they buried the cable from the tenant house to the new step office. They delivered the fiberoptic converter box to the step office and placed it just inside the door. Needless to say, the linemen were curious as to why a step office came to be installed way out in the middle of a farm, tucked in the corner of the woods.

Mr. Johns was able to obtain the battery bank from Atlanta since they were in the process of moving all of their exchanges to one central location in downtown. He obtained the car telephone line equipment as surplus locally and took it over to Steven's house and delivered it.

It was a fairly busy week at school for most of them with the normal amount of homework and tests, and all nine of them made arrangements to be at Robert's farm early Saturday morning to witness the crew from Sirius installing their part of the galactic communications device. They eagerly awaited for Saturday to come and were not going to miss the opportunity to witness this for anything.

Robert decided to call Mr. Mayfield and give him the chance to come out and witness the event. After all, he had a keen interest in the stars and planets and believed in extraterrestrials. This would definitely be of interest to him. Robert would explain more to him on Saturday.

Saturday, March 23, arrived. Fortunately, it was a nice and sunny day. All nine of Robert's friends arrived at 7 a.m., and Mr. Mayfield arrived soon after. They walked up to the woods and showed Mr. Mayfield the newly installed step office and explained to him how it worked. He was seriously impressed with it and looked forward to watching the extraterrestrial crew install their part of it.

Steven took the modified car telephone line equipment out of his car and brought it over to the rest of them at the building.

"Tell us what you did to modify it, Steven," said Robert.

"These units normally receive electromagnetic wave frequencies of around 170 to 180 Megahertz, which is above the FM band on the radio. All I basically did was to take out the receiver for electromagnetic waves and install a unit to receive and send light for the fiberoptic communication."

"That sounds easy enough," said Robert.

"Yeah, it was easy," boasted Steven. "I only spent an hour on it."

"Well, it looks really good," Robert commended.

Around 8 a.m., Mr. Johns arrived, towing his trailer, which was full of large batteries. He got out of his van and said:

"I see the crew from Sirius is not here yet. Here, let's move these batteries into the office and connect them to the power supply and to the exchange before they up and appear."

They all came over to the trailer and helped him carry the batteries in, one by one. Mr. Johns followed them into the building and showed them how to place them in series, and he went to work connecting them together. Next, he connected them to the exchange.

After half an hour, he completed that task and connected the fiberoptic converter box that tied into the five subscriber lines to be used by the extraterrestrials. Also, he installed the car telephone modified equipment to those same five lines. This left 15 lines free for local use. Robert decided to use three of the lines for connecting the two barns to the house. Another line was assigned to the step office itself, and that left eleven lines free for future use. Next, Mr. Johns connected the 10-line trunk cable from Murfreesboro, and that would handle the incoming and outgoing calls.

By now, it was nearly 9 a.m., and Morris announced that he heard Tom's voice and that he and his crew were going to arrive. Seconds later, Tom and four men appeared, suddenly and silently. Mr. Mayfield was quite surprised, needless to say. In addition to the crew, five sets of electromagnetic ring and crystal apparatuses, complete with their stands and servo motors and tracking devices, suddenly appeared in the barnyard. Each tower was 15 feet tall.

"My goodness!" Mr. Mayfield exclaimed. "That's the most amazing thing I have ever seen!"

"You're not kidding," agreed Mr. Johns.

"Good morning," Tom announced. "How are you all doing?"

"We're doing fine," said Morris, answering for everyone.

"That's great!" said Tom. "Let's go ahead and choose a location for these five units that we just teleported here."

Robert decided to give Tom the directions. "Okay, Tom, I'm sure I don't want them in the barnyard. The cattle might tear them up. Let's move them over to those limestone rocks in the woods just over on the other side of the new building."

"All right, take me over there," Tom requested, "and show me exactly where you want them to be placed." Robert, Tom, and the crew of four men walked over to the rocks, of which there were numerous rows that were naturally occurring. Most of these rocks protruded two feet out of the ground, and moss covered their sides.

"This is where I want them," said Robert, as he pointed to the rows of rocks. "I'd say place them in an array and anchor them firmly to these rocks."

"Okay, let's stand aside," said Tom, "and my crew will levitate them over here."

Robert and Tom went back to join the rest of them while the crew remained by the limestone rocks. Slowly, the towers silently left the ground and floated above the trees over to the limestone rocks, where they descended until they made contact with the rocks. The sound of welding could be heard as the legs of the towers imbedded themselves into these rocks.

"I knew levitation was possible!" Mr. Mayfield exclaimed. "I just knew it!"

"Oh yes," Tom replied. "Many things are possible that Earthlings don't know about. Earthlings used to know a lot more than they know now. You see, a lot has been forgotten here on Earth."

"I'd say I agree with you," said Mr. Mayfield. "I've got a lot of questions to ask you."

"Well, stay around and we'll have a discussion," Tom told him. "Right now, I need to direct my crew as to the connecting and operating of these five units."

"Okay, I'll be here."

Tom went to join his crew while the rest of them watched. Robert's parents walked up from the house and were amazed with the progress. Each tower had within it a two-foot tall, pyramidal-shaped, quartz crystal pointing upward. Imbedded within each crystal was a metallic-looking object several inches in diameter with a fiberoptic cable coming out of the crystal through the bottom. The crystal was mounted by aluminum angle iron and insulators and was centered within a metallic electromagnetic ring some eight feet in diameter and eight inches thick. This big ring was attached by insulators to two rotational shafts, both of them perpendicular to each other and within the ring's plane, giving the crystal two axes of rotation. Servo motors rotated the shafts, and the shafts were firmly attached to the aluminum frame tower. Two sizeable electrical cables were attached to and ran from the large ring, while more wires fed the servo motors and tracking devices.

Under Tom's direction, the crew ran the fiberoptic cables from each tower and connected them to each of the five available lines of the step office through the modified car telephone line equipment. Afterwards, Tom and the crew appeared to have a discussion in a foreign language that Robert and his friends had never heard before. Next, Tom walked over to Mr. Johns and said:

"We have a problem. We didn't teleport a power supply for these five towers because we were assuming that we would just tap into the electrical system here."

"I see," replied Mr. Johns. "I don't know if you are aware of it, but electricity costs money here on Earth."

"Oh yes, I'm aware of that. Tell me. Just for the record, how many volts does the power supply have here?"

"You can choose from 220 volts AC or 110 volts AC at a frequency of 60 Hertz," he answered.

"No, that won't work for our towers," said Tom. "In your units, they require 750 volts DC. What I'll do is send my crew home briefly so that they can obtain a solar-powered panel complete with a battery bank to supply the power at night."

"Tom, how big is that going to be?" Robert suddenly asked with considerable concern.

"Oh, don't worry. It's only 20 by 20 feet," Tom assured him.

"Oh, okay. Yeah, that's fine," Robert consented. "I was worried that it would be *much* larger."

"Remember that Earthlings," Tom explained, "have not yet figured out how to have efficient solar panels, and once they do, they will see no reason not to use solar power."

"That's a good point," Robert agreed. "I wish Earth would hurry up and be efficient."

"I don't think it will be too many more years before they will be," Tom speculated. "I'll go ahead and send my crew home."

Tom went over to his crew and gave them some instructions, and the four of them vanished. Next, he returned to Robert and the others, who were now seated on the rocks by the towers.

"They'll be gone for around 20 minutes," he said. "Do any of you have any questions while we wait for them to return?"

"Yes," Mr. Mayfield spoke out, "how fast do gravity waves actually travel?"

"Within this galaxy," Tom answered, "they are next to instantaneous, taking maybe only a split second to cross it. To other galaxies, it's a different story since they are so much further away."

"How can that be possible?" Mr. Mayfield wanted to know. "I thought that nothing could travel faster than the speed of light."

"Nothing *physical* can travel faster than the speed of light," Tom brought to his attention. "Gravity waves are waves of the actual space-time framework. Electromagnetic waves travel within the space-time framework or network and therefore travel at the speed of light, while gravity waves are a distortion of the framework, itself. In a way, gravity *is* space and time, and it originates from higher dimensions."

"Hmm . . . Yeah, that makes sense," Mr. Mayfield agreed.

Andrew had a question. "I'm sure you've accounted for the rotation of the Earth, which means that approximately half of the time this galactic communications device will be out of range of your planet, that is, on the other side of Earth from your planet. Isn't that going to be quite inconvenient for you, not being able to use this central office half of the time?"

"No, that won't be any problem," Tom replied. "We'll be able to use this central office any time."

"Oh, I see. I guess that means that you are going to have a bunch of reflector stations at different places around Earth?"

"No, that's far too complicated. Besides, we won't need any of that stuff, anyway," Tom explained. "Gravity waves travel through the earth almost unimpeded. In fact, Earth is a good conductor of gravity waves."

"How can that be true since electromagnetic waves do not travel through the earth?" Andrew wanted to know.

"You see," Tom continued, "electromagnetic waves are more like light, which is the movement of photons, and photons cannot penetrate very far. Gravity, being only a force, can travel through anything. You know it does. Think about it. If gravity did not travel through the earth itself, you and everything else not anchored to Earth would go off floating."

"Yes, that's definitely true," Andrew admitted. "I see your point."

Mr. Mayfield had a question. "Tom, did this whole project happen just because you wanted Morris to have that crystal ball?"

"It is true that I wanted Morris to have that ball," he answered. "It's very important to him in his life, and it's true that this project came about as a result of that initial deal, but I will explain it in more detail. I wanted to find a way of having a communications device built so that we on other planets in other star systems would be able to communicate with the people on Earth.

"What I did," Tom went on, "was to ask Morris to accept the ball. In addition, I gave him the ability to transmit visual images to anyone. Further, I granted Robert and nine friends of his choosing, Morris included, the gift of being able to transport themselves anywhere they thought of, including to and from other planets.

"In exchange for these gifts, Robert, Morris, and their friends would build us a telephone central office to interface with our towers that send and receive gravity waves. This would link our planet and other planets to Earth's telephone network. It looks like they've done an excellent job, and I'm very pleased with the quick progress."

"Yeah, this really is a masterpiece," Mr. Mayfield proudly said.

"Tom," Mr. Johns brought up, "we need to discuss the particulars of how a person from Earth is going to call any one of the five extraterrestrial locations. A seven-digit number needs to be assigned to each location using a three-digit Eagleville prefix. Follow me into the step office so I can explain better what I mean."

Tom and Mr. Johns walked over to the step office from where they had been sitting on the rocks, and the rest of them followed and listened to their conversation.

"As you know, Tom, this step office has 20 lines. Since Eagleville is now a subexchange of Murfreesboro, and since this step office is also a sub-exchange of Murfreesboro, it was decided that this exchange would also have the Eagleville prefix of 274 since we are somewhat in the Eagleville area. The numbers assigned to this exchange range from 274-7000 through 274-7019 with the area code of 615 in front of it. Each one of your five extra-terrestrial locations needs a phone number."

"Okay," said Tom, "I'll take 274-7015 through 274-7019."

"All right, I'll connect your five fiberoptic cables to those particular terminals in conjunction with the modified car telephone line equipment. Now tell me, who or what will the people of Earth be calling when they dial any of these five numbers?''

"We will station a person or an operator at the extraterrestrial end of the line," Tom replied, "to receive any calls at any time around the clock. It will be done similar to how operators work here on Earth with eight-hour shifts."

"I see. That's easy enough," said Mr. Johns. "Tell me, how is this operator going to get a dial tone and place calls by dialling direct to anywhere on Earth?"

"Through constant tracking devices mounted on the five towers here and on our similar towers on each of the five extraterrestrial locations," Tom explained, "the ring and crystal units on the towers will always be facing one another. That's the purpose that the two rotating shafts and servo motors serve, to keep the units on the towers facing one another at all times."

"What sort of telephone instrument or equipment will your operator use on your extraterrestrial locations to pulse out the digit train of the phone number you may be calling on Earth?"

"It might be best for us to use a good, dependable rotary dial telephone," Tom replied. "What style or model do you recommend, Mr. Johns?"

"I recommend the Western Electric black desk rotary dial phone, and I recommend one of the earlier versions with a black metal dial, if possible. You don't want any of the newer stuff. They're cheaply built and don't last long. The old Western Electric rotary dial phones last for many years."

"That's what my parents use," Robert announced. "Come on down to my house, Tom, and I'll show it to you."

"If the crew shows up," Tom told the others, "tell them I'm down at Robert's house for a few minutes."

Tom and Robert walked quickly down to the house, and Robert took Tom inside and showed him the telephone instrument. His parents had recently gone to town to do some errands. Tom picked up the black bakelite handset of the telephone and listened to the sound quality of the dial tone and tested out the dial's ability by dialling a few digits. He was quite impressed.

"Robert, this type of telephone will serve me very well. What I want to do is to take it outside and duplicate it several times and then teleport a bunch of them back to my planet."

"Okay, be my guest. Could you also make me some duplicates while you're at it?"

"Of course," Tom answered. "Let's take this phone up to where the others are, and I'll have the crew duplicate it. Then we'll bring it back."

They walked out of the house and back up to the step office and saw that the crew had already returned. A section of solar panels and a battery bank sat in the barnyard. Tom walked over to them with the Joslin's telephone and gave them instructions as to what he wanted them to do.

"How many phones do you want for yourself, Robert?" Tom called out.

Quickly, Robert asked his friends if any of them wanted a phone like this one. They all told him yes.

"Twenty," Robert called out.

The crew set the telephone on the ground in the barnyard, and it slowly started to rise and move to one side. As it did so, a duplicate phone appeared in the space where it had just been. This process continued until there were 121 telephones in a long line, all of them floating. Next, all of them gently descended to the ground. Robert and his friends were appalled.

Tom called out, "We made 100 duplicates for ourselves to teleport home."

"That beats all I ever saw!" declared Mr. Mayfield.

"You're not kidding!" the rest of them remarked.

"Tom," Mr. Mayfield called out, "how did your crew duplicate those phones?"

"As we move the phone at a constant velocity which you saw, we also move the phone back in time once every second, and that's why you kept seeing a duplicate phone appear in the place where the original phone had just been. All 120 of these phones are exactly like the original phone, because all of them *are* the original phone, only moved back in time. Jesus Christ had this same ability, which is why he could 'create' food in abundance."

"That's amazing!" declared Mr. Mayfield.

Robert and his friends went and got the original phone and twenty duplicates and carried them away from the remaining 100 phones. The crew went over to them and levitated them until they were all arranged in a 10-by-10 configuration a few feet above the ground, and they suddenly vanished.

"The telephones are already on Sirius B," Tom informed them.

"Just like that?" Robert asked.

"Oh yes. Teleportation is instantaneous," said Tom. "Now, I will direct the crew as to where to set the solar panels and the battery bank."

"Okay," said Robert, "place them over there by the towers on some more of those limestone rocks."

Tom gave the crew directions, and they levitated the panels and the battery bank to their designated location. Next, they ran cables to each of the five towers. Upon completion, Tom walked over to Mr. Johns and said, "I am now going to direct my additional crew on Sirius B to connect one of these telephones to a power supply and have them dial this step office."

"I guess that you are already aware that telephones operate on 48 volts DC," said Mr. Johns.

"Yes, I am. Is the step office up and working?"

"Yes," Mr. Johns replied. "Everything is connected and the power is up, as far as I know."

"Okay, what is the phone number of this step office?" Tom wanted to know.

"I've designated the main number to be 274-7000."

Tom appeared to meditate for 20 seconds and said, "They know the number now."

"You mean you can think that information to them, all the way to another star system?" Mr. Mayfield asked, seemingly surprised.

"Oh yes, we do that all the time," Tom replied.

"Then why bother with all of this complicated communicating equipment?" he further asked.

"As you know," Tom explained, "most Earthlings do not have the ability to communicate with each other by thought as do all of us on Sirius B. We are fully conscious humans, and Earthlings used to be until several thousand years ago when their ability was disconnected by Atlantean genetic experiments. As you know, Atlantis sank some 12,000 years ago, leaving the remaining humans on Earth with only some of their prior abilities intact.

"Earth is somewhat in a state of going into a new evolution, as you might have guessed. You've seen the population double just in your lifetime. Some of our beings from Sirius have recently incarnated, that is, in the last 30 years as humans here on Earth, and they forgot their purpose for coming. With only some of the abilities of the physical human being intact, it's easy to realize that they would have no memory of their lives prior to birth.

"We have not been able to awaken those Earth-incarnated Sirians," Tom went on, "not even through their dreams. Therefore, we figured that by dialling them directly through Earth's telephone network, we would be able to re-establish and maintain contact with them since they cannot communicate by thought."

"They may think you are a prank caller," Mr. Mayfield brought up. "How are you going to convince them that you are authentic?"

"If that problem arises, I and possibly my crew will make an appearance before each one of them that doesn't believe us and perform some 'miracles' if necessary to prove our authenticity."

"Yeah, that will work," Mr. Mayfield agreed.

Most of Robert's friends, although very interested in the events that took place today, had not really had any questions. They mostly observed.

Morris had a question for Tom. "Tell me, how did that crystal ball get on top of the battery bank over at the Eagleville exchange?"

"I teleported it there," Tom answered. "I see the future as you do to some degree, and I could see that you and your friends were going to be there later that day."

Suddenly, the telephone rang inside the step office. The operator on

Sirius B had dialled the number successfully. For the first time in history, a telephone call had been placed to Earth from another star system.

Mr. Johns walked inside and answered the phone. "Hello?"

"Is this the step office on planet Earth?" said a voice with a foreign accent on the distant end of the line.

"Yes, it is," Mr. Johns replied. "Are you calling from Sirius?"

"That is correct," the operator confirmed. "May I speak to Tom?"

"Yes, here he is."

Tom took the handset of the phone and began to speak in a language of which no one was familiar. He appeared to be overjoyed with happiness to see that the galactic communications device was working and was a complete success.

"So, I see that the Sirians have their own language," Mr. Mayfield remarked.

"Yes, it's much different from our language, isn't it," Robert agreed.

Tom spoke for a few minutes, evidently talking over plans with crew members on Sirius B. Then he handed the handset to one of the crew members here who also spoke to one of the crew members on Sirius B. Tom informed the others that his crew was talking over plans and that they were enjoying the uniqueness of using a telephone. The other crew members took turns talking on the telephone. Approximately 15 minutes later, the last one hung up.

"Now," Tom announced, "they want us to call them to test it out for two-way capability."

Tom picked up the handset and listened for the dial tone, after which he dialled 274-7015. The ringing could be heard over the line.

"click...BBBBBB...BBBBBB...Hello?"

Tom began speaking in his foreign language and spoke for half a minute and hung up.

"It's a success!" he shouted. "I'm so pleased with your quality work and with this step office! You have done a superb job in constructing this whole central office and with making it compatible to interface with our receiver-transmitter towers."

"We were glad to do it," said Mr. Johns, speaking for everyone. "I'm glad you like it."

"Oh, I do indeed," Tom assured him. "This whole galactic communications device is wonderful. I'm really looking forward to re-establishing contact with those of us here on Earth."

"I'm sure you are," said Mr. Johns. "Now, Tom, are you going to need or want any sort of a central office on each of the extraterrestrial locations?"

"No, we won't need that. Any time any of us wants to call a person on Earth, we will just teleport ourselves to the telephone station on that planet and use it to call Earth. It's no trouble for us to just think ourselves from one location to another."

"Okay, then it looks like our work is finished and that everything is up and running here," said Mr. Johns. "What are the other planets or star systems that will be having phone lines?"

"Here, I'll write it out on a piece of paper for you." Tom took out a piece of paper and wrote five lines of information and handed it to him. It read:

Sirius B **615-274-7015**
Sirius B (Galactic Federation) **615-274-7016**
Sirius B (storage facility) **615-274-7017**
Vega, Lyran Constellation **615-274-7018**
The Pleiades .... **615-274-7019.**

"Well, well, would you look at that!" Mr. Johns declared. "It looks like we have a galactic step office. And I'm the first Earthling to see a galactic phone directory. By the way, Tom, where is Vega, and where is the Pleiades?"

"Vega is in the Lyran Constellation and is 25 light years from here. We are in close communication with the humans in that star system. All humans on Sirius B originated on Vega before colonizing Sirius some 4 million years ago. The Pleiades are also known as the Seven Sisters, and those stars range from 360 to 365 light years from here. Their culture has had a lot of influence here on Earth for the past 6,000 years. They are also humans."

"That's really interesting," Mr. Mayfield declared. "I somehow thought that humans inhabited other star systems and not just Earth."

"Has the equipment been set up on Vega and on the Pleiades?" Mr. Johns wanted to know.

"Not yet," Tom answered. "My crew will teleport themselves and the equipment to Vega and then to the Pleiades to install the towers and the telephones. It will take a few days' work to complete it. I will accompany them and will call you from each location upon completion. What is your home telephone number?"

"274-5050," he answered. "Just dial the seven-digit number. By the way, let me give you a local telephone directory. It gives instructions on when to dial one-plus for long distance and when to dial the area codes. Plus, it tells you how to place international calls. William," he called out, "go and fetch me a phone book out of my van so I can give it to Tom, will you?"

William walked over to the van, found a phone book inside, returned, and gave it to him.

"Thanks, son. Here, Tom, take this with you, and you'll understand how our phone system works." Mr. Johns handed him the telephone directory. "Also, I will inform the phone company that 274-7015 through 274-7019 are to be absolutely toll-free for placing calls to any location."

"How can you possibly do that?" William asked his father.

"As far as the phone company is concerned, those five lines are special-use lines that are not for use by ordinary subscribers. Therefore, there will be no charge to those five numbers for service and equipment nor for any calls placed through those same numbers. Also, 274-7000 will be a free-use number because it belongs to the step office itself.''

"That's great!" exclaimed William. "I wish I could have free phone service and free phone calls to anywhere in the world."

"Yeah, you and all of us," Paul added.

"Now, I'm sure you realize," Mr. Johns explained, "that if we gave totally free phone service to everyone, we would not be able to stay in business. It's just that those five lines belong to subscribers in other star systems, and we certainly can't expect them to pay us, of all things, in U.S. dollars."

"That's true. You have a point there," Paul admitted.

Robert started thinking about the fact that the towers and solar panels were not protected from the weather and decided to say something about it.

"Tom, I'm sure you realize that we have fairly severe weather here at times, including hail storms with golf ball size hail stones on occasion. That might wreck havoc on your solar panels and on your crystals."

"The solar panels are made out of shockproof plexiglass," Tom informed him, "but the crystals on the towers might be more vulnerable. We could put some sort of a shield over each tower. I'll send my crew home to fabricate some weather shields to bolt onto the tops of the towers. They'll come back later this week to install them. Thank you for bringing that up. I had not even thought about it since we do not ever have severe weather on Sirius B.''

"Yes, I'm glad I told you," said Robert. "I would not want to see your fine equipment damaged by one of Earth's severe storms."

"You know," Tom suddenly realized, "I haven't yet introduced you to my four crew members. I guess we were so busy installing all of the equipment and getting everything straight, that it just slipped my mind."

He motioned to his crew to come over. They walked over to Mr. Johns, Mr. Mayfield, Robert, and his friends. Tom introduced them.

"I want you all to meet my crew. Their names are fairly complicated to say or spell out in English, so I'll just leave it at that."

In his foreign language, Tom spoke to the crew, introducing them to Robert and his friends. Each of the four crew members extended his right hand, and Mr. Johns, Mr. Mayfield, Robert, and his friends all walked by them, greeting each one of them and shaking hands. It was really unique to all of them to meet these extraterrestrials, and they somehow had the feeling that they were meeting long-lost brothers. In reality, they and all Sirians were their distant cousins.

After their formal introduction, Tom gave the crew more instructions, and they walked over to the towers where he pointed to the tops of them, explaining to them, no doubt, about the need for protective shields over each tower. Afterwards, the crew walked further into the woods and instantly vanished. Tom returned to have further conversation with Mr. Johns.

"I'd say when you call me from the Pleiades later this week," said Mr. Johns, "that *that* will be the most distant phone call ever placed."

"From an Earth standpoint, it certainly will be," Tom agreed.

"I'm looking forward to it," Mr. Johns told him. "Tom, I've enjoyed working with you on this project. My work here is finished except for maintaining this step office on a regular basis."

"It's been a pleasure for me too, Mr. Johns. I'm going back to Sirius B now. I'll see you again sometime." He walked into the barnyard and instantly vanished.

"Boy, that was something else, seeing the installation of this equipment!" Steven remarked.

"That's true for all of us," said Eric.

"We've witnessed a very significant piece of history today, haven't we," Mr. Johns commented.

"Yeah, to say the least!" James added.

"Robert, thank you very much for inviting me out here to see this today," said Mr. Mayfield, as he shook hands with him. "Today's activities have answered a lot of questions for me."

"I'm glad to show you," said Robert. "Now remember, everyone, that this whole project is to be kept a secret among us. That's very important. If the government finds out what's going on here, there's no telling what would happen."

"You have our word on that," everyone told him. "We won't tell anyone."

"Thank you all for your help," said Robert, "and especially for yours, Mr. Johns."

"You're welcome, Robert."

It was lunchtime, and everyone decided to go home. They had really enjoyed seeing the morning's activities.

7 The Meeting

Nearly a week had passed, and the galactic communications device was now in full operation with all five extraterrestrial phone lines in service. The crew from Sirius B had returned earlier in the week to install the shields on top of the towers. Many calls had been placed from Sirius B to the people on Earth whom the Sirians had not been able to contact previously. People on Vega and on the Pleiades were overjoyed at this wonderful opportunity to telephone people on Earth, and numerous calls started going through the step office from those star systems also.

Needless to say, those five extraterrestrial lines were in constant use, and when Robert had walked into the step office to admire it a few days earlier, plenty of clicking and clacking sounds from the Strowger switches and electro-mechanical hardware could be heard. Everything worked, and Mr. Johns would be coming by once every two weeks to check on it and to perform maintenance, such as keeping the moving parts oiled.

It was Saturday morning, March 30, and Robert and his friends had arranged to have a meeting to discuss the particulars of where they would like to travel this summer with their new ability to transport themselves anywhere they desired. They were going to discuss how long they wanted each trip to be, what type of equipment they would need to take with them, and who would be available for each trip.

Around mid-morning, they arrived in their cars over a range of 20 minutes, and they walked up into the woods. Robert led them to the top of the knob in the middle of the woods. This was the highest point of land on the Joslin's farm, and the top was a huge table of limestone bedrock with rows of crevices running through it. Some of the crevices allowed access to some interesting small caves, one of them large enough to hold several people.

As the 10 of them sat in a circle facing each other on the huge limestone bedrock, Robert began the meeting.

"Okay, everyone. As you know, we have all gathered here to discuss our plans for this summer, now that we have this new ability since four weeks ago to transport ourselves at will. Also, you know that Morris, here, can transmit visual images to us of many extraterrestrial locations that he has seen in his dreams, giving us many more choices of places to travel.

"We have recently found out that human beings who are our distant cousins, reside on Sirius B, Vega, and the Pleiades, and that there are probably more star systems and planets with humans on them as well. We have an adventuresome and exciting summer ahead of us, and we are about to go places and do things that others would be willing to give anything to do also. Let's each of us give some suggestions of possible places to travel."

Paul decided to speak first. "First of all, I'd like to know of how many extraterrestrial places Morris has seen in his dreams."

"Yes, that's a good point," Robert agreed. "Where are some places you have been to in your dreams, Morris?"

"Oh, I've been pretty much all over the galaxy," Morris replied, "and sometimes in other galaxies as well. Many planets, of course, cannot support physical life, and they appear lifeless. However, there are far more planets *with* physical life on them than astronomers ever hoped to give credit for.

"I've been to several star systems with our cousins, the humans, inhabiting them. Certainly, Vega, Sirius B, and the Pleiades have humans on them, and many others do also. I've also seen places with reptilian-like humanoids, and they appeared to be up to a lot of evil, as I could see them waging huge wars. I wouldn't recommend our going to their areas of this galaxy.

"In addition to that, I've dreamed that I've been to places that have the cousins of dolphins and whales as their dominant intelligent species. In other places, I've met amphibians and reptiles. The list goes on. I can't think of it all right now."

"You *do* have some dreams, *don't* you!" James remarked.

"That's right," Morris replied, "and I reckon most of it really exists, as

I proved to every one of you two weeks ago when we were at Savage Gulf."

"Oh, yeah. That's right," James recalled. "Didn't you already know about the psychic woman in the hut before we went there?"

"Yes, I did."

"Morris' ability to have such fantastic dreams," said Robert, "and to be able to transmit visual images of what he's seen will most certainly give us a much wider range of places to choose to travel to this summer. Morris, how about transmitting some of those visual images of places you've seen in your dreams, so that we may know what they look like?"

"None of you have seen Sirius yet, have you?" Morris checked.

"No, we haven't," said Robert, answering for everyone.

"Okay, here is a scene from Sirius B."

Soon, everyone could see in his mind what appeared to be a very volcanic landscape. The color of the soil ranged from red to orange, and shrubs partially covered the ground in certain areas. Plants that looked somewhat like Cactus grew in other areas as well. Robert recognized the shrubs and said, "Those shrubs look a lot like Tamarisk shrubs."

"I was going to say either Cypress-Pines or She Oaks, both of which grow in the form of shrubs in the Australian Outback," James added. "In fact, that scene could pass for the Outback."

"This planet revolves around Sirius B, which is a small white dwarf star," Morris explained. "Sirius A is the large star in the system. This planet is mostly desert-like, and has been volcanic. Around 20 million humans live on this planet, and this is where Tom, the galactic salesman, is from."

"Isn't that amazing how you can place these images in our mind!" Robert remarked.

"Okay, here's one from Vega," Morris continued.

Everyone began to see a scene of mostly barren landscape with shrubs dotting the area, similar to Sirius B.

Greg was the first one to speak. "How do we know that this is not just a scene from Sirius again, or for that matter, just a scene from another part of Earth?"

"You know," Morris explained, "when you're dreaming, you can usually sense where you are, even though no one tells you. It's just something that I sense or already know while I'm having the dream. Lots of scenes on other star systems look a lot like Earth. After all, this is all one universe under the same laws of physics."

"Yeah, you have a point there," Greg admitted. "I guess it wouldn't look all that much different. Show us a scene of the reptilian-like humanoids."

Morris transmitted an image of several beings standing by each other, and they looked just like little lucifers who would be expected to hold a pitchfork.

"Hey!" Chris spoke out. "They look just like little devils. I guess they don't look very friendly, do they?"

"That's right, and they're not, from what I've observed," Morris informed them. "Now I will show you a scene from the Pleiades."

Everyone soon received a scene of a deep and lush forest with tall trees that looked somewhat like Palms in that the branches were attached only to the upper one-fourth of the trees. They must have been 200 feet tall, and the branches, instead of having palm-like leaves, had leaves that looked like entire fern plants.

"What a fantastic looking forest!" James exclaimed.

"I've never seen anything quite like it," said Robert. "That's definitely a virgin forest."

"These trees are endemic to this planet in the Pleiades," Morris explained. "I've never seen any trees like these anywhere else except in the Pleiades, so I believe they are endemic to there. These trees, as I have noticed, serve to filter out the negative energies from above, so that by the time these energies reach the inhabitants below, they are harmless."

"What do you mean by that?" Andrew wanted to know.

"Well, these energies are not negative, as in bad, but they are somewhat harmful to the residents that live on the forest floor. You know, they may be harmful like the rays of the sun are harmful if you are out in the sun too much."

"Oh, I see," said Andrew.

"I could show you scenes all day," Morris continued, "but keep in mind that we are still limited as to where we can travel because the atmospheric content of the planets we may choose to visit must be fairly similar to ours. We cannot, for example, transport ourselves to Mars, short of wearing a space suit, or we would die in seconds upon our arrival."

"That's true," Robert agreed. "It's very important that we use our gift wisely and carefully so that we don't make any fatal mistakes and die for it."

"I have a suggestion," James announced.

"Yes, James."

"I think it would do us well to have something like a series of trips, each one being from around one to two weeks long, and for some of these trips to be to selected areas here on Earth. That way, we might be able to make a better comparison of the flora and fauna of Earth with that of other planets in other star systems."

"That is an excellent suggestion," Robert remarked, "and I agree that we would learn a lot more by including some trips to various places on Earth. Thank you, James."

William started thinking about the supplies and said, "I guess that there are certain supplies that each of us will need to bring with us for each of these trips. What do you suggest, Robert?"

"I'd say that each of us needs to travel with a backpack loaded with at least a week's supply of food and all other equipment and clothing that you would use on a week long backpacking trip in the wilderness. Most or all of us already know what that requires, and we already have those things."

"That's easy enough," said Steven. "These trips we have planned are beyond temptation, and I'm just going to go for it and come with you all. I haven't really had a desire to travel before, always feeling like it was wrong in an unknown way, but Virginia caused me to realize what that tinge of guilt carried over from when we all visited her two weeks ago on Lopeia. I now see no reason to resist coming, and I can't wait for this summer!"

"That's great!" said Robert. "There's no need to feel guilty, and I don't even believe that temptation needs to be an issue."

"Absolutely!" agreed Steven in an exclamatory tone.

"It's too bad that Greg and I can't join the rest of you on everything," said Eric in a regretful manner. "Greg finishes his summer course at the end of July, and August is one of the slower months in the pottery business. Maybe we can join you for the last month before school begins in September."

"I'm sorry you can't join us for the whole summer either," said Morris, replying for everyone. "However, I can bring you up to date with the rest of us in August by meeting with you two and transmitting the visual images of where we will have been so that you can have a better idea of what we will have experienced."

"Okay. That sounds good," said Eric.

"As you know," Andrew brought up, "the only people besides us who know about our new gift and of our travel plans are Robert's parents, William's father, and Mr. Mayfield, and hopefully they will keep it a secret. I think it would be best if we didn't tell our parents our true plans of travel. For these past few weeks, they think we've just been gathering and having a good time doing things together. I think we need to stage it so that it appears like we are taking a long road trip out West or something like that."

"Yes, that's a good idea," Robert agreed. "We could act like we are all taking a trip in my car out West and just leave it at that. Now, what am I supposed to *really* do with my car?"

"Well, now," Chris answered, "we could leave the car here by hiding it or something like that."

"Yes, we could," said Robert, "but what are we going to do about our parents seeing us drive off after they will have brought us out here in their cars?"

"I guess we'll have to actually load the car, trailer, and everything, and drive out of here," Paul suggested. "Then you could go around on the road to your other entrance and drive into these woods on your rough dirt logging road, wait an hour or so, and then carefully drive back to your house and hide your car in the barn."

"Yes, that will work," said Robert. "Then we could just unload the car, put on our gear, and transport ourselves to the first place of our choice."

"Right, but we are going to have to return here once a week for more food," Morris brought up.

"That's true," Robert admitted. "How are we going to get around that one? Does anyone have any suggestions on how to solve this problem?"

"Sure," William answered. "We've all saved our money for this trip this coming summer, and on that trip we were planning, we were going to buy food each week anyway, weren't we?"

"Yes, that's right," said Robert.

"Well then," William went on, "with our new gift of transporting ourselves, all we need to do is to think ourselves to a grocery store somewhere out West, or just buy from this area for that matter. We can just buy our food each week or whenever we need to."

"Yes, of course!" exclaimed Robert. He thought for a few seconds. "That will work fine, except that we wouldn't want other people seeing us making our appearance."

"Oh, yeah. That's true," William admitted, not having thought about that.

"Robert," Steven suggested, "why don't we just tell our parents the whole thing and not worry about it?"

"How many of you think that your parents would really and truly understand or even believe us?" Robert asked.

Only Steven and William raised their hands.

"That's what I thought," said Robert. "If too many others find out about this, it's going to leak out, and soon everyone will know. The government would be on our backs and then some. Soon there would be reporters out here and everything. This has got to be kept a secret among us. I trust my parents, Mr. Mayfield, and your father, William.

"Morris, with your intuition and your abilities, can you locate some store somewhere in the western United States with a woods nearby so that we can make our appearance without ever being seen?"

"Yes, I reckon I could," Morris replied. "I'll see what I can do. I'll check around and will let you know."

"Great!" said Robert with a sense of relief. "I'm glad you'll be able to."

"Really," Robert continued, "I think it would be best if none of us told our parents what we're really going to do. We're not doing anything wrong. My parents had to know for obvious reasons. William, your father had to know, of course. I chose to tell Mr. Mayfield, but if any more are told, it may leak out and severely jeopardize our plans and our future. If any of you really trust your parents to truly believe you and not tell others, then go ahead and tell them, but don't blame me if it leaks and the word gets out about what we're really up to."

"I'm in agreement with Robert," James announced. "For our own good, we don't want what we're doing to leak out."

Everyone soon joined in and agreed not to tell anyone, not even their parents. They might tell them several years in the future but not for now.

"Now, I have another subject to bring up," Robert continued. "We need to discuss the possibilities of our possible girlfriends, if any of us have any now or later, coming with us on our summer travels. Is there anyone here who is dating steadily at the present time?"

No one spoke.

"Does anyone want to make any comment at all?" Robert asked them.

"Well, I've had girlfriends in the past," Andrew told them, "but for the past year, I just haven't been so lucky."

"Actually, when I was a child," said Morris, "most of my good friends that I played and ran around with were girls. Most of them have moved away, or we've grown apart. So, at this present time, I don't have what might be called a *sweetheart*."

"I've had several back in Tasmania," said James, "some of them, really good friends, but when I left to come here with my family, the one I was dating rejected me."

"Sorry to hear that, James," said Robert. "Maybe you'll find a replacement here in this country."

"Oh, it doesn't matter," he told everyone. "After the way she treated me, I'm in no hurry to date or fall for any women!"

"I've had some casual friends who are women," said Chris, "but nothing serious."

"That's about the way it is for me," said Robert.

"My last girlfriend was a year ago," Steven informed them, "and we decided to call it off."

"You already know what Virginia told me," Paul reminded them. "I'll just wait till later before I start dating."

"I haven't done a whole lot with women yet," said William. "I sort of agree with Paul. That's something I'll do later on."

Greg and Eric didn't volunteer any opinions.

"Well, I guess it looks like we'll be going by ourselves and that no women will come," Robert concluded. "It's just as well. Since none of us seem to have any serious girlfriends right now, we won't have to worry about telling them our secret."

"Who knows," William speculated, "we may meet some young women this summer during our travels."

"Maybe one of us will fall in love with an *alien*," Chris suggested.

"There you go, Chris," said Paul. "That'll be the day."

"Okay now," Robert continued, "let's go back to what James suggested about our travelling to places on Earth in addition to other planets. James, what places do you have in mind?"

"Actually, there's a really fantastic walk that runs from Cradle Mountain to Lake St. Clair in Tasmania. It's around 100 kilometers long, or just over 60 miles in your units, and runs through both forest and open meadows. The views of the surrounding mountains and valleys are simply wonderful when the weather is good. Mind you, it's going to be cold because it's nearly winter in early June."

"Is it going to be loaded in snow or just cold?" Robert wanted to know.

"There might be a little bit of snow, but it won't be like a snowpack," James replied.

"Spring Break starts a week from now on April 6th," Morris brought up. "Why don't we go down there for Spring Break before their winter sets in?"

"Yeah, that's a super idea!" Steven exclaimed. "How's the weather there in April, James?"

"Quite good. Early April is like late summer, and it won't be crowded with tourists like it usually is in January. There are huts along the way, and we may even have them to ourselves."

"That would be really nice," said William, "and if we have a few days left, we could see other parts of Tasmania or even Australia."

"Oh yes, certainly," said Robert. "Well, I guess that about takes care of our plans for Spring Break. How many of us can go?"

All of them raised their hands except Greg and Eric.

"My family and I have to go down to Florida, so that's where I'll be," said Greg.

"My father needs me to help him make pottery for most of that week," said Eric.

"Sorry you two can't come," said Robert. "So, that leaves eight of us going, right?"

They nodded yes.

"What other places starting in June would we like to visit on Earth?" Robert now asked.

"I think a week or so in the western United States would be fantastic," Steven suggested. "We could go hiking on something like the Pacific Crest Trail."

"All right, that sounds good," said Robert. "With the three months of summer, we could spend three or four weeks each on a choice of three or four star systems, couldn't we?"

"Yes," Morris replied, "and that would give us long enough to really have a good look at each planet of our choosing."

"That's true," said James, "and maybe we could also have a good look at the flora and fauna of each planet we visit and compare them to what Earth has."

Andrew brought up a comment. "I don't know if we could make a good comparison by visiting just two general areas of Earth: Tasmania and the western United States.''

"That's true,'' James agreed, "but there are always books to read that detail the types of flora and fauna for various parts of Earth. I'd say with that, we'll be able to make a pretty good comparison.''

"Yeah, that's true,'' Andrew admitted.

"These plans sound good enough for now,'' Robert announced, satisfied with the progress of the meeting. "We can make more detailed decisions closer to the time. After all, there's no need to set anything down in stone right now.''

Paul started thinking about the step office and changed the subject. "I wonder how the Sirians are doing on contacting the people they'd lost contact with on Earth?''

"I don't know,'' Robert replied, "but I do know that they've made a bunch of calls because the equipment has definitely been used a lot this week. I walked into the step office a few days ago, and the whole room was filled with the sounds of clicking and clacking.''

"I'm telling you what!'' William remarked. "Those Sirians get busy and really get things done! Tom called my father from Vega on Monday evening and from the Pleiades on Tuesday evening, informing him that all of the towers and telephone instruments were set up in their designated extra-terrestrial locations.''

"That's amazing!'' Paul remarked. "But when they have the ability to levitate, teleport, and duplicate items like they did before our eyes last week, I can understand why it didn't take them very long.''

"I'll bet the Vegans and the Pleiadeans were overjoyed to suddenly have the ability to literally call people on Earth by telephone,'' said Andrew.

"You know,'' Robert suddenly realized, "we need to call Tom and find out the exact locations of the towers on all five extraterrestrial locations so that during our travels, we might be able to call my parents and let them know we're okay, that is, when we may be in that vicinity.''

"Yeah, let's go call him,'' William agreed. "We haven't even placed a call through the step office yet.''

"No, you all haven't, have you?'' said Robert. "Come on. We'll call him now.''

They all decided to walk down to the step office at the foot of the woods, and they arrived in 10 minutes. Robert picked up the handset of the phone inside the step office and dialled 274-7015.

"click...BBBBBB...BBBBBB...BBBBBB...BBBBBB...''

"Come on. Answer,'' said Robert, wondering if the call was really going through.

"...BBBBBB...BBBBBB...Hello?''

"Hello. This is Robert Joslin. Am I speaking with the operator on Sirius B?''

"Yes, you are," said the operator in a foreign accent.

"Is Tom there?" Robert wanted to know.

"No, he isn't right now. Hold the line a minute, and I'll send word for him to teleport himself here so he can speak to you."

Robert waited on the line for a minute, and suddenly a voice came on the line saying:

"Hello. This is Tom."

"Hello Tom. This is Robert Joslin. My friends and I are here today, and they haven't yet spoken over our newly installed telephone network. Each of us wants to speak to you."

"Okay," said Tom. "Put each one of them on, and I'll speak to them."

Over the next five minutes, everyone took turns speaking to Tom. It really was a strange feeling to be talking to someone over eight light years away, when by conventional electromagnetic waves, this conversation would have taken at least 16 years. Tom sounded as though he were in a tunnel, but the phone connection was crisp and clear.

Morris was the last one on the line and told Tom what they needed to know. "As you know, Tom, we are planning on spending several weeks on other star systems including Sirius, Vega, and the Pleiades. We need to have a good visual memory of the locations of the towers so that we may be able to call Earth to let Robert's parents know how we are during our travels."

"You could just transport yourselves home and let them know that way instead," Tom suggested.

"Yes, we could," Morris admitted, "but I think that would interrupt our trip too much. We'd rather just transport ourselves to the telephone tower and make the call. Besides, it would be different and unique for us."

"Yes, you have a point there," Tom admitted. "I'll just teleport myself down there, Morris, and give you the visual images. I need to check the towers and equipment anyway. I'll see you in a minute."

"Okay, thanks. See you shortly."

"Bye."

Morris hung up the phone and said, "He's coming to check on the towers and equipment and to give us the images we need. He will be here in just a minute."

They walked out of the step office and soon saw Tom instantly appear in the barnyard. He walked toward them saying, "So, you all had a meeting to make plans for this summer."

"That's right," Robert replied.

"That's good. It's always good to make plans for whatever you do. I'll just take a few minutes to check over the equipment and towers to make sure they are operating all right, and then I'll transmit those images to each of you." He walked over to the towers and looked them over carefully and saw that everything appeared to be in order.

Then he returned to the barnyard and said, "Now, Morris, I'm going to transmit the images of the locations of the towers in the following order: Sirius B (general use), Sirius B (Galactic Federation), Sirius B (storage facility), Vega, and the Pleiades. Please make a mental note and remember this visual data."

"Believe me. I will!" Morris affirmed.

"The rest of you will also receive the same transmission of data that I am about to send."

Tom appeared to meditate, and Morris, Robert, and their friends received all five visual images clearly and in perfect detail.

"That's amazing!" Greg remarked. "That's even clearer than what Morris transmits. Not that his isn't already clear, but yours is incredible!"

"All right, I must return to what I was doing on Sirius B," Tom announced. "Come and visit me when you come to Sirius. You'll be welcome to stay a while if you like."

"Thank you, Tom," said Morris, answering for everyone.

"Okay, I'll see you this summer. Call me by telephone when you plan to come, or transport yourselves to the telephone station on Sirius B, and they'll send for me. Happy travels."

"See you later, Tom," they all said.

Tom walked away from them and suddenly disappeared.

"He's already back on Sirius," said Morris. "And to think that Earthlings think that the only way to travel to other star systems is to ride in a spacecraft for 100 years or so. How absurd!"

"I'm telling you what," said William. "Earthlings have a lot to learn about how long distance travel is really done. We do it all the hard way."

"*Almost* everyone," Paul reminded. "How nice it is that we don't have to do it that way anymore."

"That's true," James agreed. "We're very lucky."

"That we are," said Robert. "Okay, I guess that about wraps it up for our meeting."

"I'm really looking forward to our travels," said Andrew.

"Me too," Chris added.

"I guess we'll go ahead and leave now," said Steven. "We'll pack our backpacks for the exciting Spring Break, actually Fall Break, in Tasmania."

"Okay, good. I'll see you all later," said Robert.

Robert's friends went to their cars, got in, and drove off. They just couldn't wait for Spring Break to arrive, and they looked forward to the fun times they were going to have in Tasmania.

8 The Trip to Tasmania

It seemed as though the week at school would never get over as Robert and his friends were eagerly awaiting Spring Break so they could take off on their first major adventure. They didn't tell anyone what they were really going to do, and those who asked were told that they were planning a trip to the mountains of Georgia. In other words, they weren't told the truth. Everyone had his backpack completely packed and ready several days before school let out.

James had cleverly remembered that food prices were considerably lower in Australia than in the United States and told each of them the following:

"Look, let's wait until we get to Tasmania before we buy our food. Prices on average are 60 percent of what they are here, and they have a great selection of food at Coles New World supermarket in Devonport. There are plenty of cereals, for example, to choose from, including Kellogg's brands, which are free of BHT in Australia, by the way. Also, there are cereals made by Sanitarium Health Foods, and there are plenty of muesli cereals, some of which are sugar-free. Furthermore, you're not charged that 8 percent tax."

Everyone agreed that Australia's food stores had a much better deal and took his suggestion.

Saturday finally came, and Robert's friends showed up in their cars and parked them around to the left, outside of the yard. Robert took his car and hid it inside the barn and covered it so that if any of the other parents were to come, they would have thought that they all went in his car.

They took their loaded backpacks out of their cars, and Robert said, "James, where is a good place in Tasmania for us to arrive?"

"How about let's arrive at my friend's house just outside of Devonport. After all, we're going to need our week's supply of food from Coles New World. Can I ring him up from here?"

"Oh yes, of course, but let's call him from the step office telephone," Robert suggested. "That way it won't cost us anything."

"Good point. Okay, I'll call him from there."

Robert's parents came out to see them off and wished them a good trip, saying to Robert, "Good luck, son, and be careful." They said goodbye and began walking toward the woods.

Once at the step office, James made his call to his friend, Mark Peters, telling him that eight of them were about to arrive in his backyard and for him to make sure that no one would see them making their appearance.

"You're joking!" Mark exclaimed, certainly being in a state of disbelief. "You mean you're actually coming here?"

"That's right, Mark," James insisted. "Now, is the yard clear of anyone who may be watching?"

"Uh . . . yeah," Mark stammered. "Yeah, it's clear at the moment."

"Good. I'm going to hang up the phone now. We'll be there in 20 seconds," James told him in a perfectly serious manner.

He hung up the phone receiver and stepped outside to join Robert and the others as they formed a ring with James supplying the mental forces of the visual location where they were to arrive. The whirring wind noises began, and a pink glow overcame them as they vanished.

Meanwhile, Mark raced out into the backyard as soon as James had hung up on him so that he could witness the event. He was astounded beyond belief when he started hearing the sound of whirring wind, seemingly out of nowhere, and seeing a ring of pink glow appear and become brighter, soon revealing the eight of them. As they made their appearance, the wind and the pink glow faded away.

Immediately, James called out, "G'day, Mark. How are you going?"

"But . . . But how?!" Mark gasped, still stunned with amazement.

"It's a long story, Mark, which I'll explain later," James answered.

In Tasmania, it was 1 a.m. Sunday morning, April 7. James had waked Mark out of bed when he had called him from their step office in Tennessee a few minutes earlier. The weather was sort of cool and breezy, and the sky was clear, as the stars could clearly be seen.

"Good gracious!" exclaimed Mark. "This is a surprise to see you here!"

"I'm sure it is," James calmly replied.

"You've got your gear and everything. How long are you over for?" he wanted to know.

"This is our Spring Break, and we're going to do the Overland Track and see some other areas as well," James explained. "Everyone, this is Mark Peters, one of my best friends."

They all greeted him and introduced each other. Mark was a thin, sort of wiry, black-haired fellow who always seemed full of energy and was enthusiastic.

"It's too bad, but I've got school this week, or I'd join you," said Mark. "Come on inside the house. My parents are away this weekend."

They followed him in and sat down to visit. "I just can't believe you're actually here!" Mark carried on. "I must be dreaming."

"No, this is for real, Mark," James assured him.

"How in the world did you just . . . *show up* . . . like that?" he wanted to know.

"Oh, we've been granted a gift," James explained. "See, Robert Joslin, here, had this dream last month that he and the rest of us could transport ourselves to and from any place in mind by thought or at will. Morris, here, had the same dream but continued dreaming and made a deal with a galactic salesman so that we could have this ability in real life . . ."

James and the rest of them told Mark the whole story including the building of the step office and their building of the galactic communications device and the building of the receiving and transmitting towers by Tom and his crew. Much of this was far beyond the wildest dreams that Mark had ever had, and he just couldn't believe his ears.

". . . and this is absolutely top secret among us and only a few others in the United States. We don't mind telling you, being this far away from Tennessee, but please don't tell anybody. If this information leaks out to the general public, we'd probably be inundated by reporters and no telling what else!" James concluded.

"I won't tell a soul. No worries at all," Mark promised. "Look, I'm too excited to go back to bed tonight with you all here and everything. How about let's go outside and take a walk up the hill in the field behind us?"

"That sounds great. Let's go," James eagerly said.

"Okay. I'll change clothes, and we'll go."

After Mark changed into some daytime clothes, he grabbed a flashlight, which he called a torch, and they walked out into the field behind his house and up the steep hill. Five minutes later, they had climbed quite a bit and had some fine views of the surrounding countryside, even though it was dark. The Bass Strait, a few miles to the north, could be seen stretching out into the darkness of the horizon. To the east of them could be seen the lights of a large town.

"What's that town east of here?" Steven asked.

"That's Devonport," Mark replied.

"Are we near the ocean here?" Chris asked, as he was looking to the north.

"That's the Bass Strait to the north," Mark answered. "It separates us from the mainland of Australia, although we call Tasmania the mainland and Australia the island. The Bass Strait has some of the roughest waters in the world."

"Is that right?" Robert asked. "Do boats or ships cross it?"

"Oh yeah. They cross it," said Mark. "The Abel Tasman goes across it every night. It takes 15 hours to get to Melbourne. Just eat your meal and go straight to bed, though, so you won't get seasick."

"I don't doubt it if the waters are as rough as you say they are," William commented.

"My! Look at how vivid the Milky Way Galaxy looks!" Paul remarked.

"Yeah, the Southern Hemisphere is known for that," Mark agreed.

They spent several minutes looking in all directions from here.

"Tell you what," Mark offered, "let's walk through that field east of here, turn left on the road, and we'll walk down to the sea."

Around a half hour later, they reached the rocky shore just on the other side of the highway connecting Devonport to Ulverstone. The small waves could be seen breaking and lapping onto the rocks of the shoreline. Every now and then, a car or truck would go by on the highway. Eventually, they walked along a lower, more direct road back to Mark's house.

For the rest of the morning, they just sat up and visited, talking about different things. James, most of all, enjoyed the visit, catching up with the events and things of the land that he had left in December. Daylight finally arrived, and Mark said, "I can offer you all breakfast, if you like. What would you like?"

All of them wanted cereal, and Mark took out of the cabinets, all of the types of cereal in the house, including a 500-gram box of Kellogg's Sultana Bran. Robert noticed the price tag and said, "You mean this box only cost $1.88?"

"That's right," Mark answered.

"This stuff costs around $2.50 back in Tennessee," Robert told him. "What's the exchange rate?"

"I believe it's around $1.45 Australian to the U.S. dollar at the moment," he answered.

Robert did some figuring in his head. "That means this box of cereal only cost around $1.30 in U.S. dollars. You were right, James. I'm glad we waited until we got here to Tasmania to buy our food instead of having brought it with us from Tennessee."

"Yeah, you're not kidding," Paul added.

"If you like, I'll take you all into Devonport, and we can have a look around," Mark offered. "There's a big Coles New World store, and right next to it is another big store called Roelf Vos. They are always in competition with each other, so you can stock up there. My parents took the car and left the Ford Spectron van parked here this weekend. I reckon I can haul all eight of you in it. It will be a bit tight, but I believe we can manage, no worries at all."

"Thanks very much, Mark," said James.

"Would you like to have some toast with Vegemite?" Mark offered.

"Sure," said James, not bothering to tell the others how bitter they might find it. "Fix up some for all of us."

Mark took out 10 slices of bread and toasted them, after which he spread a nice layer of dark brown Vegemite, pure yeast extract, on each toasted piece. He handed all eight of them a piece, keeping two for himself. Everyone, except James, received a shock at how bitter it was and spit it out in a hurry. They were expecting it to be sweet and taste like chocolate pudding.

"What's the matter?" asked Mark in complete surprise.

"I don't know what it is," replied James, "but none of the Americans like Vegemite. They think it tastes bitter. You and I and the rest of the Australians were brought up on it and like it, but the Americans weren't. Please excuse them."

"Sure. No worries, mate," said Mark.

"Here, you can have my piece, Mark," Robert offered.

"Mine too," said Chris.

Everyone handed his piece to either Mark or James, and they each had five slices, as it turned out.

"Mark," Robert brought up, "we've got a problem. All of us have U.S. dollars, and this being Sunday, I'll bet all of the banks are closed."

"Oh, I can buy 'em off ye, if you like," Mark offered. "I've been saving to come to the States, anyhow." Mark picked up a basket of apricots from the counter, brought it over to the breakfast table, and set it down. "By the way, here are some apricots. I'll just be a minute while I go get some cash." He went to another part of the house and returned. "I've got $300 cash. That'll probably do you for a week's worth of food."

Robert took a piece of paper and a pencil and calculated how many U.S. dollars that would be and said, "If my calculations are correct, I come up with U.S. $206.90. Here, we'll just give you $210." All of them took cash out of their wallets, giving it to Mark until he had U.S. $210.

"That's great! I can't wait to come and see the States," declared Mark, as he handed them $300.

Once everyone had finished breakfast, they all piled into the van, leaving their gear at his house to be picked up later that day. He took them to Devonport on more of an inland road instead of on the coastal highway. Mark sat on the right and changed gears on the floor with his left hand in this 5-speed van.

He first drove further inland on a small, winding, paved road with woods on the left and marsh on the right. Soon, they came to an intersection.

"This is Forth," Mark announced. "Do you see that road that goes to the left on the other side of that bridge to the right of us? That road goes up to the Cradle Mountain area. For now, we'll turn left here and go to Devonport via Don."

He turned left and took them on a narrow two-lane road with curves and hills which went on for the few miles to Don, a small community on the west side of Devonport. Robert agreed with James that this road did indeed have similarities to Highway 99 from Murfreesboro to Eagleville.

Mark showed them around Devonport including a look at the Mersey River and the pedestrianized street in the town center. Across the road from there in a huge parking lot was Coles New World supermarket with Roelf Vos right next to it. Although the parking lots were right next to each other, one could not drive from one lot to the other without having to go out onto the road because there was a concrete wall dividing them.

Everyone went inside and stocked up on enough food to last for a week. Some went over to Roelf Vos to compare their prices with Coles New World's and found them to be basically the same. They were overjoyed to find that the price of food was almost half of what it would have cost in the United States.

Morris came over to Robert and said, "Robert, as far as a grocery store in the western United States with a woods near it is concerned, the best I could come up with was Cascade Locks, Oregon, but the prices here are so much cheaper, and they have more of the types of food that we like. Why don't we just come here once a week and stock up during our summer travels?"

"That's good thinking," Robert told him. "That's a great idea! You know, maybe just one of us, James, for example, could come and buy the food for all of us. He could exchange money at the bank, buy the food, and return with it to wherever we are."

By this time, James had walked over and was listening to their proposed plans. "Why, yes! I reckon that would be a great idea!" James exclaimed. "We could visit one of the extraterrestrial telephone stations once a week, whichever one is closest to us at the time. I could call Mark to verify that no one's watching, and make my appearance at his place. He could take me to Devonport, and I would exchange the money, buy the food, and return to you. That would also give me a chance to visit here and to stay caught up on the events here in Tasmania. Yeah, I'd be glad to do it."

"That's great, James!" said Robert. "It looks like we've got it all figured out then. Just be sure that you're not seen when you leave here to return to us after you go through the checkout line. Find a good place to hide."

James understood the importance of not being seen while appearing or disappearing. Also, he and all of them were certainly honest, and it would never have crossed their minds to do something like gather food from the shelves and disappear with it, never going through the checkout line. All of them realized that such an action would be misuse of the gift that they had been granted and could well be grounds for having the gift removed by Tom and the Galactic Federation. Besides, they were morally honest to begin with because they knew that was the right thing to be.

After having a ball comparing the differences in prices and food selection between Australia and the United States, they checked out, and Mark took them back to his house where they loaded the food into their packs.

James had brought with him a map of Cradle Mountain-Lake St. Clair National Park, and they looked at it and made plans as to where to stay each night along the Overland Track. They decided that taking it easy and spending six nights along the way would make for a great hiking adventure and would get them in shape for the coming summer.

Mark offered to drive them up to the trailhead, and was it *ever* a tight fit into the Ford Spectron van when all eight backpacks had to be crammed in also! They managed, however, and left for Cradle Valley, nearly an hour's drive away. The paved road was winding and curvy as it climbed from Forth through mostly Eucalyptus forest. After some time, the road leveled out and crossed mostly uninhabited meadows with Mountain Rocket shrubs and patches of trees here and there.

For the last several kilometers, the road's pavement ended, and it became such a narrow gravel lane that it looked like a trough. Had a bus been going down this lane, its sides would certainly have scraped the banks on both sides of the lane. Robert and the others just couldn't believe that this was the only road that went to Cradle Valley, but this was it. Two cars certainly could not have passed by each other, but there were passing places every so often.

They arrived at the end of the road at Waldheim Chalet. James was glad to see that the park headquarters had already closed up for the season, which meant that each of them would save the $10 walker's fee. Mark helped them unload their backpacks and said:

"I wish I could join you this week, but I've got to go back home and go to school. The forecast is quite good for this week, so I'm sure you'll enjoy it. It was nice meeting you, and have a great trip."

"Thank you for all your help," said Robert.

"No worries at all," Mark replied. "All the best."

"By the way, Mark," Robert brought up, "what was all of that laughing and cackling we heard at the crack of dawn in the woods next to your house?"

"Oh, those were Kookaburras, a member of the Kingfisher family."

James and the others thanked Mark, and he drove away back to his home. They heaved their heavy backpacks, stuffed with over a week's supply of food, onto their backs and walked over to some picnic tables there at Waldheim Chalet, which was a collection of wooden guest cabins at the road's end. There was a small gravel parking lot, and the cabins were situated in a small forest of Myrtle Beech trees, King William Pines, and Pencil Pines.

"Look at these little kangaroos all over the place," Steven commented, as they were setting their packs down by the picnic tables to eat lunch.

"I know," said Robert, "and I can pet them, too. Look." He reached down and gently stroked one of them on the back.

There were seven or eight of them in the area, and most of them came over to them at the picnic table.

"Those are Bennett's wallabies, a smaller version of the kangaroo," James explained. "They are well known for their tameness."

"Oh, I wish I could take one of these back home with me," said Chris.

"What are those black crow-like birds that keep calling out their grating, scratchy sounding notes?" Andrew wanted to know.

"Those are Clinking Currawongs," James answered. "Around here, they love to snatch people's food during their picnics. So, let's be careful while we eat lunch here."

It was now early afternoon, and everyone was hungry and eager to dig into their recently purchased food from Coles New World and Roelf Vos. Sure enough, the Clinking Currawongs snatched a few pieces of food in the blink of an eye, and the wallabies looked so gentle and attractive as they began to beg in an irresistible manner for pieces of food.

"It's not good to feed the wallabies bread and crackers because it's bad for their teeth," said James. "However, a few of our nuts and grains are fine for them."

"Ohh . . . Aren't they cute," Chris commented.

"Yeah, really," said Paul. "It would be nice if we could take some of them home with us."

"I know, but they have their place here," James told them. "This is their home."

"Look," said Andrew. "This one's got a little one in its pouch."

"They call them joeys," said James.

Andrew was able to pet the little one in its mother's pouch.

They finished lunch, packed up again, and began hiking south on the Overland Track. The weather was cloudy bright with high, thin clouds, and it was cool and breezy, perfect weather for going hiking.

As soon as they began, they left the patch of forest and briefly descended into a large, brownish, open meadow on a man-made boardwalk that soon ceased to exist as they continued. In the distance ahead of them could be seen the smooth, rounded mountains with just a tiny glimpse of Cradle Mountain behind these closer ones. Eucalypts and other trees dotted their sloping, weathered landscapes, and the higher elevations were mostly exposed with rounded rock. This was only the start, as the scenery would prove to be even more spectacular further on.

When the boardwalk ended, they were walking on dark, peat-like ground which at this time of year was not a problem for walking, since it had been relatively dry for the past few weeks. However, in wetter times, this could be like walking through a quagmire and be difficult to traverse, to say the least.

It was not long before they entered the sparse forest of mostly Eucalyptus trees, also known as Gum trees. Other trees grew here as well. James had hiked through here two years earlier with his father and, for the most part, served as the guide for the other seven.

Robert began to ask James questions. "James, what are these other trees growing in here with these Eucalyptus trees?"

James walked over to a plant that looked like a Yucca shrub. "Here is an interesting one," he announced. The rest of them looked on with interest. "This is called *Richea scoparia*, also known as Alpine Heath. It is one of the largest Heaths in the world, the largest of which is the Pandani tree, *Richea pandanifolia*. They are much taller than these, and we'll see some of them later on.

"Over here," as James moved to another tree, "is a Celery Top Pine, *Phyllocladus aspleniifolius*, which has leaves similar to a Ginkgo tree, only this is a relative of the Podocarp family." James continued moving from tree to tree. "These trees that look like Japanese Cedars are King William Pines, *Athrotaxis selaginoides*. This is a Myrtle Beech, *Nothofagus gunnii*, also known as Southern Beech, as they are relatives of the Beech trees that we just saw in Savage Gulf last month."

"How did a relative of the Beech tree show up down here?" Andrew inquired.

"Oh, keep in mind," James answered, "that trees and seeds migrate over the millions of years, and as they move on to different places, they change and evolve to new types as they adapt to the environment. See, many millions of years ago, all continents were connected, and trees and plants migrated without the barriers of the oceans to stop them."

Andrew pondered about what James had just said. "I don't know if I believe that continents can drift like that."

"Well, they do," James insisted. "Look at South America and Africa, for example. You can see on the map how well they used to fit together in the past, and look how northwestern Africa and the east coast of the United States would have fit together. Also, what do you think causes earthquakes today. There's just way too much evidence to deny that continental drift is a reality."

"I agree with you, James," said Robert.

"Yeah, I suppose it could be true," Andrew somewhat admitted. "I'll have to think about it."

As they continued through the shallow forested ravine with increasingly better views of Cradle Mountain, which displayed its furrowed and jagged slopes above everything else, they soon came out onto the shores of Dove

Lake. The weather had cleared to blue sky, and the wind blew fairly fiercely off of the lake.

From there, they followed the track around the right side of the lake and entered the "Ballroom Forest" which contained King William Pines (King Billy Pines), Southern Sassafras (*Atherosperma moschatum*), Alpine Heaths, Pandanis, and Tea-trees (*Leptospermum genus*). Sure enough, James noticed the Pandanis and said to everyone:

"Here, everyone, is a Pandani tree, the largest type of Heath in the world. They grow up to six meters high. Over there you can see some Pencil Pines, the same type of tree that I pointed out to you over a month ago."

The going became rough, and Chris said, "This trail is in terrible shape! It's almost straight up and full of roots."

"Oh, this is just a bit of a rough section," commented James, proud of the ruggedness of Australia's wilderness. "No, don't worry. It gets better after this."

They continued to pick their way over roots and boulders as the trail ascended steeply, winding its way out of the forest into open, rocky terrain. Some of the slopes had sandstone rock faces. No more than they crested than the trail made a steep descent and then climbed up again! Everyone was pretty disgusted with this "track" by the time they had climbed up onto the rocky shores of Lake Wilks, a small lake on the north face of Cradle Mountain.

"I'm telling you what!" gasped William. "Whew-wee! I've never seen such a rough going trail before, if that's what you want to call it."

"You're not kidding!" Robert agreed. "But it's worth it to see Cradle Mountain towering in front of us like that."

"Look at Dove Lake behind us," Morris brought up.

"And there isn't a house on it," Paul added.

"Yeah, that's really great!" said Steven.

"Okay, everyone," James informed them, "from here we'll pick our way along the foot of Cradle Mountain over to Kitchen Hut." Suddenly, he noticed a bunch of blooming Grass Trigger Plants (*Stylidium gramnifolium*). "Hey, look! Robert, take a small grass blade and gently poke it inside one of those blooms."

Robert did as James requested, and as he inserted the blade of grass, a hammer-like column, formed from the stamen, swung up and tagged the grass blade.

"Well, I will say!" exclaimed Robert, surprised at the flower's ability to do that. "Isn't that something!"

"That's a Grass Trigger Plant, and they do like that when an insect feeds on the flower's nectar," James explained. "The insect's back receives pollen and carries it to the next flower where the same thing happens, ensuring cross pollination."

"That really is amazing!" said Paul.

Everyone had to see it for himself, so each of them took a thin grass blade and gently poked it inside different blooms and marveled at the phenomenon.

"Australia really has an interesting list of biology and very unique at that," Morris stated.

"Oh yes. It's quite unique," James agreed.

After picking their way over boulders through a treeless terrain having nothing more than shrubs, they finally arrived at Kitchen Hut. Most of them were exhausted, and it was shortly after 5 p.m. Sunset would be near 7 p.m.

Kitchen Hut was a small wooden building that sat on the northwest foot of Cradle Mountain in a treeless, exposed area. There were plenty of Mountain Rocket shrubs (*Bellendena montana*) which had the same foliage as the Celery Top Pines. Also, there were some Cushion Plants that looked like giant pincushions.

"Who wants to go up Cradle Mountain with me?" Robert asked everyone.

Only James and Morris took Robert up on his offer, leaving the other five to fix supper for everyone. After setting their packs inside, the three of them took off, seemingly tireless after the long day which, for all eight of them, began around midnight, Tasmania time, when they had gotten up in Tennessee.

There was barely enough time as the trip to the summit and back would take just under two hours with a 10-minute rest on top. The climb to the summit was steep and difficult as they scrambled up the loose, rocky slopes. Robert led them as they picked their way between many rocky boulders to a small saddle with a short climb to the summit after that.

Pillars of sandstone-like rock stood upright all over the summit, and the views were spectacular! A plaque was imbedded into one of the rocks, and it displayed the names and directions of all of the surrounding mountains including the distances to them. Patches of orange colored lichen could be seen on every rock and boulder.

"What's that mountain west of here standing all by itself like a butte?" Robert asked James.

"That's Barn Bluff," James answered.

"It sort of looks like a scene out of the Old West," Robert commented.

"Yes, it does," Morris agreed.

Further to the west could be seen a mass of clouds rolling in, and it signalled that the weather might not be so good the next day. They could see for many kilometers in all directions with fantastic views of the rolling hills and terrain, dotted with lakes and covered with forests and meadows.

"This is really a spectacular view!" James exclaimed. "It's far better than I've seen during any other climb up here in past years. I wish the other five had come also."

"Me too," Robert agreed. "They really missed out on this one."

James looked at his watch and said, "I guess we'd better go back down now, or we might get caught out in the dark."

All of them took in a final glimpse of the spectacular scenery and made their way back across the boulders to the saddle and then down through the crevice to continue descending on the loose, rocky slope to Kitchen Hut. They made it back 10 minutes before it got really dark, just in time, and they told the others about the wonderful scenery they had missed.

The other five had prepared supper for everyone, and they ate well. Kitchen Hut was a small wooden shelter, and it had a nice upstairs loft just large enough to sleep all eight of them. Once it became dark, everyone set out their bedrolls and sleeping bags.

It wasn't long before the nocturnal animals started stirring. A quoll or marsupial native cat scurried around and was mostly tame, as it was used to visitors. It had spots on its back and was quite a subject of amusement to them as they drifted off to sleep.

The west wind could be heard howling through the night.

Everyone certainly slept well following the very long day they had just had. Most of them were still in somewhat of a state of disbelief that they were actually in Tasmania. For them, this Spring Break was far better and more exotic than anything they had previously thought possible. How thankful they were that they had this rare and unusual gift of being able to transport themselves wherever they desired.

Morning arrived, and everyone woke up to find that the clouds from the west had rolled in. Cradle Mountain could not be seen as it was foggy and drizzling. Everyone ate breakfast, packed, and soon left.

As they left, the drizzle stopped, and they hiked around the right side of the mountain on a somewhat boggy and muddy track, ascending at first and then descending as they turned right and walked away from Cradle Mountain. As they descended, they emerged just below the clouds and had a wonderful view of the Buttongrass plain ahead. To the left, the whole plateau dropped sharply at a 45 degree angle into the valley way below, and the Overland Track ran right along the edge of this dropoff.

They eventually veered left, still following the edge of the plateau and soon descended sharply into Waterfall Valley which had some exposed rock faces and dropoffs into gullies which had been eroded into the otherwise level terrain. Pencil Pines and Tasmanian Snow Gums (*Eucalyptus coccifera*) grew in patches.

Waterfall Valley Hut and Cirque Hut were in this general area. After hiking for six kilometers this morning, they arrived at Cirque Hut and entered through its back door. This turned out to be a great place for lunch, and no one else was there. Barn Bluff could be seen to the north, and clouds covered its summit. The area around Cirque Hut was wet, as there was a small creek and gully next to it. Myrtle Beeches and Pencil Pines were the main trees in this area.

After a relaxing and restful lunch, everyone set out again and hiked for six more kilometers to Windermere Hut. The weather was still mostly cloudy, but the sun occasionally broke through the clouds and was a welcome sight when it did.

Most of the track passed through open Buttongrass plains and also passed through occasional patches of Tasmanian Snow Gums, Myrtle Beeches, and Deciduous Beeches. Here and there could be seen some Alpine Heaths and Grass Trigger Plants. Small lakes and tarns dotted the scenery, some of them with Pencil Pines growing in scattered patches around their shores.

"This is it!" Paul suddenly exclaimed, seemingly for no apparent reason.

"What is?" Robert asked.

"This is where we came over a month ago the very first time we transported ourselves, isn't it?" Paul continued.

"That's right," James confirmed. "You're very perceptive to realize that, since it was dark when we came here."

"I'm glad to see it in the daylight this time," Paul added.

"Yes, it really is beautiful, isn't it?" said Morris.

"That's true," James agreed, "but I can't say that this track always is.

When it rains steadily, this track gets so muddy that you can sink up to your thighs unexpectedly.''

Most of them found that hard to believe since the ground was only spongy in bare spots between the tufts of Buttongrass, but they could see multiple foot paths that had previously been used to bypass wet areas of the original track.

After more hiking, they arrived at Lake Windermere, which afforded them spectacular views of Barn Bluff, seen across the lake's surface. Pencil Pines, Tasmanian Snow Gums, and Heath shrubs grew in areas along the shore. Around the right side of the lake and a few hundred meters away was Windermere Hut situated at the foot of a hill in a beautiful patch of Myrtle Beeches, Eucalypts, and Tea-trees.

It was only 3 p.m., but everyone decided to stop there for the night and take it easy this afternoon after the very long day yesterday. Two other fellows, brothers in their early twenties, were already there and spoke with English accents. These were the first people they had seen since leaving Waldheim Chalet the day before, and they introduced themselves as Chris and Richard Bell from Lewes, Sussex, England.

Robert, James, and Morris sat down inside the hut, visiting with these two characters from the south of England. The other five went outside, exploring and looking around the lake as Clinking Currawongs, Ravens, and various other birds made their calls.

Chris and Richard were on a year's trip around the world and were spending quite a while in Australia, already having spent three months in New Zealand. They had only recently arrived in Australia, purchased a car on the mainland, left it with a mechanic at his garage near Sydney, and had come to Tasmania for six weeks. They enjoyed hearing Chris and Richard tell of their adventures they had already had in New Zealand and found them to be quite friendly and hospitable. *How nice,* Robert thought, *that two brothers were such good friends that they would travel together for a whole year.*

It turned out that Chris and Richard were only resting and intended to push further north to Cirque Hut to stay there overnight, so they decided it was time to leave. Robert asked them for their address in case he might venture to England one day, and they gladly gave it to him along with their phone number. Robert, James, and Morris gave them their addresses also. They wished one another well, and Chris and Richard put on their packs and left the hut.

Morris decided to quietly venture outside very soon after they left. Without Chris and Richard knowing about it, he kept an eye on them as they walked down the track.

"Ha! I knew it!" Morris suddenly yelled out. He had just witnessed Chris and Richard suddenly and silently vanishing as soon as they had walked around 100 meters up the track. "I just *knew* they weren't really Earth people! I just knew it!"

Robert and James heard Morris shouting outside and rushed out to see what it was all about.

"Sorry, what was that, Morris?" they both asked him.

"It's about Chris and Richard. I just saw them disappear."

"You *what*?!" exclaimed Robert, utterly amazed.

"I just witnessed them as they suddenly vanished 100 meters up the track."

"But that can't be!" James insisted. "They had perfect English accents."

"That's right," said Morris. "They've evidently spent a lot of time in England, just visiting and checking it out. It doesn't take them very long to pick up a language or an accent and speak it perfectly."

"Uh . . . What do you mean?" Robert wanted to know.

"They're from another planet, just like Tom and his crew," Morris explained. "You saw how well Tom could speak English, didn't you? You see, they're fully conscious beings."

"So, that means they gave us a false address, didn't they!" declared Robert in an angry tone.

"They sure did," said Morris. "I'll bet you that Grafton Terrace they gave us in Lewes, Sussex, doesn't even exist."

"I can't figure it out. Why didn't they just tell us the truth?" Robert wanted to know.

"They didn't want to stir people up and make anyone freak out. See, they are here on a vacation trip from whatever they do on their home planet, and they just came here to have a good time and casually associate with various other Earthlings, and that was it."

"How did you know, Morris?" James asked.

"Oh, I could sense it, intuitive as I am. My guides sort of give me ideas without actually telling me in words."

"Boy, I wish I could sense those things accurately," Robert wished out loud.

"Maybe you will soon," Morris speculated.

"I hope so."

"We had just become friends with them!" James declared.

"I know, but that doesn't really matter for them," Morris explained. "They live only for purposes, and we've already served that for them. So, that's all we are to them. See, friendships are not valued and treasured for them like they are between the eight of us here, plus Greg and Eric."

"Of course, you know, we're always open to making new friends," said Robert.

"That's right, but they're not," Morris went on, "especially with those on Earth, since they see no point in establishing close friendships with people like us who live on a different star system from where they live."

"That's too bad," James commented. "It seems sort of sad to me. I wish I had gone down to the lake with the others instead."

"Well, there may have been a purpose for your having been with us in the hut and having met them," Morris explained. "Who knows. There may be a time in the future when you may not realize just how valuable it is to have friends. I don't mean to be too critical, but I can sense that there are times when you don't take a person's remarks with a grain of salt, and you may discredit a friend when all he's doing is explaining something to you."

"What do mean by that, Morris?" James asked.

"Well, it doesn't mean the person wouldn't be a friend of yours," he continued. "It's just that he may want to be open with you and let you know what he thinks about something or how he feels about it. There's nothing the matter with that, and I think the purpose of Chris and Richard's visit was to remind you of the true value of friendship."

"But how can that be a purpose for Chris and Richard?" James wanted to know. "I thought you said they didn't value friendships like we do."

"Yes, that's true," Morris admitted, "but they served several purposes while they were here, and they wouldn't necessarily *know* what all of them are. As you see, their visit has caused us to have this important discussion, which otherwise would not have taken place."

"Yeah, I guess I see your point," James admitted. "I'll keep that in mind and will do my best to take things with a grain of salt."

"That's good," said Morris.

"What caused you to bring up that point, Morris?" Robert wanted to know.

"There are times in people's lives when they need to be reminded of certain things, and I could sort of sense that James needed to be reminded about the value of friendship, especially when he brought up that he would rather have been down by the lake running around with the others."

"You *are* good at philosophy, aren't you," James remarked.

"Yes, I am, and I've always had an interest in it. Whenever I see the opportunity, I use it to help out others by explaining what I think, just like I did with you."

"Thanks for telling me, Morris," said James. "I really appreciate that."

"What star system do you think they live on?" Robert asked, now changing the subject.

"I'm not really sure, but I lean toward Vega. They're probably just having a good time learning about how their fellow humans are living out their lifetimes here on Earth."

"So, in a sense, they are travelling like we are," said James.

"Exactly," Morris agreed.

"Boy, I wish Chris had been here with us," said Robert. "He'd have had a ball analyzing those two characters with his interest in philosophy."

About this time, the other five returned from the lake, ready to relax and eat supper. Robert, James, and Morris told Chris and the others about the interesting story of Chris and Richard Bell, and wasn't Chris sorry that he hadn't stayed to see the course of events, especially their sudden disappearance! Morris and Chris had a lot in common since they both had analytical minds when it came to philosophy.

They enjoyed an early supper and went outside to see if they could pet the wallabies and the pademelons, which were sort of like a cross between a wallaby and a rabbit. For some reason, the pademelons were far less tame than the wallabies, and no one succeeded in petting one.

Once it got dark, they went inside and talked for a while with each other. They were still in a state of amazement that they were on the other side of the Earth. No one else stayed here overnight, and they had a peaceful night's sleep.

It was now Tuesday morning, April 9, the third day for them on the Overland Track. The skies had totally cleared, and the sunlight was just beginning to shine through the trees. Ravens, Clinking Currawongs, and other birds could be heard making their calls, definitely loud enough to wake everyone up. What a wonderful day it was with no rain and plenty of clear weather to afford them the best views possible. They got up, ate breakfast, packed, and left, eager to see what lay ahead of them.

The track soon emerged from the forest, which later included Tasmanian Snow Gums, into a small alpine meadow, affording clear and spectacular views of Barn Bluff and Cradle Mountain. Alpine Heath shrubs and miniature ferns inhabited this meadow along with plenty of Buttongrass. After passing through a final row of Myrtle Beeches and Celery Top Pines, the track dropped sharply into a large, open meadow for the next few kilometers.

There were creeks to cross, and some places were boggy. The wind was nearly calm on this bright, warm sunny day.

Mt. Pelion could be seen ahead with views of Mt. Oakleigh, Pelion East, and Mt. Ossa further away and to the left. A few Pencil Pines grew next to a shallow lake, which they passed near the end of the meadow.

Abruptly, the track entered a thick forest as it crossed a creek. There were plenty of Myrtle Beech trees, Tea-trees, Pandanis, and Eucalypts. Further on, just before they emerged from the forest again, they passed through a pure stand of Pandani trees, some of them six meters high. Everyone noticed as James pointed them out.

"Here is an excellent stand of Pandani trees," he announced. "This is the best stand of them that you will see anywhere on this walk."

Needless to say, the rest of them agreed, as this stand looked really unique.

After the Pandani stand, the track passed through mixed meadows and forests with small ponds or tarns. Pencil Pines were interspersed here and there. Eventually, they entered more forest and hiked through it to Frog Flats, which had a campsite situated in an open forest of mostly Eucalypts. From there to Pelion Hut, the track was mostly a deep muddy ditch skirting along the edge of a forest with Pelion Plains to the left. Mt. Oakleigh could clearly be seen across this grassy plain.

They arrived at Pelion Hut at 3 p.m. after 14 kilometers of hiking. No one else was there. This green hut with metal siding was situated in an open forest of mostly Swamp Gums (*Eucalyptus delegatensis*). Just further on was a sizeable creek where everyone went and splashed around. Wallabies and pademelons could be seen hopping about from place to place among the Myrtle Beeches and Tea-trees.

Again, Robert, James, and Morris had the urge to climb another mountain, this time Mt. Oakleigh, which was to the north of them. It looked too irresistible to the other five to pass up this one after they had passed up the chance to go up Cradle Mountain. So, all of them packed their daypacks and left their backpacks inside the hut while they set out to go mountain climbing.

As they were walking across the grassy plains, James commented, "This is one of my favorite mountains in Tasmania, and the views are absolutely amazing from its rocky summit!"

Everyone followed him to the foot of the mountain slopes where the forest began. Plenty of Grass Trigger Plants could be seen growing all over the wet, spongy ground. The forest contained large Eucalypts, Myrtle Beeches, Southern Sassafras, King Billy Pines, and a few Waratah shrubs (*Telopea truncata*). Much of this forest floor was carpeted by moss. Pandanis grew up to six meters with their large tufts of Yucca-like blades growing only on their tops.

Higher up, as the track climbed steeply up and over boulders, there was a pure stand of Pandanis and Alpine Heaths that nearly blocked the way and made the going difficult. Soon, they emerged from this tangle and arrived at a saddle where they turned left, climbed over more boulders, crested, descended through mostly open meadows to a creek, crossed it, and made a final ascent to the summit of boulders. This summit had plenty of tall, vertical columns of sandstone-like rock.

"This is really neat!" Chris remarked.

"I know," agreed William. "We can see all around us up here."

"I'm glad I came up here," said Paul. "How does this compare to Cradle Mountain?"

"Oh, this is better," James answered.

"I can see why this is your favorite place, James," Robert told him.

The skies were still perfectly clear, and the sun now sat low on the western horizon, causing views of Mt. Pelion West to be a little hazy. Mt. Pelion East and Mt. Ossa could clearly be seen to the south across Pelion Plains with the forest beyond that.

"This was definitely worth coming up here!" Steven remarked. "After views like this, I'll always have a desire to travel."

"That's great," said Robert. "You'd be surprised at what you'll learn just by travelling."

"I'll say!" Steven agreed.

"I'd say travelling is an education in itself," Chris added.

"I wish we'd brought our camping gear with us so we could have camped up here tonight," Andrew brought up.

"Yes, that would have been good," Morris agreed.

It was nearly 5 p.m., and everyone decided that it was time to return to Pelion Hut if they wanted to return before dark. As they began to leave, Andrew asked, "James, what are those mountains way off to the east of here?"

"Those are the Walls of Jerusalem, and at the foot of them is Dixons Kingdom Forest, which is an ancient stand of Pencil Pine trees. It's really a beautiful place. After we finish this hike, we can go there, if you like."

"Yes, let's all go there just before returning home," Robert suggested.

They arrived back at Pelion Hut just in time, as it became totally dark only 10 minutes later. Everyone was really hungry after their vigorous, long day, and they ate well. Pelion Hut had two layers of bunks in its rear, and there was more than enough room to sleep them all. Again, only the eight of them were here with no one else.

"This is really great how we have this whole track nearly to ourselves," said Robert. "We've only seen two people since we began."

"Yes, it's the end of the walking season here," said James. "Most people have already taken their holidays for the year and are now back at work. Now, mind you, January's a different story altogether. It's really crowded then, and the huts are almost always full."

"I don't doubt it," William agreed. "I'm glad we didn't come then."

It wasn't long, and they all drifted off to sleep, having walked nearly 22 kilometers today.

When everyone arose the next morning, they noticed how cold it was. There was a light coating of frost over the Pelion Plains. However, the weather was still perfectly clear, and it would soon be a nice, warm sunny day. As soon as they ate breakfast, they put on their backpacks and set out for another day's adventure. They were only just now getting used to the fact that they were really and truly in Tasmania.

The Overland Track gently ascended for quite a while through mostly forested areas of Myrtle Beeches, Tea-trees, Eucalypts, Pandanis, and a few King Billy Pines. There were some waterfalls along the way, and the forest became thinner as it opened up to Alpine Heaths and Tasmanian Snow Gums. Eventually, the track crested at a four-way intersection with tracks going to Mt. Ossa on the right and to Mt. Pelion East on the left.

"Let's go up Mt. Ossa!" James suddenly suggested. "It's the highest point in Tasmania at 1,617 meters, and the views are excellent!"

They set down their packs and packed a lunch along with some emergency supplies into their daypacks and made a run for the summit. After ascending the slope, which had plenty of Snow Gums, they came to steeper and rockier terrain. It became somewhat of a scramble with a sheer rock cliff to their left and a huge rock face on their right.

"This looks a lot like Stone Door," William brought up.

"Yeah, it sure does!" agreed Robert. "At least it reminds me of it."

As Paul was looking down from where they had come, he exclaimed, "Boy, some of that land is *way* on down there now!"

After ascending the top level of the rock face, the going became easier with only a gentle slope to the summit. Again, some of the rock had the appearance of vertical pillars or columns. The summit itself was a pile of large, rounded boulders, and the rest of the area around the summit was a mixture of small alpine meadows and boulders dotted with several small tarns.

"You're right, James," said Morris. "These views are excellent!"

"I wish I'd gone up Cradle Mountain with you three," said Chris, "but this will make up for it."

"Yeah, that's for sure," William agreed. "I wouldn't have missed this for anything."

"Me neither," said Andrew.

Now that everyone had reached the top, James told them about the area. "Okay everyone, I'll tell you what the surrounding mountains are. To the southwest, you can see Frenchman's Cap, and it's properly named because it looks like one. To the south is the Acropolis and other mountains near Pine Valley. To the southeast is Cathedral Mountain. Mt. Pelion East is east of here. I'm sure you already know the ones sort of northeast of here: Barn Bluff and Cradle Mountain. Looking even further, you can just get a glimpse of the sea."

Everyone really enjoyed the scenery, and they stayed up there an hour while they ate lunch. The weather remained clear in all directions, except for a few puffy clouds way off to the west, and the air was almost still with hardly any breeze. What a wonderful day is was, and how nice it was to be spending Spring Break in Tasmania.

After lunch, they descended and returned to their packs at the track intersection and continued south on the Overland Track, descending gently most of the way. Most of the terrain was open Buttongrass plains with patches of mostly Eucalyptus trees here and there. One place afforded a spectacular view of Cathedral Mountain in the distance with its rock cliffs visible across the plains with patches of Eucalypts.

The track was a little more muddy than in other areas, and there was a really muddy area just before crossing a creek and arriving at Kia Ora Hut. This hut was situated by the creek and at the edge of a forest, as the rest of the Overland Track south of here would be mostly forested. Two Bennett's wallabies greeted them as they arrived. Pademelons could also be seen hopping about. Clinking Currawongs and other birds made their calls throughout the afternoon.

It was late afternoon, and they decided to call it a day after walking more than 14 kilometers. They ate some supper and enjoyed being able to pet the wallabies. Robert and Chris had the most fun associating with the wallabies, and they gave them some nuts out of their trail mix. Again, none of the pademelons were tame.

Overnight, it became cloudy, and it became quite cold again. The next morning, frost covered the mountain slopes north of this area. Mt. Ossa and Mt. Pelion East were covered by clouds, and the frost seen on their slopes under the clouds really made for a unique and spectacular appearance. Tasmania had lots of varied scenes and weather to offer, and it was a place to which they were glad they chose to travel. Clinking Currawongs and other birds made plenty of morning calls.

As they packed and left, it looked like it would begin raining any minute, but it held off all morning. Most of the track was level but was somewhat muddy as it crossed a couple of creeks. The forest had Myrtle Beeches, Eucalypts, Tea-trees, Waratahs, and a few Banksias.

After a few kilometers, they emerged from the forest into a small grassy meadow with the ruins of a hut. This was DuCane Hut, and a nice large Leatherwood tree (*Eucryphia lucida*) grew near it. A few of the white blooms still remained on the tree this late in the season. Even a few Silver Wattles (*Acacia dealbata*) were growing in this area.

As they continued south, there were plenty of Leatherwoods and Southern Sassafras trees along with Myrtle Beeches and increasing numbers of Celery Top Pines. It was a deep, thick forest, and Chris commented, "This forest looks just like the forest seen on *Snow White and the Seven Dwarfs*."

"Yes, you're right. It does," Andrew agreed.

"I was going to say that too," Robert added, "except I was going to say *The Rescuers*."

"Yeah, that too," William agreed.

After a while, they came to a turnoff to the left that led them to several large, spectacular waterfalls. The stream above the lower falls ran right between two rocks faces that were close enough together for someone to jump from one side to the other. A large rock ball had wedged itself between the two sides some two meters above the water. These falls were large, up to 25 meters high, and on one of them, the water plunged to the left, bounced off some rocks, and then plunged to the right. Pencil Pines and King Billy Pines grew in this area. They enjoyed exploring the area and then returned to the trail to continue south.

"Ooohh! Get it off me!" Chris suddenly yelled out.

"Ooohh, nasty!" exclaimed William.

They had gotten into a patch of leeches which thrive in deep, moist forests. Several of them were discovering these leeches crawling up their legs. Leeches look sort of like a slug, are brown in color, and move like an inchworm. They are bloodsuckers.

"I can't get it off!" Chris exclaimed.

Luckily, James brought some salt with him. "Here Chris," James offered. "I'll just put a bit of salt on it. Leeches are quite common in damp, dark areas like this place, and they're even more prevalent on cloudy, non-sunny days." James applied some grains of salt, and the leech immediately let go of Chris' leg and dropped to the ground, squirming as if it was really suffering.

"That'll teach him!" said Chris, relieved to have the nasty thing off of him.

Robert checked his legs. "Hey James. I've got one on me too."

"Me too," said Paul.

"And me too," Steven added.

"Here, everyone," James offered. "Take some of this salt and get them off. Let's get out of here before a whole slew of them get on us!" Everyone did as he directed. "You will have a little bit of bleeding, but don't worry about it. It will soon stop. Leeches inject an anticoagulant when they suck the blood."

Immediately, they got out of there and continued further south through the forest, soon passing another turnoff for Hartnett Falls, which they went and saw. They ate lunch there. After this turnoff, the track climbed to Ducane Gap, cresting at just over 1,000 meters in altitude. Large Swamp Gums, Tea-trees, some Waratahs, and a few Hakeas grew in this more open forest. As they ascended, there were plenty of sandstone rock outcroppings.

Once they crested and began to descend, Banksia trees became more common, and after a fairly steep descent, they arrived at Windy Ridge Hut on the right. It began sprinkling, and some of them considered staying there for the night, but it was only early afternoon. After talking it over, they decided to push on to Narcissus Hut on the northern end of Lake St. Clair.

The terrain was mostly flat, and much of the track contained boardwalks as it passed through partially open meadows with some patches of mostly Eucalyptus forest. At one place, they crossed a major creek on a narrow suspension bridge.

Narcissus Hut sat right on the forested shore of Lake St. Clair. Clinking Currawongs dominated the sounds throughout the area with their calls. They arrived at 5 p.m. after hiking just over 20 kilometers. No one else was there, and up to this point, the only people they had seen since Waldheim Chalet were Chris and Richard Bell, whom they had seen at Windermere Hut.

"I'm really amazed at how few people we've seen on this popular walking track," James declared. "It has to be the time of year because during the summer there are just droves of people up here!"

"So, we chose a great time of year to come," said Robert.

"I'm so glad it didn't rain a lot this week," said Chris.

"Me too," Steven agreed. "I was sort of worried that it would go to pouring back there at Windy Ridge Hut, but it only sprinkled."

They explored the area, looking around the lakeshore, climbing over tree roots, and skipping rocks over the water. Soon, they fixed supper and ate well, after their long hike. After looking around the area some more, they went on to sleep, not long after dark.

It was now Friday, April 12, their last day on the Overland Track, and it was a warm clear day. During the summer, the National Parks ran a ferry service to and from the other end of the lake, but that service had stopped for the season a week ago, and everyone now had to walk around the shore for the last 16 kilometers. They wouldn't have taken the ferry anyway because that would have been like cheating.

Around 9 a.m., they left Narcissus Hut and began hiking around the right shore of the lake. The first kilometer was mostly through an open meadow, and a nice, elevated boardwalk made the going easy until it abruptly ended at the edge of a thick forest dominated by Eucalypts.

This was the thickest forest that they had seen, and some of the Swamp Gums were huge with trunks up to three meters in diameter! Myrtle Beeches were very common, and there were also some Leatherwoods, Southern Sassafras trees, and a few Pandanis. Celery Top Pines showed up in increasing numbers.

"Wow!" Andrew exclaimed. "Look at the size of these trees!"

"I know," James agreed. "These are some of the largest trees in Tasmania."

"I'm telling you what," said William. "I don't doubt it."

"These are the largest trees I've ever seen!" Robert exclaimed.

"You're not kidding!" Paul agreed.

"Look at this moss," Chris pointed out. "It's on the forest floor everywhere."

"I know. It really is a sight to see," said Morris.

"This really rounds our trip off to see this wonderful forest," Steven declared.

"Mine too," said Robert. "It's so nice that it's all protected."

They continued for several kilometers through this thick forest and crossed tiny creeks every now and then. One section of the track nearer the shoreline passed under a canopy of understory shrubs, making it seem like a tunnel. Soon after this, they arrived at Echo Point Hut.

It was now lunchtime, and they stopped to eat while resting at this hut that was right on the lakeshore. It was the smallest hut they had seen, even smaller than Kitchen Hut. Again, Clinking Currawongs made their scratchy sounding calls which dominated the sounds of the area.

From there further south, the walking was not so pleasant because two large formerly forested areas had been burned up by bush fires a few years earlier. Plenty of shrubs had taken over along with ferns up to one meter tall. As a result, the track was choked with vegetation and difficult to walk through.

They eventually bashed through, and the track improved after the burned area, giving them one last look at this beautiful forest. The track climbed a short while and crossed a creek on a large wooden bridge and finished its last kilometer on a gravel lane to Cynthia Bay at the south end of Lake St. Clair.

There were some day tourists along this lane, none of them venturing further than the wooden bridge. A paved road accessed Cynthia Bay from the main highway a few kilometers south of here. More tourists came to this end of the Overland Track than to the north end of it for obvious reasons due to easier road access.

They all arrived at Cynthia Bay in the mid-afternoon and found several buildings in the area including a ranger station and a showerhouse. Weren't they glad to find the showerhouse still operational this late in the season because they had not had a proper shower or bath since leaving Tennessee nearly a week ago! All of them felt much better after having showered.

There were plenty of wallabies hopping about from one tourist to another, irresistibly begging for food. These were more pet than any they had seen, and some of them sat on the short grass in such a way that they looked like a woman lying on her side at the beach with her head propped by her arm, her elbow resting on the ground. Some of these wallabies seemed almost human, and to stop and rest by one of them made it seem almost as though one were resting and having silent conversation with another person instead of a wallaby.

"Okay, James," said Robert, "you're our tour guide on this trip. What do we do next?"

"You know," he replied, "Mark Peters may have some time off this weekend and might enjoy showing us around a bit. Tell you what, I'll ring him up and see what he's doing. I'd say he's just now getting home from school."

James went to a pay phone that happened to be at this road's end. It was a green, cast steel, vandal-proof, 60 kg CT3 rotary dial pay phone, standard for Australia. James dialled Mark's number. The ringing could be heard over the line.

"click...pop...PRR ^ PRR...PRR ^ PRR...PRR ^ PRR...Hello?"

"Hey, Mark. How are you going?"

"Hey, James! How are you?"

"Just fine. We had a wonderful walk through the Overland Track and just got out a few minutes ago."

"Oh right! Yeah right!"

"Say, have you got most of the weekend off, Saturday, at least?" James asked.

"Yep, almost no homework, mate."

"Great! We were wondering if you'd like to show us around a bit, maybe see Hobart or something like that."

"Oh right! Yeah right," said Mark. "Sure James. I reckon I can do that.

Tell you what. I'll just pack a few things and come on down to collect you straight away."

"Oh, that'd be great! Thanks, Mark," said James.

"No worries, mate."

"See you then."

"Okay, bye."

-click-

James hung up the handset of the pay phone realizing how fortunate he was to have such a kind and generous friend as Mark Peters. He walked over to tell the others that Mark was coming.

"We don't have to transport ourselves out of here," James announced, "nor do we have to pay for eight bus fares. Mark's coming to collect us, and he's going to take us around Tasmania a bit."

"Oh, that's great!" Robert exclaimed.

Mark arrived shortly after 5 p.m. in his family's Ford Spectron van. His parents had gladly loaned it to him so he could fulfill his kind gesture of hospitality to his Tennessee friends.

"How's it going, Mark?" Robert asked when he arrived.

"All right, how are you?"

Everyone else greeted him and piled into his van, and they drove the few kilometers south to the Lyell Highway, the main highway from Queenstown to Hobart.

"Where's the nearest Golden Arches?" Chris brought up.

"Golden Arches? What's that?" Mark asked, as he had never heard of it.

"Oh, MacDonald's," said Chris.

"Oh right," said Mark. "The nearest one's in Melbourne."

"You mean there's *no* MacDonald's in Tasmania?" Robert interjected, quite surprised.

"That's right," confirmed Mark, "and proud of it, we are! No Mac-Donald's in Tasmania, at least not yet, anyway."

"Well, I will say!" Chris remarked.

"Those fast-food chains just pack everything in polystyrene," Mark explained to them, "and then they just chuck all that rubbish out on the roadside. We don't want them coming here."

"I see your point," said Robert. "You know, you're right. If it weren't for all that fast food, there would be a lot less litter, especially on the roadsides."

By now, they had reached the Lyell Highway. Mark turned left, and they were on their way to Hobart.

"I rang up my uncle in Hobart, and he said that all nine of us could stay over at his place," Mark announced. "He's got a fairly large house, and we can all spread out on the floor."

They had conversation for the next two hours and arrived just before 8 p.m. The two-lane winding road steadily improved as it approached Hobart, becoming a motorway for the last several kilometers. Upon arriving at his uncle's place, they unloaded their backpacks and placed them in his living room.

His uncle, George Peters, was a husky, weathered man of stocky build, quite the opposite of the thin, wiry appearance of Mark. George welcomed everyone and took them into his backyard where he had a fire going in his barbecue grill. Two large pots were filled with pumpkin, potatoes, and carrots in boiling water. To the side were plenty of Aussie style sausages frying in the flat-surfaced grill. This was a typical Aussie barbecue. Everyone enjoyed the plain meal, even though it was missing potato salad and potato chips. No one had ever eaten pumpkin as a vegetable, and they certainly were surprised to find it as sweet as sweet potato.

"That's butternut pumpkin," said George.

Everyone had a good feed, visited for a while, decided what to see in Hobart the next day, and went to sleep on Mr. Peter's living room floor. What a fantastic week they were having! They wished it would never end.

The next morning, everyone got up and had Weetbix and toast with Vegemite. Robert and his friends couldn't believe that anyone could possibly like Vegemite, and they spread a very light layer on their toast. George wished them well. Mark and the others thanked him and left to have a look around Hobart.

He left the van parked at his uncle's house, and they walked into the city center, going from place to place and looking at different sites. They also visited shopping malls including Cat and the Fiddle Square. James made sure to take everyone to the royal botanical gardens, which was one of the best ones in Australia. There were plenty of Australian natives and also plenty of trees from all over the world, including a lot of North American natives.

After a good morning, looking around Hobart, Mark led them back up to George's house, and they piled into the van once again. From there, Mark took them along the two-lane winding Tasman Highway that ran along the east coast. They had some really nice views of the offshore islands in the vicinity of Maria Island and Freycinet National Park. Everyone was surprised at how natural the entire coastline was: no large hotels and no development. All of it was either farmland or small towns.

At St. Mary's, he turned inland and took them to Launceston and then to Deloraine. James mentioned that Walls of Jerusalem National Park would be a great place to visit before returning to Tennessee. Mark took them to Lake Rowallan and delivered them to the trailhead for the trail that went to Mt. Jerusalem and Dixons Kingdom.

Everyone had a great time, and they expressed their sincere thanks to Mark for having shown them around Tasmania. Mark was glad to do so and bid them farewell saying, "All the best." People in Tasmania were very kind and hospitable.

Mark had some things to do on Sunday, or he would have joined them for the hike. James also explained that they would be in there until Monday afternoon and would simply transport themselves home to Tennessee when that time came. Until then, they would see and do as much as possible.

It was late afternoon, and they hiked up the track through forests of mostly Eucalypts to a small, rustic hut where they camped for the night. The weather had been fantastic and warm all day. Only a gentle breeze could be felt.

They woke up to another beautiful clear day, and it wasn't even cold this morning. Everyone ate some breakfast and soon left the small hut, continuing the ascent on the forested track until it finally leveled out.

From there, the terrain was mostly meadows with plenty of shrubs and some patches of Eucalypts and Pencil Pines. They later passed a medium sized alpine lake with mostly rocky shores and Pencil Pines growing on all sides of it. Here, they stopped for a rest.

"This really is a beautiful lake," Paul commented.

"Yes, even more so than Lake Windermere," Robert added.

"I wouldn't say quite that much," said Steven.

"And this one's got plenty of Pencil Pines, too," Chris pointed out.

"If you think there are plenty of Pencil Pines here," said James, "wait until you see Dixons Kingdom."

"You mean there are more there than here?" Robert asked.

"Oh yeah," James answered, "and they are a lot older and larger as well."

After a short rest and looking around the lake, they continued along the fairly level terrain, which appeared somewhat monotonous until they climbed for a while and passed between two mountains, arriving at Lake Salome. To their right was the west wall of Walls of Jerusalem. Ahead of them was a large valley of mostly light alpine scrub with occasional patches of Pencil Pines. Across the valley was The Temple, elevation 1,446 meters, and slightly to the left and further back was Mt. Jerusalem, elevation 1,459 meters.

Much of the meadow contained Buttongrass, and there was plenty of underground water to be seen as they made their way across this beautiful valley. Several times they crossed tiny streams or walked by tiny water holes.

As they reached the other end of the valley and passed through The Gate of the Chain, the face of Mt. Jerusalem was clearly visible. It rose up out of the valley in a nearly vertical manner. However, the whole mountain still had a rounded weathered appearance. Everyone understood why this national park was called Walls of Jerusalem.

As James guided them, they turned right just before Mt. Jerusalem and walked between it and The Temple, passing through Jaffa Gate. Ahead of

them was Dixons Kingdom mostly to the right and down the hill. This was one of the largest Pencil Pine stands in the state of Tasmania, and it was a pure stand. Tussock Grass grew on the forest floor, and there were plenty of small water holes throughout.

Dixons Kingdom Hut was a small shelter of logs and wooden shingles designed to sleep six people. It was located at the lower end of the Pencil Pine stand. The lower slopes of Mt. Jerusalem rose up from it to its east. Tasmanian Snow Gums grew on the lower slopes of this hillside while the upper slopes were more rocky and barren.

All of them stashed their belongings inside Dixons Kingdom Hut and had a look around this ancient forest. James had been here before and had plenty to tell the others about the trees and features of the area. Some of the Pencil Pines were more than a foot in diameter, which is nearly half a meter. This was large for a Pencil Pine.

"These trees really do have some similarities to the Eastern Red Cedar," Robert commented.

"Yes, I agree," said William. "The bark is sort of soft and looks like it could peel off in strips just like the Cedar back in Tennessee."

"At a glance, I don't think even I would know the difference," James admitted.

"How about let's go up Mt. Jerusalem?" Steven proposed.

"Good idea!" said James. "After all, the weather *is* excellent, isn't it."

From Dixons Kingdom, the climb was fairly easy as they headed in a northwesterly direction. It was now early afternoon, and the climb took less than an hour. Mt. Jerusalem was the highest mountain in the whole area. To their left and below them was the steep rock face that was called the East Wall of Walls of Jerusalem.

The top of Mt. Jerusalem consisted of mostly rounded rocks and boulders, and the views were spectacular on all sides. To the west, they could see the mountains of Cradle Mountain-Lake St. Clair National Park. All of them were visible and had the appearance of a row of jagged peaks in the horizon. Further to the right, they could see Barn Bluff and Cradle Mountain with a view of the West Wall and Lake Salome in the foreground. Not a cloud could be seen.

The land to the east of them looked flatter and drier. Most of it was rocky and barren with very little vegetation. There must have been a thousand tiny lakes across the whole landscape. James explained to them that a fire had swept through the land east of here a few years earlier, and many Pencil Pines were lost at that time.

"We certainly have been lucky about the weather," Robert brought up.

"Yes," James agreed. "This time of year is usually drier. Also, the further to the northeast you go in Tasmania, the drier it gets. The southwest portion is the wettest area of the state while the Midlands, east of here, enjoy hot, dry summers."

Everyone took in the scenery for a while and eventually returned to Dixons Kingdom for the rest of the afternoon and evening. Some of them still felt energetic and continued having a look around, exploring this ancient forest. They were getting the most out of their Spring Break.

It was now evening, and they cooked supper, ate, and rested for a while under some of the Pencil Pines. Bennetts wallabies could now be seen hopping about, and some of them were tame enough to come right over and be petted. Since the weather remained clear, they decided to sleep outside under the trees and stars. As they visited, they had conversation about various topics.

"Morris," Chris brought up, "Tell us more about your crystal ball."

"Well," he began, "I've been experimenting with it, and it's helping me relate the past with the present. Also, I am better able to see the future. Most of all, I believe it helps me think more clearly and to be able to transmit visual images to other people. It's helping me in many ways. If I want to reach a certain destination, this ball can help me find my way there by giving off a faint visible glow, while if I get off course, the glow will fade."

"How can that be?" Chris asked.

"All I have to do is to think in a certain way of a place I want to go to, and this ball sort of knows what I think. I believe I could find my way in the thickest fogs or could probably do it even with my eyes closed just by feeling the glow of this ball in my hand."

"That really is something!" Robert declared.

"And to think that you initially weren't interested in having that ball," Paul added.

"I know it," said Morris. "I could kick myself for waking up on Tom the first time he offered it to me."

"Well, at least he offered it to you again, and you have it now," said Paul.

"Oh yes, and I'm glad of it!" Morris declared. "I don't see how I ever did without it."

"It's amazing what came out of that deal you made with him," said Andrew. "I mean, he wanted you to have that ball for sure. In addition to that, he gave you the ability to transmit visual images and gave all 10 of us the ability to transport ourselves by thought."

"And then in exchange for that, he had us agree to help him build the galactic communications device," Robert added.

"Which we did," said Steven.

"Yeah, I really enjoy having a step office at my place," Robert commented.

"I wonder what all of those people thought," Steven speculated, "when they suddenly received a phone call from Tom or from some of the others on those other star systems."

"I'll bet it's the biggest surprise they ever got!" James remarked.

"Or practical joke, depending on how they took it," Paul added.

"I know this," said Robert, "It certainly *was* the most long distance phone call they ever received!"

"You got that right," William agreed.

"I'm sure that those who didn't believe where their calls really came from," said Morris, "probably received a personal visit from Tom or somebody."

"That'll teach 'em to believe, won't it!" Andrew remarked.

"It certainly will," Morris agreed.

"You know," William brought up, "why didn't Tom and his people just go and personally visit those who they needed to contact in the first place?"

"They could have," Robert answered, "but there would have been no way for the people, once contacted, to have been able to call Tom. Through that galactic communications device, it's like a two-way street of communication."

"Also," Morris added, "I'm sure it's easier for Tom to ring up those people instead of having to make personal appearances in front of every one of them."

"True," said Robert. "I know that the step office was busy during its first week of operation. All five extraterrestrial lines were in constant use."

"I wouldn't be surprised if they're going to want more lines," said Paul.

"No," Morris disagreed, "I believe they will think they have enough. After all, each new line requires a whole tower with a crystal inside of a large metal ring."

"That's true," Paul admitted.

"Yes, March 23rd, 1985, a very special day for planet Earth," Steven declared.

"And most Earthlings don't even know what it was," Robert added.

"But all of us here know what it was," said Paul. "It was the first day in the history of the world for a galactic phone call to ever be placed."

"I'm glad we were a part of it," said Chris.

As they were continuing this discussion, Morris suddenly got a strange ringing in his ears.

"Everyone, quiet for a minute," he said. They all waited patiently and silently for Morris to continue. "I hear Tom speaking. He says he sensed our talking about him, and since he happens to be in Launceston at the moment, he's going to pop over and give us a visit."

"Is that right?" Robert asked. "He's in Launceston?"

Ten seconds later, Tom made his appearance behind them and emerged from behind a large Pencil Pine. All of them turned around as soon as they heard him walking toward them.

"How are you doing, Tom?" said Steven, speaking for everyone.

"Doing fine, Steven," he answered. "How is everyone?"

"We're all doing fine," Morris answered.

"Yes, like I was telling Morris telepathically, I was in Launceston visiting one of our people. We had lost contact with him as soon as he was born 30 years ago, and he certainly was a difficult one to convince! He didn't believe in any extra stuff whatsoever, and I had to bring in my crew to perform some miracles to prove our legitimacy."

"What did he do when he saw your performances?" Robert asked.

"He was so surprised that he just about had a blue fit! He wanted to know why we were bothering him. So, I told him that he had made a pact with the Sirians to let us know how things were during his lifetime in the Launceston area, and we had not heard a peep out of him since his birth 30 years ago. While we realize that his telepathic mind is switched off for his lifetime, we informed him that he could reach us by phone and asked him to please call us and give us a report every few months. After explaining our reasons to him, he agreed."

"That's good," said Morris.

"Thankfully," Tom continued, "the others that we have contacted through the galactic communications device have been easier to communicate with. So, tell me. What have you been doing lately?"

"We came down here to Tasmania for our Spring Break to do some hiking and exploring of the wilderness," James answered. "We had a wonderful week's walk on the Overland Track through Cradle Mountain-Lake St. Clair National Park, and now we have come up here for a couple of days to relax in this wonderful grove of Pencil Pines before transporting ourselves home tomorrow night."

"I agree," said Tom, "that this ancient grove is really a nice place to come and relax, collect one's thoughts, meditate, and recharge one's self."

"As you know," said James, "I'm from Tasmania, and this is one of my favorite places to visit in this state."

"Yes, I can imagine," Tom agreed. "Well, I just came by to sort of check on you all and see how things were going since I was in the area anyway. I must return to my home on Sirius B, but first, I believe I will go into this forest and meditate for 10 minutes."

"Thanks for stopping by, Tom," said Andrew.

"That's okay. Give me a phone call if any of you need me, and have a great time here."

"Oh, we will," said Morris.

With that, Tom walked into the forest behind them.

"I declare," said Steven. "Wasn't that a surprise! We really have had a fantastic Spring Break, and I'm glad that I came along."

"Yeah, for you and all of us," Paul added.

"Let's see," said William, "if Tasmania's 16 hours ahead of us at this time of year, that would mean that we need to return to Tennessee by just before midnight tomorrow night, Tasmania time, to make it to school on time by 8 o'clock Monday morning, right?"

"Right," Robert answered. "So, we have all day tomorrow, and if we sleep for five hours early tomorrow evening, at least we won't be completely heavy-eyed at school on Monday."

"Okay, let's leave around 11:30 tomorrow night," Morris suggested, "and we'll make it to school just in time."

"Sounds good," said Robert.

With all of this straight in their minds, they all called it a day and went to sleep under the stars. The night was quiet, and the air was still. The only sounds that could be heard were occasional thumping noises from the wallabies hopping about. This was probably the most peaceful night of their trip, and what better place was there to spend it than camping in an old-growth forest of Pencil Pine trees?

The next morning brought another day of fine weather with hardly a cloud in the sky. It was a fairly cold morning but not cold enough for a frost. All was quiet with only the faintest breeze. There were no birds calling this morning.

It was Monday, April 15, their last day of Spring Vacation, and everyone intended to make the most of it. After eating breakfast in the company of their friends, the wallabies, they decided to climb The Temple whose slopes rose steeply behind them from Dixons Kingdom.

They ascended the steep slopes, which afforded them an aerial view of Dixons Kingdom forest below. It was a large patch of green surrounded by meadows and valleys colored with a mixture of yellow and brown. Above the forest and meadows, the slopes were mostly rocky with only some patches of grass. They continued ascending until they soon reached the rocky summit.

The views up there were nearly as good as they were on Mt. Jerusalem the day before. To the west, they could see the West Wall with Damascas Gate between it and The Temple. Mt. Jerusalem was clearly visible with its East Wall to the east of them. To the northwest, they could see all the way to the mountains of Cradle Mountain-Lake St. Clair National Park.

Down the slopes from them on the other side of The Temple from Dixons Kingdom, they saw a small stone hut, but it was in ruins. They decided to walk down to it and investigate. Upon arriving, William announced:

"You know, what do you say we restore this ruin to good condition? With the eight of us working on it, I don't see it taking us over two or three hours."

The others agreed to it, and they went to work, gathering fairly flat or rectangular-shaped stones from the vicinity of the hut until they had quite a large collection piled up next to the ruin. Next, they cleared the rubble of the ruin and prepared the site for the new building.

It turned out that Robert had a good sense of where to place each stone, and all eight of them started placing stones in a circle around four meters in diameter. Robert oversaw the structural integrity and made sure the stones had a good fit as they added to the walls. Leaving a door as the walls went up, they capped it with a long stone and continued building up the walls but curved them inward in a conical fashion until they placed a last stone on top of it all.

"That's a real work of art," Robert commented.

"Yes, and now people will have a place to take emergency shelter if they need it," James added.

"I don't think this building will be going anywhere anytime soon," said Paul.

"That's for sure," Morris agreed. "This really looks sturdy with walls nearly a meter thick."

"There certainly were a lot of stones lying around up here," Chris remarked.

"Yes, and just perfect for building this new hut," Steven added.

"This hut looks sort of like one of those cones on a castle," Andrew brought up.

"Yes, I agree, now that you mention it," said Robert. "Building in the shape of a cone eliminates the need for a roof."

"I'm telling you what," William declared. "When we set our minds to something, we certainly get it accomplished in short order!"

"That's true," agreed Robert. "It only took us three hours to build this whole shelter, just as you thought."

"We'll have to return and spend the night up here sometime," James suggested.

"Maybe Tuesday morning, Tasmania time," Robert suggested, "after school's out this afternoon, Tennessee time, we can transport ourselves back here and catch up on our sleep by taking a nap here."

"Plus, we can show Greg and Eric our work as well as a part of Tasmania," Morris added.

All of them admired what they had just built and then returned to the summit of The Temple for a last look around the countryside. They next descended west to Damascas Gate and returned to Dixons Kingdom for a late lunch.

With a few hours left, they took off exploring more hillsides and valleys and even took a hike east of Dixons Kingdom to visit the barren rocky landscape dotted with many small lakes. There were lots of dead trees standing, and they were mostly white, as their trunks and limbs had faded in the sunlight.

Near evening, they returned to Dixons Kingdom and ate supper. They talked about their adventures this week and went to sleep early, right at sunset. Also, they had cleaned up as best as they could since they would not be taking the time to go home for a shower before arriving at school at 8 a.m. Those who had alarms on their watches set them for 11:30 p.m., which would be 7:30 a.m. Monday morning in Tennessee. It was a still and peaceful night with clear skies, and the stars were clearly visible.

At 11:30 p.m., William and Robert's watches sounded their alarms, and everyone woke up. By the time everyone had packed his bedroll under starlight, 10 minutes had passed.

"We're not going to have time to drive our cars from my place to school by 8 a.m.," said Robert, realizing the time.

"I believe," said Paul, "we're going to have to make our appearance on the banks of the Stones River across the road from Riverdale."

"Tell you what," Morris offered, "why don't I go there and make sure no one's watching, like a fisherman or somebody, and then return and tell you?"

"Better yet," Robert suggested, "could you tell us if it's all clear by using your crystal ball?"

"Good idea," said Morris. He took his ball out and stared at it and soon received a visual image in his mind of the forested banks of the Stones River and could not see anyone in the vicinity. Next he transmitted this visual image to the other seven. "Has everyone received the visual image? It appears to be all clear."

Everyone answered yes.

By this time, it was 11:45 p.m. All of them placed their hands by their sides and thought of the scene by the Stones River. As they transmitted the energy through their hands, the pink glow overcame them, and the sounds of whirring wind became louder as they disappeared.

They successfully made their arrival to the Stones River. Across the road and out of sight from them was Riverdale. Lots of cars could be heard arriving and parking in the parking lots. With their backpacks on, they walked across the field, leaving the Stones River. As they crossed the road, they happened to see Greg and Eric just arriving in their separate cars.

Immediately, they rushed over to where Greg was parking and intercepted him.

"Hey Greg!" Robert shouted.

Greg was just closing the door to his station wagon as he heard his name called out. He turned to look. "Well, I will say! Did you all wait till the last possible minute to return here?"

"Yes, we did," Robert answered, as they were all quickly approaching him. "All of our cars are still at my place. Can we stash our backpacks in your car for the day?"

"Yes, certainly," Greg consented.

By this time, Eric had seen them and was walking over to them.

"Hey Eric," said William. "How's it going?"

"Just fine," said Eric. "How was it?"

"Fantastic!" Steven exclaimed, answering for everyone.

As they were stashing their backpacks in Greg's car, James made an offer in a low voice so as not to be overheard.

"How would you and Eric like to join us this afternoon after school's out for a quick look at one of my favorite spots in Tasmania? We just came from there."

"Well, sure!" said Greg.

"Yeah, I'd be glad to," said Eric.

"Okay, meet us out here at 3 o'clock, and we'll walk across the road to the banks of the Stones River. From there, we'll transport ourselves."

"Sounds good," said Greg. "We'll be here then."

By now, it was five minutes till 8 a.m., and they all walked inside and sat down in class only 20 seconds before the beep for first period began. The day at school went like any normal day, except that people were asking Robert and his friends how their trip was. They answered that they had a nice trip down south.

After school, Greg and Eric met them in the parking lot and they waited until most of the students had left. Then they put on their backpacks, and Greg and Eric went with them, carrying only daypacks. Once they reached the banks of the Stones River and made sure that no one was in sight, Morris checked his crystal ball and made sure that Dixons Kingdom was clear also. It showed clear, and he transmitted the visual image of Dixons Kingdom to Greg and Eric.

"Oh, by the way," Robert brought up, "did everyone phone his parents and tell them that we're safe from our trip and didn't have time to more than go straight to school after arriving here?"

Everyone answered yes.

"Good," said Morris. "Let's go."

Everyone disappeared and soon arrived at Dixons Kingdom. There were a few high clouds that had come in overnight, and it was now 7:15 a.m. The wind had picked up, and it was breezy.

"We're here!" exclaimed Greg.

"Wow! Look at this forest," Eric remarked.

Everyone showed them the large stand of Pencil Pines. There were also some wallabies, and they came up to everyone and greeted them in their silent way. Next, they climbed The Temple and reached the summit. To Greg and Eric, this was a fantastic afternoon tour of a place on the other side of the world.

"You see that conical-shaped stone hut down there?" Robert pointed out. "We just built that yesterday, and it took the eight of us three hours. There used to be an old ruin there."

They walked down the slopes to look at it and were impressed.

"You all built this in three hours?!" exclaimed Eric in a state of disbelief.

"That's the truth," Robert confirmed. "You remember how fast we built that concrete block building for the step office building last month? This was no more difficult."

"Oh, yeah. That's right," Eric recalled.

"This is really something!" Greg exclaimed.

"I'm sure you realize that we are still used to Tasmania's hours, being eight hours behind Tennessee at this time of year," James brought up. "The eight of us got up at half past eleven last night, and first period began at midnight for us. We need to take a nap and catch up on our sleep. Feel free to have a good look around the area while we honor this new hut's existence by being the first ones to sleep in it and use it."

"Yes, certainly," said Eric. "Greg and I will explore the area. We can return here in three hours to wake you. How does that sound?"

"That sounds fine," James agreed.

"Good, we'll return here around 8 p.m., Tennessee time."

James and the other seven entered the hut and set out their bedrolls and sleeping bags. They were glad to be able to catch up on their sleep. Greg and Eric were so intrigued by the scenery that they ran from place to place, seeing as much as possible. They even descended The Temple and raced up Mt. Jerusalem, after which they returned to Dixons Kingdom to admire more of the old-growth forest of Pencil Pines.

By the time they returned to the stone hut, they were exhausted. They awoke the others and told them, quite to their amazement, all that they had done in the three hours.

"Let's give you two 10 minutes to rest before we transport ourselves back to Tennessee," said Robert. "We don't want you getting caught up in some unknown place, you know. You must have enough energy to properly transport yourselves."

After resting, they proceeded to transport themselves from just outside the stone hut. Robert and the seven of them went to his place in the woods. Greg and Eric went to the Stones River, walked to their cars parked at the school, and drove home.

In the corner of the woods where the eight of them made their appearance, Robert went to check the step office. Everything looked fine. It wasn't as busy as it had been during its first week in operation, but calls were still going through as there were some clicking and clacking sounds from the Strowger switches.

All of them walked down to their cars parked by Robert's house and drove home. Robert went inside the house and told his parents all about their trip to Tasmania. They agreed that the eight of them had a fun-filled, inexpensive, and adventurous week. The trip had given all of them a great desire to travel, and everyone was eager to take off travelling again as soon as school would be out for the summer. Most of the student body would have been envious beyond belief had they found out the truth of where they had been during Spring Break. Word did not leak, and it remained a secret among them.

9 Another Visit to Riverdale

More than a week had passed since their trip to Tasmania. It was Wednesday, April 24, and Robert and his friends were seated in Mr. Vance's American history class. The discussion today concerned the United Nations and which countries had joined it and why. In the latter part of the period, the discussion shifted to which countries were more intelligent. Different people and cultures were compared until Mr. Vance brought up the intelligence of the cetaceans.

"Okay, ladies and gentlemen, since we have been discussing intelligence levels of different people and cultures, I think it would be appropriate to discuss the cetaceans, that is, the dolphins, whales, and porpoises and their intelligence in comparison to humans. What do you think if you had to compare? Would you say humans are more intelligent than whales or dolphins? What's your view of it, just anything you want to say? Yes, Mr. Wilson."

"Well," said Paul, "I don't think we really have any way of measuring whether or not the dolphins and whales are more intelligent than humans because I don't *think* any human that I know of has gone down and had a lengthy discussion with any of them."

"So," Mr. Vance inquired, "you mean you think it's impossible to measure that?"

"Well, I'll admit," Paul went on, "that they do show evidence at being intelligent, but we have no way of testing them. We can barely manage to test human intelligence, let alone dolphins and whales."

"Have you all thought about that?" Mr. Vance asked the class. "Do you agree with him that there's no way to test them? Do you have any sense that one or the other might be more intelligent than human beings from what you know about them? Yes, Miss Walton."

"I think the only reason we might consider ourselves more intelligent is because we have studied ourselves more. We ourselves are mammals, and so are the cetaceans. If we were to study the other species as much as we study ourselves, we might find them equally or more intelligent than most humans give them credit for."

"So, Miss Walton, it could be just a lack of understanding on the part of the humans since we've studied ourselves more, right?"

"Exactly," she replied.

"All right, what about the sounds they make?" Mr. Vance wanted to know. "Do you think the sounds they make *are* communication?"

"Yes," another student answered.

"Okay, why do you think that, Miss Childress? I mean, what is there about these sounds that makes you think it's communication and not just . . . something else?"

"I don't know if I've read it before," she answered, "but it seems like I've heard that porpoises and dolphins use sonar or something like that. Scientists did a study and determined that it *was* communication. What else would it be?"

"Well, it could be used in finding objects sort of like bats do," Mr. Vance pointed out. "Do you all agree with her? Yes, Miss Leathers."

"They make different sounds and obviously react differently to each type of sound they make. I mean, it's gotta be communication," she insisted, "because we react to different sounds, and they do the same."

"Okay, good point," said Mr. Vance. "Anybody else on that? Yes, Mr. England, what do you think?"

"The problem with a lot of humans," said Morris, "is that they automatically assume they are above all other species of mammals. They think since they are humans that they are the only species capable of communicating even though many other species of mammals do indeed communicate. I strongly feel that humans are not more intelligent than the cetaceans. In fact, I think humans are still young in their evolution and that the cetaceans are very wise and advanced. They are very tolerant and understanding and are here to help us improve with time."

"That's a very interesting point, Mr. England. That brings me to another question. Do you believe that the cetaceans, whether it regards dolphins, porpoises, or whales, communicate telepathically? Do you also believe that humans communicate telepathically?"

"I'm sure they do," Morris replied.

"Okay, we'll come back to you in just a minute, Mr. England. Yes, Mr. Price."

"Not only do I think they communicate telepathically," Steven replied, "but I also believe that dolphins, for example, are presently reincarnated humans that once lived in Atlantis. By being dolphins now, they are physically unable to carry out the experiments they once did as humans on Atlantis."

"That is a really interesting comment," Mr. Vance told him. "Anyone else? Yes, Mr. Westfield."

"In my opinion," said James, "we can speak telepathically, and if we can do so, why can't the dolphins and whales?"

"Okay, good point, Mr. Westfield. Yes, Mr. Joslin, what do you think?"

"I also agree that they can communicate telepathically. I have some friends in Miami, Florida, and their father is keenly interested in dolphins and whales. He studies voice patterns of human speech by looking at a voice print or graph. He also does the same for dolphins."

"Is that right?" Mr. Vance asked. "So, not only do they communicate, but their sounds are being recorded, graphed, and studied. Am I right?"

"That's right," Robert confirmed.

"Does anyone else have any comment? Yes, Mr. Nelson."

"Well," said Greg, "it's a known fact that human beings are the only species on Earth with any technology at all. I mean, I've never seen a dolphin or whale with a computer. I'd say they are just like any other mammal, be it a cow, dog, or cat."

"Yes, you do have a point there," Mr. Vance admitted. "Any more comments? Yes, Mr. Tomlin."

"I agree with Greg that we humans are the only ones with technology. After all, I've never seen dolphins and whales partaking in wars with each other. They have no fame and glory like we do."

"No, I've never seen a famous dolphin or whale. Okay, Mr. England, I know you've been very eager to tell us what you think. Go ahead."

"Just because the cetaceans don't show any physical evidence of technology doesn't mean they aren't intelligent," Morris explained. "In fact, they are so intelligent that they don't need all of that technology. Furthermore, they're not nearly as foolish as the humans are by partaking in wars. Also, they have their own modest sense of fame and glory that does not carry with it the ego of the humans.

"I don't think everyone in the class will agree with this, but the cetaceans are mammals because their ancestors also used to live on the land over 35 million years ago. They were gray in color, bi-pedal, and were very intelligent creatures, and they had physical civilization with technology then."

"So, you think they used to have an advanced civilization millions of years ago here on Earth?" he asked Morris. "Where is their land civilization now?"

"No," Morris clarified, "they had an advanced civilization in another star system, *before* they came to Earth. A major catastrophe occurred, resulting in the destruction of their old home planet, and they had to flee. To answer your second question, when they arrived here, they chose to live in the sea."

"How could you possibly know this, Mr. England?"

"This may come as a surprise to most of you, especially to you, Paul, but I, myself, communicate with whales and dolphins telepathically."

-Beeeeeeeeep-

"So," Mr. Vance concluded, "we have somebody right here in the class who *has* had a lengthy discussion with the cetaceans. That's very interesting. Thank you all."

Everyone got up and left class. Many of them went on to Mr. Mayfield's chemistry class. Paul walked over to Morris.

"Morris," he said to him, "I didn't know you could communicate telepathically with whales and dolphins."

"Oh yes, I do," he confirmed. "There are a lot of things I know that I don't really tell anyone. I just decided that the time was right to surprise the class today and tell them what I told them."

"You did *that* all right!" Paul agreed. "Tonight, I'll be having crow for supper."

They both laughed a little and went on to chemistry.

Today, Mr. Mayfield had a class discussion, mostly a question-and-answer session concerning one of the chapters. He finished covering the chapter a few minutes before the end of class and decided to talk about why people or objects vanish.

"Well, it looks like we've got a little time on our hands," Mr. Mayfield announced to the class. "I'd like to talk to you about the possibility of people or objects vanishing. Have any of you ever seen someone or something vanish?"

Robert and his friends began to get a little anxious that Mr. Mayfield would spill the beans and accidentally tell the whole class something about the galactic communications device or about the travelling they were doing. Fortunately, he did not, and the discussion went well.

Robert was the first one to reply to Mr. Mayfield's question.

"Yes?" said Mr. Mayfield.

"I'll relate to the class my most strange experience with someone vanishing," Robert explained. "Two years ago, I was backpacking alone for a few days and camped alone way up on a mountain in an open meadow between two small ridges. At 1:30 a.m., I was awakened by a person's voice outside my tent. I could hear him walking around, and his footsteps crunched the fine gravel near my tent as he paced around. I reached for my flashlight, turned it on, and reached for my tent zipper. The sound just . . . ceased. I never heard anyone or anything walk or run away. It just . . . vanished silently. When I got out of my tent, I looked around and could see no one."

"Huh!" exclaimed Mr. Mayfield. "That is something! I wouldn't be too surprised if that was something like an extraterrestrial. Did you say it seemed human?"

"Yes," Robert replied. "It walked around like a person does."

"Well, I will say!" he exclaimed. "You know, I think there's something to teleportation, and I believe that there are beings from other star systems who can travel by that means. It seems evident, based on stories in the *Bible*. Teleportation would explain a lot of what we consider to be 'miracles' today."

Although Chris, along with the rest of Robert's friends, knew that teleportation was indeed a fact since they had personally witnessed it, he acted

like he didn't know and asked Robert, "You don't think you were just *dreaming*, do you?"

"No, I wasn't," Robert insisted. "I know the difference. I was waked up and definitely heard the footsteps cease some 15 seconds after I awoke. If I'd dreamed I'd done it, I would have had strange things happen that would have been dream-like."

Mr. Mayfield continued, "Has anyone else had any experiences that he or she would like to share with the class?"

Morris raised his hand.

"Yes, Morris?"

"I was hiking with some others just this Spring Break in the mountains of Georgia," said Morris, as he altered the location from Tasmania on purpose, "and two brothers from England happened to be hiking in this area also. They visited us at our campsite one night. They were very friendly and decided to push on further that night, which I think was ridiculous, as it was already dark. They bid us farewell and walked on down the trail. The others I was with thought no more of it, but I quietly followed them a short while without their knowing it. I'll be a monkey's uncle if they didn't just *dis-ap-pear!*"

"Yeah, you've got something there," said Mr. Mayfield. "I really do believe that extraterrestrials are watching over us and checking on us to see to it that we don't do something crazy."

James decided to add a comment since he and Robert were actually there when Morris witnessed the event. He raised his hand.

"Yes, Westfield?"

"I somewhat agree with you. I was with Morris when that happened, only I wasn't looking down the trail when they vanished. I believe that beings from other star systems take on human form and visit us for fun and good times and also to check on us and learn about us. They don't want to tell us the truth because they don't want anyone to freak out."

"Yes, that's a good point," said Mr. Mayfield. "I'm glad you brought that up."

A lady in the class raised her hand.

"Yes, Walton?"

"I think extraterrestrials may be sort of experimenting with us. Maybe they have a secret plan that they don't want to reveal to us."

"That's very possible," Mr. Mayfield agreed. "I'd say you're probably right. They're keeping themselves in hiding and are probably in on a lot of the control about what happens through our government and all over the world for that matter. I believe that everything is already predetermined.

"I've seen the world population double in my lifetime and have watched technology advance in greater proportions in my time than in any period before that. I don't see how there can't be some plan for it all, and I think this world's a cradle. It probably won't be too long before the people of Earth will be dispersed to areas all over the galaxy. In the near future, I predict that there will be less than 100,000 people on Earth, and the rest will be gone to elsewhere."

"How do you think they'll leave?" Greg asked.

"Oh, I think they may be taken away in large spacecrafts, or there may be mass teleportations to occur. Yeah, there's a lot out there that we don't know. I don't see how anybody can be bored with so much to ponder and wonder about."

"Mr. Mayfield?" Steven asked.

"Yes."

"Have you ever seen anything or any person vanish?"

"Well, let's see," he answered. "Back 10 years ago, I was walking out in a field on my farm and . . ."

-Beeeeeeeeep-

"We'll continue this discussion later. See you tomorrow," he concluded.

As they were leaving class, Eric walked over to Morris and quietly said, "Boy, I sure am glad he didn't say too much."

"Yeah, I'll say!" Morris agreed. "He's so interested in that type of thing that he could have spilled the beans without realizing it."

"Thank goodness he didn't," said Robert, as he was just approaching them, "but he's pretty careful about what he says."

They walked on to fourth period.

Lunch at Riverdale High School lasted for half an hour and took place somewhere within fourth period. Robert and most of his friends had lunch at the same time, and the cafeteria was a large, square-shaped, open room with brick pillars interspersed to support the ceiling. Today, Robert, Chris, Eric, Greg, James, Morris, and William were eating lunch together. Andrew, Paul, and Steven had different classes, and their time for eating lunch this year was also different.

When Robert and the other six arrived at the lunch table, a tray was already sitting on the table. They thought nothing of it, moved it aside, and sat down to eat.

"This certainly has been an interesting and unique day, hasn't it?" Robert brought up.

"It definitely has," Morris agreed, "and I sense that there is more to come before the end of sixth period."

"What do you mean?"

"I'm not sure," Morris replied. "I can't detect any details, but there's going to be some trouble with it."

"You don't think our classmates got any ideas about us, due to Mr. Mayfield's discussion, do you?" Chris asked.

"No, ah-ah. It's not that," Morris assured him. "We'll just have to wait and see."

"Mr. Mayfield gets off the subject about every other week," Greg pointed out, "but I've never seen Mr. Vance get off the subject until today."

"Yes that *was* an interesting discussion," Morris agreed.

"And you really communicate by mental telepathy with whales and dolphins?" James asked.

"That, I do," Morris answered. "I've always had an interest in them, and I know a lot about their history and their origins."

"Maybe when this summer's said and done," said William, "we'll all be able to communicate by mental telepathy."

"That may actually happen," said Morris.

About this time, Riverdale's principal, Mr. Howard Stockard, came by. He, along with a few coaches, patrolled the cafeteria during lunch to guard against possible food fights.

"That tray was here before you boys got here, wasn't it?" Mr. Stockard asked them in a declarative manner.

"Yes, it was," William answered for everyone.

"Well, just make sure it's gone when you leave," he firmly told them.

With that, Mr. Stockard walked off to patrol other areas.

None of them thought any more about it, and they continued their lunch, talking at the same time. Morris didn't pick up on the tray being the source of the trouble that was to come before the end of the day.

"What were we talking about?" Chris asked everyone.

"Dolphins," said Greg.

"Oh, yeah," said Morris. "Let me tell you that mankind needs to consider that there are other sentient and intelligent species on Earth, namely the cetaceans, and that interrelationship with those diverse species is very important in the future."

"Why's that?" Greg wanted to know.

"They have a lot they can teach us about how to live and how to take care of this planet which, unfortunately, human beings are far from doing at the moment."

"But they don't have any technology!" Greg insisted.

"They don't need any physical technology," Morris explained. "For the cetaceans, it's all in their minds since they are fully conscious beings."

"Yeah, okay. I sort of see what you're talking about," Greg partially admitted.

"That's about all I want to tell you right now," said Morris, "in case anyone may be overhearing us."

"Well," said William, "I guess I'll head back to class."

"Me too," said Eric.

Over the next few minutes, the rest of them finished eating lunch. None of them had taken that extra tray up to the counter. So, Robert, being the last one to leave, took it with him to the counter. Mr. Stockard saw him coming and said:

"No, that's okay, Robert. You don't need to take that tray up there. I'll just find out who left it and punish him."

"Are you sure?" Robert asked him.

"Yes," he answered.

Robert returned the tray to the table, placed his empty lunch sack in the trash, and returned to fourth period.

An hour later, when Robert was in fifth period electronics class, he received a note to go to the principal's office. He had no idea what it was about, having thought nothing more about that tray. His classmates kidded him and said:

"Whew-wee! You're in trouble, boy!"

He walked to the principal's office and found one of the assistant principals standing in the hall.

"Yes, what's the matter?" Robert called out to him as he approached him.

"Mr. Stockard wants to see you," he replied, pointing his finger in the direction of the cafeteria.

Robert continued down the hall and rounded the corner as he came into view of the cafeteria and was utterly amazed to see Mr. Stockard standing by the table that still had that same tray on it! Six of his friends were already there and seated. As Robert neared the table, he said:

"You called us out of class for this? I offered to take it up to the counter for you, but you told me to put it back on the table."

"I know I did, Robert. Have a seat," he told him.

For the next 20 minutes, Mr. Stockard had a lengthy discussion with Robert and the six of his friends, all in an effort to find out who in the world left that tray on the table. Before Robert had arrived, Mr. Stockard had taken 20 minutes just to find all seven of them in their different classes. He hadn't known all of their names, but with the help of some of them, he had found out.

"Now, let me get this straight," Mr. Stockard began. "This tray was already here before any one of you got here to lunch. Am I right?"

"That's right," Robert answered.

"Did any of you see a person leave this table when you first came to lunch today?" he asked.

"No," everyone answered.

As he continued asking questions, he realized that he was not going to be able to find out the answer about who left the tray.

"I've just got to find out who left this tray here!" he carried on. "If everyone did this, there would be a huge pile of them by the end of fourth period. I've got to find the culprit and punish him."

"I wish we knew who did, but we don't," Robert told him.

"It really irritates me when someone is irresponsible enough to leave a tray on the table and not bother to take it up to the counter like he's supposed to do!" Mr. Stockard declared.

"I know what you mean," said Chris.

"Do any of you have any friends who eat here before you all do?" he wanted to know.

"No, not really," James answered. "We pretty much have the same lunch period."

"Does anyone besides Chris know anyone who eats in here earlier?"

"Actually, *I'm* Chris," Chris corrected Mr. Stockard. "He's James Westfield."

"Oh, okay," said Mr. Stockard. "You two *do* look alike, don't you."

"Yeah, we do, come to think of it," Chris admitted.

"You're the exchange student from Tasmania, aren't you?" Mr. Stockard asked James.

"That's right, Mr. Stockard, except that my family and I have moved here for good."

"Is that right? Tell me. What's it like down there?"

James and Mr. Stockard had a nice five-minute discussion about Tasmania and Australia while the others listened in on it. Mr. Stockard soon forgot about the tray as he listened with interest to James' description of Down Under.

"That will be all, everyone," Mr. Stockard concluded. "Let's not worry about the tray anymore. We've got better things to do than waste valuable classtime over a thing like this. You all can go back to class now."

With that, he picked up the tray and took it to the counter himself. Then he went back to his office as Robert and his friends returned to their separate classes. Morris and James had the same class at this time, and on their way back, Morris said to him:

"That tray was the source of trouble that I said I felt was coming to us this afternoon. I wish I'd realized it earlier."

"Oh, that's okay," James assured him. "That only made our day more interesting."

"Thanks for getting him off track about Australia, or we might have been there a lot longer."

"No worries, mate," James told him. "Quite ridiculous, raising a fuss over a stupid tray, isn't it!"

"You got that right!"

They entered their class and took their seats.

Robert returned to electronics class and told them the story of Mr. Stockard wanting to know who left that tray on the table. Much of the class roared with laughter.

The teacher said, "I agree with Mr. Stockard 100 percent. People need to be responsible enough to take their tray up to the counter when they're through eating."

Class resumed with a discussion about circuits.

10 A Few Days in England

A month had passed. School was out for summer vacation on Friday, May 24, and Robert and his friends were really looking forward to their travels and adventures. Robert, Chris, Morris, and Steven were ready to start immediately. William, Andrew, James, and Paul would have been ready, but they needed to take care of a few matters before breaking away for the summer. Greg was getting ready to leave to go to summer school out of state until August. Eric had to help his father in making pottery. So, Robert, Chris, Morris, and Steven decided to go to England for a few days and bicycle around the countryside.

Morris had been to England before and had seen quite a lot of it. Not all 10 of them had bicycle touring gear, but Robert and Steven did. Steven knew some other bicycling enthusiasts who let Chris and Morris borrow some racks and panniers. After quickly packing their gear on their bicycles on Friday afternoon, they came out and spent the night at Robert's place.

On Saturday morning, they got up early and sat on top of their bicycles. Morris transmitted a visual image of High Street in Cheltenham, Gloucester near the Welsh border in England.

"This is High Street in Cheltenham," Morris announced. "We need to go there first so we can exchange some money for the next few days, and I believe the banks are open on Saturdays in larger towns and cities. Now, do you see that alley over to the right? That's where we will arrive so as not to be seen by anyone."

They took their hands and placed them on either side and proceeded to transport themselves, keeping the visual image in mind and hoping that their bicycles and touring gear would come with them.

"Oh, wow! We're here!" Robert exclaimed.

The transportation was a success, and their bicycles had come with them, complete with the touring gear. It was early afternoon and was warm and sunny.

"How nice it is to return here," said Morris. "It's almost as if I feel at home in this country."

"Yeah, I can see what you mean," Chris agreed.

"I can't wait to start riding," Steven eagerly said.

They emerged from the alley onto High Street, which was the main road through the city as it ran from northwest to southeast. They were presently on the northwest side of the city. As they walked their bicycles on the sidewalk of this busy street, Robert couldn't help but notice a shop on the north side of the street called The Telephone Store.

"Hey! Look at all of those old phones in the store window," Robert pointed out as they were approaching the store. "Come on. Let's have a look." The four of them walked inside.

"Good afternoon," said a man at the far end of the room. "Can I help you with something?"

"Yes," said Robert. "I noticed all of these old phones and had to come inside and have a look."

"Well, I'm glad you did," he told him. "My name's Malcolm Percival. You all are from America, I presume?"

"Right. We're from Tennessee. I'm Robert Joslin. My friends here are Chris Chanford, Morris England, and Steven Price. As you can see, we came over to do some cycling."

"Oh, *have* you?" Malcolm remarked. "Well, that's great! I hope your trip goes well."

"Thanks," said Robert. "Tell us about your phones."

Malcolm showed them the various bakelite telephones including crank phones and newer dial telephones in various colors of modern plastic.

"These bakelite dial phones with the handset on the pedestal are 232's, made by GEC of Britain. They are over 50 years old. The next style made was the 332 which looks less stylish. The newer ones of various colors are 706's and 746's. If you like, I can show you my warehouse across the street."

"Okay, sure," said Robert. "What about you all?" he now asked Morris, Chris, and Steven.

"Sure," they answered.

"Wigg!" Malcolm yelled upstairs. "I'm just taking some boys over to see my phones across the street. I'll just be a few minutes, if you could come down and watch the door for customers."

"All right, I'll be right down," called out a voice from upstairs.

They left their bicycles inside the store and Malcolm led them across High Street to a large building whose entrance was on the side. He inserted his key and opened the large door.

"Wow!" exclaimed Robert. "I've never seen so many phones! Just think what Tom would say if he saw this, Morris."

"Who's Tom?" Malcolm asked.

"Oh, he's a friend of ours back in Tennessee," Robert informed him. "We and some other friends helped him build a communications device by building him a step office. Also, he purchased a bunch of dial phones to use with it."

"Is that right?" Malcolm responded. "So, you *are* really into telephones."

"Oh yes," Robert answered.

All four of them entered as Malcolm showed them around. He had a little of everything in this warehouse. There were many types of crank phones and dial phones including some from other countries. There were also some button A, button B pay phone boxes which were used before the present day pay phones of Britain.

"This is really something!" Robert remarked.

"Yes, I'm the largest distributor of old telephones in Britain," Malcolm told them.

"I'll buy one of those black 706's and a 332," said Robert, as he picked up one of each from the pile and checked both phones for defects. "We haven't been to the bank yet and only have U.S. dollars."

"Yes, and they're closed today," said Malcolm.

"Oh, I thought banks were open on Saturday," Morris told him.

"Not in Cheltenham, anyway," replied Malcolm. "Tell you what. I'm going over to America in a few weeks to trade telephones. I can buy some dollars from you, if you like. How much do you need to exchange?"

"I'd say $100 will do us."

"Okay, that will come to around £70," said Malcolm, as he pulled out his wallet and handed Robert the money.

Robert and his friends gathered a total of $100 from their wallets and handed it to Malcolm.

"Those 706's are £5 each, and the 332's are £10 each."

"Okay, here's £15," said Robert, as he handed Malcolm the money.

"Right you are. Thank you very much," he told him.

"You're welcome, Malcolm. It was a pleasure doing business with you."

Malcolm saw them out of the building and locked up. They walked back across the street and into the store. Wigg was at the counter.

"Thanks, Wigg," said Malcolm. Wigg returned upstairs.

"Anyway fellows, have a nice cycle tour in Britain," Malcolm told them. "Come again sometime."

"Thanks, Malcolm," said Robert. "I'm sure we will."

They took their bikes out of the store and continued down the street.

"Morris," said Robert, "I believe I'll quickly go home and deliver these phones to the step office."

"Good idea," he agreed. "You don't want to carry all that weight for the next few days."

They found a narrow alley and Robert entered while Morris, Chris, and Steven made sure no one was watching. The traffic from the cars and trucks (lorries) were loud enough to drown out the sound of whirring wind that was created when Robert briefly transported himself home.

Upon arriving with the two telephones, he went to the door, opened it, and entered the step office. Calls were still going through from other star systems, and the sounds of clicking and clacking filled the room. Robert set the phones on a table in the corner of the room, went back outside, closed the door behind him, and transported himself back to the alley off of High Street in Cheltenham.

Once Robert returned, they left the alley and bicycled southeast down the left side of High Street until it became a pedestrian way through the city center. The street was covered with a brick patio, and many people were walking to and from different shops. As they walked their bikes through here, they noticed all of the different shops including several camping stores and pastry shops.

"Say," said Steven, "let's have a look at this camping store."

"Okay," the others agreed.

They walked in to browse. Robert walked to the back of the store where they were selling camping stoves. He couldn't help but notice the EPI gas camping stoves made by Taymar Industries in Stockport, England. One model, the EPI gas 3002 HP, was small enough to fold up conveniently into the palm of the hand, and it screwed onto and off of the self-sealing EPI gas fuel stove cartridges, which were scarcely larger than a tea cup.

A young clerk walked over to them saying, "Can I help you with something?"

"Yes, I really do like this stove," said Robert. "I must say I've never seen anything so nice and compact. I wish we had these in America."

"You don't have these in America, do you?" he asked with a British accent.

"No, we sure don't."

Chris, Morris, and Steven were looking at other equipment throughout the store.

"These 220 gram EPI gas 250 cartridges operate the stove continuously for two and a half hours. They're quite efficient, actually," the clerk told him.

"Yeah, I'll say!" Robert agreed. "This is the best little stove I've ever seen. I'll buy one. I'm going to need it this summer."

"You're going to do some camping, are you?"

"Oh yes. I sure am."

Robert handed him £14 for the packaged unit that came with an EPI gas 250 cartridge.

"Right. I'll just get your receipt for you," said the clerk.

Robert followed him to the counter where the clerk gave him his receipt.

"Have a nice cycle tour," he told Robert.

"Thanks. Have a good day."

Chris, Morris, and Steven hadn't bought anything, and they all walked back out onto the pedestrianized High Street.

"Look at this nice little stove I bought," Robert told them as he showed it to them. They looked at it, impressed with how small and efficient it was.

"That will serve us well this summer," said Morris.

They continued southeast along High Street, the pedestrian way ending after 10 blocks, and they rode for probably two miles until they turned left and went up a side street near the edge of the city. The side street climbed rather steeply as it entered farmland and became a road. They had to dismount and walk their bicycles, as it was too steep to ride.

After at least a mile, the road crested. They were well above Cheltenham, which was behind them, and they could see for miles in all directions. This was the Cotswolds Range, and they noticed a public footpath called the Cotswolds Way crossing the road.

It was now late afternoon, but the sun was far from setting, as it would not be dark until 10 p.m.

"Hey, why don't we see a little of the Cotswolds Way?" Robert called out to the others.

They agreed and hid their bicycles in the bushes by the roadside. Not too far to the south, they could see Dowdeswell Wood, which was a nice hardwood forest. After a few minutes' walk, they arrived at the edge of this impressive native forest and entered. The trees they saw were European Beech (*Fagus sylvatica*), English Oak (*Quercus robur*), Ashes (*Fraxinus* genus), Sycamore Maples (*Acer pseudoplatanus*), Plane trees (*Platanus* genus), Lime trees (*Tilia* genus), and other shrubs.

"These trees are very much like trees back in Tennessee," said Robert.

"That's right," Morris agreed. "When I came over with my parents earlier, I noticed that. Most of Britain's native forest has been cleared over the millennium for farmland. There isn't nearly as much forest as in Tennessee."

"Well, at least some got left," said Chris.

Steven looked at the different trees of the forest, noticing the similarities as well.

They walked back to their bicycles and continued east along the country road through the towns of Syreford and Shipton as the terrain gently rolled up and down. Between Shipton and Northleach, they had to ride on the A 40, the main highway from Cheltenham to Oxford, and that was a busy two-lane road. There were no shoulders and plenty of large trucks passing by.

They were relieved to turn right onto another country road that took them south of Northleach where they crossed the A 429 and now rode in a southeasterly direction as the terrain went up and down. After a mile, they crested and saw a lone farmhouse and barns on the left. Since they were ready to call it a day and camp, they decided to ask the farmer if they could camp on the land. Robert went to the door and knocked, and a man came and answered it.

"Good day," said Robert. "May we pitch our tents and camp on your land?"

"Well, it's not my land," he answered. "It's not my permission to give."

"You're kidding!" exclaimed Robert. "There's not another house in sight."

"I know, but the land owner lives over the hill behind me. He's the one to give the permission."

"Thanks anyway. We'll just continue on down the road," Robert concluded.

As they continued, the road descended and came upon a small farm on the right-hand side. It was titled Saltway Farm, and a small dirt lane led them right to the front yard of the house. Dogs were barking at them, and a lady came out and hushed them.

"Hello there," she called out. "Nice evening for a ride, isn't it?"

"Yes, it is," Morris answered. "We were wondering if it would be all right for us to camp on your land overnight."

"Why, yes. That will be fine," she consented. "You can pitch here in the yard, if you like."

"Okay. Thank you very much," said Morris.

They entered the yard, and she took them around and helped them choose a site. The yard was amazingly well kept with plenty of flowers throughout. There was a row of both Lawson Cypresses (*Chamaecyparis lawsoniana*) and Incense Cedars (*Calocedrus decurrens*), both natives of California and Oregon. They chose a spot in the front yard.

"My husband's out feeding the pigs," she told them. "He'll come in shortly. We're about to have supper. Would you like to join us?"

"Yeah, sure," Steven responded, before the others could say anything. "Thank you very much."

"That's quite all right," she said. "I'm Nell O'Connell. What are your names?"

"I'm Robert Joslin. My friends here are Chris Chanford, Morris England, and Steven Price. We're from Tennessee."

"Oh really?" she said. "My cousin lives in Tennessee, over near Selmer."

"Yeah, I know where that is," said Robert. "It's in West Tennessee. Isn't that something!"

"It's a small world, isn't it," she commented. "Anyway, set up your tents and come inside, if you like. I'm going inside to fix the meal." She walked back in the house.

"Isn't she a nice person," Steven remarked, as he was setting up the tents.

"Yes," Morris agreed. "I believe we found a nice place to stay for the night."

After five minutes of setting up their equipment, they walked inside for supper. Mrs. O'Connell had a big pot of vegetables boiling on the stove and bread rolls in the oven. Her husband walked in.

Seeing the four of them, he said, "Well, good day. How are you? My name's Henry O'Connell."

They introduced themselves.

"You're over from America, are you?"

"That's right," Robert answered. "We're from Tennessee."

"Oh, right! Nell's cousin lives in Tennessee."

"Yes. She was telling us. Selmer, right?"

"That's right," he answered. "Where have you come from today?"

"Cheltenham," Chris answered, not revealing the part about coming from Tennessee only hours ago.

Nell soon brought the food to the table in the middle of the house and served everyone. They enjoyed the meal and the visit, talking about various subjects of both the English and American way of life. After a couple of hours, Robert and the others decided to turn in for the night. They went out to their tents and quickly fell asleep.

It was Sunday morning, May 26. They woke up fairly early in the morning, as many birds were calling. It felt as if it were 2 a.m. because of the six-hour time difference, but they got up anyway and packed their things.

Nell came outside to greet them and asked them inside for breakfast, which they gladly accepted. She boiled them some porridge and served them slices of fresh fruit, as well. Henry had already eaten and was out taking care of the pigs. They enjoyed the breakfast, thanked her, walked outside, and prepared to leave.

"Oh, wait!" she called out to them. "I've got some sandwiches for you to take with you."

"Why, thank you," said Robert. "That's very kind of you."

She handed them some sacks of sandwiches, and they gladly inserted them into their panniers.

"If you're through this way again, call in."

"Thanks, Mrs. O'Connell," said Morris. "The same is true for us if you're through Tennessee."

"That's kind of you. Thank you," she said.

They bid farewell and rode out on their bicycles. Today they decided to ride mostly south, and it was another nice, warm sunny day. Again, they followed mostly backroads which passed through beautiful farmland that was not entirely level. At Poulton, they crossed the A 417 and continued, veering southeast, and passed through Castle Eaton and Hannington.

Upon arriving at the B 4019, they turned right and headed to Broad Blunsdon, a community just north of Swindon. It looked attractive, so they decided to turn right on the street leading into the town and check it out. As they rounded a curve to the left, they passed by a church that was just letting out its members after a service.

Robert and his friends stopped to speak to some of the people, and they started carrying on conversations with several of them, exchanging ideas and finding out more about England. Some of them also wanted to know more about America. The minister or vicar walked out of the church and headed toward them.

"Well, hello there!" he called out to them. "Out for a cycle holiday, are you?"

"Yes," Robert answered. "We four are from Tennessee."

"Is that so?" he asked in a friendly manner. "Welcome to Broad Blunsdon. My name is John Ware. I'm the vicar of the Parish church here, and I live in the large rectory on the other side of the church."

"Nice to meet you," Morris spoke first.

They introduced themselves.

"Would you like to have a look at the church and go up into the bell tower?" he offered them.

"Yeah sure," Steven quickly answered before the others had a chance to speak.

John Ware led them inside the church after they secured their bicycles. Inside, at the back of the church, he opened a hidden door and led them single file up a very narrow stone spiral staircase. They arrived at a platform and climbed a series of ladders, finally arriving at the bell room.

The bells were huge and must have weighed several hundred pounds each. They were hung on shafts supported by a very sturdy wooden structure. Ropes, attached to the bells via weights and arms, went through holes in the floor to the bottom of the tower. John led them, as they carefully picked their way over the structural support, to a final ladder where they climbed out onto the roof through a trap door. The roof was made out of lead, and it was surrounded by a stone wall.

"Isn't this an excellent view from up here?" John asked them.

"Yes, very. I agree," said Morris.

"Are those the Cotswolds to the northwest?" Robert asked.

"Yes, they are," he answered. "Quite magnificent, aren't they."

They could see far and wide across the English landscape of fields and villages. Swindon could be seen to the south with the North Downs, a range of hills, beyond that. Further south, beyond the North Downs, was the Salisbury Plain where Stonehenge was.

"Well, I will say!" Steven exclaimed, as he noticed the roof he was standing on. "This roof is made out of lead!"

"That's right, and it's been here for over 200 years," John told him.

"That's amazing!" said Steven.

"Yes, this church is very old and is all original."

John continued pointing out places that were visible and then led them back down the tower through the bell room and the stone spiral staircase. As they were mounting their bicycles and preparing to leave, he said to them:

"All four of you be my guests. Come and have lunch with me and my family."

"Why, thank you," said Morris. "That's very kind."

"That's my house, the Rectory, behind the church," as he pointed in that direction. "My wife's just preparing the meal."

They followed him over, taking their bicycles with them, and entered the large, gray, stone house. Once inside, he took them to the kitchen.

"I want you to meet my wife, Phillida," he told them as he introduced them. "I've just found four Americans outside our church," he now told Phillida, "and I've taken them up into the bell tower."

"Oh, that's nice," she commented.

"I've asked them to join us for lunch, if you could prepare a place for them also?"

"Yes, certainly," she answered.

They introduced themselves.

"Most of my children are away at the moment, visiting neighbors," John informed them, "but I believe Andrew's around here some place." At about this time, a fellow the age of Robert and his friends came down from upstairs. "Oh, there you are," he said to Andrew. "I want you to meet Robert Joslin, Chris Chanford, Morris England, and Steven Price, all from Tennessee. Have I got your names right?"

"Yes, exactly," Chris answered.

All of them greeted each other and sat down to lunch. Phillida Ware had prepared a nice meal of different pastas along with mixed vegetables and different salads, as well. Water was served as the drink. Everyone enjoyed visiting with one another, exchanging ideas about their countries and cultures. They were glad to meet Andrew, a person their own age.

After lunch was over, Robert said, "Thank you very much for lunch and for everything, Mr. Ware."

"You're welcome, Robert. It was a pleasure, and it's all better for British-American relations, isn't it."

They all swapped addresses, bid each other farewell, and left.

From Broad Blunsdon, they decided to ride in a southeasterly direction, missing Swindon, and passing through South Marston, Hinton Parva, and Aldbourne, crossing the M 4 motorway on the way. From Aldbourne, they followed the B 4192 for a mile and then turned right on another country road as they passed through Ramsbury and crossed the River Kennett.

It was mid-afternoon, and they were now southeast of Swindon. Since the main highways were fairly busy, they decided to stay off of them as much as possible. They bicycled through some narrow winding backroads and crossed the A 4 highway, and as they continued south, they passed through Great Bedwyn and later crossed the A 338 at Marten.

Steven decided that it was time for them to pull over for a rest and take a look at the road atlas. They knew that they wanted to see Stonehenge, so they now took a backroad in a southwesterly direction to put them on course toward Amesbury, a small town just east of Stonehenge. By now, it was becoming late afternoon, and the four of them decided to look for a place to camp.

Shortly after passing through the village of Wexcombe, they saw an attractive farmhouse set back off the road down a winding gravel lane. Morris felt like this would be a suitable spot, and they turned and bicycled in. A barn sat on the left a couple hundred yards down this driveway, and there was a gate to open to continue another 200 yards to the farmhouse, which was nearly hidden by some trees. Robert placed his bicycle just inside one of the barn halls while he went to open the gate for the other three to ride through. About this time, they heard a car start up at the farmhouse and begin to come toward them.

"Oh my goodness!" exclaimed Steven.

"Don't worry, Steven," Morris assured him. "It will be all right."

Robert went ahead and opened the gate, and they quietly waited while the car approached them. It was a convertible with the top open, and two friendly looking round-faced ladies who appeared to be in their sixties were in it. Upon seeing the four of them standing by the open gate, the car stopped.

"How's it going?" called out the lady who was driving.

"Fine how are you doing?" Robert quickly answered, his words running together.

"Just fine," she calmly replied.

"We were just . . ." Robert started to explain.

"Oh, that's okay," she assured them. "You don't need to explain. You're certainly welcome to camp overnight here, if you like."

"Why, thank you very much," Morris said.

"I'm Mrs. Forvueweb, and this is the Forvueweb farm. This is my sister here with me. We live in the farmhouse, as you might have guessed. We were just on our way to the local market to buy some goods. If you like, you can go on back to the farmhouse and pick a spot to camp. There won't be any dogs to bother you, either. We'll be back soon." With that said, she and her sister proceeded in her car to the road.

Robert and his friends walked their bicycles back to the farmhouse, and they picked a nice spot under a huge English Maple tree. This was a beautiful farm with a small brook nearby which ran parallel to the driveway. Trees lined the creek as well as the fencerows throughout this farm, and the terrain was mostly flat.

"Those ladies were friendly enough," Chris commented while they were setting up their tents.

"Yes, they sure were," Steven agreed. "What did she say her last name was?"

"I think she said Forvueweb," Robert replied.

"Never heard of it," said Steven. "Let's see if I've got it right. For - view - web, with the accent on the first syllable?"

"Yes, that's right."

They finished setting up their tents and bedrolls and rested under the trees. After a few minutes, Mrs. Forvueweb and her sister returned from the market and parked their convertible under the garage.

"Well now," she said, stepping out of the car, "I see you all are nicely settled. Come inside and have a cup of tea."

They obliged and followed her and her sister inside the wooden farmhouse. As they became seated at the table in the kitchen, she asked them, "How would you like your tea?"

"Actually, we don't drink tea or coffee," Robert replied, "but water will be fine."

"Oh! Well, that's simple enough."

She filled four glasses with water from the tap and handed them to them. While her sister had gone to rest in a different part of the house, Mrs. Forvueweb sat down at the table to visit with them.

"So, you're over for a cycling holiday, are you?" she asked them.

"That's right," Morris answered. "We've come over for a week."

"My! That's such a short time!" she exclaimed.

"Oh, it's no problem for us," Robert explained. "We can come any time we like."

"Is that so?" Mrs. Forvueweb stopped what she was doing and thought for a few seconds. "Did you four simply pop over to England . . . by thought?"

Robert and his friends felt a rush of anxiety go through them. How could she have guessed? They didn't know what to say to her. She picked up on their expressions and continued.

"That's what I thought. Now don't worry. I've been travelling by the same method for years, now."

"You . . . you HAVE?" Robert stammered.

"Oh yes," she answered, "and isn't that pink glow the most interesting thing?"

"And the whirring wind as well," Morris added.

"Yes, that also," she continued. "I tell you. It all started for me some 20 years ago soon after my husband suddenly passed away. I had this dream that I was travelling by thought from place to place, including to and from other star systems. A pink glow would overcome me along with the sound of whirring wind, and I would transport myself in seconds."

"That's the same sort of dream I had!" Robert exclaimed.

"Oh my goodness!" Steven exclaimed, almost laughing. "That's exactly how it works for us!"

"I knew I felt compelled to have us turn and come in here for some good reason," Morris declared. "What other planets have you travelled to?"

"I've only been to a few, but the most interesting one I've visited is the

Planet of the Islands, as I call it, and I believe it revolves around the Garnet
Star on the other side of the Little Dipper. It is very Earth-like."

"Is that right?" Chris asked her.

"Listen, I feel I must show you one of the old Roman roads near here,"
she brought up, changing the subject. "We can discuss the planets later, but
it's getting on in the evening. I'll just ring up my friend, Erica, and see if
she'll be able to take us in her mini-bus."

Robert and his friends remained silently seated, going along with her
idea while she got up and dialled her number on her black bakelite 332
rotary dial desk phone. The ringing could be heard over the line.

"click...BBB ^ BBB...BBB ^ BBB...BBB ^ BBB...Wexcombe
3657."

"Hello, Erica? This is Mrs. Forvueweb."

"Oh, yes! How are you?"

"Doing fine. Listen, I've got four American bicyclists visiting me at the
moment, and I was wondering if you could take us on the old Roman road in
your mini-bus and show it to them."

"Why yes! Certainly," replied Erica.

"Oh, thank you."

"I'll be right over. Give me 10 minutes."

"Lovely. See you then."

"Okay, bye."

-click-

"Erica lives just up the road in Wexcombe," she told them. "You
passed her place on the way to here. She'll be here in 10 minutes. I must pack
a picnic for all of us. All seven of us, including my sister, are going. Alice!"
she called out to her sister. "Erica is going to take me and the four Americans on the old Roman road. Would you like to join us?"

"Yes," she answered from a different part of the house. "I'll just get
some things ready."

"How many people on Earth do you think can travel by thought?" Chris
asked her.

"Oh, I'd say there are less than 100," she answered, as she was scurrying about, gathering items for the evening picnic. "I've only met three or
four in my life, that is, before I met you four."

Erica soon arrived in her Ford Transit van or mini-bus and tooted her
horn outside. Mrs. Forvueweb and her sister and the four boys rushed out of
the house. Erica was seated on the right side of the van, waiting for them.

"Hello, Erica," said Mrs. Forvueweb, as she reached the van. "I want
you to meet . . . You know, I just realized I haven't even found out your
names!"

"Oh yeah," Morris realized. "We never did tell you."

They introduced themselves.

"I'm pleased to meet you. I'm Erica Grinstead, and I live in Wexcombe, just up the road. Hop in, and I'll take us along the old Roman road. It's quite scenic, you know.''

Everyone climbed in. Erica moved the floor shift lever into first gear and proceeded.

"You're in for a real treat, seeing the old Roman road," Mrs. Forvueweb told them.

Erica turned left and drove to the A 338, turned right, followed it for a mile, and then made another right followed by another left, after a mile. They were now on the old Roman road, heading in an easterly direction. It was a very winding, ancient road built out of stone blocks as it climbed through the gorge to a plateau. Sheep could be seen grazing the lush, green hillsides on either side of this road. There were occasional stone walls which divided the grassy hillsides into large fields.

As Robert and his friends were looking at the scenery, Erica said, "Many of our ancestors built this road."

"When was that?" Morris wanted to know.

"Oh, I'd say it was at least 1,500 years ago."

"Our ancestors must have been a hardy and tenacious race," said Mrs. Forvueweb, "to have set all of these stone blocks into place."

"I'll say!" Chris agreed.

"How high up does this road go?" Robert asked Erica.

"We'll crest just up the road at Inkpen Hill," she answered.

As they climbed steadily, they crossed a couple of paved roads along the way. Most of the terrain was open, grassy farmland, but the road dipped in and out of hardwood forests on occasion. After crossing the second paved road, the Roman road became more treacherous, climbing quite steeply at times. Erica used first gear in this section and crawled along at 10 mph. The stone blocks made for a somewhat bumpy ride, and much of the road was now lined with stone walls on one or both sides.

Steven looked out of the rear window. "Oh, wow!" he exclaimed. "That's quite a view back there, isn't it?"

"Oh, yes," Mrs. Forvueweb replied. "Like I said, you are in for a real treat."

"Yes, this is quite scenic," her sister, Alice, added.

They finally crested at Inkpen Hill and continued now on more level terrain. The views of the surrounding hillsides and scenery were incredible! Most of it was still grassy meadows, and there were patches of trees tucked in the small gullies at the base of many hillsides. Flocks of sheep could be seen grazing.

On the right, there was a small turnout. "Let's park here, Erica," Mrs. Forvueweb requested, "and we'll have our evening picnic."

"Yeah, good idea," said Chris. "I am getting hungry."

After Erica parked, everyone got out of the van, crossed over the rock wall on a wooden stile, and walked to a large Ash tree situated at the bottom of a hill across the field some 200 yards away. The weather was cooler at this higher altitude, and the wind blew with considerable strength. Once at the base of the tree, sheltered from the wind, Mrs. Forvueweb unfolded and spread out a tablecloth on which she placed her large picnic basket and spread out its contents.

"There are ham and cheese sandwiches for everyone, and I also brought along some hard-boiled eggs," she announced.

"There are some cans in here as well," Alice added. "Help yourselves."

"Thank you," said Morris, answering for everyone.

"This is one of my favorite spots to come to," Mrs. Forvueweb told them. "I feel as though I'm young again when I come up here."

"I can imagine," said Steven.

They enjoyed the picnic as they had conversation about various subjects, and half an hour later, she announced that it was time to return to Erica's van and continue. After climbing back into her van, Erica continued in an easterly direction on the old Roman road. The terrain continued in a fairly level manner for another mile while the road was mostly straight. After passing under a stone archway on which there was another road, they began to descend.

The road dropped quite sharply as it wound its way through a native hardwood forest of Ash, Beech, Maple, and Oak trees, and there were some hairpin curves as well. Erica kept it in first gear, and she rode the brake when necessary. To Robert and his friends, this was quite a thrill, as it was sort of like riding downhill on a roller coaster in slow motion. Had it not been for the large stone blocks, this road would have eroded into a deep, impassible trench.

After nearly a mile, the steep descent lessened, and they emerged from the deep hardwood forest. The road veered toward the southeast as they passed by more farmland with grassy hillsides. They passed by Pilot Hill and Coles Wood, another native hardwood forest, and soon arrived at the A 343. The tour of the old Roman road was complete.

"Thank you for taking us through there, Erica," said Robert.

"That's okay. I'm glad to have shown it to you all."

"That was really something!" Morris exclaimed.

"I told you it would be a treat," said Mrs. Forvueweb.

"Yes, I take great delight in taking visitors through there," Erica told them.

"Sorry James wasn't with us to see this also," Chris brought up.

James, of course, was one of the five back in Tennessee and was still packing and preparing for their summer adventures.

"I can imagine the comment he would have made," said Steven.

" 'That was really scenic and unique!' " Robert quoted.

They laughed a little, and Erica took the A 343 Southwest to Hurstbourne Tarrant and took a paved country road that wound its way back to the A 338 at Marten. From there, she turned left and soon made another left and returned them to Mrs. Forvueweb's farm.

"Thank you very much for taking the boys through the old Roman road," Mrs. Forvueweb told her. "I know they enjoyed it."

"You're very welcome," said Erica. "I'll be going now. It was nice meeting you four. Enjoy the rest of your holiday."

"Nice meeting you too," they told her.

Erica drove off as Mrs. Forvueweb and the others walked back into the house.

"England really is a quaint and scenic country," Steven commented, "and the hospitality really is nice."

"Oh yes," said Mrs. Forvueweb's sister. "Well, we enjoy having visitors and showing them a bit of the countryside as well."

"Have a seat," said Mrs. Forvueweb, "and I'll tell you about the Planet of the Islands." They did so, and she began. "This planet is full of islands of all sizes and is mostly ocean, otherwise. Many of the people live on large ships, and the climate is mostly temperate, like it is here. When I arrived on one of these islands, I found the people to be of only one race and one language. They have no emotional upset or stress like we have here on Earth, and they live from 2,000 to 3,000 years. Some of them are actually immortal. Further, they are free of all diseases as they've learned how to ward them off.

"I found the trees to be similar to the ones in the temperate area of Earth, and there were both conifers and hardwoods. It really was very Earth-like. I would have thought I was still here on Earth, but the people told me that I was on a planet around the Garnet star on the other side of the Little Dipper and that I was approximately 3,000 light years away from here."

"What language do they speak?" Morris asked her.

"Oh, English," she answered.

"How can that be?" Steven wanted to know.

"Many of them teleport themselves to Earth and visit us," she explained. "They learn a lot from us and obviously learned English while they visited some time in the past. That's my theory. Anyway, it's getting late, and I need to turn in. You're welcome to some breakfast in the morning. I'll be glad to tell you more about my extraterrestrial visits then."

They bid each other a good night, and Robert and his friends went outside and camped in their tents pitched in her yard. It was nearly 10 p.m. and was just getting dark.

As they were waking up the next morning, Mrs. Forvueweb came outside and called to them, informing them that there was breakfast for them.

"Thank you, Mrs. Forvueweb," said Robert. "We'll be right in."

When they walked inside several minutes later, there were four bowls set out on the table with a choice of Kellogg's Corn Flakes or Weetabix cereals. A platter with slices of toast and various jars of jam sat in the middle of the table. Robert and his friends ate a good breakfast as she visited with them. Mrs. Forvueweb's sister, Alice, had not yet awakened.

"Tell us more about your travels to other planets," Steven requested.

"I'll tell you about Vega. It's mostly desert-like with no real trees, as we know it, but more or less shrubs. Actually, there is a planet around Sirius B that is very similar to it. In other words, Vega and Sirius B are very much alike. Also, several years ago, I toured Australia, and I was surprised to see that it, too, was very similar to Vega and Sirius B.

"Both planets are limited on the water content," she continued, "since they are so desert-like, but there are around 20 million humans living on each one. It's been theorized that humans came to Earth over 2 million years ago from Vega and Sirius B by some means of spacecraft or teleportation."

"Yes, we're in communication with a galactic salesman named Tom," Morris informed her, "and he's from Sirius B."

"Oh, right," she said. "A galactic salesman, is he? How quaint! Anyway," she went on, "if you like a hot desert environment, Vega and Sirius B are definitely worth seeing. I spent just a few days on each one, and the humans there were very kind and helped me get over the loss of my husband."

"I have heard that they are a kind and loving people," said Morris.

"Oh, that they are," she agreed. "I miss their company sometimes, and when I feel a strong urge, I just transport myself there by thought. I tell you, the few that have seen me arrive and leave get the biggest laugh out of seeing that pink glow and hearing all of that whirring wind. See, nearly all of them just teleport themselves to and from places instantly and silently."

"That's how Tom does it, instantly and silently," said Robert.

"Is that so?" she asked. "Tell me, how did you all receive the ability to transport yourselves like I do?"

"Well," Robert began, "I had a dream back in early March sort of similar to what you had. My friends and I were transporting ourselves to other planets. Morris had the same dream but dreamed longer than I did. He made a deal with Tom, that galactic salesman, and he granted us the ability to transport ourselves in real life. In exchange, Tom had us help him build a galactic communications device using a telephone exchange and other sending and receiving equipment to link Earth's telephone network to Vega, Sirius B, and the Pleiades. We've had a great time working with him and going travelling when we weren't in school. We just got out for summer holidays a few days ago."

"That sounds like a great project you boys have worked on," she commented.

"Oh yes," said Robert. "We're very pleased with the device, now that it is in operation. Many calls have gone through as the Sirians have re-established contact with those whom they had previously lost contact."

"That's great!" she said. "Communication is very important, you know."

"Yes, very. I agree," said Morris.

"Well, it's getting on in the morning, and I have a few errands to run in Wexcombe. Alice is still asleep, so I'll come outside and see you off."

They had just finished breakfast. They thanked her, got up from the table, and walked outside. She followed them outside and saw them off as they packed their gear onto their bicycles.

"Enjoy your travels this summer," she told them. "If you're through this way again, please call in."

"Thank you," said Morris. "We will. We may also transport ourselves here if we want to discuss other planets with you later this summer."

"That will be fine," she said. "I look forward to seeing you sometime in the future."

They said farewell, mounted their bicycles, and rode down the driveway, passed the barn on the right, and returned to the road.

As they turned right, Steven remarked, "What an interesting pair of ladies, especially Mrs. Forvueweb. I'm glad we got to meet them."

"Yeah, me too," Robert agreed.

"That *is* strange how she had travelled to other planets like we're going to do," said Chris.

"Yes, that is," Steven agreed.

"Let's go see Stonehenge," Robert suggested. "You want to?"

"Sure!" Steven eagerly said. "Let's go."

They bicycled in a southwesterly direction and passed through more farmland of rolling hills. Upon reaching the A 342, they rode over to the A 338 and bicycled into North Tidworth. When they reached the town center, they saw several banks. Robert wasn't sure if he wanted to exchange any money, but he wanted to check the exchange rate, anyway. Among the banks seen were Barclays Bank, Lloyds Bank, National Westminster Bank, and the Royal Bank of Scotland.

"Let's go into Barclays," Robert suggested to the others.

They locked their bikes and followed him in. To their surprise, as each customer waiting in line was about to be served, he or she would pitch a canned drink and a sack of food to the teller. They watched a young man at the head of the line pitch a can and a sack of food to a male teller, and he began munching away while he served this customer.

"Good gracious!" Steven quietly exclaimed. "I'm not believing this!"

"I've never seen *this* done at any bank in England before," Morris added.

"I wonder why they're doing that?" Robert wanted to know.

"I guess it gives this bank more of a relaxed or home-type atmosphere," Chris speculated.

"I don't know about you all," said Morris, "but they must be stuffed by the end of the day! I'm surprised they're not all blimps!"

"Oh, I'm sure they don't do it all day," Robert assured him. "Surely, they do this only during lunchtime, which it nearly is by now."

Robert and his friends reached the head of the line and walked up to the male teller.

"Sorry I haven't got any food or drink for you," he told the teller.

"Oh, that's okay. I've had enough already. Quite silly games, aren't they."

They both laughed a little at his comment.

"Yes," Robert agreed. "I was just wondering what the exchange rate is for the U.S. dollar to the British pound."

"I'll just have a look for you." He pulled out his chart from under the counter and checked. "A dollar fifty-two to one, at the moment."

"Thanks," Robert told him. "Have a good day, and happy eating."

"And you."

They walked out of the bank, got on their bicycles, and rode out of town. Upon reaching an intersection at South Tidworth, they decided to consult their atlas.

"Let's see," said Steven. "If we hang a right and then an immediate left, then we'll leave town and head toward Bulford. It looks like a dirt road."

That seemed okay with everyone, so they made the necessary turns, and the pavement soon ended next to a golf course on the right. On both sides of them, there were M.O.D. (Ministry of Defense) signs posted, warning them of the danger areas until they arrived at Bulford. From there, they continued south for another mile and crossed the A 303 four-lane superhighway, very soon after which they turned right and took the old A 303 into Amesbury.

Amesbury was a nice small town that they pretty much passed through without stopping since they were set on seeing Stonehenge. They continued west on the old A 303 as it climbed uphill and crested. After descending for a while, the road merged with the new highway, and just ahead at the bottom of the hill was the turnoff for Stonehenge. They could see it up on the next hill.

The A 303 was quite busy to cross as they turned right on the two-lane highway that led up to Stonehenge. It sat on the left a quarter mile up this road, and the National Trust had gotten hold of it and was charging admission. The entrance to Stonehenge was on the righthand side of the road with a tunnel passing underneath it to reach the site.

"You know," Robert brought up, "I don't like the idea of anyone having to pay to go and see Stonehenge. I can see it well enough from the road, here."

"Let's just transport ourselves over to it," Morris suggested. "There aren't that many people up there right now."

"Good idea," said Steven.

"Well, okay, but let's not get caught," Chris agreed, with apprehension in his voice.

They parked their bicycles by the fence on the roadside.

"Okay," said Morris, "here's the plan. We'll just wait until there are no cars seen on this road and until there is no one looking our way. Let's arrive just on the other side of that boulder on the left side of Stonehenge. I'll say, 'Now!' when the time is right."

After waiting for a couple of minutes, there was an opportunity. Everyone happened to be on the right-hand side of Stonehenge, and no cars were seen.

"Now!" Morris quietly told them.

They transported themselves, and the whirring wind and pink glow overcame them. In a few seconds, they materialized behind that boulder on the left. No one had seen them.

"We did it," Robert quietly told the others.

Immediately, they walked over to and got on the designated path, glad to have gotten in for free.

"How do you think Stonehenge got here?" Chris asked.

"I don't know," Steven answered, "but it must have been a lot of hard work, manhandling these huge stones into place."

"Oh, that's not how it was done," Morris told everyone. "These stones were set into place by levitation. These large stones are not local, in case you didn't know. They were quarried in Wales and are called bluestones. Really, can you imagine how difficult it would have been to lug these huge stones over here by cart or to drag them over? It had to be levitation."

"You mean they were sort of air lifted over here?" Chris asked.

"That's right," Morris answered. "They were floated over in mid-air."

"But how?" Steven wanted to know.

"There is a theory," Morris explained, "that through the benefit of crystals and of a vocal sound with the sound of OM-1, to be precise, which was tuned to the crystal, the stones were levitated and set into place. This use of sound for levitation is a form of what is known as psychokinetic energy."

"How do you know about all of this, Morris?" Robert asked him.

"I do considerable research in my dreams, and there is so much that I want to know. I still have much more to learn despite the fact that I already know a lot. Still, the fact is that these stones are not local. Further, from the modern point of view, why did an ancient Earth civilization bother to erect such a structure as this here Stonehenge?"

Robert, Chris, and Steven pondered for half a minute on Morris' question.

"You know," Steven finally spoke, "I'll bet you that Stonehenge was an earlier form of a galactic communications device suitable for its time."

"Now, you're onto it," said Morris, as he encouraged him to come up with his own answer.

"I'd say that these stones were placed in a circle or ring," Steven went on, "to act as some sort of a sending and receiving station . . ."

". . . to link up Earth with some other star systems," said Robert, finishing his statement for him.

"You're right on track," Morris confirmed. "There were no phones back then, so it's not like the one we just built. This Stonehenge probably used crystals of some sort like ours does, but the sending and receiving was probably done more on a spiritual level or different plane of existence or even in other dimensions for that matter. In higher dimensions, there are shortcuts, in case you didn't know that."

"That really is interesting," Chris remarked. "I never thought about it that way before."

"Yes, that's my theory," Morris went on, "and it was probably used for several hundred years, after which the descendants of the civilization forgot how to use it or lost the ability to use it."

"I'd say it's possible," Robert added, "that it was used long enough for the extraterrestrial civilization to maintain communication with the new group they had just brought to Earth. They probably trained them in various ways and helped them along, here on Earth, until they could completely take care of themselves. Once they reached this stage, Stonehenge probably ceased to be used and became the ruin that it is today."

"That is an excellent theory," Morris declared, "and I'd say you're probably right."

"And may I add," said Steven, "that I don't think the Sirians will be using our step office and sending-receiving towers forever, either."

"That's very true," said Robert, "but they'll probably use it for most of our lifetimes to maintain communication with many Earthlings."

"Anyway," said Steven, "I'm glad we came to see this. It really is an outstanding wonder to many people."

With no one watching, he quickly jumped the rope, left the path, and tagged one of the stones, after which he quickly returned to the path. Robert, Chris, and Morris soon followed and did the same. What satisfaction they received out of *touching* one of the stones of Stonehenge!

"Well," Robert asked, "where would we like to go from here?"

"Let's ride to Salisbury," Morris suggested, "after which we can transport ourselves to the very north of England and walk a couple of days on the Pennine Way. I've been there before, and I'm sure the caravan park at Byrness would let us leave our bicycles at their place."

"That sounds fantastic!" Steven exclaimed.

"Good then," said Chris. "Let's go."

The four of them walked out on the path, went through the tunnel walkway under the road, and passed out of the gate at the ticket counter. They returned to their bicycles parked by the roadside, turned around, and rode back to Amesbury.

Just before arriving at the town center, they turned right and followed a scenic, winding backroad, which followed the River Avon, toward Salisbury. Much of the road was fairly level, but there were stretches that went up and down some steep hills and passed through some deep, scenic forests as well. This was England, a country of scenic farmland, farmhouses, cottages, narrow and scenic country roads or lanes, and small quaint villages.

A few miles north of Salisbury, they found a nice patch of woods and decided to enter them and hide. Morris transmitted a visual image of a Spruce forest on a steep hillside just north of Byrness. As soon as they saw it, they proceeded to transport themselves, bicycles, gear, and all. They arrived successfully with a steep stretch of the Pennine Way nearby.

"Let's make our way down to the highway," Morris told them, "and turn left. About a half mile down on the right is the caravan park that I was telling you about."

They made a steep descent, crossed a gravel lane, and emerged out of the forest onto the A 68 highway. They easily found the caravan park on the right and decided to stay overnight. There was a nice bunkhouse with two rooms and a small kitchen. The bathroom and showers were around to the side of the building.

The family that owned the caravan park said it would be fine for them to leave their bicycles there for a couple of days. They were friendly and asked them inside for the evening meal. They had a nice discussion about America, Britain, and Australia and what it was like in each country. Also, the caravan park owners told them that George Washington's ancestors came from this area.

The next morning, May 28, Robert and his friends left their bicycles in the large garage or workshop of the caravan park. They took out their day-packs and strapped their sleeping gear to them the best way they could and set out walking down the highway back to the Pennine Way.

After turning right, they climbed steeply through the Spruce forest and continued climbing even more steeply, now in open, treeless terrain. It was a scramble to get to the plateau above, and some of the large boulders had miniature peat bogs on them.

There was a Ministry of Defense (M.O.D.) base nearby, and fighter jets could be seen shooting across the sky, sometimes quite loudly as they were only a few hundred feet overhead. The caravan park owners had told them that during some practices, it sounded like a war zone.

They crested at Byrness Hill with views of Byrness and the valley behind them. Much of the land below them was forested with coniferous tree plantations. The terrain was rolling and hilly with mostly grassy fields, and there were almost no rock walls. A few barbed wire fences could be seen, and much of the Pennine Way followed these various fencelines.

The weather was very windy, and it blew so hard at times that they felt like they might possibly get blown down. It was partly cloudy, and some of the clouds were dark and hung low. Rain showers could be seen dropping from these darker clouds, and they displayed a unique appearance that they weren't used to seeing back in Tennessee. Through the day, they got caught in a few of these showers, each one lasting around 10 minutes. Storms came and went quickly due to the high winds.

They turned left and followed along the edge of the grassy plateau, ascending to Windy Crag and then to Ravens Knowe. They came to a fenceline and followed it most of the way, occasionally leaving it to cross open grassland. There were no trees whatsoever. All of it was grass with occasional sheep grazing. Most of the trail was in good condition, but there were a few muddy places.

They walked near a coniferous forest plantation just down the hill to their left and later left the fence and headed cross country to the ruins of the Roman Camps. Several Roman roads, overgrown with grass, ran through this area. Dere Street ran north from here, and The Street crossed the Pennine Way at a point further north. Clennell Street was further north above that. The Roman Camps sat sort of in a gully with a stream next to it. No ruins could be seen, as everything was covered over with grass. However, Dere Street could be seen and had the appearance of a large ditch, and the Pennine Way followed it north for a while.

"Those Romans must have been a hardy race to come all the way up here and set up a camp," Robert remarked.

"Yes, they were ambitious," Chris agreed.

"Tell us, Morris," Steven asked. "What do you see with your crystal ball?"

Morris took the ball out of his leather pouch and looked into it. He began receiving a visual image of the activities that used to take place during the Roman times. People could be seen running about. There were stone huts for the residents. Large carts were used to haul goods.

"Yes, I see plenty of activity going on. This was around 400 AD. I'll transmit the visual images I see, so that you can see them for yourselves." Morris appeared to concentrate.

"That really is amazing," Steven commented, upon seeing the visual images, "that they used to come all the way up here. I guess it was all part of patrolling what was theirs."

"Yes, they had their reasons. I'm sure," Morris agreed.

"Come on," Robert urged them, not being as interested in the activities of the Romans as the others were. "Let's keep moving."

They proceeded north on Dere Street from which they later deviated as they walked up and down rolling hills and across boggy terrain in other areas. Along the way, they crossed one stream. As they crested a hill, the fence made a 90 degree left turn, and they followed alongside it downhill to a small mountain refuge hut that was approximately 8 by 12 feet in size and made out of wood. It was firmly anchored to the ground by steel rods imbedded in a concrete pad.

Robert lifted up the wooden latch and was the first to enter. The others soon followed.

"Let's stay here tonight," Steven suggested, even though it was only 3 p.m.

"Yes, I agree," said Robert. "That's a good idea, seeing how the wind is blowing so hard."

"The next hut is another nine miles north of here," Morris informed them, "and we wouldn't get there until late tonight."

"Okay, then I guess it's settled," Robert concluded. "We'll stay here tonight. Is that okay with you, Chris?"

"Fine with me," he answered.

They set their packs down by the benches lining the walls and began to prepare an early meal.

11 The Earth Museum

"I have a feeling that more people will be coming here this afternoon or tonight," said Morris.

"Is that right?" Chris responded.

He barely got his words out before two young fellows arrived and opened the wooden door. Robert and Morris stared at them briefly, wondering why they looked so familiar.

"Chris and Richard Bell!" Robert suddenly exclaimed.

"Well, I will say!" Morris declared.

Chris and Richard stared at them briefly. "Oh, right. You're Robert Joslin, and you're Morris England, and we met you in Tasmania, didn't we?"

"That's right," Robert answered.

"Oh, yeah," Chris Chanford recalled. "I heard about you two and was sorry I didn't get to meet you. I'm Chris Chanford, and this is Steven Price. We were both running around down by the lake while you two were visiting with Robert, Morris, and James."

"Nice to meet you," said Richard, speaking for both of them.

"This really is a surprise to see you two again!" Robert told them. "Now, please don't disappear. We're okay, but there is something we want to talk to you about."

"What's that?" Richard asked, completely puzzled.

Morris took over from here. "We know your intentions are good and that you are good people, but we know you're not really from Lewes, Sussex. You're from somewhere else and are just visiting Earth, aren't you? I saw you two instantly and silently disappear up the track from Windermere Hut, as I went outside and watched you two walk away."

Chris and Richard both turned a little red in the face from embarrassment, knowing that they had been found out.

"Now, don't worry. We won't tell anybody," Morris assured them. "We, ourselves, have travelled to other planets since three months ago."

The redness in their faces quickly vanished as they showed looks of surprise and relief at the same time.

"Is that so?!" Chris Bell asked them with a tone of astonishment.

"Yes," Morris answered. "We were granted a gift of transport by a galactic salesman in early March."

"Oh, really?" Richard eagerly asked. "Tell us. Tell us all about it."

"Now, wait just a minute," Robert interjected. "Before we go any further in telling you things, we need some truth from you two, namely your correct address. Where are you two *really* from?"

Chris and Richard looked at each other and decided to tell them.

"We reside on a very Earth-like planet around the Garnet Star around 3,000 light years away. It is mostly islands and has a temperate climate."

"Is that the Planet of the Islands?" Steven asked.

"Yes. That's right," Richard answered, quite surprised. "At least, many people refer to it as that. How did you know?"

"We met a Mrs. Forvueweb in Southwest England who said she'd been there."

"Oh, right," said Richard. "We actually know her. She's been to visit us on our home planet and was one of the first to tell us about Earth. She and my parents are good friends, by the way. She lives on a farm just outside of Wexcombe, right?"

"Well, of all the coincidences in the world!" Steven remarked.

"Small world, isn't it," said Robert.

"Or galaxy, as you might call it," Morris added.

"Well, I don't guess you have a mailing address since you don't live on Earth," said Robert. "You still have ours, I guess."

"Oh yes. We still have it," said Richard. "Please forgive us for giving you a false one earlier. We didn't mean to put you off or get you angry, but it's just that most Earthlings don't believe in life from other planets and star systems, and we didn't want anyone to freak out. We have to be very careful, you know."

"Oh, that's okay," said Morris. "We understand why you did it now. After you two disappeared on that track near Windermere Hut, I was speculating on where you were from, and I leaned toward Vega. I guess I don't get everything right."

"No, not everything," said Richard, "but you were very intuitive to think to watch us leave so that you would see us disappear."

"There must have been some reason for that," said Chris Bell. "After all, we've now crossed paths again."

"Let's make a deal," Robert offered. "You be totally open and honest with us from now on, and we'll do the same."

"Fair enough," Richard agreed. "Chris and I accept your offer and will be."

"Good," said Morris. "We'll go ahead and explain to you how we acquired our gift of transport." Morris went into a 15-minute explanation, telling them about the dream, the galactic salesman, his mission, and the galactic communications device.

"That is most interesting!" declared Richard. "You all, along with a galactic salesman and his crew, built a galactic communications device?"

"That's right," Steven answered, "and it looks good, too."

"I wonder why they left us out?" Richard asked his brother.

"I don't know," he answered, "but after all of the trouble we've had, I'm not the least bit surprised."

"Trouble?" Steven asked. "Tell us. What sort of trouble have you had?"

"Chris and I live with our family on a fairly large island at a latitude of approximately 60 degrees south, and we are very interested in life on other planets and what these other planets have. We have a very large museum that we've created from items we've collected and teleported back to our home planet. One section of the museum is about planet Earth, its flora and fauna, and its technology.

"One of our main subjects in our museum is communication. Around a year ago, we decided to obtain surplus telephone equipment to build an exchange to show the locals who are interested just how telephones on Earth are used and how their calls are placed. The only problem is that we have been unsuccessful, as yet, in being able to secure such equipment."

"Sorry to hear that," said Robert. "Mr. Johns, a telephone technician friend of ours, had no trouble at all in getting us what we needed out of Eagleville, Tennessee, which cut over back on March 3rd."

"Is that right?" Richard asked, quite surprised. "That really is amazing! Maybe that's why we've crossed paths again."

"It could be," said Morris. "Explain to us why you've had so much trouble."

"Last year, in June 1984," Richard began, "we began our efforts to obtain step-by-step equipment, and we wanted some that had recently been taken out of service where the exchange had been cut over to a newer system. We've been communicating with Allied Telecom, a small phone company that had recently bought out some small exchanges in Georgia and North Carolina. Of course, when they bought them, they didn't realize what they were getting, as most of the exchanges were on step-by-step. Immediately, they went to work, converting those exchanges to digital. At present, there are only a few left yet to convert.

"Every one of those Allied Telecom employees has been giving us the run-around and has never failed to pass the buck onto someone else, who, needless to say, has done the same also. No one seems to have the authority or say-so to release the equipment to us, and we want it for a very good reason, to display to others in our Earth museum.

"We got very irritated around three months ago in late February when one of the maintenance supervisors told us to come on down to one of the exchanges that had just cut over in Georgia and get what we want. We went to the trouble and expense of hiring a large U-Haul truck and driving it to the exchange to meet him at a specified time. He showed up and started backing out and then said, 'No, I'm not going to do anything for you now.'

"I said, 'Look here. You said we could come and get what we want.'

"He told us, 'I told you exactly that, but if the tear-out crew finds any of this stuff missing, my goose is cooked!'

"We told him, 'We went to the trouble of hiring this truck and everything.'

"He told us, 'Makes no difference to me. Life is tough, isn't it.'

"Needless to say, we were angry enough to spit nails, and he accused *us* of having an attitude, of all things! Also, he told us that if it were up to him, he would load the whole exchange on our truck, but it wasn't up to him, obviously, and we got nothing. We even offered him money, and he said he didn't even want to hear about money."

"Golly!" Robert exclaimed. "What a jerk!"

"You got that right!" Richard agreed.

"I can't believe he did that to you!" declared Morris.

"What a shame!" Chris Chanford added.

"Oh, it's happened to us a lot," Chris Bell told him. "We've seen all types here on Earth, and we've experienced many differences in hospitality as well."

"Wait," said Robert. "I'm confused. I thought you had been travelling in New Zealand for several months before we saw you in Tasmania."

"You see," Chris Bell explained, "we had to cover up our true extraterrestrial identity. Both of us agreed on a story to tell anyone we might have met. After that joker pulled the rug out from under us, we threw up our hands on ever getting our step office and took off travelling, first to New Zealand, and then to Australia and Tasmania. Anyway, the travelling has done us good, and we feel ready to get back to work again. So, we were actually there, in New Zealand, but not for as long as we said we had been."

"What sort of work do you do?" Steven asked them.

"Oh, we run the museum," Richard replied. "Our parents tend to it and keep it open while Chris and I travel all over the galaxy, looking for items, subject matter, and ideas to display in it."

"That's really great!" Robert remarked. "I'm glad a family like yours cares enough about things to preserve them in a museum, especially items concerning communication."

"Oh yes," Chris Bell agreed. "We have one of the most complete museums in the galaxy, that is, if we can ever lay our hands on a step office."

"Chris and Richard, I believe we can help you out," Robert offered. "After all, it's foolish to see all of it go to waste with no one at Allied Telecom caring about it. I'm sure they're just going to junk it, anyway, aren't they?"

"Yes, I'd say you're right," Richard replied.

"I believe we're going home tomorrow," Robert continued, "and you two can come with us, if you like. All we have to do is to pick up our bicycles at the caravan park in Byrness, just south of here, before going home. Morris will transmit to you tomorrow the visual image of our step office, the receiving and transmitting towers, and the woods. That's where we will arrive back in Tennessee. You can teleport yourselves there and wait for us while we transport ourselves to Byrness and then home. We'll meet you there. We'll show you what we have, and you can see if you want something similar. If Mr. Johns can't help us, we'll call Tom, the galactic salesman, and see if he can duplicate our step office for you to teleport back home to your museum."

"Tell you what," Steven suggested, "why don't we see if Tom and his crew can meet us at one of those Georgia step offices that has just recently converted to digital. After all, they'll be complete with 1,000 lines or more instead of just 20 like ours. Tom and his crew can probably teleport to your home planet everything you need out of there."

"But that would be stealing," said Chris Bell.

"Not if we leave, say, $250 on the floor to pay for it," Steven cleverly pointed out. "That's more than Allied Telecom probably gets for each step office from the tear-out crews that bid on them."

"Yes, you do have a point," Chris Bell admitted. "There's no official way to get it, so we'll just take it and pay for it and leave an anonymous note telling them that the discontinued step office disappeared mysteriously for top-secret reasons."

"Really," Steven told them, "as long as they get paid for it, they won't care. Besides, it will save them the trouble of having to get it manually torn out, and the equipment will be put to good use, promoting communication in your museum."

"Plus, if you like," Robert added, "we can get Tom to include your planet with Sirius B, Vega, and the Pleiades and have him and his crew install another receiver-transmitter tower on our galactic communications device."

"That sounds great!" Richard enthusiastically remarked. "I really appreciate this. Please accept my apologies for having given you all a false address and phone number earlier. If only we were more intuitive, we'd have known better."

"Oh, that's okay," Morris assured them. "Forget it. At least we've met up again, and we can help you out."

"Thank you," said Richard. "That's very kind of you."

"Are you going to spend the night here with us or do you have to move on again, like last time?" Robert asked them.

"Oh, we'll stay here, if that's okay with you all."

"Good. We'll be glad to have your company," said Robert. "I was just about to go get some water down the hill when you two arrived. Do you want to come along?"

"I will," said Richard. "Both of us need water, so I'll come with you and collect it."

The two of them went outside, crossed the border fence into Scotland, and descended the steep hill into the gully below. The views of the Scottish countryside to the north were magnificent as the sunlight shined through the partly cloudy sky and brightened certain hillsides. A strong wind blew through the area from the west. Water was available from a spring at least a quarter mile down the hill.

"This land has some similarities to New Zealand's south island," Richard commented.

"I haven't been there," said Robert, "but based on pictures I've seen, I agree with you."

They collected the water and returned to the hut. As they entered, Morris said to them, "Tell us how you found the people during your trip to New Zealand, Australia, and Tasmania."

Chris Bell went into a long explanation while the others listened.

"Between Australia and New Zealand, Richard and I found the Australians to be just slightly more hospitable, even though many New Zealanders we met were very friendly also. Mind you, we met all types. Some were friendly, and others weren't."

"I guess that's true for anywhere," Chris Chanford commented.

"Right," Chris Bell agreed. "There were times when families, especially in New Zealand, would ask us inside and even ask us to stay the night with them, offering us a bed, along with breakfast the next morning. The same was true in Australia, but not as often."

"Then why do you rate the Australians as more hospitable?" Robert asked.

"Because in New Zealand, their kind hospitality, in some cases, is just a front to their true characteristics. In other words, they are hospitable for up to a few days only, maybe a couple of days. Some of them really get unhappy if you stay for a week, even if they had previously asked you to stay that long. We stayed with one family in the South Island for a week after the father in the family had invited us to stay that long. His wife wasn't pleased at all with that, and we noticed. In New Zealand, they'll tell you to make yourself at home, but what they really mean is for you to come inside and make yourself comfortable, nothing more.

"In Australia, you'd be able to spend a week with a family, and they'd be glad to have you. They didn't ask us in as often because we travelled by bus or train in Australia as compared to bicycle in New Zealand."

"That is strange, the differences you saw," Chris Chanford remarked.

"Yes, and that's not all," Chris Bell continued. "I don't mean to sound too negative, but we were visiting one family near Lawrence in South Otago. We had stayed with them a couple of days already when the mother in the family served us lunch on that particular day. Her son was around 30 and was married, living down the road, and was eating lunch with us. There was no bread served with the meal, so I asked for some. The son said no. I thought I misunderstood him, so I asked for bread again. He got irritated and rudely told me:

" 'Look, if I were at *your* house, I would eat what was put before me! I wouldn't ask for more!'

"I said, 'And if you had visited us, we'd have been glad to have given it to you.'

"With that, Richard and I got up from the table and left. The son was right in the middle of watching a cricket match on TV and couldn't be bothered with courtesy. We packed our belongings on our bicycles and rode out of there. He was too proud to come out and apologize, and the parents didn't even come outside to see us off."

"I can't believe it!" Morris declared. "If they'd been of the friendly sort, they would have been glad to serve you bread when you asked for it."

"Yeah, really," Chris Bell agreed.

"I can understand why you rate Australians as more hospitable, then," said Robert.

"Yes," said Chris Bell. "Now don't get us wrong. What I just told you is not the norm. Nearly everyone else we stayed with in New Zealand was very nice to us, and they were interested in what we were doing and told us about their way of life as well. We've enjoyed meeting many families during our travels and will probably look some of them up in the future."

"You might even be able to call them by telephone once you get your step office installed in your Earth museum," Steven suggested.

"That's true," Richard agreed. "It will be nice when we have that up and going."

"Didn't you say you had bought a car in Sydney?" Morris asked them.

"Yes, we did," Richard replied. "We left it with a mechanic up there while we saw Tasmania for three weeks. When we returned, the car had been vandalized."

"Oh, no!" Steven exclaimed.

"The mechanic was truly sorry it happened but took absolutely no responsibility for it. We had only paid $400 for it in the first place, so we just left it in his hands to dispose of it."

"That's too bad," said Chris Chanford.

"Oh, it doesn't matter that much," said Richard. "We learned more about the ways of life on Earth through that experience."

"Yeah, I guess that is about the best way of looking at it," Morris agreed.

"Tell us more about your Earth museum," Robert requested, changing the subject. "What types of things do you have in it?"

"Actually, the Earth museum is only one section of our complete museum, which includes items from all over the galaxy," Richard explained. "Our parents have been collecting for many years, and we started travelling and collecting for them around five years ago.

"The most important part of our complete museum is our arboretum which includes trees and plants from all over the galaxy. They come only from Earth-like planets and then only from an environment that is temperate like ours is. We have the arboretum separated into large sections, each section being from a different planet, and we also have some smaller members of the native wildlife for each planet. Each section is around 100 acres in size, and they are securely fenced off from one another to keep incompatible wildlife from mixing with those from other planets.

"The other part of our museum displays the ways of life of intelligent species from many planets in our galaxy. In our Earth museum, for example, we have a display of the technology of the human species including a history on how it came about. We have displays on some of the major events of Earth and have a strong emphasis on communication instead of wars. We have noticed that most of the history books on Earth harp on the details of wars while they would do a lot better to harp on communication instead. We emphasize communication in our museum because if there were more of it, there would automatically be more understanding and peace. People on Earth act before they think or communicate, and that's why we feel so determined to have a step office in our museum."

"That sounds great!" Robert told them. "We'll be glad to come visit you this summer and see this museum of yours. In fact, it would be a good idea for the eight of us, including those back in Tennessee, to see your museum at the start of our summer travels later this week."

"Yes, we'll be glad to have you come and visit," Richard told them.

"Thanks. We'll come, then."

"I guess you've noticed," Morris brought up, "that people are different from one another in many ways. Some are genuine and straightforward while others will tell you one thing and then do another."

"Oh yes! We've noticed," Richard replied. "Based on our experiences, I'd say that probably one in four people we've met are willing to help us upon request. The other three are usually the type who give lip service."

"We call them fair-weather friends," said Chris Chanford.

"That's right," Richard agreed, "and when it goes to clouding up and raining, and you really need their help, they won't come through for you. They'll make up every excuse in the world to keep from doing it."

"We've all seen enough of those types," said Robert.

"Back on our home planet," Chris Bell explained, "everyone is genuine and is willing to help. If a person has fallen under hard times, his neighbors will pitch in and help, and they'll be glad to do it. After all, they too, may fall under hard times and need help in the future."

"That really is a good system of welfare," Steven commented.

"Yes, it is," said Chris Bell, "and that's why it's so difficult for me and Richard to understand the fact that so many people on Earth are not willing to help one another and that there is such turmoil and emotional upset in many places."

"I have a theory for that, if you'd like to hear it," Morris offered.

"Yes, what is it? I'm all ears," said Chris Bell.

"It is my theory that the human species originated here on Earth several million years ago, even though Tom has told us that they originated on Vega. In actuality, the ones who, quote, originated on Vega probably came from here before that and continued evolving on Vega after having been transported or teleported there by extraterrestrials millions of years ago."

"And I'd say that around 2 million years ago," Robert interrupted, "some of them were brought back to Earth from Vega or even Sirius B."

"That would explain the missing link!" Steven suddenly shouted.

"That's right," Morris continued. "Over a course of time, the humans, being left on their own here on Earth, became advanced and took off travelling to other planets and star systems. They settled many areas, one of them, your home planet, the Planet of the Islands. Some of those advanced civilizations have returned to Earth in the last few thousands of years to check on us and make sure we were okay.

"As for the turmoil and emotional upset that exists here on Earth, it's my theory that more aggressiveness was purposefully bred into us by extraterrestrial humans to give us, here on Earth, a better chance to survive. After all, the Ice Age was pretty severe, and survival must have been pretty difficult in those days."

"That is a good theory," Chris Bell admitted. "I'd say I agree with you. Richard, I'd say that what Morris has just told us is worthy of writing down for display in our Earth museum. What do you think?"

"Yes, I agree. That is a good theory. Let's mention it to our parents and see what they think. Thanks for telling us that, Morris."

"Oh, it was nothing, really. I'm glad you agree with it."

"Oh, it was more than nothing," Richard insisted. "I'd say it's true."

They continued visiting and discussing various subjects until it began to get dark around 10:30 p.m. It never did get totally dark, being this far north, and a considerable glow could be seen in the north sky until sunrise around 2 a.m.

The next morning, Wednesday, May 29, was beautiful and clear. The wind had stopped blowing. Chris and Richard Bell were still there and had not mysteriously disappeared during the night. Everyone had breakfast and packed to leave.

"Okay, Chris and Richard," Morris announced, just before they all left, "I will now transmit to both of you the visual image of the corner of the Joslin's woods where the galactic communications device is. It is there that I want you to teleport yourselves. We will meet you there in half an hour, as we have to transport ourselves to Byrness and collect our bicycles and gear beforehand." Morris proceeded to transmit the visual image.

"Oh, wow!" exclaimed Richard.

"It's as clear as a television picture!" Chris Bell remarked.

"That's amazing!" Richard went on. "I can see the woods, building, towers, and everything."

"Look at those rings and crystals," Chris Bell pointed out.

"I know. I see them too," Richard confirmed.

"Okay, Chris and Richard," Morris continued, "I can tell that you've definitely received the image accurately. We'll see you there."

Everyone stepped outside.

"See you in half an hour," said Richard. With that, they instantly and silently vanished.

Robert, Chris, Morris, and Steven transported themselves, creating the sound of whirring wind and the image of the pink glow as it overtook them, and they disappeared. They arrived in the Spruce forest up the hill from the highway and walked back to Byrness Caravan Park and collected their bicycles and gear after informing the owners. They rode back to the Spruce forest and transported themselves and their bicycles back to Tennessee, arriving at the corner of the Joslin's woods. Chris and Richard were sitting in front of the step office building, waiting for them. It was 3 a.m. and was dark.

"Oh good! You made it here," Steven declared upon seeing them.

Chris and Richard looked at the four of them and remarked, "That really is something, the way you transport yourselves with that pink glow and whirring wind like that!"

"You mean you haven't seen that method of transport before?" Robert asked.

"No, we haven't, actually," they told him.

"What about Mrs. Forvueweb? She travels that way."

"We've never seen her arrive or leave," Richard explained. "Evidently she has a hiding place where she makes her appearances and disappearances. However, she does come by to visit us whenever she's on our planet."

"I guess our appearance just now was quite a sight, then," Robert mentioned.

"Yes, we didn't know what in the world that pink glow and whirring wind was until we saw you four begin to materialize!"

They all laughed about it.

"Richard and I already walked inside your building. That's quite an impressive step office in there. You and Mr. Johns did a great job putting that back together after it was torn out of Eagleville."

"Thanks," said Robert. "I'm glad you like it."

"Oh, we do," Chris Bell insisted. "We definitely want to tie into this exchange as soon as we have our step office up and working in our Earth museum."

"Come on inside," Robert offered. "I'll call Mr. Johns, and you can tell him what you want."

Robert led everyone inside. He picked up the handset of the phone and started dialling his number. Suddenly, he hung up. "What am I doing? It's 3 a.m. over here, and I was about to call him!"

"Oh, yeah. That's right," Morris realized. "I'm glad you caught yourself and didn't let that call go through."

"That makes both of us!" Robert agreed. "Would you like to have a look around the place while we wait for sunrise?"

"Sure," said Richard. "Show us your woods here."

Robert, Chris, Richard, and the others grabbed their flashlights out of their panniers and walked up the trail to the large flat bed of limestone at the top of the knob. Robert pointed out the various trees and plants to them on the way up. Chris and Richard were fascinated with the variety of trees in these woods and were especially intrigued with the fossils that were imbedded in the limestone bedrock at the top.

"These crinoid stems are very impressive!" Chris Bell remarked. "Something like this would be great for our museum."

"It would," Robert agreed, "but I don't want anything leaving here. I do have some limestone rocks with some crinoid stems in them down at the house. You're welcome to take one of them back with you."

"Robert and the rest of us had a meeting up here back in late March," Chris Chanford informed them. "We discussed our plans for our summer travels. At that time, we didn't know about the Garnet Star, and we definitely want to go there now."

"It's a really great place to visit," Richard told him, "and it's peaceful and quiet. There's no hustle and bustle with technology there, like there is here on Earth."

"Peace and quiet is what we want to see," said Morris. "We're not after the city life like so many others are."

They looked around the top of the knob for some time, peering down the crevices and exploring the small caves nearby. Eventually, they returned to the step office building. It started to become light outside, so they showed them around the farm, including the barns.

After Chris and Richard had a good idea of what a farm looked like in Tennessee, they finally went inside the Joslin's house, as it was now a decent hour in the morning. Robert's parents had just gotten up and greeted everyone as they entered.

"How are you doing, Robert?" his father asked him. "How was England?"

"I had a great time!" he answered.

"It was fantastic!" Steven declared.

"Come on in, everyone," said Mr. Joslin, as he offered his hospitality to them. "My wife's just fixing breakfast. Who are these two you all have brought with you?"

"These two are Chris and Richard Bell," Robert informed him, "and they're supposedly from England. Actually, they are from a planet 3,000 light years away."

"Is that right? Hello, Chris and Richard. I'm Bob Joslin. I'm pleased to meet you."

They greeted each other and shook hands. Everyone entered and walked through to the kitchen where Mrs. Joslin was preparing breakfast. She served them a variety of cereals, toast, and cantaloupe, along with orange juice. As they ate their breakfast, they became more acquainted with each other, and Chris and Richard explained what they did back home on their planet.

"Oh, by the way, Robert," his mother brought up, "Mr. Mayfield called a couple of days ago. He said he wondered if he could travel with you to some of the places that you're going to travel to this summer."

"Hmm . . ." said Robert, thinking it over. "He hasn't been granted the gift. I'll have to talk to Tom and see if it's okay with him. I've already granted the gift of transport to nine others, and that's my quota or limit. Only Tom can grant Mr. Mayfield the gift, so it's up to him."

Robert walked over to the phone and picked up the handset to make a call. "I better call Mr. Johns before he goes off to work." He got him on the line.

"Hello?"

"Hello, Mr. Johns. This is Robert Joslin."

"Oh hey, Robert. How's it going? How was your all's trip to England?"

"We had a great time bicycling around."

"Well, good. I know William wanted to join you all, but we had a few things that needed doing around here, you know. He's packed and ready now and can't wait to join you all for the summer."

"Great! I've got something to ask you," said Robert. "Are you able to get any more step office equipment? I've got two fellows with me that we met in England . . . well, actually Tasmania, but that's a long story. They are from a planet around the Garnet Star 3,000 light years away and on the other side of the Little Dipper, and they want to build a step office in their museum and hook into our exchange as well."

"Is that right?" Mr. Johns asked with surprise. "Let me see what I can do. I'm not sure if I can get any more of that stuff or not. I probably could eventually, but if you need it right away, your best bet might be to talk to Tom and see what he can do. I'm just not sure how easily I could lay my hands on any equipment since it would now have to come from outside of my area. Eagleville was the last one to cut over in my district. I'm sorry I can't be of better help than that."

"That's okay. Tell you what. I'll let you speak to Chris and Richard, the two I was telling you about." Robert motioned to them to pick up and speak to Mr. Johns. Chris used the extra phone. Richard came over, and

Robert handed him the phone he was using. Both of them explained in some detail what they wanted to do. Mr. Johns offered his help in any way possible and recommended that they consult Tom first to see what he could do, especially if they needed it pretty soon.

Chris and Richard hung up and looked somewhat concerned. "It looks like Tom, the galactic salesman, may be our only hope," said Richard.

"I feel sure he can help you out," Morris assured them.

"I certainly hope so."

"Don't worry, Chris and Richard. He will, really," Robert reassured them. "Tell you what. Let's go ahead and call Tom right now."

Robert dialled 274-7015. The ringing could be heard over the line.

"...pop...BBBBBB...BBBBBB...BBBBBB...Sirius B."

"Yes, this is Robert Joslin. Is Tom there?"

"Hold the line while I send for him," said the female voice on the distant end of the line. Thirty seconds passed.

"Hello. This is Tom."

"Yes, Tom. This is Robert Joslin. How are you doing?"

"I'm doing fine. How is everything there?"

"We are all fine and are getting ready to begin our summer travels. Some of us have already visited England for a few days. While we were there, we met two fellows who reside on the planet around the Garnet Star, and they've come home with us. They were wondering if . . ."

"The Garnet Star," Tom interrupted. "That sounds familiar, but I can't quite place it."

"It's a star on the other side of the Little Dipper, and it's around 3,000 light years away."

"Oh my goodness!" Tom exclaimed, as if he'd made a terrible mistake.

"What is it?" Robert asked with some concern.

"I *knew* I forgot something! I just knew it!"

"What's that?"

"They were supposed to have been included and linked up to the galactic communications device. It completely slipped my mind. I can't believe I left them out! Did you just tell me there are two fellows with you that are from there?"

"Yes."

"Oh, thank the lucky stars!" Tom declared. "Tell them to stay put. I'm coming right now. I want to talk to them. Are you at your parents' home?"

"Yes."

With that, Tom hung up the phone on Sirius B before Robert could say another word.

"Tom said he's coming right now," Robert informed the others.

Little did he finish his sentence than the doorbell rang. Robert went to answer it. There was Tom, already at the door, still in his white robe and holding his walking staff. He greeted him and let him inside. Everyone else waited in the kitchen. Tom entered and had a seat.

"You must be Tom, the galactic salesman," said Richard as he got up and extended his right hand to greet him. "I'm Richard Bell, and this is my brother, Chris. We reside on the Planet of the Islands as Robert has already told you."

"I'm very pleased and feel very fortunate to meet you," said Tom. "First of all, may I apologize for leaving your planet out of the galactic communications device. I didn't do it on purpose. It just slipped my mind."

"Oh, that's quite all right," Richard assured him. "We really appreciate your coming because we need your help in acquiring some step-by-step central office equipment for use in the technology section of our Earth museum on our home planet. My parents run the museum, and Chris and I travel all over the galaxy, collecting items for displaying in it."

"Is that right?" Tom asked him, quite surprised. "That's amazing! I declare that sometimes the universe is really perfect! At times, the pieces of a puzzle fall right into place, like clockwork. Here I've come to talk to you two about linking your planet to our galactic communications device, and you've also come to me to consult my help in obtaining surplus central office equipment. It is therefore in the best of both of our interests. I am therefore at your service. How can I be of help?"

Chris, Richard, and Tom seated themselves at the Joslin's kitchen table while Robert and his friends sat in the same room and listened. Richard did most of the talking while he and his brother explained to Tom the details of the trouble they had been having in obtaining the surplus step office equipment from Allied Telecom. Tom listened intently, already thinking of possible ways to help them.

". . . and that maintenance supervisor that backed out on us told us, 'I ain't got no time to baby-sit no endeavor of yours!' " Richard concluded.

"I am really amazed at all the trouble you've had," Tom commented. "Also, Mr. Johns just told you that he couldn't get any more of it, at least not now. That's what you said, right?"

"Right," said Richard.

"Let's see. How can I help you?" Tom thought for a minute.

Steven spoke up with his idea. "Tom, I was telling Chris and Richard that maybe you and your crew could visit one of these step offices just taken out of service and teleport the equipment out of there and leave, say, $250 on the floor with an anonymous note, saying that it mysteriously disappeared for top-secret reasons or something like that."

"I don't know," Tom hesitatingly said.

"Really," Steven insisted, "Allied Telecom won't care as long as they get paid for it, and they don't get any more money than that from the tearout crews that bid on them. Besides, teleporting the stuff out of there and paying for it will save Allied Telecom the trouble of having to have it manually torn out."

"I see your point," said Tom. "That's a good suggestion and idea, but I will have to check with the Galactic Federation to get their approval. If it's okay with them, I will return here, and we'll get started. Meanwhile, Chris and Richard, I need you to call Allied Telecom and find out which step offices have recently been cut over and are therefore still intact. Be careful not to let on that you're really serious about obtaining this equipment. We don't want to raise any suspicions."

"Actually, I believe I'll have someone else check on this for me," said Richard. "If a third party checks on it, they'll never link it to us."

"That's a good idea," said Tom with a tone of approval in his voice. "Meanwhile, I must return home and get the Galactic Federation's approval. It could take the rest of the day. I'll plan on returning here late this afternoon or evening."

"We really appreciate this," Richard told him.

"That's quite all right," said Tom. "After all, I want your planet to be linked up to our galactic communications device. I'll see you later today."

"See you then," said Richard.

With that, Tom instantly disappeared, right in front of everyone.

Robert's parents had been in another part of the house and now returned to the kitchen.

"I believe I'll quickly go home," Richard announced. "Chris, you stay here with the others. I'm going to bring Mother back with me, and I'll have her call and find out which step offices are just taken out of service. That will cover us. I'll be back soon." With that, he instantly disappeared.

"My goodness!" Mrs. Joslin exclaimed. "He can disappear, too?"

"Yes, he and Chris teleport themselves," Robert answered.

"Ever since that dream you had," she remarked, "you've been meeting all kinds of people. Things are happening so fast!" She sighed and then added, "Robert, you might want to call Mr. Mayfield while you're waiting for Richard to return."

"Oh, yeah. That's right. I'll call him now." Robert dialled his number and got him on the line.

"Hello?"

"Mr. Mayfield? This is Robert Joslin."

"How's it going, Robert?"

"Fine. How are you?"

"I'm doing okay."

"I heard that you called a couple of days ago to see about travelling with us," said Robert.

"Yes, I did. I was just wondering if I could come see some of those places you're planning on transporting yourselves to? I've always been curious about life on other planets. If you all could get me there, I could go off and do things while you all do your things."

"It's fine with me and fine with the rest of us, Mr. Mayfield, but I could only grant the gift of transport to nine others, and I did that the first day I had the gift back on March 3rd. It would be up to Tom, the galactic salesman. He might be able to help you."

"Oh, really?" Mr. Mayfield asked enthusiastically.

"Yes, I believe so," Robert answered. "Tom will be here this afternoon or evening, and we're going to Georgia. That's a long story, but if you want to come out here when Tom is here, you can ask him if he will grant you the gift."

"Okay, Robert. Thank you very much. So, you'll call me when Tom returns?"

"Yes. I'll do that, then."

"Okay, I'll make sure and be here to take your call."

"Okay, bye."

-click-

Robert hung up and said to his friends, "Mr. Mayfield wants to travel with us, at least to get to some of those other planets, at which time he will go about his way while we go about ours. What do you think?"

"I have no problem with it," said Steven.

"Fine with me," said Chris Chanford.

"If Mr. Mayfield comes with us, it will be like having a chaperone," Morris pointed out. "That may actually look good in the eyes of some of our parents, but that's probably irrelevant. After all, we are 17, most of us. Some of us are still 16. I have no objection to his coming, if that's okay with Tom, that is."

"Okay," said Robert.

"Robert," Steven suggested, "Let's call the others and see if they want to join us and come with us to Georgia."

"Yeah, good idea," Robert agreed. "Here's the phone, Steven. I'll let you call them. I'm going to have a seat at the table and relax."

Steven walked over to the phone and called William Johns, Andrew Tremain, James Westfield, and Paul Wilson. As he reached each one of them and carried on conversations with them, telling them about their fantastic few days in England, Robert sat down at the table with the others.

Suddenly, the doorbell rang. Robert went to answer it. Richard Bell had already returned and was alone.

"You're back already, Richard? Where's your mother?"

"She wouldn't come. She said it would be best if I, myself, go ahead and call the same people at Allied Telecom and tell them that we'd given up on getting any step office equipment but had come to the conclusion that we still needed it and wanted it. So, I'll just call them and find out which step offices have recently been converted."

"Richard, if you call them now, and one of their discontinued step offices disappears mysteriously, they're going to come to you, saying, 'Where is it?' You don't want that happening."

"Remember," Richard reminded, "we *are* going to pay for the equipment, and even if they want to come after Chris and me, they won't be able to do anything since we don't live on Earth. If they arrest us, we'll just teleport ourselves away."

"Oh yes, of course," Robert admitted. "Okay, then. Go to it, and call them. Now remember, my friends and I don't know a thing about this, and we've never heard of you two, as far as Allied Telecom is concerned."

"Right. I understand," Richard assured him.

They both walked into the kitchen, and Richard made several phone calls to various people at Allied Telecom in Georgia. Robert explained to the others that Chris and Richard's mother had decided not to make the calls for them.

After Richard hung up from his last call, he said, "They've told me that Kingston Park in Southwest Georgia just cut over night before last and that Appleton in Central Georgia will cut over tonight."

"Kingston Park," said Morris. "That sounds familiar. I wonder why."

"I don't know," said Robert. "I've never heard of it, myself."

"Let's get the map out and find it," Steven advised everyone.

As Robert reached for the road atlas, he said, "I believe it would be better for us to go to Kingston Park. Everybody and his brother, including politicians, will probably be in Appleton tonight, since they're cutting it over."

"Here it is," Chris Chanford announced, as he placed his finger on it. "It's in the Albany area."

"None of us have been there," Robert realized. "How are we going to transport ourselves there?"

"Good question," said Steven. "I don't actually know. Morris, do you have any ideas?"

"What about that crystal ball?" Chris Chanford asked. "After all, you said it sounded familiar."

"Maybe you can see it *that* way," Robert suggested.

"Okay, let me look and see," Morris consented, as he took his crystal ball out of its leather pouch. "Chris and Richard, I need you two to sit across from me and let your minds and thoughts wander. What I'm going to hopefully do is to latch onto some visual information and, with a good bit of luck, see a visual image of at least something in Kingston Park, Georgia. Once I've caught it, I can transmit it to the rest of you, and we can go there."

They followed his instructions and sat across the kitchen table from Morris. Everyone else sat quietly in other parts of the room and observed the event. After three minutes of concentrating, Morris announced:

"I've got it! I'm sure of it. I see a road sign saying, 'Kingston Park City Limits.' Right beside it is a sign saying, 'Speed Limit 35.'"

"Good work, Morris!" Robert exclaimed.

"That's amazing!" Steven added. "You really do have psychic abilities."

"Oh yes. I'll admit that I do," said Morris, "when I set my mind to it."

"If Tom gets approval, we'll go there tonight," said Richard.

Robert's father had not really made any comment to their plans, having been in and out of the house, doing outdoor farm chores. He now came over to them at the table and said:

"Robert, I feel like I must talk to you about your plans to help Chris and Richard get this step office out of Georgia. I'm really concerned about it. I mean, if they catch you, they could arrest you for stealing and put you all in prison for life. I'm pleading with you to . . ."

"Oh, don't worry," Robert reassured him. "We're just going to observe it. Chris and Richard will have the equipment, not us, and Tom will actually be doing the taking as he teleports it out of there. Besides, they're going to leave money to pay for the equipment and an explanatory note. So, it's not really stealing."

"I see your point," his father admitted, "but no one has been given the approval by Allied Telecom. Anyway, it might be better if you stayed here, but if you decide to go, be careful, and station someone outside the building to watch for potential telephone company workers. I just don't want you getting in any trouble, son."

"Don't worry. I'll be careful," Robert reassured his father.

"All right. Good luck."

Mr. Joslin walked back outside with a look of concern and worry on his face.

"Steven," Robert asked, "what time are the others coming here to meet us?"

"They'll be here around 4 p.m."

"Okay," said Robert, "I've got a few farm chores to do around here, including mowing the lawn. If you all need to go home and unpack, go ahead. Chris and Richard, if you want to hang around here or go with them, either choice is fine with me.

"Morris," Robert requested, "could you transport yourself to Kingston Park and find the telephone exchange building in that town? That way, we could transport ourselves directly to the building instead of to the town limits and therefore minimize our chances of being seen and raising suspicions."

"Yes, that's a good idea. I'll go ahead and do that."

"I believe Richard and I will go with Morris," said Chris Bell.

"All right," said Robert, "I'll see everyone back here at 4 o'clock, right?"

"Right," they answered.

With that, everyone left, and Robert went outside to do farm chores.

Morris took Chris and Richard to Kingston Park, and they walked all over that town, looking for the telephone exchange. Finally, they located it in the south side of town down a side street and under a group of Live Oak trees. As soon as they found it and picked a good arrival spot, they returned to Tennessee.

At 3:30 p.m. Tom returned with an answer from the Galactic Federation. "They have given me approval to help Chris and Richard obtain the step-by-step equipment, so long as I leave an anonymous cashier's check made out to Allied Telecom for $250."

"That's good," said Robert. "Tom, my parents, especially my father, are worried about my well-being and that my friends and I may be arrested and go to prison if we're in on it."

"Ease your mind, Robert," Tom assured him. "Let's go talk to your parents about this."

They walked into the house. "Mother, Father," Robert called out.

"Yes," they answered from a different room.

"Tom is here and wants to talk to you about what we're going to do tonight."

"All right, we'll be right there. Meet us in the living room."

Robert led Tom into the living room, and they had a seat. His parents soon entered.

"Oh, yeah!" Robert suddenly realized. "I need to call Mr. Mayfield. I told him I'd call him when you arrived, Tom. I'll be right back." Robert ran into another room to use the phone. A few minutes later, he returned and had a seat with his parents and Tom.

"Let me assure you," Tom began, "that Robert and his friends will in no way be responsible for the removal of the step office equipment in Georgia. I will take full responsibility and can assure you that they will be completely innocent and will be nothing more than bystanders to witness the event."

"I certainly hope so," said Robert's father.

"Everything will be fine. I promise," Tom reassured them. "It's for a good cause. Things aren't always done in a totally proper manner, but I will be paying Allied Telecom more for the equipment than the potential bidders and tear-out crews will pay."

"Please, let me go with them," Robert requested of his parents.

"Hmm . . ." said Mr. Joslin. "I just don't know. It's like you and your friends will be accomplices to the 'crime', as Allied Telecom might call it. Well . . . okay. I guess that will be all right. Just be careful, son. Be sure that you and your friends don't touch anything inside that building. Tom, thank you very much for reassuring me. I still feel uneasy but not as much as I did. I'll just be glad when it's all over, and you all are safe."

"Everything will be all right, Mr. Joslin," Tom assured him. "I'll make sure that only Chris, Richard, and I touch the equipment inside that step office building."

"Very good, Tom," said Mr. Joslin as he and his wife got up from their seats. "My wife and I will go back to cleaning in the back of the house." With that, they walked out of the living room.

"Do you have the cashier's check, Tom?" Robert asked.

"Yes, I've already been by a bank to obtain it." Tom pulled the check out of one of his pockets inside his robe and showed it to him.

"I'm glad you've already done that because the banks just closed."

"Yes, I was aware of that, and that's why I've already obtained the check."

"My friends and also Mr. Mayfield will be arriving any minute now. By the way, Chris and Richard found out that Kingston Park, Georgia just cut over to digital night before last. It's in Southwest Georgia near Albany, and that's your best bet."

"How am I going to teleport myself there?" Tom asked him. "I've never been there before, nor have I seen it."

"Morris managed to obtain a visual image of the town with the help of his crystal ball and Chris and Richard letting their minds wander. I believe the three of them went to Kingston Park today to locate the building."

"Excellent!" Tom declared. "That crystal ball really is something, the way it can help a person visualize. That's great! I'll just have Morris transmit the visual image to me."

Cars started arriving outside. Robert looked out the window. "William's here. So is Paul. That's Andrew's car coming down the driveway. Let's go on outside to meet them."

They walked into the front yard and greeted them as they stepped out of their cars.

"How's it going, Robert?" said Paul. "How was your trip?"

"We had a great time. Are you packed and ready to come with us this summer?"

"Oh yes," Paul enthusiastically told him. "My father's all caught up at the plant, and I'm free for the entire summer."

"Great!" said Robert. "As soon as everyone arrives, we'll go on up to the woods, and Tom will tell us his plans."

Chris and Richard suddenly appeared in the front yard, followed by Morris arriving with a pink glow and whirring wind. James and Mr. Mayfield arrived separately a few minutes later.

"Where are Steven and Chris?" Robert asked the others. At that moment, their cars came into view as they crested the hill on the Joslin's driveway. "Oh, here they come."

Once they arrived, all of them walked up to the step office building in the woods. Tom announced to everyone his plans.

"What I am about to do is in the best interest of Chris and Richard Bell and their Earth museum on the Planet of the Islands around the Garnet Star, 3,000 light years away and on the other side of the Little Dipper. The Galactic Federation has given me approval to go with Chris and Richard to Kingston Park, Georgia, where I will personally teleport the discontinued step office equipment out of the building and leave an anonymous cashier's check made out to Allied Telecom for $250.

"Let me assure all of you that only Chris, Richard, and I will be responsible for the disappearance of the equipment from Kingston Park. No one else will be liable. You are welcome to come with us and be bystanders to witness the event, but make sure you don't touch anything unless it's step-by-step equipment. In case Allied Telecom doesn't take too kindly to the loss of their equipment, even though they will have been paid for it, we don't want any fingerprints, except mine, left in that building."

Tom now turned to speak to Chris and Richard standing beside him. "The next thing I need to do is go with you two to the Planet of the Islands and see your museum and determine the site where we want this equipment to arrive."

"Okay. That will be fine," said Richard.

"Okay, everyone," Tom continued. "I'm going to transmit the visual image of the Planet of the Islands to you." He paused for a moment. "Wait. I haven't been to your Earth museum, Chris and Richard. Can either one of you transmit visual images?"

"No, I'm afraid we cannot," Chris Bell answered.

"Would you like me to grant you the ability to do so?"

"Yeah, sure!" they both eagerly replied.

"Okay, stand still, and I'll grant it to both of you." Tom moved to a position around 10 feet away from them and faced them. He appeared to meditate and used his walking staff to help him as he appeared to scan them with it, pointing it in their general direction and waving it around. "Okay, now see if you can transmit visual images. Just meditate and think of your Earth museum. Transmit the data to all of us here."

Chris and Richard began, and soon everyone began to see the scene of their island and the numerous sections of woods and buildings, each section divided by tall concrete walls.

"Look at those sections of forest," Robert remarked.

"I know, and those walls look like they're nearly a hundred feet high," William added.

The view transmitted to them was an aerial view. Chris and Richard now transmitted an image at ground level next to their museum. "It is here that Tom, Richard, and I are going," Chris Bell announced. "How many of you would like to come with us?"

Everyone, including Mr. Mayfield, raised his hand.

"Tom?" Mr. Mayfield spoke out.

"Yes."

"I was wondering if it would be possible for me to be able to transport myself like Robert and his friends do, not that I would tag along with them everywhere they go, but so that I could go see these places myself."

"Yes, I believe that will be all right," Tom replied. "Let's go into the step office and call the Galactic Federation for approval. You can speak to them and ask them what you just asked me." With that, Tom walked into the building with Mr. Mayfield following him.

Five minutes passed while the others discussed what it was like at Chris and Richard's Earth museum. Then Tom and Mr. Mayfield emerged from the building. "Mr. Mayfield has been given approval to receive the gift of transport," Tom announced. "I grant you the gift." With that, Mr. Mayfield felt a jolt or a thud go through his body.

"What was *that*?" he exclaimed.

"That's the attachment of the etheric silver platter," Tom replied. He continued as he gave Mr. Mayfield instructions on how to transport himself and what to expect to feel while he did so. "I will come with you and transport you myself this first time so you can get a feel of what it's like."

Tom now looked at everyone. "If everyone is ready, let's all go to Chris and Richard's Earth museum. I'm going to personally transport Mr. Mayfield." All of them proceeded to transport themselves, and a few seconds later, they materialized at the Earth museum on the Planet of the Islands.

Mr. Mayfield was speechless. ". . . Well . . . I will say!" he finally exclaimed. "I used to think your telephone duplication act beat all I ever saw, but this takes the cake! Am I really here?"

"You're here, all right," Tom confirmed. "We're all here."

Robert and several others looked around and took in the scenery and the many different types of trees from the temperate climate back on Earth. They were standing by a large concrete block building that would soon house the Kingston Park, Georgia step office. In all other directions, the area was forested with trees that the Bell family had planted in the past. It was a beautiful area and far exceeded any botanical garden that they had previously seen on Earth.

"We are here at the site of our Earth museum," Richard announced. "Come inside, and I'll show you what we have in mind." He opened the door and led everyone inside. "This is the room we've designated for the step office. We plan on displaying telephones around the wall in the room next to this one."

Tom looked the room over very carefully, thinking of how to teleport the equipment into there. "This room will definitely be large enough. What I'll do is place a force field over everything that I teleport here so it won't fall over upon arrival. Immediately after I teleport everything, I'll teleport myself here. You two come with me. The rest of you can come if you like, but please arrive outside the building, after which you can walk in. If everyone is ready, let's go to Kingston Park."

"Wait, Tom," Morris interjected. "Back on Earth, it's around 6 p.m. in Georgia, and it won't be dark for three more hours. We're all liable to be seen in broad daylight. I think it would be a lot better and safer for all of us to wait until it gets dark before we go there."

"You have a good point there," Tom admitted. "Morris, while I'm thinking of it, may I see your crystal ball? I need to look into the future and see if the building will be clear and free of Allied Telecom workers tonight."

"Certainly." Morris handed him the ball. "Now, let me make this very clear. As far as everyone is concerned, I didn't do anything to help, and I'm not liable."

"That's fine, Morris. You're protected," Tom assured him.

Tom peered into the crystal ball, and then he looked at Chris and Richard and said, "I need the visual image of the Kingston Park step office building."

"Of course," they answered, and they transmitted the image to Tom and to everyone else as well.

As soon as Tom had received the image, he meditated briefly as he continued peering into the ball. "It's clear between the hours of 7 p.m. and 8 p.m. Eastern time. That is the largest block of time I see with no one in the building. At all other times during the night, there isn't as much as a 20-minute period available without some Allied Telecom worker in there, taking care of line troubles and working out some minor problems with the new digital switch."

"That's an hour from now," said Paul.

"Tell you what," Tom offered. "Why don't you all take a look around the museum and the arboretum while I stay here with Chris and Richard and make preparations?"

"If it's okay with you, Tom," said Chris Bell, "I'll take the others on a tour of the place for an hour while you and Richard make the preparations."

"That will be fine, Chris."

"Wait, Tom," said Robert. "It looks like we'll be going to Georgia when it's still daylight this evening. We might be seen arriving outside the building."

"Don't worry, Robert," Tom assured him. "I'll check that with Morris' crystal ball, and we'll arrive outside the building when no one is looking."

"Oh, okay."

"Go on with Chris and the rest of them, and enjoy the tour of their arboretum."

"Okay, Tom," said Robert.

With that, Chris Bell led Robert and his friends and Mr. Mayfield out of the building and took them for a walk through the forest. Robert and James had the most fun as they ran from tree to tree, identifying as many of them as they possibly could.

"Chris, this is a superb forest!" James complimented.

"Yes, thanks, and we're proud of it, too."

The hour went by before they realized it, and Chris announced that it was time to return to the building where Tom and Richard were. Upon entering, Steven suddenly remembered something and asked, "Tom, what about your four crew members? Aren't they coming with us?"

"No, not this time," he answered. "In actuality, what I'm about to do is not 100 percent up front and honest, and even though I have been given approval by the Galactic Federation, I didn't want to risk any other Sirian's well-being. Chris and Richard will be my crew for this one."

"Oh . . ." said Steven, sort of surprised. "But what about all of us?"

"Oh, don't worry," Tom insisted. "I've got you all covered, and I'll take full responsibility if any trouble comes out of this."

"Okay, Tom," Richard told him, "I believe we've got everything ready to receive the equipment when you teleport all of it here."

"That's good," said Tom. "Okay! I believe we're now ready to transport ourselves to Kingston Park. The force fields are set up here, ready to receive everything. Is everyone ready?"

"Yes," they answered.

"Morris," Tom asked, "is the space under the Live Oak trees by the building clear of anyone watching?"

"I don't know, Tom. You still have my ball."

"Oh, yeah. That's right. Here, I'll just check it myself." Tom peered into the ball and saw that it was completely clear of anyone who might be watching them. "It looks all clear, everyone. Here's your crystal ball back, Morris." He handed it back to him. "I will now transmit the visual image to all of you, in case any of you missed it when Chris and Richard transmitted it earlier." He transmitted the image, making sure that everyone received it.

"All right, let's hurry on down there before someone sees us," Tom directed.

They proceeded to transport themselves, and all 12 of them successfully arrived under the group of Live Oak trees behind the Kingston Park telephone exchange building. Upon arriving, they immediately walked to the building's back door.

"Blast it!" Tom declared. "It's locked! I keep forgetting that people lock everything on Earth. Does everyone know what it looks like inside?"

"No," Mr. Mayfield answered.

"All right, here's the image." Tom transmitted it for everyone to receive in case there were any others who didn't know. As soon as he finished transmitting it, he commanded, "Let's transport ourselves inside immediately before we're seen!"

They proceeded to transport themselves and successfully arrived along the back wall where there was some space. Luckily, each one of them arrived in a slightly different position instead of on top of one another.

"Robert," Tom requested, "I need you to show me which equipment belongs to the discontinued step office. I want to be sure I don't take any of the new digital equipment with us."

Robert took Tom between the rows of equipment, pointing out what would go and what would stay. Chris and Richard helped. Andrew and Steven also had their input, being more technically minded in electrical equipment.

"Okay, Tom," Robert began, "every row having these metal covers that look like mailboxes goes. Here are your line-finder switches and banks. Two rows over are the connector switches. Over there in the back and hanging from the ceiling are the 1st and 5th selector switches."

"One of those battery chargers goes too, doesn't it?" Richard asked.

"Right, one of them, but I believe the batteries stay," Chris Bell told his brother.

"Tom, I believe this whole row in the middle, with the boxes of relays and square metal covers and other equipment, also goes," Andrew pointed out.

"Yes, and there's more," Robert continued, as he pointed to yet another row. "This whole row of metal boxes to produce the dial tone, ring back tone, busy tone, and the ringing voltage, all goes. Actually, everything in this row goes."

"Robert, what about the main frame?" Steven asked.

"Yeah, that too," Robert agreed. "The old one's on the left, and the new one's beside it on the right, and only the old one goes, of course."

"What about the cables up above in those racks?" Andrew asked Tom.

"I'm going to let my forcefield trace every wire connected to this discontinued equipment, and all necessary wires will automatically come with it, leaving all new wires beside it intact and on the cable racks."

"That's incredible!" Andrew declared. "But what about the cable racks themselves?"

"I believe they'll have to be left here," Tom admitted. "Chris and Richard, do you have access to any cable racks, or can you make some?"

"Oh yes," Richard replied. "That won't be any problem."

"Good."

They spent 20 minutes as they hurried about from one piece of equipment to another inside the building, making sure they didn't leave anything out. Robert and his friends were careful not to touch any of the new equipment for fear of leaving fingerprints. Mr. Mayfield, not having gone with the rest of them to see the Eagleville exchange back in March, was impressed with the amount of equipment it required to run a thousand-line telephone exchange. He walked between the rows, just looking at all of it.

"Okay, everyone," Tom announced. "We're ready. Robert, I want you and your friends to stand over in that space by the old main frame. Chris and Richard, stand behind me. I'm going to tag each piece of step office equipment with my walking staff, or wand, as you might call it, and will transport all of it by an older method. Actually, it's the same method that you and your friends use, Robert."

Next, Tom withdrew an envelope from his robe. He positioned the cashier's check for $250 so that it stuck part ways out of the envelope and set it on the floor at the end of one of the new rows of digital equipment.

Suddenly, everyone heard a faint on-off high pitched beeping sound coming from the new digital equipment.

"Uh-oh," Robert declared with some concern in his voice. "That sounds like an alarm."

Morris quickly became anxious. "Tom, I get the feeling that Allied Telecom workers will soon be here to answer that alarm."

"Yes, it sounds like someone has some line trouble," Tom agreed. "Well, they're not supposed to be here until 8 o'clock. It's only 7:30 right now."

"I know, but I don't think that crystal ball is always 100 percent accurate," Morris insisted. "I can feel that someone will be coming very soon."

"Okay. Everyone stand back," Tom ordered them. "Time is of the essence. Here goes!"

As soon as everyone had moved back against the back wall, he proceeded to tag each row that was to go, using his walking staff to direct the energy as needed. He never had to place his hands on either side of the rows, like Robert and his friends had expected he might. Over a period of 30 seconds, Tom tagged everything that was to go. As he tagged each piece, the familiar pink glow enveloped it, and the sound of whirring wind increased for each piece tagged. When the last piece was tagged, Tom meditated, and every piece of step office equipment left the Kingston Park telephone exchange simultaneously over a period of five seconds.

Immediately, Tom commanded everyone to return to the Earth museum on the Planet of the Islands. Tom, Chris, and Richard instantly disappeared while the others transported themselves, using the pink glow and the whirring wind.

Little did they realize that they had narrowly escaped being caught by an Allied Telecom employee who entered the building only two seconds after they had disappeared. As he was unlocking the door, he had wondered what

all of that whirring sound was. By the time he entered, the sound had just
ceased, and everyone was gone. Two fellow employees followed him inside.

"What in the world?!" the first one exclaimed, shocked beyond belief
when he noticed that all of the discontinued step office was completely gone.
"Where in the *world* is the old step office?"

"Let's call 911," another one suggested.

"How can this . . .?" the first one asked the others.

"I'm not believing this! This can't be," another one remarked.

"I don't know," the first one said, "but they sure did a neat job of it.
There isn't a single bracket or bolt left on the floor!"

"Hey! What's this?" the third one asked the others. He had found the
envelope with the cashier's check made out to Allied Telecom.

Meanwhile, Tom, Chris, and Richard were inside the Earth museum on
the Planet of the Islands, securing the equipment. Everything had successfully arrived to the forcefield that Tom had earlier placed inside the building,
and each piece or row was floating in mid-air. Robert and his friends had arrived just outside the building as Tom had requested, and they were now inside helping the others. They lowered the step office from the forcefield,
piece by piece and row by row, until all of it was sitting on the concrete
floor. As each piece was lowered, they bolted it to the floor. The entire step
office now sat intact, ready for use in Chris and Richard's Earth museum.

"Oh, this is excellent!" Richard declared. "Tom, I don't know how to thank you."

"It's quite all right," said Tom. "I'll bring my crew later this week, and we'll install two towers or two lines to your step office. One will link you to Earth, and the other will link you directly to us at Sirius B."

"That sounds amazing!" Chris Bell exclaimed. "I'm almost in disbelief that we actually have our step office. Thank you very much for your help."

"No, really, I want to thank you two for your willingness to have a complete step office and for making it possible for us at the Galactic Federation to connect our planet with yours."

"Well, it's been a real pleasure working with you," said Richard.

"The same is true for me," Chris Bell added.

"Yes, I also have enjoyed working with you," Tom admitted. "Anyway, I must return home and file a report to the Galactic Federation, informing them that the transportation of this equipment was a complete success. Like I said, my crew and I will return here in a few days to install the receiver-transmitter towers."

"See you later, Tom," said everyone.

Tom instantly vanished.

"Well, I guess we all better return home to Earth," said Steven. "It's been a very long day for some of us here, and my parents are expecting me home for supper tonight."

"I guess the same is true for all of us," William agreed.

"Our parents only think we met this afternoon to discuss our plans for this summer," Paul mentioned.

"Except for my parents," Robert added.

"Well, Chris and Richard," said Morris, "It's been a pleasure for us to work with you on this project. I'm sure we'll come back to see you later this summer."

"Give us a phone call when they connect you to our galactic communications device," Andrew requested.

"We certainly will."

"I can't wait to see the rest of your trees," said James.

"We'll be glad to show you," said Richard.

"Can I stay on?" James asked Chris and Richard. "My parents aren't expecting me for dinner like the others are."

"Sure," Richard consented. "Come on, and I'll show you around."

"I wish I could stay on," said Robert, "but I better go home and assure my parents that nothing went wrong on this project."

As Chris and Richard began to give James Westfield a tour of their arboretum, the others, including Mr. Mayfield, transported themselves back to Earth. Upon arriving in the Joslin's woods by the step office building, they walked to their cars and drove home.

Robert entered his home and told his parents the whole story while they ate supper. Weren't they relieved, especially his father, that everything had gone so smoothly. Robert didn't mention their fears that an Allied Telecom worker could have walked in and caught every one of them.

It had been a very long day for Robert and some of the others. All of them slept soundly at their separate homes for the night. Robert, being used to the time in England, awoke at 2 a.m., but he was so tired that he soon drifted off to sleep again. He awoke again shortly after 7 a.m.

It was Thursday, May 30, and he was looking forward to the adventures that he and his friends were going to have this summer. They were going to leave home in just a few days. He got up and walked into the kitchen and fixed himself a bowl of cereal. His parents were already up, watching the 7 a.m. national news. The usual take-it-for-granted news was being reported, and Robert, as usual, didn't pay it any attention. He went into the room next to the den and ate his cereal.

"Oh my goodness!" he suddenly heard his mother scream.

"What?!" Robert quickly answered with a tone of alarm in his voice.

"You're not going to believe it! Come in here now!" she ordered.

Robert rushed into the den and saw the report on the news.

"A most mysterious event has taken place in a small Southwest Georgia town called Kingston Park. Authorities are investigating the sudden and unexplained disappearance of some telephone central office equipment in . . ."

"Oh, no!" Robert exclaimed. "They'll . . ."

"Wait! Listen," his father requested.

"Here with us is Jerry Pike, a maintenance supervisor for Allied Telecom," said the reporter. "Mr. Pike, what do you make of all this?"

"At around 7:30 last night, I and two others went to answer an alarm for some line trouble with the new digital switch. As I was unlocking the door, I could hear a weird humming or whirring noise, but as soon as I had entered, the sound was gone. I don't know *what* that sound was! That was nothing compared to the surprise we got when we walked inside and found every scrap of the discontinued step office *gone*! There wasn't even a bolt or screw on the floor! They were very neat, whoever took it, because all of the new digital equipment was left intact and unharmed."

"Do you think that Allied Telecom is going to find the perpetrators and prosecute?" asked the reporter.

"No, I don't, because there was an anonymous cashier's check made out to Allied Telecom, paying for the old equipment," Mr. Pike replied.

"Is that so?" asked the reporter in a surprised tone.

"Yes. Whoever they were that took this equipment evidently meant no harm, as they left the digital equipment intact. Furthermore, they paid for the equipment, and I think they needed it for something because they left an explanatory note saying that it had been taken for top-secret reasons."

"Yes, but they didn't ask Allied Telecom before doing it," the reporter brought up.

"I know, but to be straightforward with you, no one at Allied Telecom cares anything about that old step office equipment, anyway, and we were just tickled to find it gone, to tell you the truth. It saved us from having to go to the trouble of having a tear-out crew come in here and manually tear it out. We're glad to have it all out of the way. Whoever wanted it that badly was welcome to it, as far as I was concerned. Like I say, since they paid for it, even though they didn't ask first, I'm sure that Allied Telecom is not going to press charges."

"How do you think they knew which building to come to or which town to find the step office equipment in?" the reporter asked.

"Oh, that's pretty easy. Whenever an exchange cuts over, it's usually in the newspaper, or word gets out, and everyone soon knows. Kingston Park cut over two nights ago, and like I say, that old equipment was in our way. It was crowded in here, having two exchanges in one building."

"I see," the reporter realized. "Well, thank you for your time, Mr. Pike."

"You're welcome."

"This is Irving Lawrence, reporting live from Kingston Park, Georgia."

★ ★ ★

"I can't believe that made national news!" Robert declared.

"Well, it did, and I'm glad we saw it," said his father. "It looks like you're safe. Allied Telecom is not going to press charges."

"Yes, that's a relief for me and all of the others," Robert admitted.

"Son, please don't get into any more projects that could possibly get you in trouble. You may not always be so lucky."

"Yes, I agree," he told his father. "I don't want to get in trouble either, and I'll make sure that we stick to adventures only."

"Very fine, son. I'm glad to hear that," Mr. Joslin told him with a sense of relief in his voice.

At that moment, the phone rang. Robert answered it. It was Steven.

"Robert, did you just see the national news?" Steven asked.

"I did. I couldn't believe it!"

"What a relief that we're off the hook!" Steven added.

"You got that right," Robert agreed.

They went on talking for a few minutes. Many of the others called, and those who had missed the broadcast soon found out the surprising and good news. James had spent the night with the Bells, as it turned out, and he returned home this morning, relieved to find out that all of them were off the hook.

Two days later, Chris and Richard called Robert by phone, informing him that Tom and his crew had successfully connected their exchange to the galactic communications device. They had a little trouble supplying the power to operate the whole exchange, but after some help from Tom and his crew, they managed to get the necessary power by means of solar panels and batteries.

This was, by far, the most distant phone call that had ever been placed, as far as Robert knew, and there would possibly be even more distant calls placed in the future.

12 The Trip to Sirius B

It was Monday, June 3, and everyone was now packed and ready to go. The weather was hot and humid as the sun rose and shined through the hazy blue sky, which was typical for Tennessee's summers. Robert had his 1979 Ford LTD wagon all ready to go, and Paul's father had loaned a trailer to them for their trip. Robert felt a little strange, borrowing a trailer when he knew that they were just going to park the car and hide it anyway. How nice it would be, he thought, if they all could just tell their parents the real truth, but they couldn't afford to risk the exposure and publicity that would likely befall them.

Robert's friends arrived between 7 a.m. and 8 a.m., their parents having brought them. They loaded their backpacks and gear into the car and trailer. It was somewhat of an emotional scene with the goodbyes and farewells as their parents saw them loading the car to leave. When all the farewells were said, the eight of them climbed into Robert's car, and they drove out of the Joslin's long driveway.

Once out of sight, Robert picked up speed to be sure they would stay ahead of and out of sight of any possible parents who might have immediately gotten into their cars to also leave. At the road, he turned right and drove the two miles around to the Joslin's woods where he entered on their dirt lane. They had not been caught, and they drove the mile through woods on this narrow winding dirt lane, emerging from the woods at the step office building. He carefully checked that no one was watching and drove his car and trailer into the side hall of the big barn and parked. All of them got out, taking their backpacks with them. Next, they hid the car by throwing down some old bales of hay and straw from the loft and surrounded the car and trailer entirely. Once Robert was satisfied, he announced, "Okay, let's *really* leave."

"All of us know the location where we're going, right?" Morris checked.

"Right, the telephone station at Sirius B," Paul confirmed.

"Is everyone ready?" Robert asked.

All of them answered yes, so they proceeded to transport themselves. The pink glow and whirring wind overcame them, and they, in seconds, arrived on planet Sirius B. It was mid-day there, and the weather was hot and dry. The sky was a lighter color and had more of a reddish tinge to it than the blue sky of Earth. The terrain was somewhat hilly with valleys and coves in several directions. Much of it was reddish-orange in color. They had arrived on top of a small hill next to the receiver-transmitter tower and the small building by it.

Tamarisk shrubs (*Tamarix* genus) grew here and there along with Juniper-like shrubs. Various other desert-like plants grew in the vicinity including Cactus. As they looked around them, peering into the valleys and coves below, several groves or clusters of these coniferous-like shrubs could be seen. Many of them grew on the hillsides between the many red rounded boulders also imbedded in these hillsides.

"Wow! We're really here!" Andrew exclaimed.

"I'll say!" Steven agreed.

"Yes, we made it," said Robert. "Here, let's go see the operator and have her send for Tom."

They walked over to the small building and were greeted by a female Sirian in a white robe that looked less elaborate than Tom's.

"You must be the group of teenagers from Earth," she said.

"That's right," Robert answered.

"Tom has told me so much about you and your wonderful help in making actual communication possible with the people of Earth."

"Oh really?" Morris asked.

"Oh yes," she answered. "Anyway, I'm Manta, and I'm very pleased to meet you all. Tom has said you are just beginning your summer travels."

"That's true for some of us like me," William answered. "We just began today."

"Well, I'm sure you'll have a wonderful and unique time. Let me send for Tom, now." She meditated for 10 seconds, and Tom made his sudden and silent appearance just outside the building 20 seconds later.

As he approached them, he said, "Hello, everyone. Welcome to Sirius B."

"Thanks, Tom," said Robert.

"I'm glad you've chosen to come visit," Tom kindly told them. "I'm sure you're going to have some wonderful adventures during your summer holidays. By the way, where's Mr. Mayfield? Didn't he come along with you?"

"He's on the Planet of the Islands," Robert answered. "I spoke with him just a couple of days ago, and he decided to spend the summer there, exploring the area and going fishing. I went with him and saw to it that he arrived okay. If he has any trouble or something like that, he can always use the telephone at the Bell's Earth museum to call home to Earth."

"True enough," Tom agreed. "I'm happy for him and am sure he will have a great time."

"What do you suggest we do with our time here?" Chris asked.

"Well, the first thing I suggest is for you all to come to my place of residence and spend the night. I'll tell you more about our planet and what it's like here."

"Where do you live?" Andrew wanted to know.

"I live, in your units, around 20 kilometers from here in an underground dwelling."

"Underground?" Andrew asked with surprise.

"Yes," Tom answered. "Almost all of us do, as it's quite hot here. Most of Sirius B is a desert environment, which by now, I'm sure you've guessed."

"Yes, we've noticed," said Morris.

"Anyway," Tom offered, "I'll transmit the visual image of the aboveground scene just outside my residence, and we'll transport ourselves there." He meditated briefly, and everyone soon received the image. "Does everyone have it now?"

Everyone answered yes. With that confirmed, Tom and the eight of them transported themselves to his place of residence.

As soon as everyone had materialized, Steven commented, "This is really a pretty place, and these rocks are so red!"

"We have a lot of iron in our rocks and soil here," Tom explained. "Come on inside and have a rest for a while."

They obliged and followed him inside. Tom lived by himself, never having mated with anyone, and he therefore didn't have a family. The dwelling consisted of three medium-size rooms carved out of the deep red rock. It was a beautiful place, and the furniture was simple and ordinary. There were a few natural rock shelves carved into the walls, and these shelves contained some of his material possessions, including two natural quartz crystals.

"Oh, you have more crystals!" Morris remarked upon noticing them.

"Oh yes," Tom admitted, "but no round ones like yours."

"Then why did you give me your only round one?" Morris asked him.

"Oh, I greatly benefited by having done that," he explained. "My transaction with you has brought lots of progress to our race, and I'm not talking about technological progress because that depletes natural resources. Think about it. Because of my transaction with you, the galactic communications device has been built, and now, we Sirians have a direct link to Earth through their telephone network. The communication barrier we were experiencing has been overcome, thanks to your help, all of you. This has been a great time for all of us here, and my mission is accomplished."

"So, back on Earth," Steven brought up, "we might say that your whole purpose has been a mission of a galactic salesman."

Everyone had a good laugh at Steven's cleverly worded phrase, and after the laughter died down, Tom said, "That's very true indeed. You're very perceptive to realize that."

"Thanks," said Steven.

"Tell us about your two crystals here," Robert requested.

Tom walked over to his natural rock shelf and picked them up. Each one was the size of a hand. "This one is called red quartz, as it has a lot of iron in it. It is native to this planet and comes in the form of large geodes. This is part of the inside of a geode." He showed it to them, and each one of them looked at it and its dazzling red display of colors. It was a very unique crystal that looked like nothing any of them had ever seen on Earth. Its main feature was the pyramid-shaped point in the center of it, and it was not artificially cut that way.

Next, Tom handed them a purple crystal. "This one, you are probably more familiar with. It's called Amethyst and is from Brazil." Everyone looked at it, also. Tom continued. "I keep these crystals because they most closely fit my vibrations, and they help me be better able to think and to stay attuned to myself, my surroundings, and other people."

"Very interesting," Andrew remarked.

Paul had an uneasy look on his face, and Tom picked up on it and asked, "Paul, is there something you want to say to us about these crystals?"

"No, nothing really," he commented.

"Yes there is," Tom insisted. "You want to make a comment about my red one, don't you."

Paul gave him a look of complete surprise. "How did you know?"

"Remember, I read people's minds," Tom reminded him.

"Go ahead, Paul," Robert urged him. "Tell him what you're thinking. The rest of us would like to know."

"All right," he agreed, "I'll tell. Tom, back on Earth, the color red is associated with evil or dark forces. Some say it represents 'Satan'."

"That's what I thought you'd say," said Tom. "I can tell you all this much. At least from the standpoint of everyone here on Sirius B, colors have no bearing on whether something is good or bad. We 20 million humans operate only with the intention of good, and colors make no difference to us. As you've certainly noticed, we have a lot of iron in our rocks and soil. So, naturally, our rocks and crystals will be of reddish color.

"I believe you may know that many Earthlings," Tom went on, "associate the color red with evil because many believe that the entity that they call 'Satan' lives deep down within the Earth and lives among fire, which has a reddish color. It's a shame that so many people rule out red just because of their belief systems."

"You know," Paul realized, "I never gave it much thought before, but you're right, Tom. Associating red with evil is a ridiculous concept."

"Yes, and red," Tom told everyone, "like any other color, is a beautiful color."

"Anyway," said Tom, now changing the subject, "enough of that. Come on outside, and I'll show you around and tell you a little bit about our planet and star system."

They all went outside and climbed a nearby hill. When they reached the top, Tom began explaining about the Sirius star system. "The Sirius star system is a binary star system, as you may already know. We are 8.8 light years away from Earth. This planet goes around the star, Sirius B, which is a type A white dwarf star, and this is the only planet that revolves around it, completing a revolution in around four Earth days. We are 7,800,000 kilometers from the Sirius B star.

"As we are in a binary star system, we receive most of our light and energy from Sirius A, which is a type A hot white star. It takes two months for our planet to spin on its axis, but that doesn't matter since our planet revolves around Sirius B star in just four days. I'm sure it's strange compared to Earth, but it works fine for us, and we've adapted to it fairly well. Like I said, we are the only planet around Sirius B star, and Sirius A has no planets. Also, the two stars, Sirius A and Sirius B, sort of revolve around each other like two dogs chasing after or circling around each other. I believe some people on Earth call Sirius A the dog star. Anyway, due to the complex interaction between Sirius A and Sirius B, we actually have, on average, days and nights that are four Earth days long each."

"You know," said Morris, "I believe I've heard that before, that Sirius A is called the dog star."

"This planet is smaller than Earth," Tom continued, "having a circumference of around 16,000 kilometers, but it is more dense and therefore has nearly the same gravitational attraction as that of Earth. As you already noticed, our mean temperature is higher than that of Earth's, and we therefore have a desert-like environment. Our temperatures here on Sirius B do not vary to such extremes due partly to the fact that our off inclination is 14.38 degrees, less than yours on Earth of 23 degrees."

"Are there any oceans or seas?" Morris inquired.

"There are no oceans or seas, large ones, that is, but at our north and south poles, there are a few large lakes, some of them nearly 100 kilometers across. Most of them exist in the north at a higher altitude, nestled within a beautiful mountain range. The most beautiful one is near our north pole at a latitude of around 85 degrees north. Even though the terrain is nearly tree-less, there is an abundance of surface water, and the ground and rocks stay moist most of the time."

"I'd like to go there and have a good look at that," Robert mentioned.

"Yes, definitely go there, all of you," Tom urged them, "and visit the mountains and lakes for several days."

"Tell us about the trees and plants here," James inquired.

"Right," said Tom, "our main trees are coniferous-like, the main ones being Tamarisks and Cypress-Pines, both native to your planet Earth. When humans settled here 4 million years ago, they visited Earth and brought some specimens here to this planet. At the same time, they took specimens of many different varieties of Cactus plants, native to here, and planted them in the drier climates of Earth."

"Oh, yeah!" Morris exclaimed. "That makes sense, because I read an article not too long ago that said that there was no fossil evidence for Cacti. That would explain it, even though Earth has many varieties."

"Yes," agreed Tom. "It's amazing what people can learn by travelling and talking to others."

Meanwhile, James was stunned with the knowledge Tom had just told him, and he pondered for a few moments while the new information sank in. "That's amazing!" he came around to declare. "I'm glad I asked you, Tom."

"How do you have enough water for everyone?" Paul asked.

"Oh, that's not a problem since we only have 20 million people on this entire planet," Tom answered. "However, we do have an abundance of water underground, and to further add, we monitor it to make sure that it re-supplies itself naturally at a faster rate than we consume it. Our wells go down a few hundred meters into the ground, and we use them to irrigate our gardens and small crops in places."

"Is there any native wildlife?" William asked.

"We humans are the only mammals on this whole planet, and as you know, we are not endemic to this planet. The dominant wildlife is mostly reptilian, and most of them are various forms of lizards. Their ancestors go back millions of years, both here and on Earth, and they easily adapt to whatever environment they live in."

"Are there any insects?" Robert asked.

"Yes, there are certain types here, but not as many as on Earth. One of interest is in the bee family, and we call them Ariaba bees. They are smaller than the common honey bee of Earth, but they are stingless."

"That must be nice," Steven commented.

"Yes, it is," Tom agreed, "and they also make honey in a fairly similar manner to the honey bees of Earth."

"I assume that all of this transference of life was done by teleportation?" Andrew asked.

"That's correct," Tom confirmed. "We never have used spacecrafts since, to us, having the ability to teleport ourselves or other objects, the use of spacecrafts would be absurd." All of them pretty much agreed with that, even though they made no comment.

The terrain was far from flat where Tom lived. There were plenty of hills, gullies, and small valleys in all directions. Cactus plants grew more on the hillsides while Tamarisks and Cypress-Pine shrubs (*Callitris* genus) grew more in the protected areas. Here and there, they would see a lizard scurry across the ground, racing from the shelter of one rock to another. In addition to the shrubs and Cacti, there were some other plants that were not really Yucca-like but still somewhat similar to them. They had long, pointed, broad and drought-resistant leaves that were thick like that of a Yucca plant.

"What are those broad-leafed plants?" James asked. "I've never seen anything like them before."

"Those are what we would best call in your language a Xantoe," Tom answered. "They're native to Sirius B, and I don't believe any specimens have ever been taken to Earth. I'm glad we have them because they are the only type of broad-leafed shrub on this entire planet."

"This planet doesn't have the variety of life that Earth has," Robert commented.

"That's true," Tom admitted. "Your planet Earth is one the most extraordinary planets in the entire universe, and as one looks over your whole planet, there are different areas that compare to almost every planet in the universe, both in appearance and in the lifeforms that they have."

"That's great!" Steven remarked.

"I know," said Tom remorsefully, "but it grieves me that mankind on Earth is ever more quickly using up the natural resources there and that native lifeforms of all types are being swept aside and/or obliterated in certain areas. Earth has been like a museum of life for the whole universe, or at least this galaxy, and I'm worried it may soon be all gone."

Nearly everyone felt a sharp sense of emotion at what Tom had just said. His words hit home, and they thought, *Why has mankind been scurrying around, using up so many natural resources when there might be a much better and more conservative way to still enjoy the luxuries of life?*

"Tell you what," Andrew suggested. "Maybe now, since you Sirians are linked up to Earth's telephone network, you all can help awaken them to realize your good intentions and cause it to turn for the better."

"Yes," Tom agreed, "I believe we may be able to. That, my friends, is the rest of my mission, to save planet Earth from destruction. I only hope that I and others succeed in this task before it is too late."

Tom took them on a walk around the vicinity, telling them more about Sirius B. He lived several kilometers from the nearest neighbor, as did many of the Sirians. However, there were some towns where many lived, and they all lived underground. He led them into one small cove just down from his residence, and they all picked vegetables out of his garden. Once finished, they returned to his underground residence, and he proceeded to cook supper for all of them.

They seated themselves at a large table inside his kitchen-dining room. He cooked over a fire, and the smoke was vented through a vertical shaft to the air above ground. "Most of the time," Tom explained, "I just mix my vegetables and eat them uncooked, but knowing how Earthlings usually cook their food, I've decided to do the same for you. Even though I live alone, I have numerous guests come to visit from time to time, which explains why I have such a large table."

"Yes, we were wondering that," Steven responded.

"There's a friend of mine I'd like you to meet," Tom later announced when he had just about finished cooking supper. "Let me call him." Everyone instinctively expected him to use a telephone to dial his number, but then they realized differently when Tom appeared to meditate silently, calling his friend by mental telepathy.

"Oh, yeah," William realized. "I keep forgetting that they don't need phones up here, except to call people on Earth."

Thirty seconds later, a young man with dark brown, medium-length hair, appearing to be in his twenties, instantly appeared in the room. They were a little startled by his sudden appearance.

"My friends," Tom announced, "I want you to meet Caymar, a very good friend of mine. He is the one who actually suggested that I make a deal concerning my former crystal ball, now Morris' crystal ball."

"Is that right?" Morris eagerly asked.

"That's true," Caymar verified. "I made that suggestion nearly half an Earth year ago during a meeting of 12 of us. Anyway, I'm pleased to meet you all. Tom has been very praising of all the help you have been in making his proposed galactic communications device a physical reality. All of us were literally overjoyed that it actually came into existence."

They all introduced themselves, and when they shook hands, a strong sense of true friendship was transferred from Caymar and felt by the eight of them. Caymar's handshake was neither a vice grip nor too weak, and when he shook hands with them, the best possible combination of friendship and peace of mind was immediately felt. Everyone felt at ease around him, and it was as if they had known him for years. For the next several hours, they enjoyed visiting, exchanging ideas, and finding out more about each other's worlds.

A few minutes after they had been visiting and talking, Morris started thinking. Then something dawned on him. "Caymar," he spoke out, also getting everyone else's attention at the same time.

"Yes," he answered.

"You know, I believe I actually heard part of the conversation going on during that meeting of 12 you just spoke about. Robert, William," Morris now directed at them, "do you remember when we were sledding down Versailles Hill this past January?"

"Yes," Robert and William both answered.

"And I'm sure you remember when I heard that faint message from what I thought was another star system, right as we were on the hilltop."

"Oh yes, we do," Robert answered.

"Tom, was that meeting about proposing a way to communicate with Earthlings with whom you had lost contact?" Morris asked. "Further, I believe a group of 10 people was needed to help on a project of some sort, am I right?"

"Yes," Tom verified, "we had a major meeting of 12 of us, and it *was* in later January, Earth time. That's when we made the initial plans for the galactic communications device."

"And we decided what to do with your former crystal ball," Caymar said to Tom.

"You mean you tuned into and *heard* that?" Tom asked Morris with surprise.

"Yes, it was sort of like a ringing in my ear, and I faintly heard voices in my head. I didn't hear very much of it before it faded, and I lost it."

"Well, isn't that amazing!" Tom declared. "I knew I gave my crystal ball to the right person; you, that is."

"That proves you're definitely authentic," Paul said to Morris.

"More than that," Caymar added, "Morris has the ability to communicate telepathically, a rare thing among Earthlings."

"I'll say!" William agreed.

Caymar, as they found out, was one of Tom's nearest neighbors, living only a few kilometers away in the next range of hills. He and Tom helped each other out on many things, and even though they weren't brothers or close relatives, it was as if they were.

"Tell you what," Caymar offered. "While you're here on Sirius B, I highly recommend your visiting and walking around the magnificent mountains and lakes in the far north."

"Oh, yeah," Robert recalled, "Tom was telling us a little about that."

"Well, it's one of the most beautiful areas to visit on this planet, and if you like, I'll be glad to come with you and show you around for several days. After all, travelling like you're doing opens the mind."

"Thanks, Caymar," said Morris, "and I do agree with you. Travelling opens the mind."

"That's right," Robert agreed. "Might I add, travelling opens the mind to new ideas."

"Not only that," Caymar continued, "travelling is an education in itself."

"Yes, please do come with us and show us around the far north," Steven insisted.

"All right, if you like," Caymar offered, "we'll leave here in the morning."

"Sounds good," said Paul. "We're ready."

As they continued visiting, Tom served all of them supper. Robert and his friends were a little surprised at the blandness of the vegetable mixture, but they ate well, as they didn't want to be hungry later. They were glad, however, that they had brought just over a week's supply of Earth food with them. James had popped down to Devonport, Tasmania a couple of days earlier and had purchased all of the groceries needed. When they would run low on food, James had agreed he would return to Tasmania to buy more.

They all had a good night's rest, and they noticed how peaceful and quiet it was, sleeping underground in what they considered to be a cave. Tom had them put out their bedrolls and sleeping bags on the living room floor. He would have joined them and Caymar for the next several days in the far north, but he had some work to do with the council and also had to make some transactions.

The next morning was a beautiful and sunny day. In actuality, the sun (Sirius A) never set, but Tom and the others on planet Sirius B were used to sleeping several hours out of every 25 hours. The star, Sirius B, stood out like a large moon in appearance, and it gave off a faint white glow in comparison to Sirius A.

Robert and his friends pulled some breakfast out of their backpacks and ate some cereal and fruit. Tom had another serving of the vegetable mixture, and so did Caymar.

As soon as they finished breakfast, Caymar announced, "Now everyone, I am going to transmit to you the scene where we will begin our walk of several days." He meditated and everyone received a visual image of a fairly level landscape dotted with occasional coniferous-like shrubs. The scene was at the foot of a very large mountain that loomed ahead of them. "You are looking at the southern edge of the mountain ranges of the far north. We will arrive at the place you've just seen, and we'll begin our several days' walk from there. Has everyone received the image?"

Everyone answered yes.

"Good, I'm ready when you are," said Caymar.

They said goodbye to Tom and thanked him for his kind hospitality, and they all walked outside, their backpacks on their backs. Once outside, they proceeded to transport themselves to the far north.

A few seconds later, they all materialized at the location Caymar had shown them. The weather was much cooler and was a welcome relief to the hot dry climate much further south from where they had just left.

"Huh!" Steven exclaimed. "The ground is actually moist here."

"Yes, there is quite an abundance of water up here," Caymar informed them. "Also, since the rays of Sirius A are never direct, the result is a much cooler climate. The same is true in the far south, but the scenery here in the north is far more spectacular. The water from here flows underground, and it supplies everyone across the whole planet."

"Why didn't you have us materialize up there near the mountaintop?" James asked.

"If we were to materialize up there," Caymar explained, "it would take all the fun out of climbing this entire mountain. Besides, there is much to observe and learn about while we make the climb through this day. This will give us a sense of adventure and accomplishment."

"It's just such a long ways," James whined.

"And you were the one who boasted about how the climb out of the Ballroom Forest was just a bit of a rough section," Robert reminded him. "So, what are you complaining for?"

"Let's look at it this way," Caymar told them. "Everyone will have something to boast about when we reach the top. Like I said, you'll feel a sense of accomplishment."

Robert looked way up at the top of the mountain and could just see a little snow near one of the peaks. "Is that snow way up there?"

"That it is," Caymar confirmed.

"I don't know about you all," Robert said to the others, "but I'm going for the adventure. I wouldn't miss this chance for anything." With that said, all of them began the climb up the fairly steep rocky slopes.

"At what altitude is the valley or plains, as you may call them?" Andrew asked.

"Well, that's a difficult one to determine since our planet has no oceans to reference elevation to," Caymar replied. "However, I can tell you that the total elevation difference from the plains we just left to the highest peak is around 5,000 meters."

"Wow!" Andrew exclaimed. "Will there be enough air on top for us to breathe?"

"Oh yes, there's still enough air on top to breathe," Caymar assured him.

"How far are we from the area where you and Tom live?" Paul asked.

"We live almost due south from here, and we live approximately 25 degrees north of the equator. So, the distance is around 3,000 kilometers from here."

They spent all day climbing the mountain, noticing that the temperature gradually became cooler as they ascended. Sirius A hung low in the sky for the whole time. The rocks and soil were not nearly so red as they were further south where Tom and Caymar lived. As they climbed, the redness in the rocks became even more faint, and the dominant color was now a light orange. Much of the ground was moist but almost never muddy, and there were occasional streams to cross as well. In a few selected areas that were wetter, there were shrubs, most of them being Tamarisks. No Cactus plants grew in the far north at all.

As they reached higher altitude, the slope of the terrain finally gave way to more level ground, at least for a while. It was a relief to them, as they had been hiking for a total of eight hours, and they had climbed a total of 2,000 meters in altitude, still less than halfway to the summit.

"I'm telling you what," William remarked. "That sure was a long steady climb!"

"Yeah, no kidding!" Steven agreed. "I'm tuckered out."

"Well, at least that part's behind us, and we've conquered it," said Paul.

They looked behind them from where they had just come. The plains stretched out from the foot of this large mountain range. They looked flat and desolate, and they faded into the distant hazy horizon.

"Caymar," Robert asked, "Are there any people living down there on those plains?"

"Almost no one," he answered.

"Why would that be?" Robert wanted to know. "The ground is wet enough."

"That's true," Caymar admitted, "but I'm sure you notice how desolate the terrain is. There is almost no plantlife further away from this mountain range."

"Why's that?" Andrew now asked.

"I don't believe the soil is quite right for it," he answered. "Further, the energy must not be right to support growth. So, nothing grows there."

"That is strange," Chris remarked.

"There is still a lot that we don't know," Caymar informed them.

They proceeded a little further, and the terrain leveled into a small cove. Caymar announced that they would set up camp and rest for the night, only Sirius A would not be setting. However, it passed behind the peaks of the mountain range, affording them shade for the next several hours. A small stream ran nearby, and everyone went to collect water.

Robert and his friends unpacked their backpacks and set up their tents on the most level places they could find. Next, they prepared a supper over their EPI gas stoves and ate well, for they were hungry after the long climb. Caymar had also brought a backpack, and it was made on planet Earth. Tom had obtained it for him. His food consisted only of a mixture of chopped up vegetables that were uncooked.

"How do you stand to eat that stuff?" Steven asked him.

"To us, it's quite good. It keeps our energy flowing and doesn't interfere with our ability to think, which many prepared foods of Earth do."

"Is that right?" Steven asked.

"Yes, that's right," Caymar confirmed. "Many prepared foods have too much salt, sugar, or food additives. If I were to eat that food, I would notice a big difference in my clarity and ability to think."

"I don't have any trouble thinking, and I eat anything!" Steven insisted in a defensive manner.

"That's true," said Caymar, "and I can see that you are one of the luckier ones who aren't sensitive to foods. However, you may not always be if you continue to eat anything."

"Actually," Robert brought up, "I do notice a difference in my mental awareness, depending on what foods I eat. Some foods make me feel ill, and I'll bet food additives are the main cause. I'll have to be more careful of what I eat in the future."

"I'd say I agree with you," said William.

"I don't know about you all," Paul added, "but food means a lot to me. I love to eat."

"I didn't imply that I didn't like to eat," said Robert. "It's just that I need to be careful and eat the right things that are good for me. After all, a person is what he eats."

"That's very true," said Caymar.

"Robert, why not enjoy life and eat whatever is available?" Andrew asked him.

"Because if I did that, I would *not* enjoy life, and that's because the foods I would eat would make me feel ill. You know as well as I do that a person cannot enjoy life at all when he's sick."

"Yes, you have a point there," Andrew agreed.

"Down in Australia," James mentioned, "they have strict rules about what food additives get put into certain foods, and there is better quality food available there than in the States, from what I've noticed so far."

They carried on about food, its importance, food additives, and so on. Finally, everyone was tired enough to sleep for the next eight hours.

Sirius A just peeked around the right side of the mountain peaks, signalling to everyone to get up and continue climbing the mountain. They had breakfast, packed up, and left the nice sheltered cove. The day was beautiful with not a cloud in the sky.

For four more hours, they continued climbing up the seemingly endless slope. The coniferous-like shrubs became smaller and more sparse until, finally, there was no plantlife. In places, the rocks were wet, and most of them were of a light orange color. They realized that they were above the tree line, if that's what it would be called on this planet.

Finally, the steady slope arrived to a gentle and narrow ledge that was around the width of a one-lane road. On the upper side of this narrow ledge, between them and the upper slopes of the mountain, stood a vertical wall or cliff blocking their continued ascent. They turned left and walked along this ledge to hopefully find a way to negotiate their way around or over this seemingly impenetrable cliff. As they continued along, they soon found a gap that allowed them to pass between the rock faces. It was a fairly wide gap at five meters, but it had not been visible until they were upon it. Caymar already knew of this gap but had not said anything.

From there, they left the ledge and picked their way through a fairly treacherous boulder field. All of the rock was orange in color, and some of the boulders were the size of cars. The gap veered to the right, and they followed it and ascended, picking their way over large and small boulders. To their right was a sheer rock face, and because it was there, it had served to catch all of these boulders when they had tumbled down from the higher slopes over the past many years. In some ways, this area was scenic, and most of them considered it an adventure to negotiate this boulder field.

After around 100 meters of climbing, there was another rock face in front of them. However, to their left, the gentle slope continued, and they turned in that direction, still picking their way over orange boulders. Finally, after a few hundred more meters, they left the boulders, and the terrain became easier.

The grade of the slope became more gentle as they continued ascending, and they noticed that the ground was almost entirely moist and was covered with wet shale-like rocks, quite a change from the orange boulders that they had just climbed over. These wet rocks were mostly flat and mostly dark gray in color, and they shined with a dull finish as the light of Sirius A struck their surfaces. Water seeped out of the ground in many places, but it was not muddy due to the many rocks covering the ground.

"How high up do you think we are now?" Robert asked.

"I'd say we've climbed anywhere from 1,200 to 1,500 meters this morning," Caymar answered.

Robert looked at his watch. "Earth time, it's 2 p.m., and it's Wednesday, June 5th."

"There's a stone hut around two kilometers further up this slope," Caymar informed everyone. "I recommend we stay there and set up camp before going any further."

"Sounds good to me," William agreed.

They continued ascending the gentle slope, all of which was covered with wet shiny rocks. After nearly an hour of walking, the stone hut came into view. Further up, they could see the summit of the mountain, its upper slopes and peaks covered with snow in places.

"How did that stone hut get put there?" Morris asked.

"Oh, many of us on Sirius B like to get away from our normal routine," Caymar replied. "This is a great place for us to come and relax and enjoy something different. It's a lot cooler here, and we feel refreshed by the time we return to our normal lives. To answer your question, a group of us met here several years ago and built this shelter for our convenience and also for emergency use if necessary."

They were now within 100 meters of the stone hut. Just briefly after Caymar had finished answering Morris' question, they suddenly heard the most awful rumbling and crashing sounds imaginable, coming from further up the mountain. All of them looked up.

"Oh law!" Robert quietly exclaimed.

"Uh-oh!" Steven remarked.

"Quick! Run for the shelter!" Caymar commanded.

A whole mass of rocks and boulders of various sizes was tumbling down the steep mountainside directly toward them from further up. Everyone was struck with sudden terror, and they quickly made a run for the stone shelter, hoping to reach it before the mass of boulders did. If they could just reach the lower side of the shelter, they were thinking, then the boulders would go around them and miss them. Some of the boulders were the size of small cars, and the mass of them was quickly approaching.

Thoughts were constantly racing through their minds as they struggled with all their might to reach the stone shelter in time. They barely made it, and Chris had a narrow escape, having been the last one to reach safety. A boulder around one meter in diameter just barely missed him, whizzing by him in excess of 100 km/h. The burst of wind it created nearly knocked him down, but he didn't fall, and he managed to reach safety.

"Golly! What was that?" Chris exclaimed just as he reached the others now crouched by the lower wall of the shelter.

"You almost bit the dust!" Paul informed him. "That boulder barely missed you!"

Chris had not actually realized how close it had been for him. All he had noticed was the sudden burst of wind on him.

"Really?" Chris asked.

"Yes, really," William confirmed. "I saw it, too. It was very close."

Most of the rocks missed the shelter, passing by on the uphill side of it, but a few of them slammed into the upper outside wall, and some of them, like the one that barely missed Chris, passed on the downhill side of the shelter. The eight of them watched as the mass of boulders tumbled further down the slopes that they had just ascended. It was quite a spectacle, seeing how they violently bounced their way downhill, some of them staying airborne most of the time. Finally, they passed out of sight, but the rumbling could be heard for several minutes way below.

As they collected their thoughts, James commented, "I'm thanking my lucky stars that we didn't arrive here any later. That lot of boulders would have put us away for sure, if we had still been coming up that slope!"

"I'm telling you what," William added. "That was a close one for all of us!"

Morris looked around. "Where's Caymar?" he asked the others.

They looked around and also realized that he was nowhere to be seen.

"I don't see him either," said Robert.

"He must have teleported himself out of here," Steven declared.

"Why didn't *we* think of that?" Andrew asked everyone.

"I guess we were so concerned about reaching safety that transporting ourselves out of here just slipped our minds," Morris replied.

"Well, we're safe now," Robert assured everyone, "but if we run into any more problems, let's always remember that we have the gift of transporting ourselves out of wherever we may be."

"Where's the door to this hut?" Paul asked, not having seen it at all.

"It must be on the uphill side," said William.

About this time, Caymar walked around from the upper side of the shelter and saw that all eight of them were crouched by the stone wall and were fine. "Oh, thank heavens you are all right. Sorry, I forgot to mention or remind you to transport yourselves out of that dangerous situation."

"That's okay," said Steven. "At least we're okay now, and it's behind us."

Everyone got up and followed Caymar to the door on the upper side of the shelter and entered it. Inside, there were stone benches lining the walls, and there was a fairly large table on the downhill side. The shelter had one window, also on the downhill side, and it afforded spectacular views down the mountain and of the other mountains in the distance. They were now nearly 4,000 meters above the valley floor where they had begun their climb. The summit of the mountain appeared to be an additional 1,000 meters further up.

As they rested inside with the narrow escape still fresh on their minds, William declared, "Boy, that was *some* rock storm!"

"Yeah, really!" Paul agreed. "That's a good name for it too. Rock storm."

"I'd say we're going to have some hair-raising stories to take back home with us," said Robert.

"Yes, but remember," Morris reminded, "we can't tell anyone that it was here, but instead that it was somewhere out West."

"Yes, of course," said Robert. "We'll just say it was somewhere like Mt. Shasta in California."

"How often does this sort of rock storm happen up here?" James asked Caymar.

"A rock storm of the scale you just saw occurs a few times a year," he replied. "When the conditions are right, such as temperature and the angle of light from Sirius A, the snow melts and starts an avalanche. As the snow slides, it dislodges rocks and boulders, and down they all come."

"How does this hut survive all that?" Robert asked.

"We built it with thick walls, as you can see, and we come up here from time to time and keep it maintained," he explained. "As you notice, we didn't install any windows on the side of the hut facing the upper side of this mountain, and now you know the obvious reason why we didn't."

"Yes, that was very wise," Robert agreed.

"Does the sun ever set up here, I mean, Sirius A?" Chris asked.

"Since we are approximately 85 degrees north," Caymar explained, "it remains light for half a year at a time. Then it becomes dark and remains so for the other half."

"Then how can the Tamarisks and the others plants and shrubs near the foot of the mountain survive for that long a period of darkness?" James wanted to know.

"It snows a lot in this area during our winters, and the plants and shrubs just become dormant and hibernate, as you might call it. Think about it. Back on your Earth, many mountains become covered in heavy snowpacks, covering the younger trees for the entire winter. They do just fine, don't they?"

"That's true. You have a good point," James admitted.

"I don't know about the rest of you, but I'm starved," Paul announced to the others.

As he started digging food out of his pack, the others did the same.

Soon, Sirius A disappeared behind the mountain peak from which the rock storm had come. A mass of clouds entered the valley between them and the next set of mountain peaks. It was a spectacular sight as the clouds surrounded the distant mountains, their peaks exposed. The phenomenon caused the peaks to appear as if they were floating. All of them admired the view, and some of them went outside to have a better look at it.

"You know," Morris said to Robert as they were standing outside with some of the others, "I just realized that I haven't seen or heard any birds at all since we've been on this planet."

"Yeah, you're right. I haven't either," Robert agreed. "It's amazing what's taken for granted and how long it sometimes takes us to realize that something is missing."

"Hey Caymar!" Morris shouted into the hut, as he had remained inside. He came to the door, and Morris continued. "Are there no birds on this planet, because I haven't heard or seen any?"

"No, there aren't any at all," he answered. "There never have been any birds on this planet. At least, there is no fossil evidence of any having been here."

"Why weren't they brought here when some of Earth's trees were brought?" Morris asked.

"They were very careful about what they teleported here, and they must have had a good reason not to have brought birds. We've honored their decision and have never introduced them to this planet."

"That's too bad," Morris remarked.

"Oh, it's okay with us," said Caymar. "There are plenty of birds to enjoy on other worlds, and when we want to see some birds, we just teleport ourselves there and do so. Many of us take vacations to other worlds. Doing so expands our horizons and views."

They pondered what he had said and realized how wonderful this gift of transport really was. In addition to their adventures, this summer was going to be a wonderful experience. *How many Earthlings,* they wondered, *had the opportunity to expand their horizons to a galactic level?*

Both William and Chris had brought decks with them, and everyone decided to play some cards. After a while, tiredness set in. They laid out their bedrolls and sleeping bags on the hut's benches and went to sleep.

The next day started out cold. It had frosted while Sirius A had remained behind the mountain peak. As it peeked around the mountain's right side, the light struck the frosted rocks and created a dazzling display of reflections from their surfaces. The clouds still blanketed the valley below.

"This is incredible!" William remarked, as he stepped outside to admire the scenery.

"It's worth every bit of our climbing over the past two days to be able to see this," said Robert.

Caymar stepped outside to join them. "Views like this give us an exhilarating burst of energy. That's why I like coming up here and being in the mountains."

"Yes, I can see why you would," Paul agreed.

"I've rarely seen better than this, even in my dreams," Morris commented.

"What are the plans today?" Steven inquired.

"If you like, we'll climb to the summit," Caymar offered. "We can leave our packs here and return, or we can take them with us and continue further, going down the other side of the mountain and into the next valley."

"Let's take our packs with us and go for it," James eagerly urged everyone.

"I tell you, it's cold this morning!" Andrew declared, changing the subject.

"I know," agreed Robert, "but it will soon warm up."

They went back inside, ate some breakfast, packed their packs, and left. Caymar led the way as they continued ascending, leaving the stone hut behind.

The slope became steeper, and the rocky terrain continued to be wet. Soon, they reached patches of snow, and each patch became larger as they climbed higher up the mountain. The last kilometer of the ascent was completely snow-covered, and after struggling uphill, being careful not to fall on the wet, slippery snow, they arrived at the rocky, exposed peak. The summit was actually a rim of exposed jagged rocks that surrounded what appeared to be a snow-filled crater. The rim was 200 meters across, and they decided to walk out onto the snow that was filling the crater and explore the area.

They had climbed 1,000 meters in elevation from the hut and were a total of 5,000 meters above the valley floor where they had initially started.

"This looks a lot like an old volcano," Chris mentioned to Caymar.

"That's right," he told them. "This mountain range is old, however, and the volcanoes are now extinct."

"I have a headache," Robert announced.

"It's the high altitude," Caymar explained. "The air is thin up here. Take a lot of deep breaths, and your headache will go away."

Now that they were at the summit, they could see further into the mountain range. There were many snow-covered mountains, some jagged and some rounded, stretching to the horizon. In addition to that, Caymar told them that there were some beautiful lakes lying between some of the ranges, even though they couldn't yet see any. Between them and the next range further on, there was a fairly deep valley or gorge with a river running through it. It emptied to their left into the plains, 5,000 meters below them, and they could see those flat lands stretching for probably 100 kilometers into the horizon. To their right, up the gorge, they could hear the water falling off distant hillsides into the river.

"On the other side of the next mountain range is the largest lake on this planet," Caymar informed them. "If you like, we'll go there next."

"Yeah sure!" Steven remarked enthusiastically.

"Sounds good to me," William calmly agreed.

"Is it warm enough for swimming?" Andrew asked.

"I'm not sure, but I'd say it might be," Caymar answered.

"Good, let's go there next," said Robert.

Everyone took an hour's rest on this mountain summit, and they enjoyed the scenery while they ate some lunch. A cool breeze swept over them.

After lunch they explored more of the rim and played on the snowfield in the old crater. They noticed if they ran too much that they easily got out of breath. Finally, they were ready to leave.

Caymar led the way as they descended the steep side of the mountain on the other side from where they had come up. The next range of mountains was clearly visible nearly 15 kilometers away, and they were going to have to drop nearly 2,500 meters to cross the upper part of the gorge nearest them to access the next range. As they descended, they kept to the right.

It took them several hours to descend the 2,500 meters to their destination, and they stopped along the river. Most of the terrain was solid rock, but there were a few areas with silt deposits, and a few Tamarisk shrubs and other smaller plants were growing in these few select areas. Even in this gorge, none of the plants reached over two meters high, due to the harsh climate of the winters.

When they reached a nice large siltbed by the river, they decided to stop and set up camp, pitching their tents between the shrubs. The river flowed fast as it descended the steep valley, and the rush of water was enough to drown out other sounds. Most of them were pretty tired, so they ate some supper and went to sleep. Sirius A slid behind the next mountain range, giving them shade for the "night."

The next day was clear and sunny, and they got up, ate breakfast, and continued walking, with Caymar leading the way again. He knew the way to the largest lake, so they all let him be their guide. They appreciated his friendship and kindness, and they wondered how many people they knew back on Earth who would be kind enough to take a group of people hiking for several days and really enjoy doing it. Actually, they were able to think of some who they thought would have done so.

For several hours, they climbed several hundred meters in altitude, most of the time walking on fairly level terrain. At times, the grades were steeper. For the most part, they were crossing the upper part of the valley, which, oddly enough, was wider upstream from where they had camped. As they approached the steep sides of the next mountain range, they kept a little to the right, heading for a visible gap where they would climb and pass over into what lay beyond it.

When they reached the range, it still looked like a wall ahead of them, and they made a scramble for several hundred meters as they ascended it. As they picked their way over boulders lying here and there, they were cautious not to stumble or fall. When they crested, they discovered that the terrain did not drop back down like they had expected but continued ascending, only this time more gently. There was no view of any lake in sight.

"Where did you say the large lake was?" Robert asked Caymar.

"It's just over this next rise around a kilometer from here," he assured everyone.

At least the final ascent before reaching this large lake that Caymar was telling them about was a gentle one. They made their way across the wet, rocky terrain, mostly gently ascending and sometimes briefly descending. There were a few areas that were boggy, and small streams ran through the area as well. No plantlife grew anywhere, and most of the rocks were of a dark gray color.

They didn't know why, but they felt lighter than usual, and they sometimes ran across the rocks. They didn't even get out of breath. Finally, a kilometer after the gap, like Caymar had insisted, they came into view of the large lake, right as they crested a gentle rounded ridge of bedrock. Its shore was only 100 meters down the hill. It looked like a sea, as its waters stretched to the horizon. Small waves lapped the shoreline of gray sand.

They set down their packs and ran for the water's edge. As they entered, it felt somewhat cold, but they went swimming anyway. Robert was the first one to taste the fresh water, expecting it to be salty like Earth's oceans.

"Say! This water's dilute," Robert remarked.

"That's true," Caymar agreed. "Our lakes and waters are not nearly as salty as Earth's. This lake does have a slight amount of salt, but it probably seems like nothing compared to Earth's oceans."

The waves were too small to ride or to do any body surfing, but they did enjoy a nice swim for some time. The water was perfectly clear and appeared to have a tinge of blue to it, similar to Earth's waters.

"Are there any fish in this lake?" Paul asked.

"Yes, there are, actually," he answered. "Did any of you bring a fishing rod and line?"

"No, none of us did," Paul admitted. "We didn't even think about fishing. I guess we forgot."

"If you all will set up camp," Caymar offered, "I'll teleport myself home and retrieve my fishing rod and equipment and will return here within an hour."

"Sounds great!" said Paul. "We'll be here."

While they waited, they set up their tents on the upper part of the gray shore at the base of the rounded ridge of bedrock. They unpacked their packs, took out some food, and ate supper, hoping for some fish as a treat to round off their meal. In half an hour, Caymar returned with three rods and lines and other equipment.

He, Paul, and Andrew did most of the fishing, and they caught four large fish, each one nearly half a meter long.

"I believe that will be plenty enough for all of us," Paul remarked.

"Yes, I agree," said Caymar. "Let's cook them and eat them."

As they cooked them over two of their EPI gas stoves, Robert asked, "What is the name of this sea or large lake?"

"There is no name for it," Caymar informed him.

"No name?" Robert asked with surprise.

"What about the mountains?" Andrew asked.

"The same answer," he continued. "You see, we people have never bothered to name pieces of land or water because we don't own them. It's more like we are a part of this planet, and therefore we don't express ownership by naming everything in sight, like Earth people do."

"I see," said Robert, "but this planet has a name, Sirius B."

"That had to be named," Caymar explained. "The Galactic Federation required that for the purposes of identification."

"What about the trees, shrubs, and plants?" James brought up. "They have names."

"That's true," he admitted. "The way we see it, trees and plants come and go, and we therefore feel all right in naming them. Further, we have names for each person to ease in identification among us, but for land masses and bodies of water, we consider them to be more permanent and therefore don't name them."

"When you're talking to others," Steven asked, "how can you specify which mountain, for example, you're talking about?"

"Most of us have seen them, not physically, but in the mind," Caymar replied. "Remember, we transmit visual images to each other for much of our communication. Those images are as clear as what you might call a television picture back on Earth."

"Oh, yeah," Steven recalled. "I forgot about that."

"Since the eight of you are more used to communicating by speech," he told them, "I choose to speak to you instead of transmitting and receiving images."

"By the way," Morris told Caymar, "I actually transmit visual images, as Tom granted me that gift as part of his deal."

"Oh, he didn't tell me that," he said in a surprised tone.

"Oh yes, and it's really great," Morris went on, "because I can transmit to the others, visual images of places I've been, both physically and in my dreams and astral travel."

"His ability gives all of us a much wider variety of places to travel," Robert added.

"Would you like to communicate by transmission of visual images?" Caymar offered to Morris.

"Yeah sure. Go for it."

Caymar and Morris took turns transmitting scenes back and forth to each other, and Morris began to laugh. Everyone else could also see the exchange of visual scenes. Some of them laughed at some of the scenes they saw. Basically, the two were transmitting outdoor scenes of each other's home planet. When Caymar transmitted a certain scene of Sirius B, Morris would find the best match for it and would transmit a similar scene of a location on Earth. They enjoyed the visual exchange of communication for several minutes, and the others enjoyed the entertainment.

"That was good," Andrew told them. "I enjoyed watching that."

"It was sort of like watching a slide show in your mind," said William.

They finished eating the fish they had caught and went to sleep soon afterwards. Sirius A never did slip behind any nearby mountain ranges since they were in a more level area than they had been during the previous nights. It remained hanging low in the sky.

As everyone awoke several hours later, Sirius A had moved and was now shining across the lake's smooth surface. There was no wind, and the temperature was very mild. Sirius B had not been seen since they had left the area where Tom lived, and it could not be seen this far north at this time of the year.

Since they had spent the last four days hiking and climbing, they decided that they would like to take a rest day. Caymar agreed to the good idea and added that since they would rest a day, he would return home to tend to some matters there and check up on things and that he would return 12 hours later. He instantly disappeared. Robert and his friends were alone on the beach with the whole day to do whatever they desired.

"Let's explore the area!" James eagerly declared.

"Yeah, let's go for it," Robert agreed. "At least we'll be able to leave our backpacks here and not have to wear them."

They all placed their backpacks inside their tents and explored the surrounding hillsides near the large lake. Also, they went swimming during the warmest part of the day, even though Sirius A still hung somewhat low in the sky. For some of the time, they just rested and took it easy, so as not to be too tired for the next day when they would continue with their hiking adventure.

As they were resting by the lakeshore, Robert brought up, "Isn't this great to be visiting a lake on another planet. It's so clean and unpolluted."

"I know," William agreed, "and wouldn't it be nice if people back on Earth would show more concern for their own waters?"

"It sure would," said Paul. "If they saw this, I believe they would realize just how important clean water really is."

"Actually," said Morris, "I'm not sure if they ever will. There are too many people who just don't care enough to stand up to those major polluters and have them stopped."

"I think one day people on Earth will wake up and get things cleaned up," Robert speculated.

"It will be a miracle if they ever do," said William.

Caymar returned, and some of them fished again. They enjoyed another fish dinner along with their supper. They went to sleep for several more hours, and Sirius A hung low in the sky for the whole time. It was strange to them how it never got dark this far north at this time of year, and the only way they could keep track of the time was to use their watches.

After their sleep, they got up and had breakfast, and Caymar announced that they would go and visit some beautiful lakes higher up in the mountains. "We'll walk the shoreline on the left side of this sea for several kilometers, turn left, and climb over the next ridge. Below us, you will see one of the most scenic areas in this mountain range."

They packed up and left and walked along the smooth rounded ridge of bedrock just up from the shore. For the next five kilometers, they continued along the sea's edge, occasionally crossing streams that fed this large lake. They had decided not to walk on the sandy beach itself, since the sand was so soft that it made walking difficult.

Finally, they made a left turn and climbed gently upwards, leaving the sea. Most of the terrain was smooth rounded bedrock, and it was mostly light gray in color. Again, in many places, it was wet because water seeped out of the ground, and many small streams flowed through the area as well.

For the next four kilometers, they ascended gently and must have climbed a total of 500 meters in altitude by the time they crested at a gentle rounded ridge. Ahead of them were many small lakes, some of them nestled within the peaks of the next mountain range.

From the rounded ridge, they now descended gently for several kilometers, and they began to pass some small lakes. Many of them stopped to drink water along the way, and they filled their water bottles. Finally, they descended to a very attractive lake situated at the edge of a mountainous ridge. To the left of the lake, the land sloped sharply downhill into a gorge and the other side of the gorge was met by the steep slopes of the next mountain. Ahead of them, on the other side of the lake, the land sloped downhill sharply, again into the same gorge below.

Surprisingly, much of the rock was lighter in color than what they were used to seeing. Very little of it had the usual red color common to this planet. The landscape was absent of any vegetation, and in areas, small streams trickled down and fed the lake.

This lake was around 100 meters across and was spectacular, and there were several tiny islands in its middle. Many of them swam in the somewhat cold water and visited the tiny island, only a few meters across. It was really a great feeling to them to be able to spend the summer in a unique way, visiting and exploring other planets.

"Tomorrow," Caymar announced, "we'll descend through the gorge to our left and make our way to the valley floor again."

"How far is that?" Steven asked.

"I'd say it's around 20 kilometers, but it's easy, and it's all downhill."

"That won't be so bad," said Morris.

"How high up are we here with respect to the valley floor?" Robert wanted to know.

"I believe we are pretty close to 3,600 meters above the valley," Caymar replied.

"Golly! We've got a long ways to go down!" William exclaimed.

"You got that right," Paul agreed, "but at least we'll be going down instead of up."

"Are there any fish in this lake?" Andrew asked.

"No, there aren't," Caymar answered. "We've never stocked it. However, the large lake or sea where we just came from has always had fish ever since history began. It must have been stocked millions of years ago by visitors here, and they probably weren't even humans."

Sirius A slowly slid behind the mountain range to their right, giving them shade. Everyone decided to set up his tent and sleep for the next several hours.

The next day was their last one in this mountain range. This was their seventh day, and their food supply was about to run out. It would soon be time to send James to Coles New World and Roelf Vos supermarkets in Devonport, Tasmania for more food.

After breakfast, they and Caymar descended the gorge. At first, the descent was steep, but as the gorge widened, the slope became more gentle after a couple of kilometers. Soon, they found themselves walking alongside a small river on their right, and as they continued descending, they followed this river as it became larger and wound its way between tall mountains on either side.

Soon they began to notice vegetation and later some Tamarisk shrubs in a few places. Their numbers increased as they continued their descent until they, at times, passed through groves of these shrubs, some of them as tall as three meters.

The scenery was spectacular on either side. There were streams running down the mountain slopes on both sides of the river, and some of the streams were waterfalls. They could be heard in the distance, and their sounds filled the air.

Finally, the valley floor could be seen ahead of them when the river made its last curve and emptied into it. The valley's flatness seemed endless as it stretched out far beyond them to the horizon. Once they reached the bottom, they noticed that the river sank through the sandy soil and literally disappeared beneath it.

"As you can see," Caymar explained to them, "this mountain range is a source of many rivers, and they flow underground and supply everyone with water over the whole planet."

"Yes, I can see that," Andrew agreed.

"If everyone's ready," Caymar announced, "we can return to Tom's place."

"Okay," they all agreed, ready to go on to something else and having enjoyed their week's adventures.

Caymar teleported himself there while the others transported themselves in their usual way. When they returned, they noticed that Sirius A hung very low in the sky, much lower than they had remembered seeing it a week earlier.

"In case you didn't already realize it," Caymar informed them, "our days and nights are four Earth days long each, and night will begin in around 20 hours."

"What do you do during all that time with a night that is four days long?" Andrew asked. "That's nearly 100 hours."

"Well, it's not as bad as you think," he explained. "Sirius B is visible, at least part of the time, and it's brighter than Earth's moon. Actually, it's quite nice because the weather is cooler, and we can get a lot of work done outside, namely gardening. When both Sirius A and Sirius B are out of sight, then it is dark. We do things inside then, and sometimes we go outside and gaze at the stars in the night sky."

They had arrived on the hill just up from Tom's residence. He happened to walk outside, and he spotted them. Upon noticing them, he walked toward them with a smile on his face.

"Well, hello there!" he called out to them. "How was your walking trek in the mountains of the far north?"

"Fantastic!" Steven answered.

"We had a wonderful time," Robert answered, "except that we nearly got put away by a rock storm."

"Oh!" Tom exclaimed. "Was that up by that hut that Caymar and some of his friends built?"

"Yes," said Morris. "How did you know?"

"Those rocks go crashing through there several times a year, and Caymar has told me stories before. I don't understand why in Sirius B he and his friends had to build it in one of the most dangerous areas of the mountain, but I guess the view from that place was enough to make it worth the risk."

"It is a good view, I'll admit," said Chris.

"Anyway, come on in," Tom offered, "and tell me all about it."

All of them went inside and related their stories of what they'd done all week in the mountains.

After an hour's worth of stories, including those from Caymar, Tom asked, "How much longer can you stay on our planet?"

"I'd say about another week," Robert answered.

"Well, it's going to be getting dark here for four Earth days starting in 19 hours."

"Yes, that's what Caymar was telling us," said Morris.

"Oh, he's already told you that. Okay then," Tom continued, "I was wondering if you would like to spend those days visiting different families in one of our underground cities?"

"Hmm . . ." said Steven. "Yeah, that would be interesting."

"The nearest city to here is Ahntraytitral," he informed them, "and it's around 100 kilometers from here. Its population is close to 50,000 people, and nearly all of the residences are underground. However, the city center is built above ground and is situated in a flat area. I think you would enjoy it. What do you think?"

"Yeah sure!" Paul enthusiastically said.

"I think we'll learn a lot by staying with some natives," said Andrew, "and we'll make some friends as well."

"That's great!" Tom remarked. "I'll contact some of my friends in Ahntraytitral who have some people near your age, and I'm sure you'll have a great time. You all can rest here, have some supper, sleep, and we'll transport ourselves there tomorrow."

"Sounds good," said William.

"I'm looking forward to seeing what their lifestyle is like," said Robert.

After a good several hours of sleep, they got up, packed their packs, and prepared to leave. Tom had gone to Ahntraytitral to visit some of his friends and make arrangements for the homestays. James had decided not to go to Devonport for more food since Tom had also said that the families would gladly feed them. The four days of darkness would be starting in 10 hours. Tom transmitted the visual image of the above-ground scene just outside the city center, and they transported themselves there. Upon arriving, Tom led them toward the city center.

William stared at the center in disbelief. "That's the city center?!"

"That's right," Tom answered. "What's the matter?"

"It's all single story buildings," William pointed out, "and the streets are all dirt."

"Keep in mind, William," Tom explained, "that we don't need all that luxury and physical technology like you have on Earth. It just depletes resources. Here on Sirius B, we built these building out of naturally existing red rock and clay, and the city centers of our cities are mainly a place for people to gather and exchange food and supplies."

"Come on, William," said Robert. "You can't expect it all to be like Earth."

"Oh, I wasn't saying that," he clarified. "It's just that this surprised me.

Don't get me wrong. I'm sure I'll like it fine. We're all tough enough to handle many situations."

"That's true," said Tom. "That's one reason I chose you 10 to be part of my mission. Let's go into the city."

They followed him and soon were among dirt streets and rows of small one-room buildings, each displaying foods and supplies for trading. For some reason, all of this seemed very familiar to Robert, and he couldn't quite figure out why.

They continued as Tom gave them a tour through the streets. Many people, both men and women, wore robes, and they walked the streets carrying baskets of goods. It looked like a giant farmers market.

Suddenly, it dawned on Robert why it looked so familiar.

"William!" Robert called out to him.

"Yes, what is it?"

"Do you remember that dream to Mars that I told you about when we all camped in my woods back in early March?"

"Yes, I do," William recalled.

"Well, this place looks almost exactly like it did in that dream seven years ago," said Robert.

"Is that right?" William enthusiastically asked.

"Yes, it really does," Robert insisted, "but I wonder why I thought it was Mars."

Morris heard the conversation and answered, "When we dream, we don't always get correct information. Some dreams are more accurate than others."

"Oh, I see," said Robert.

Everyone enjoyed looking around the city center. There were no banks, no law offices, no court houses, no police stations, no government buildings of any type, no commercial establishments, no gas stations and convenience stores, and so on. Instead, the whole cluster of small buildings was set up in a farmers market style. When they asked Tom why this city lacked the typical buildings of Earth's cities, he explained that humans had existed just fine for the past 4 million years without all of that. There was no reason that they would need it now. He also explained that humans here on Sirius B never lived in fear of one another. Everyone got along fine with everyone else, and there was therefore no need for law enforcement.

After they had looked around enough, Tom took everyone to meet the families they would be staying with. He led them through underground corridors that led in every direction from the center to the residences. The ground on which the city center sat was flat, and the area surrounding it was hilly. Many of the residents lived in underground dwellings within those hillsides, and nearby, they usually maintained a small garden plot above ground.

Tom made four stops, leaving two of the eight of Robert and his friends at each location, in other words, dividing them up into four different homestays. The families were very welcoming and hospitable. For the next five days, they had these homestays and learned a lot about the Sirian way of life.

To the eight of them, the Sirians led a very basic way of life, free of technological luxuries. There were no televisions, no radios, no newspapers, and therefore no bad news. Their lives were virtually free from stress, and since they used no money, there was no economic situation to worry about. They soon came to like this way of life, and they certainly appreciated the peace and serenity that went with it.

The Sirians still had plenty of work to do, however. Either the man or the woman of the house would stay home and tend to the children, and the other one would leave, at times, to do outside work, possibly away from the city. They would usually tend to the gardens and crops, as food was their most important business. They needed that to live.

During their homestays, they swapped stories with their Sirian host families about each other's planets and cultures. They were impressed at how in tune the Sirians were with their planet and at how easily they could communicate telepathically, both by thoughts and by visual image transmission within their minds.

A few hours after they had begun their homestays, it became dark and remained so for four Earth days. Of course, the Sirians were used to this and actually looked forward to the nights because of the relief it offered them from their hot days that were also equally as long. For most of this particular night, Sirius B glowed in the sky and was visible, but it did set behind the horizon before Sirius A showed itself one Earth day later. Thus, last quarter of the night was truly dark.

The Sirian hosts took advantage of this time as well, and they showed Robert and his friends the constellations in the dark night sky. They were impressed with the clarity, as there was no pollution nor the glow of street lights.

When Sirius A broke the horizon and dawn began, it was Sunday, June 16, Earth time. It had really been a unique experience for the eight of them to endure a four-day night, and they were glad to see daylight again. The four separate families hosting them decided to gather and take all eight of them together on an outdoor tour of the desert environment just outside their city of Ahntraytitral.

They repeated some of what Tom had told them about the Tamarisks and Cypress-Pines coming from Earth around 4 million years ago. All eight of them were impressed with the varieties of Cactus plants throughout the hills and gullies. The Sirian host families also mentioned that every Cactus plant seen was endemic to Sirius B and that some varieties were transported to Earth in exchange for the Tamarisks and Cypress-Pines.

There were Cactus plants of all different sizes, and some of them had the most unusual blooms. Robert noted one that had narrow purple blooms that resembled that of a Penstemon. This particular type of Cactus, for some reason, was most attractive to the Ariaba bees, as they congregated around it, almost disregarding the other types. There were some other interesting Cactus plants that had an almost lichen-type appearance with less succulent leaves. Nearly all the Cacti they saw had spines, some longer and harsher than others.

"Why are there so many Cactus plants all over this planet?" James asked his Sirian host.

"It's my theory," she answered, "that every planet serves a purpose to this galaxy or even the universe. This one was the cradle for the Cactus plants, a very unique and special group of plantlife. It pleases all of us that they have done so well on Earth in the past 4 million years.

"I'll agree they've certainly done that," James admitted.

As the hosts continued showing them the area, they explored the hillsides and rock formations and even some small caves. All of the ground and rock had the usual deep red color, and everything was dry.

As Sirius A slowly moved higher in the sky, the day warmed and gradually became hot. They had walked for several hours during the early part of this morning, and the host families mentioned that it was time to return to their separate homes. The eight of them once again split up in the four pairs and went back with them and packed their belongings into their backpacks.

The hosts had made previous arrangements with Tom for them to meet at the city center today. When they arrived, Tom was already there waiting for them. Robert and his friends thanked their host families for their generosity and hospitality. It was sad leaving, but they knew that they could return at a later time if they so desired. As the host families stood back, they watched with curiosity as Tom disappeared, and the eight of them proceeded to transport themselves, using the pink glow and whirring wind.

They transported themselves to Tom's residence, and as they materialized, Tom was already there, having teleported himself there instantaneously. Upon arriving, Tom asked them to come inside and be seated.

"Tell me," Tom asked, "how did you like your visits with some of us, here on Sirius B?"

"I had a great time," said Paul.

"It was unique and different," Andrew commented.

"I really enjoyed meeting them and living their peaceful way of life," said Robert.

"I do want to say that life here is great without televisions, radios, and newspapers," Steven declared.

"People here have enough entertainment just by communicating telepathically," said William.

"Yeah, I'd say you're right," Chris agreed.

"Did they take you all outside during the darkest part of the night to show you the stars?" Tom asked everyone.

"Yes, they sure did," Andrew replied.

"Good," said Tom.

"The view of the stars and constellations is incredible from this planet!" Steven remarked.

"That's right," Tom agreed. "There's no air pollution here."

"Basically, we lived like one of them," James told him. "They treated Paul and me like we were one of them. We helped them out with the chores, and they fed us and looked after us. I was sort of sad to leave."

"Well, you know where they live," said Tom, "so you can just transport yourselves back to visit them at a later time."

"Yes, we had been talking about that among ourselves," said Paul.

"Also," James added, "I really enjoyed the superb tour the families gave all of us. It was quite educational to see all of those types of Cacti."

"That's good," Tom remarked. "I'm glad you got something out of it."

"The family Steven and I stayed with was excellent," said Morris. "Again, they treated us like family, and I also enjoyed communicating with them by transmitting and receiving visual images. They didn't know English that well, so I was glad to be able to communicate telepathically like that."

"I envy you," Andrew said to Morris. "We weren't able to do that with our host family. Robert and I mostly made signs and gestures since they didn't speak that much English."

"Ours spoke a good amount of English," said Chris. "William and I must have been lucky in that respect. We actually played cards with them."

"Lucky you!" declared Robert. "No, just kidding, Chris. We still had a great time with our host family. I wouldn't have traded it for anything."

"I knew I chose the right group of teenagers," Tom declared. "I've enjoyed knowing all of you, and like I said, you all have been a great help. Is there anything else you'd like to do before continuing on your galactic travels?"

"Yes," Morris answered, "I was wondering if we might be able to see the storage facility that you say is on this planet? I'm really curious about it."

"Why yes, certainly," Tom consented. "I'll just transmit the visual image to you all, and then we'll go there." He proceeded to meditate, and they soon received an image of a flat, barren landscape.

"*That's* your storage facility?" Morris asked with surprise.

"That's right," Tom assured him. "All of it is underground, and it is huge. It's located at 65 degrees south and is around on the other side of our planet. If everyone is ready, we can go there."

"We're all ready," Robert answered for everyone.

"Let's go," Tom ordered them.

In seconds, they transported themselves and arrived on the flat, barren land. Tom led the way, and they soon came to a trap door which was not noticeable until they were nearly upon it. He opened it slowly, not by physical force but by meditation, letting levitation do the work. Once the door was opened, he led them inside, and they descended many steps until they were well beneath the ground by more than 100 meters.

Tom led them down a very long corridor that had entrances on both sides leading to large container rooms. He showed them the wide varieties of goods stored, and the eight of them were impressed. Some of the rooms contained basic supplies like food and clothing, and other rooms contained technological equipment of all types.

"This underground storage facility or warehouse," Tom informed them, "is a shipping and receiving station for nearly the entire galaxy, that is, with those who want to do business with us."

"You mean there are some who don't?" Morris asked.

"Oh yes, certainly," Tom answered. "They either wouldn't get along with us, or we don't have or stock the particular goods that they would need."

He continued with the tour, telling them what was in each area, except for the rooms that contained top-secret equipment. Those rooms were marked 'confidential.' When the tour was complete, he took them back up the long flight of steps leading to the outside again.

"Thanks very much for everything, Tom," said Morris.

"You're quite welcome, all of you," he told them.

"Yeah, we've really enjoyed the past two weeks on this planet," Andrew mentioned.

"I'm glad you all have," said Tom. "Let me go ahead and tell you something while I'm thinking of it." Everyone listened attentively, wondering what Tom had on his mind. "The Galactic Federation and I have recently come to the decision that there will probably be more star systems that will want to link up to our galactic communications device on Earth at your farm, Robert."

"Tom, I don't really want a bunch more receiving and transmitting towers cluttering my woods," Robert told him.

"Oh, you don't have to worry about that," Tom assured him. "Rather than add a bunch of lines to the device on your farm, Robert, we struck upon the idea of eventually letting Chris and Richard's thousand-line step office be the main switching station or central office for potential subscribers throughout the galaxy. Meanwhile, we will still use the one at your farm, Robert. After all, we will need it to provide the link to Earth's telephone network. While we will maintain our direct lines with Earth, we will also open subscriber lines through Chris and Richard's step office."

Robert thought about it for a few seconds. "Yes, that sounds like a good idea."

"Rather than overload the central office at Robert's place," said Andrew, "you'll use Chris and Richard's instead. That sounds good."

"Keep in mind, Tom," Steven pointed out, "that no more than six calls can be simultaneously placed to Earth from anywhere in the galaxy at this time."

"That is very true," Tom admitted. "I don't believe that will be a problem, however, since that is probably all that we will need for connecting to Earth. We plan to use Chris and Richard's thousand-line step office as the main central office for intergalactic communication while only the calls intended for Earth will be switched through the device at Robert's place. At this present time, only we, the Vegans, and the Pleiadeans, and those where Chris and Richard live are making phone calls to Earth, and I believe that the other star systems will not have as much need to call Earth."

"I see," said Steven. "So, at this time, there is no urgent need to upgrade our galactic communications device."

"That's right," said Tom.

"Well, it looks like the risks we made at Kingston Park served you and the Galactic Federation more than you initially thought," Morris commented.

"Well, I will admit," said Tom, "that the Galactic Federation had this in mind when they gave me the approval to help Chris and Richard obtain the Kingston Park step office."

"Oh! I was wondering how you got approval so easily," Paul remarked with a smile.

"That's the reason," Tom admitted. "Anyway, tell Mr. Johns next time you see him or talk to him that I may be calling on him for technical assistance in the future. Also tell him that the Galactic Federation and I would make it worth his while."

"We sure will," Robert assured him. "Oh, and just for the record, Tom, I predict that this step office equipment will probably become pretty scarce by 10 years from now, even though it is actually the most dependable type of central office equipment that there is. So, you may want to consider bidding on some more exchanges as they cut them over in the future and you can teleport the equipment and store it here for future use."

"That's an excellent suggestion," said Tom. "I'll mention it to the Galactic Federation and will see what I can do. I will admit that when it comes to technological equipment made on Earth, you better stock up on extras if you like it, because it won't be long before they stop making it. Things change so fast down there!"

"Of course, you could just duplicate a lot of it," Chris pointed out.

"Oh yes, we'll be doing that too," Tom assured him, "but we may as well obtain some original pieces of central office equipment for future use so that they won't just be scrapped and melted down on Earth."

"Anyway," he continued, "keep in touch, and have a fantastic summer during your galactic travels."

Robert and his friends looked at each other with the expression on their faces of: Where do we want to go next?

"We have almost no food left," James reminded them. "Let's go to Tasmania and restock at Coles New World and Roelf Vos."

"Good idea," William approved. "Let's go."

They said goodbye to Tom and proceeded to transport themselves. Morris had forgotten to use his crystal ball, which he had brought with him, to check to see if Mark Peters' backyard was clear. Even though they hadn't mentioned Mark's place, they all knew to arrive there, which they did.

It was early morning, Monday, June 17, and the weather was cold and breezy. James went to the back door to see if Mark was there. His parents had already gone to work in Devonport for the day, and he was just getting up, himself.

"Well, hello there, James! How are you going?" said Mark with a surprised look on his face as he came to the door.

"Great! How are you going, Mark?" James answered.

Mark looked out the door. "Oh right! You brought your mates from Tennessee again."

"How are you doing, Mark?" said Robert, speaking for the rest of them.

Everyone entered, and James did most of the talking as they related the whole story of their trip to Sirius B. Mark was astounded at everything they'd done and expressed his wishes to go there himself.

"Well, I haven't actually transported another person with me," said James, "but later on this summer, we could give it a go, if you like."

"Yeah sure, mate!" Mark exclaimed. "That would be great."

After a nice visit, Mark took them in the Ford Spectron van to Coles New World and Roelf Vos to stock up on more than a week's supply of food. Again, Mark had bought their U.S. dollars and supplied them with Australian dollars.

Once they had bought all they thought they would need, Mark took them back to his place, and they packed up their packs to get ready to leave. Mark had to rush off to school this morning and wished them a great trip. The eight of them decided to visit the Vega star system next, and they transported themselves away from his backyard.

13 The Trip to Vega

Vega, according to Tom, also had humans living on it, and according to the visual image that he had transmitted to them, it seemed hot and dry. Vega was around 25 light years from Earth.

The eight of them arrived with their backpacks, stocked with 10 days of food. They were near the telephone station, and the weather was very hot. It felt like it was 50° Celsius, and it was the middle of the day as best as they could tell. The scenery appeared much like a desert and did indeed closely resemble Sirius B. Even the soil was red, and again there were Cactus plants and coniferous-like shrubs of Tamarisk and Cypress-Pine. Various types of lizards scurried across the ground.

"Golly! Another hot, dry planet!" Chris remarked.

"And this one seems hotter than Sirius B," William added.

"I don't know about you all," Steven brought up, "but this looks just like the spittin' image of Sirius B."

"Let's go down to the telephone station and let them know we're here," Morris suggested.

They walked down the hill 100 meters and reached the small building by the tower. A male operator was sitting inside and noticed them.

Robert spoke for the eight of them and said, "Hello there. We're friends of Tom, the galactic salesman of Sirius B, and the eight of us are from planet Earth." He assumed the operator would know English since he was placing and receiving calls to and from Earth.

"Oh yes," he replied. "Tom mentioned a while ago that you might be coming to visit our planet. Welcome to Vega."

They introduced themselves, and the operator telepathically sent for another person to come to the station to show them around. In five minutes, a woman in a white robe suddenly appeared just outside the station. She appeared to be in her 50's and was around the same height as they were.

Upon arriving, she walked up to them and said, "Hello, my name, as it would best be known in your language, is Ingra. I'm pleased to meet the eight of you and show you around."

They introduced themselves to her, and she began to tell them about Vega. They walked away from the station and climbed the hillside which was dotted with Tamarisks, Cypress-Pines, and various types of Cactus.

"I'll give you a brief history of our planet," she began. "The first humans appeared on the scene here around 6 million years ago, and there is no fossil record for humans or any primates on this planet prior to that time. Therefore, we know that our ancestors came from another world, and that world is Earth. Our ancestors were transported here by aliens at that time 6 million years ago, and we've been living here ever since. At the time of transport, our ancestors appeared more primitive and ape-like, but once here, they quickly evolved to adapt to the environment which, at that time, was not really so hot and dry as it is now.

"Two million years later, which was 4 million years ago, our ancestors achieved sentience, and some of us colonized Sirius B, and much later, planet Earth. That was just over 2 million years ago for planet Earth. During those times, many planets have been colonized and settled by our race."

"Yes, I pretty much thought that's how it might have been," Morris agreed.

They had now reached a hilltop and had a view of the landscape ahead of them. It was a plateau of reddish-orange colored soil with various sizes of boulders dotting the landscape, and there were hardly any shrubs at all. More shrubs grew on the sides of the slopes where they had just been.

"Anyway," she went on, "our star, as you know, is called Vega. It's a hot white star, and we are the third planet out from it, being 326,000,000 kilometers away. All in all, this system has 27 planetary bodies, including the moons. We don't have any moons around our planet, so when it's night, it's really dark.

"We orbit Vega in 748 of our days, which is just over two and a half Earth years, and our planet rotates in just over 29 hours, a little longer than an Earth day. While our planet is more massive and larger than Earth, its gravity is slightly less than Earth's due to the fact that we have a lower percentage of heavy metals in this planet's core. The circumference around the equator is 45,000 kilometers."

"Is this whole planet desert-like or just this particular area?" Andrew asked.

"Around 80 percent of Vega is desert, like it is here," Ingra replied. "The other 20 percent which is cooler is divided between the north and south poles of this world. There is a large sea at the north pole, and it's around 1,000 kilometers across it. High mountain ranges surround it and protect it, and that's one reason why it still remains, in addition to its being at the north pole."

"That sounds very similar to what Sirius B has, only their sea is not as large," said Paul.

"Yes, we are very similar to Sirius B," she confirmed. "As you notice, the plantlife is similar as well. Around 4 million years ago, our planet became more desert-like from what it was. As we scouted out different star systems, we decided to transfer from Earth, Tamarisks and Cypress-Pines to both Sirius B and to here. The Cactus plants came from Sirius B, as they are endemic to that planet."

"That's what Tom was saying," said Robert.

"Also," Morris added, "I read an article not too long ago that said that there was no fossil evidence for Cacti on Earth."

"That would be right," Ingra agreed, "because all Cacti are endemic to Sirius B."

"Don't you and the Sirians miss having the variety of trees that we have on Earth?" James asked.

"Yes, we do," she admitted, "but our climate is so hot that it won't allow many of the more delicate tree species to live."

"What about some of the Eucalypts or Gum trees, as we call them, for example?" he asked her. "Some of them thrive in the hot, dry Australian Outback."

"I was just about to get to that type of tree," she answered. "That type of tree can survive here. In fact, there are some types of Eucalypts on this planet."

"Oh really?" James asked with enthusiasm.

"Yes, they grow in certain areas further north and further south. We are near the equator here. If you like, we can transport ourselves to one of the largest groves of Eucalypts on this planet."

"Sure! Let's go," said James, answering for everyone.

"I'll transmit the visual image to you," she said. "Can you receive visual images in your minds?"

"Yes, we can," Morris answered. "Further, I transmit them as well. It was a gift from Tom on Sirius B."

"Very good then," she said. "Here's the scene."

As she telepathically transmitted the scene, the eight of them saw a beautiful forest of Eucalypts, something none of them had expected to see on this hot, dry planet. Most of the trees had lighter colored bark, and their limbs had long, slender, purplish-green leaves. James felt like he was looking at a scene from Australia for sure.

"If you're ready, we'll transport ourselves there," she offered.

"Absolutely," everyone said.

She instantly teleported herself there, and the others transported themselves, arriving a few seconds later. The almost mint-like smell of the Eucalypts filled the air when they arrived at the edge of the forest.

"I feel like I'm back home in Australia!" James shouted.

"Well, Australia has a lot to do with our past," she informed him.

"How is that?" James wanted to know.

"That's a long story that all of you will find out when the time is right," she replied. She pointed into the forest. "If you will walk that way, you will find your own answers. I must return to my place now. Have a wonderful time."

"But what about . . .?" James began to ask.

Before any of them could say any more, she had already disappeared.

"Boy! She sure did suddenly put us off!" James angrily declared.

"Now hold on just a minute," Morris interjected. "I know it appears that way, but there's no need to worry. Let's just enjoy it, and if or when we get into any trouble, we'll just transport ourselves out."

"Oh right, of course!" James realized. "I momentarily forgot about that. What do we care! Let's go have a good time."

Each of them had two liters of water, and they entered the edge of the Eucalyptus forest, soon walking on the light brown leaves that crackled under their feet on the forest floor. There was no undergrowth, and no one saw any wildlife.

"I take it that Vega has no mammalian wildlife either," William brought up.

"Probably not," said Morris.

Morris decided to use his crystal ball, and he placed it in both of his hands at times. He used it to guide them in the right direction as they penetrated deeper into this seemingly endless pure stand of Eucalypts. The shade they gave was a welcome relief from the heat they had felt back at the telephone station where they had arrived on this planet. Here, the weather was considerably cooler at only 30° Celsius.

"I'm glad it's not so hot here as it was back at the phone station," Robert brought up.

"Yeah, you're not the only one on that," Paul agreed.

"I say the same," James added. "Back in Australia, when it gets above 42° Celsius, and this doesn't apply to the Outback so much as it does to the coastal regions of Eastern Australia, the hot sun bakes the forest to a critical temperature. When this happens, whole forests can spontaneously ignite due to the high oil content of the Gum tree leaves."

"Don't tell us that, James!" Steven requested. "We *are* in the middle of a Gum tree forest."

"Oh, there are no worries here," James assured everyone. "It's not hot enough, and if we get too worried, all we have to do is to transport ourselves out of here."

"Oh, yeah. That's right," Steven realized. "At times I forget that we have that special gift."

They had been hiking for several hours now, and the terrain had been flat, and as it became late afternoon, they came to the foot of a small mountain whose gentle slopes were covered with Eucalypts. They decided to climb the slope to its top, a climb which took them an hour, and they were now 400 meters above the forest floor they had just left. They arrived at a plateau that had some hills further on, and they were forested.

There was a small natural clearing in the trees at the top, and they had an excellent view of the expanse of the forest from where they had come. The edge of the forest could barely be discerned, as it was now quite distant. In the same direction, well beyond the forest, they could see some reddish-orange hillsides.

"Boy! We've come a long ways!" Chris declared.

"Yes, we sure have," Robert agreed, "and we haven't found any answers yet."

"I have a strong feeling we'll find some answers soon," said Morris.

"I don't know about you all," William brought up, "but I'm tired out. Let's call it a day and set up camp."

"Good idea," Andrew agreed.

Everyone gave in to William's suggestion, satisfied with the place to camp, especially since it offered a great view of the forest below them. They unpacked their packs and set up their tents. Vega hung low in the sky now, and they realized that it would be dark in a few hours. They prepared a good supper from the food they had just purchased in Devonport, Tasmania.

As they relaxed after supper, waiting for Vega to reach the horizon, they realized how quiet the forest was. Only a gentle breeze blew through the upper limbs of the trees, and the sounds of the leaves could be heard gently clapping against one another. They had yet to see any birds or mammalian wildlife, and they therefore assumed there wasn't any. Occasionally, they noticed a lizard scurrying across the ground, constantly taking shelter under the dead fallen leaves of the Eucalypts.

"What do you think of the plausibility of Ingra's story?" Steven brought up. "Do you think that our ancestors and the ancestors of all humans in the galaxy suddenly came on the scene on Vega some 6 million years ago?"

"I think she might be quite right," Morris replied.

"It would explain the missing link that researchers are hard pressed to explain," Robert pointed out.

"What I can't figure out," Chris stated, "is why all sentient humans don't have much hair. I mean, really, all other primates on Earth have fur all over their bodies, and we have almost none."

"That's true," Andrew agreed, "and many people even go on to lose their hair on their head." He chuckled a little.

"I know," said Chris. "They go bald."

"I believe it must have been in the plan of some sentient race of aliens," Robert speculated, "whoever they may have been, to cause sentience to be achieved among the ape-like humans of Earth, but why would they have bothered moving a group of them to Vega?"

"Well, as anyone can see," Morris pointed out, "there are numerous species of primates and apes on Earth. So, no doubt, I believe that Earth's the cradle for all of primate life in the galaxy or even the universe, for that matter. It's possible that the aliens, whoever they were, came to the conclusion that the achievement of sentience would have been impossible on Earth due to the competition among the different species for survival. Oh, it may have happened, but it would have taken a lot longer. So, in theory, they may have taken some apes most closely fitting the requirements for potential sentience and transported them to Vega, putting them in an environment that isolated them from their cousins, the primates, and at that time, probably maximized their chances to evolve in the way that they desired. Once the aliens saw that things were going well, they probably left them here on their own. That was probably somewhere between 4 and 6 million years ago."

"But what about the fact that humans have no real fur?" Paul asked, remembering what Chris had just mentioned.

"The environment here must have been warm enough not to have required it," Morris answered. "So, they must have slowly lost it over many generations. I've also heard that the early humans may have been somewhat aquatic and swam in the oceans, which are no longer here except at the north pole, according to what Ingra said. They probably swam for clams, fish, and other food underwater. Look at the aquatic mammals on Earth. Many of them have little or no fur. Also, it could have just been chance evolution that the humans lost their fur on their way to achieving sentience."

"That sounds like a good theory," said Robert. "I'd say you're right."

"Anyway," Morris went on, "once humans achieved sentience around 4 million years ago, they started colonizing other worlds, like both Tom and Ingra have told us."

As they continued talking, Vega touched the horizon on the hill behind them, and it wasn't much to talk about. Basically, the sky turned a light orange color, and the star slowly disappeared behind the hill. There were no clouds, and a mass of darkness slowly rose at a steeper and steeper angle and approached them from the direction opposite the sunset. Over a period of half an hour, it became totally dark with only the sight of the stars and constellations visible in the sky. They got into their tents and went to sleep.

They had a little adjusting to do to get used to the 29-hour days on Vega. The night was 13 hours long with 16 hours of daylight afterwards. Some of them woke up at what to them was a reasonable hour, according to their watches, to start the day, but it remained dark for two or three more hours. Most of them needed the extra rest, so they just turned over and went back to sleep. Finally, Vega broke the horizon, and everyone got up.

Morris had a really interesting dream, and once they had eaten some breakfast and were packing to leave, he decided to tell them. "Listen, everyone. I have something to tell you. I had this most amazing dream last night." Nearly everyone was still packing his backpack.

"Yeah?" said Andrew. "This I've gotta hear. Hey, everyone! Let's quiet down and have a seat and listen to what Morris wants to tell us."

"Thanks, Andrew," said Morris. "Now, last night, I had a dream that I was walking among this forest of Eucalypts. It seemed so clear that I thought I was really doing it in real life. I could hear voices and sounds being transmitted to me telepathically and wondered where they were coming from.

"One voice said, 'Come closer.'

"I thought, *Where? What?* as I didn't see anyone. So, I said, 'Closer to what?'

"The voice said, 'To the tree nearest you, and place your hands on either side.'

"Slightly to my right, I saw a large Eucalyptus tree nearly a meter in diameter, and I did as the voice requested. It began to tell me a story as follows:

" 'We are glad you are here, Morris England, from planet Earth, for you are one of the few if not the only one who can communicate with us telepathically on a dream level.'

"I was absolutely amazed because I then realized that I was actually communicating telepathically with the *tree*! This had never happened to me before.

"I said to it, 'I would believe it for Earthlings, but all Vegans can communicate telepathically.'

" 'That is true,' the tree told me, 'but it is not in their destiny for them to serve the purpose for the story I am about to tell you. Is it true that you communicate telepathically with dolphins on planet Earth?'

"I asked the tree, 'What do you want to know that for?!'

" 'Is it true?!' the voice boomed at me.

"I replied, 'Yes! Yes, it is, but what in the world . . . What in the galaxy do dolphins have to do with you? You're a tree.'

" 'I know that!' the tree told me. 'Sit down at the base of me, and I will relate a story of many millions of years ago.'

"I did as it requested, sat at the base of this, no doubt, talking tree, and listened. It began as follows:

" 'Thirty-five million years ago, our ancestors used to live on a planet in a star system 45,000 light years distant. They were majestic trees, the largest our kind has ever known. For many millions of years, our kind had been living out their lifetimes, serving to create the finest and largest forest on that planet. We originated on that planet, and it was the cradle for all of our kind.

" 'However, at the time I mentioned,' it continued to tell me, 'our planet died when its star slowly expanded into a red giant and scorched all traces of life from its surface, after which it engulfed it. Fortunately, there were some native sentient species who were kind and caring enough to take some of our kind with them when they themselves had to flee to a new world, leaving their old, dying world behind. This new world was your planet Earth, and the sentient species that carried our kind with them were the dolphins. We first came on the scene on Earth 35 million years ago in what is now Australia, according to what our cousins there tell us.'

"I broke in and said, 'Cousins? Oh! You mean that you communicate telepathically with the present day Eucalypts in Australia?'

" 'That is correct,' it told me. 'We trees are capable of a lot more than you realize.'

"I was beside myself in disbelief because the time period that the tree mentioned coincided with what the dolphins had told me during my past telepathic conversations with them!

"Then I said to the tree, 'That's amazing because the dolphins that I telepathically communicate with have told me that they came to Earth from a dying planet 35 million years ago. They also told me that there were land-based dolphins who were bipedal, and they were called dolphs.'

"The tree told me, 'That is correct, and those dolphs lived on Earth's surface until 4 million years ago when they decided to flee from Earth, leaving only their sea-based kind to remain to the present time.'

" 'Yes!' I said to the tree. 'That agrees with what the dolphins have telepathically communicated to me, that their land-based kind fled from Earth around 4 million years ago.'

"It told me, 'You communicate with them very well. Have the dolphins told you the name of their old world and star system from where they came?'

"I answered, 'No they haven't, actually.'

"The tree told me, 'The name of the planet was Delikadove, and the star was Danetar. And let me tell you, that planet Delikadove was a beautiful place with pinkish-purple skies and purple-colored oceans. Our purplish color remains somewhat to this day, a remnant of our long ago past and of our old home. We are very grateful to the dolphins for having cared enough about us to transport some of us to Earth, thereby saving us from otherwise certain extinction.'

"I said to the tree, 'I would say you are. I will agree that the dolphins are a kind and considerate species. Tell me, how did your kind arrive here on Vega?'

" 'That is the next part of my story,' the tree told me. 'When the dolphs decided to leave Earth, they came here for a while, bringing some of us along with them to remind them of their old dead world of long ago.'

" 'Humans had been living here for 2 million years and had just achieved sentience, and the dolphs determined that it was time for them to bestow a most wonderful gift upon them. For many millions of years, the land dolphs had been living in a wonderful relationship with a silicon-based lifeform of crystals called the Shakeilar.'

" 'Oh right,' I said. 'The dolphins have told me that their land-based kind used to live inside crystal shelters which were actually living. They could actually expand and decrease in size simply by manifesting energy into matter, and vice versa, and they were portable by the dolphs as well.'

" 'All of that is true,' the tree confirmed. 'I will go ahead and tell you that it was with the help of these living Shakeilar crystals that the dolphins had us transported to Earth 35 million years ago, and they moved some of us here to Vega by the same method.'

" 'Is that right?' I said to the tree in surprise. 'Did they just conceal some of your kind inside these living crystals?'

"The tree said to me, 'Yes, they did. They transported us both in seed form and seedling form.'

" 'Very interesting,' I said.

" 'Anyway, to get on with my story,' the tree said, 'when the dolphs came here to Vega, they stayed here for several years. While they were here, they gave the humans on this planet many rudiments of civilization. With the permission of the Shakeilar race, the dolphs showed the humans how to use these living crystals to shelter and protect them. When the dolphs moved on to their new world, they left some of those Shakeilar crystals here and took the rest of them with them. To this day, these living crystals still exist and have a unique and wonderful relationship with the humans of this planet.'

" 'That's great,' I told the tree. 'I've only heard of the Shakeilar, but I've never seen any. I'm looking forward to meeting them.'

" 'Continue in the same direction you and the seven others have been going, and you will meet them soon enough,' the tree directed.

" 'Thank you,' I said. 'I will do that. Tell me this, Eucalyptus tree. Why are there no Shakeilar crystals on Earth and not even on Sirius B?'

"The tree answered, 'It was a decision made by the Shakeilar many millions of years ago that they not inhabit any planet with sentient life until this form of sentient life was proven worthy and capable of using it responsibly. At this time, their decision still stands that neither the humans of Sirius B nor the humans of Earth are as yet prepared to use them to their mutual benefit, and I stress *mutual*.'

"I asked the tree, 'What about the Pleiades or any other star systems with humans on them?'

"It answered, 'This is the only planet where both humans and the Shakeilar exist.'

" 'That's a shame,' I told the tree, 'because if there were Shakeilar on Earth, the humans would not have to exploit and deplete natural resources.'

"The tree responded by saying, 'That is the key word: *exploit*. The Shakeilar will in no way allow themselves to be exploited by any sentient race. I must go now. There is a purpose in your having been told this story, and you will know by your own intuitions what to do at a later time.'

"With that, the tree said no more. I walked around, waiting to see if I was going to hear any more voices, but none came. As I began to walk through the forest, I woke up."

Everyone had paid close attention to what Morris had told them about his amazing dream, and they were very moved by it. They were almost in a daze and were quite surprised that such clear information could have been obtained in a dream.

"Morris," James brought up, "I know a lot about the Eucalypts of Australia, and I've actually read in a book called *Forest Trees of Australia* that the Eucalypts came on the scene rather suddenly around 35 million years ago, and that there is no fossil evidence of Eucalypts anywhere on Earth prior to that time. Further, it said that there is no fossil evidence for the Acacias prior to 22 million years ago."

"Is that right?" Morris asked him. "I know I never knew that before. That means that the tree in my dream last night may be right. You know, I've never given any thought at all to the origins of trees. I'll have to include that in my quest for knowledge."

"I'm sure I've never mentioned the mysterious origin of the Eucalypts to you before, Morris," said James. "I believe you may be onto something."

"Maybe you really *did* communicate telepathically with the tree," William speculated.

"Well, even if I didn't do it in real life," Morris explained, "I know I did on the dream level."

"Morris," Paul brought up, "I thought you told us in that history class discussion back in April that the dolphins and cetaceans didn't live on the land once they came to Earth 35 million years ago."

"Oh, I've found out more since then," Morris explained. "That was their original idea, but they had a comeback for a while and lived for some time on Earth's lands."

"Oh, okay. I see," said Paul.

"What do you think your purpose is, Morris?" Robert asked.

"I don't know, really," he replied. "I'm sure of this much. I've got some serious telepathic communicating to do with the dolphins."

"What do you mean?" Chris asked.

"I mean that I still know very little about the old world the dolphins came from," he replied. "I knew they came to Earth 35 million years ago because their old planet was dying, but I've never asked the dolphins to tell me about it."

"Well, you said you've been all over the galaxy in astral body," Andrew pointed out. "Haven't you been to and seen . . . Delikadove, was it?"

"No, I haven't," Morris admitted, "and you'd think I would have, seeing that I've been communicating with the dolphins."

"I'd say that would have been too much to expect," Robert commented, "seeing that Delikadove died 35 million years ago. How could you possibly go and see it?"

"Actually, it is quite possible," Morris explained. "In the astral realm, there is no time as we know it, and I can pick and choose any time period to go and visit some place."

"How is that possible?" Robert further asked. "It doesn't make any sense."

"Oh, I realize it doesn't make any sense on this level," said Morris, "but what makes sense, here on this level, doesn't necessarily apply to other levels of existence."

"Oh, I see," said Robert.

"Anyway," Morris went on, "I've got a lot of research to do."

"Morris," said Steven, "I believe you may have just hit upon your purpose."

"You mean research?"

"Yes, that's right," Steven replied, "and you may even want to write a book about some of the things you know."

"Write a book . . . Hmm . . ." said Morris as he thought about it. "That's not a bad idea. I may actually do that. Thanks, Steven. Thank you very much."

"No problem," he said.

"Well, I guess we better start making tracks," Paul suggested.

Everyone stood up, put on his backpack, and began walking.

They started across the plateau, and once they reached the next range of hills, the terrain ceased to be flat like it had been for most of the previous day. There were small hills to climb and ridges to cross, and most of it was forested with the pure stands of Eucalypts. In some areas, rocks and boulders lay on top of the ground. Morris used his crystal ball again to help guide them in the direction they needed to go.

Their water supply was getting low, and they hoped they would soon find a stream or lake. After several hours of ascending and descending, they decided to stop for lunch. Eating lunch took the rest of their water supply, and they continued, now thirsty.

They had been walking for an hour after lunch when they, quite to their surprise, stumbled upon a water hole, an oasis in an otherwise dry forest.

What a relief it was to find water, as some of them had started seriously considering transporting themselves out. They quickly set down their packs, took out their water bottles, plunged them into the water, and gulped the water to quench their thirst.

As they were busy getting their fill of water, Morris looked up and was quite astounded to see what he thought he saw. He closed his eyes and re-opened them and still saw it. Around 20 meters into the forest sat an igloo-shaped dome made of what appeared to be smooth glass. It appeared to be three meters tall. Vega's light rays struck part of its surface, and it glistened. *Could this be a Shakeilar crystal shelter like the Eucalyptus tree had told me in my dream last night?* Morris wondered.

He pointed toward it and called out to the others, "Hey, everyone! Look over there." The rest of them looked and just stared. Finally, one of them, Chris, decided to venture over to it. The others followed him. Upon reaching the dome, Chris gently reached out and touched its surface.

Suddenly and without warning, part of the dome on one side dematerialized, startling the wits out of all of them. All eight of them jumped back in fright and landed upon one another, stunned in amazement that such a thing could possibly have happened.

The inside of the dome could now be seen, and a human who appeared to be in his thirties emerged. He was a thin man who was around their height, and he was wearing a yellow robe. As soon as he had seen the eight of them, he said, "Oh, hello there. Sorry if I startled you. I've been expecting you."

"You have? But how?" Steven asked.

"A Eucalyptus tree communicated with me in my dreams last night and informed me of your coming today," the man replied.

"Is that right?!" Morris asked, astounded at the coincidence.

"That's the truth," the man confirmed.

"How do you know English?" Robert asked him. He had to find this out.

"Nearly every one of us on Vega knows English," he answered. "We keep in contact with humans on Earth and on other planets as well. Many of us visit there in astral form. Some of us even teleport ourselves there and visit in physical form. It doesn't take long for any of us to learn a language."

"Oh, I see," said Robert. "So, you probably know many?"

"Yes, many people on Vega know many languages."

"What's your name?" Steven asked, extending his hand to greet him.

"My name is Lyro," he answered. "What are your names?"

They introduced themselves, and then Andrew asked, "You mean the Eucalyptus tree didn't already tell you our names?"

"No, it didn't tell me that much," said Lyro, "only that the eight of you would be coming."

"How could the tree know that we would be coming?" Paul wanted to know.

"Doesn't Morris have a crystal ball?" Lyro asked.

"Yes, that's right," Paul answered.

"Then, there's your answer," Lyro concluded.

"Oh, yeah. I see now," said Paul, realizing that Morris' crystal had guided them there.

"Is this an actual living Shakeilar?" Morris asked Lyro.

"Yes, you're looking at it," he verified.

"I've heard about them from the dolphins," said Morris. "I'm so glad to finally meet one! Tell me, why doesn't Earth have any Shakeilar crystals living on it?"

"The tree already told you why," Lyro quickly replied in an affirmative manner.

"Yes, that's true. It did," Morris admitted.

"How did that opening suddenly appear when I touched this dome?" Chris asked.

"All we Vegans do is hold out our hand, think a certain way, and the living crystal reshapes itself, creating an opening."

"That is really far out!" William declared.

"Amazing!" Steven added.

"Thanks to the Shakeilar," said Lyro, "we humans on Vega have had shelter and protection for the past 4 million years, and we haven't had to deplete any of the natural resources."

"That must be nice," Robert remarked. "I wish we had them on Earth."

"Well, the Shakeilar left Earth with the dolphs 4 million years ago," Lyro pointed out, "and they decided never to return there."

"That's a shame!" Morris declared.

"They made their minds up, and that's the way it goes," Lyro explained. "Anyway, it was nice meeting you. If you . . ."

"That's it?" Robert quickly broke in. "Where are you going?"

"I have to get back to what I was doing," said Lyro. "If you continue in the same direction, you will eventually emerge from this forest, and there will be a city visible in the distance on the horizon. Happy travels. Be sure and tank up on water before going." With that said, he entered the dome, and the opening suddenly rematerialized, leaving the eight of them alone again.

"Is it just me," James asked the others, "or does everyone feel put off?"

"I do too," Robert admitted.

"Me too," said William.

"Here, let's get some water and keep moving," Paul suggested.

They returned to the water hole, filled their water bottles, put on their backpacks, and continued walking through the forest.

Once they were well on their way, James commented, "I don't know about you all, but that bloke Lyro seemed to be a bit of a hermit!"

"I get the feeling we're not exactly wanted here on Vega," Robert remarked.

"Maybe receiving warm hospitality is not our purpose for being here," Chris speculated.

"I don't know," said William, "but that Lyro is a far cry from Caymar."

"The same goes for that Ingra woman as well!" James added.

"Here, here!" Morris called out to the others. "Let's not have all this grumbling and complaining. I think Chris is right. Our purpose is not really to meet people on this planet. We're here for other reasons. I mean, think about it. Look at how much we've already learned. For the first time in my life, I dreamed that I communicated with a tree. So, let's get the most out of this place and enjoy the forest as best as we can."

"I agree with you, Morris" Andrew stated. "This Eucalyptus forest is really great. So, let's enjoy it."

All of them realized the message that Morris was telling them. They released any bad feelings they had about being put off, and they continued walking through the forest. The terrain was flatter now, and every direction they looked, they saw Eucalyptus trees. Their almost mint-like aroma penetrated the air, and a light breeze blew through their upper branches.

Morris continued to use his crystal ball to guide them, and this assured that they moved in a fairly straight direction. If they moved too far to the right or to the left from their destined course, his crystal would lose its glow until they corrected their course. He was assuming that his crystal ball was heading them on course for the city beyond the edge of this large forest.

After several more hours of walking, they realized it had been 12 hours since they had left their campsite this morning. They had walked probably 30 kilometers, and their feet were telling them about it.

"Boy, we've had a long day today!" declared Paul. "Let's set up camp."

The area was flat and completely forested by Eucalypts. Many of the trees reached up as much as 30 meters above the ground. No water was in sight, but that was okay, as they had tanked up at the water hole.

Vega still hung fairly high in the sky, and they knew it would be several more hours before it would be dark. Getting used to 29-hour days was not easy. To them, it already felt like it was late at night since they were used to 24-hour days on Earth. They decided to call it a day anyway, and they set up camp among the trees. Most of them were too tired to do anything but sit down and have an evening meal.

"These long days sure are nice," Steven commented, "if only we could get used to them."

"I know," Robert agreed. "I feel like we're wasting the rest of the day, even that we've already spent a full day, according to our schedule."

"I don't guess it really matters," said Chris. "After all, we'll only be here for a few days or a couple of weeks at the most."

"Then we'll move on to another planet or star system," said Andrew.

Despite their tiredness, they spent the next few hours chatting about all kinds of things, and they told stories as well. Chris and William took out their decks, and they played cards. Finally, Vega touched the horizon, and they immediately went to sleep for the long night.

When morning arrived, they were well rested after their long sleep. No one, not even Morris, had any dreams of interest. Their watches read 5 p.m., June 18, and they realized that the time they were used to on Earth had shifted completely out of phase with the time here. They didn't notice it considerably since they had just slept 13 hours.

"I feel like we'll emerge from the forest today," Morris announced to them.

"How do you know?" Chris asked. "This forest seems never-ending."

"That is just my intuition at work," Morris replied.

"Okay, we'll see," said Robert. "Let's eat some breakfast. Then we'll pack and continue on through the forest."

They walked for five more hours through mostly flat, forested terrain. At times, some of them had slight feelings of anxiety, instinctively wondering if they were destined to remain in a never-ending forest of Eucalypts, even though they knew they had the ability to transport themselves out at any time.

When they stopped for lunch, they thought they imagined brighter light in the direction they were heading. Sure enough, after they finished lunch and walked for another 15 minutes, they emerged from the forest into a barren landscape of red dirt that was littered with various sizes of rocks and boulders. They looked ahead and thought they could just make out a flicker of light reflecting off of what could possibly be the city they had heard about. It appeared to be 20 kilometers away.

"Morris, is that the city way in the distance?" James asked.

"I'm not sure," he answered. "Let me check." With his crystal ball in hand, he faced toward the direction of the reflecting flicker of light and moved to face to the right, then to the left. The ball glowed when he faced directly toward the flicker of light. "I believe it is," he finally answered.

"Good. Let's keep moving," James eagerly said. Even though he said that, he then turned around and faced the forest. "Goodbye Eucalyptus forest. I've enjoyed walking through you, and it gives me a great feeling, knowing that some of Australia grows here also."

Everyone turned to face the forest before moving on, and they were grateful for the shade the Eucalypts had provided them. They now felt Vega's heat beaming down on them, and they knew that it would be a lot hotter than it had been in the forest.

"How are we going to cross this desert?" William asked. "There isn't any plantlife in sight."

"How much water do we have left?" Robert asked everyone.

"I've got half a liter," Chris answered.

"I've got a liter left," said Andrew.

Everyone else checked and answered, and Robert said, "I believe that will do us. Let's walk on through here as quickly as possible. If we do run out of water, we can always cheat and transport ourselves somewhere else to get more."

With that possibility at hand, everyone set out across the flat, barren desert toward the city in the distance. It was so hot and dry that after three hours, they had consumed all of their water, and they soon afterwards became thirsty. Basically, they had decided to push on until they became noticeably uncomfortable before cheating and transporting themselves out.

When they were just about to give up, they were quite surprised to come within view of a fairly deep gorge that had not been visible until they were within a few hundred meters of it. This gorge was cut right into the flat, barren land and was a welcome relief to Robert and his friends. At the bottom of this gorge, probably 300 meters below, a small river flowed.

"All right!" James shouted with joy. "It's water!"

"Whew-wee!" William yelled.

All of them gave out screams of joy and carefully made their way down the steep bank to the river. Cactus plants grew in this gorge along with Tamarisks and Cypress-Pine shrubs.

Upon reaching the river, they found a nice flat spot by its edge. They set down their packs and jumped in for a swim in the cool, easy-flowing water. The river's width was around 10 meters, and they enjoyed floating down it, walking upstream, and repeating the same action, over and over.

"What a nice reward after our past three long days of hiking!" Steven exclaimed.

"I'm glad we came after all," said James.

As Vega moved lower in the sky, it disappeared behind the steep bank of the gorge, giving them shade for the rest of the day. As the light reflected off the sunny side of the gorge, the views, as they looked up and down the river, were spectacular. Much of the gorge was reddish-orange, and in some places, the river had cut away at the rock, creating cliffs and drop-offs in those areas. They were smooth and curved due to having been worn by the water.

"Let's go ahead and camp here overnight," Robert suggested.

"Good idea," Chris approved.

"I wish we'd remembered to bring some fishing rods," said William, "but then, since we didn't, I guess we'll just skip it."

"The swimming is good enough for me," said Morris.

"Yeah, me too," James agreed. "Let's go in for some more."

After having crossed the hot, dry desert for the past several hours, it seemed that they just couldn't get enough of swimming. Over and over, they floated downstream, swam across the river, dived underneath the water, and explored the banks as well.

When they noticed that Vega was fairly low in the sky, as the opposite banks were now almost completely shaded, they decided to prepare and eat supper, after which they set up camp. As soon as it became dark, they went to sleep for another long night. Most of them slept right through the whole night.

When it became light the next morning, everyone arose, refreshed and ready to walk to the mysterious city. They ate breakfast, packed up, and left as soon as possible to get an early start before it would become too hot. There was not a cloud in the sky, and they had not seen any clouds at all since arriving on Vega.

The climb out of the gorge was steep and difficult, but everyone was careful, and no one slipped and fell. Once out of the gorge, they were back on the flat, barren landscape which was still littered with various sizes of rocks and boulders. The view of the city showed that they were closer to it, and it now appeared to be 10 kilometers away.

After having walked for a couple of hours, Vega was higher in the sky, and they were beginning to notice the heat. At least they were glad to have a full supply of water, thanks to the river back where they had camped.

By now, the city appeared to be only two kilometers away, and they could now see that it was a large dome that reflected Vega's rays of light into a dazzling display of colors.

"That is definitely a city made out of Shakeilar," Morris commented. "I'm really looking forward to seeing this."

Curiosity was building up in all of them. There was so much to look forward to, and it lay only a short distance ahead of them across the flat, barren terrain. Everyone eagerly walked toward it. In some ways, it appeared somewhat exotic and precious, like a huge gem or an oasis in the desert.

Finally, they were within 100 meters of the huge shining dome of various colors of crystal.

"This city looks incredible!" Paul remarked.

"I'll say!" Morris agreed. "It must be a kilometer across and 300 meters high at the top center."

"How many people do you think live inside?" William asked everyone.

"Oh, I'd say around 50,000," Robert answered. "That's my best guess."

"That's what I was thinking, too," said Andrew.

"Well, let's go on up and see if anyone is home," Chris suggested.

"Okay, here goes," said James.

Everyone set down his pack, and they walked over to the huge structure. No real entrance could be seen. Instead, it appeared to be a huge vertical wall. Finally, James reached out and touched the surface while everyone else watched, hoping that an opening would suddenly dematerialize, granting them entry.

James touched the surface with his right hand, and suddenly, the entire city vanished, dematerializing instantly and silently! For an instant, everyone was in a state of shock, not yet realizing that it was actually gone. James was beside himself in disbelief.

"No way!" Steven exclaimed.

"That's impossible!" Robert remarked.

"It's . . . It's really gone!" declared Chris.

"Blast it!" James angrily shouted. "I'm not believing this!"

"Talk about putting us off . . ." William began.

"I know," James continued, "and all I did was gently touch it. What an insult!"

"You know," said Robert, "I really wanted to explore this place."

"Yeah, you and all of us here," Paul agreed.

"Morris, where did it go?" Andrew asked.

He sighed. "How would I know that?!" he angrily told them.

"Well, come on!" Chris urged him. "You're the one who communicated with that *Eucalyptus* tree in your dream the other night."

"You have a better chance of knowing this than the rest of us do," Robert added.

"Why has the city put us off?" James wanted to know.

"All right! Enough already!" Morris shouted. "Look, I'm not going to tell you what I think about it or why, for that matter."

"What do you mean you're not going to tell us?" James quickly asked.

"I'm telling you all no!" Morris insisted. "I'm just not going to tell you, and that's that."

"Just like that?" James asked.

"You know something, don't you!" Chris declared.

"Morris, what are you doing us this way for?" Robert asked. "What did we ever do to you? Look, we've done so much to help you out with your deal with Tom. We all built that building for the galactic communications device before any of us ever saw Tom at all. None of us ever dreamed about him. Only you did. Also . . ."

"Stop!" Morris angrily commanded. "Don't start going into all of that now! That's not very nice! I've already had enough abuse to last 10 people two lives."

Robert and the others looking on just couldn't believe Morris' sudden change in attitude toward them for the worse. He looked at the others with an expression of, Did I abuse him? They signalled that no, they didn't think so. Morris' comment made Robert feel as bad as if he had killed someone, and his anger started to rise as a result.

"Abuse?!" Robert yelled. "Of all things! What abuse? I'm not abusing, for goodness sake!"

"Yeah, really, Morris!" James added. "We just wanted to know why the whole bloomin' city disappeared."

"What do you know that we don't know?" Chris asked Morris.

"Look, I told you all that I'm not going to tell you!" Morris rudely told them. "Don't you *ever* pester me about it again, or I'm going to transport myself out of here. It's that simple."

"Hey look!" Robert pointed out. "If you think you felt abused, you just made me feel as guilty as if I had killed someone, accusing me of abusing you, and I don't like that!"

"That's it," Morris declared. "I'm out of here!"

He placed his hands on either side of himself and began to transport himself away to who knew where.

"Oh no you don't!" James declared. "You're not going anywhere!"

Just as the pink glow had begun to envelope Morris, the seven of them rushed over to him and piled on top of him, knocking him to the ground, thereby stopping the transport process. As they all pinned him down, Robert got out of the pileup and said:

"Look, I know you're upset about the Shakeilar city disappearing on us, but don't take it out on us. We're you're friends! At least I hope you think we are, and where in the world did your hospitality go? Do you even trust us anymore?"

"I haven't stopped trusting any of you," Morris struggled to say, under the weight of the others. "Will you get off of me?"

"Will you tell us why the city disappeared?" James asked right back.

"All right! All right, I will!" Morris shouted, giving in to the others.

They all got off of him, allowing him to get up off of the dry dusty ground. He sort of brushed himself off and collected his wits again. "Since you're *that* insistent, I'll go ahead and tell you."

"Good. We're all ears," said Robert.

"I actually don't know the whole answer to the mysterious disappearance, but it was not our fault. I do know that much. My feeling is that the city contained knowledge that we weren't supposed to know, and we evidently are not ready nor prepared to see what is within those walls."

"You mean what *was* within those walls," Andrew corrected.

"No, it still *is*," Morris insisted. "It's just that it moved itself up to a higher vibrational level, another vibratory level, and disappeared, undetectable by us and unaffected by our presence here."

"Thank you," Robert declared. "See, that wasn't hard, was it?"

"No, it wasn't. I suppose you're right," Morris admitted.

"What was all that you said about being abused?" William asked Morris.

"You never told us you were abused," Paul added.

"Whoops!" declared Morris. "I guess it slipped out. I wasn't ever going to tell you all about that, but yes, I was abused physically by my father until I was 15 and strong enough to overpower him. The mean old jerk that he was would take a belt to me around once a week for just petty, worthless reasons. Finally, when I was 15, I'd had enough of it!

"I'll go ahead and tell you what happened. He sent me to my room because I'd made a casual comment that he didn't like. A few minutes later, he entered with his belt in hand as usual, ready to wear me out. Well, I had decided that he wasn't going to get his wish this time. To his surprise, I rushed up to him and swiftly kicked him in the balls as hard as I could with my foot, and that disabled him. Next, I slammed my bedroom door closed and knocked him to the floor. I ripped the belt away from him, and I mean to tell you, I *wore him out*! I took out the 11 years of beltings he had given me, and I turned it back around on him. I didn't let him get up as I kept whipping the daylights out of him. I tell you, I was angry!"

"Good gracious, Morris!" Robert declared. "You sure were!"

"Anyway," Morris went on, "my mother and my siblings heard the event and rushed in to see what was wrong, and they were horrified! They had to pull me off and restrain me."

"Golly! What happened then?" James asked. Everyone was listening to Morris' story with completely undivided attention.

"Well, I didn't know it at the time, but I had knocked my father unconscious. I was so angry at him that I don't know how long I would have continued whipping him, probably quite a while. He was in shock, and Mother had to call an ambulance. It came, and they rushed him off to the hospital. He was there a week, getting over his bad bruises and injuries, and it was two days before he even woke up."

"Golly! That's awful!" Chris exclaimed. "What did they do to you for that one?"

"There were no charges ever filed because Mother, bless her soul, took full responsibility for my actions. She had always been against corporal punishment, but she had never had the guts nor the strength to stop him. She walked over to me as we were standing around the hospital bed and sincerely thanked me for knocking the stuffing out of him, and she gave me a hug. It was all too much for me to bear, and I had strong feelings of guilt. Nevertheless, we all rejoiced that the days of abuse from my father were over."

Morris choked up, and he broke down and sobbed, right there in front of everyone. They gathered around him, hoping to cheer him up.

"It's okay, Morris," James assured him. "Those days are behind you. We're your friends, and we hope you'll get over your emotional trauma soon."

Morris carried on sobbing for a few minutes before he cleared up. Robert stood back and just watched. He didn't know what was appropriate to say, so he said nothing.

"I don't like to even think about it," Morris told them, still choking on his words. "I've never told anyone outside the family before."

Andrew walked over to him and said, "I know it's hard for you, but it's great that you are talking now and are working this out with yourself."

"What about your siblings?" William asked. "You're the oldest, right?"

"Right," Morris confirmed. "I think my father is mortally afraid to ever lay a hand in anger on any of my siblings again for fear of their lashing out at him as violently as I did."

"Yep, that will do it," said Paul.

"I believe what you did to your father," said Robert, "was a valuable lesson for him. It's a shame it had to be done that way, but he had it coming."

"Yes, I'll agree to that," said Morris. "I know I taught him never to whip me again."

"Corporal punishment has got to be the stupidest method of punishment that there is," Robert declared, "and it's just a cop-out and an easy way for the parents."

"If parents really loved their children, they wouldn't whip them, would they," Morris pointed out.

"That's right," Paul agreed. "I despise corporal punishment."

"I'm going to add," Chris brought up, "that any father who is going to use corporal punishment on his children is, in a way, asking them to eventually lash back at him."

"I know," James agreed, "and if the mother does it, she's asking for the same."

"When is this society ever going to learn that corporal punishment only feeds hate into the children?" Robert asked everyone.

"I don't know," said Morris, "but I vow up and down that I won't be using it with my children."

"Good for you, Morris," Robert approved, "I won't either, and I hope none of you all here ever do either."

"Let's remember Morris' story," Andrew suggested, "and when we may have children in the future, let's love them and find another way, a better way, to make them behave when we need them to."

"Everyone," Morris announced, "please forgive me for being so rude and unsociable about not telling you why I thought the city disappeared. It's just that I too was very upset and insulted at its disappearance, and I was so looking forward to seeing it and finding out all about it. Anyway, I took out my anger and frustration on you all, and that was wrong."

"Well, okay Morris," Robert calmly said. "I'm going to have to tell you this, that there is no way in the world that I can possibly imagine that telling someone how I helped him or reminding someone that I helped him, is in any way abusive. It can't be abusive because it was nice of me to give the help in the first place."

Morris thought about it and realized that Robert was right. "You're right," he admitted, "and I was about to discard every one of you from my list of friends over such a petty issue. Please forgive me. I just overreacted."

"That's okay," Andrew assured Morris, patting him on the back. "You're still getting over the terrible abuse from your father."

"Also, everyone," Morris went on, "I'm glad you pounced on me and prevented me from transporting myself away. I wouldn't have been doing the rest of you right, and that would have been selfish of me. There's no telling where I would have gone, and that would have been a cop-out for me. It's best we worked the whole thing out, and now the cat is out of the bag about my childhood. You all know."

"Yeah, I don't guess any of us knew you back then, since we didn't really meet until we got to Riverdale," said Paul.

"I don't know about you all," William brought up, "but I'm ready to leave this planet and go on to another place."

"Yes, I agree," said Chris.

"I believe I even agree with that," said Morris. "This city's obvious disappearance is a sign for us to leave. Let's put our backpacks on and go."

"Let's go back to Robert's woods and arrive on the top of the knob on the big limestone table of bedrock," Steven suggested.

"Good idea," Robert agreed. "We'll make more plans once we get there."

They walked back over to their backpacks, put them on, and transported themselves out of there. In seconds, they materialized on the top of the knob in the Joslin's woods in Tennessee. It was 4 a.m., Thursday, June 20, and there was a faint glow of light in the east sky. Still, it was quite dark, and they could barely see their way around. All of them took off their backpacks and became seated. The cool humid morning was a welcome relief to the heat back on Vega.

After resting in silence for a few minutes, Morris began the conversation. "I've decided that some time this year, probably this fall, I'm going to do some serious research into this whole thing about dolphins, dolphs, their origins, and exactly what they had to do with the mysterious Shakeilar. We obviously know very little about it at this time, but I'm going to find out."

"That's good," Robert commented. "After all, that Eucalyptus tree told you there was a purpose for your having heard that story it told you. I really think you're right on track to research it and possibly write a book about your findings. More power to you."

"Thanks, Robert," said Morris.

"You *are* going to continue travelling with us this summer, aren't you?" Chris asked with a concerned tone in his voice.

"Oh yes, I am," Morris assured him. "After all, you need my transmission of visual images from time to time and the use and help of my crystal ball as well. It's important that I stay with you all during our travels this summer.

"Besides," Andrew added, "you'll probably learn a lot toward your research just by travelling with us."

"That could well be true," Morris agreed. "I wouldn't miss this opportunity for travel, anyway. I enjoy it and learn a lot from it."

"As Caymar said," Paul quoted, " 'Travelling opens the mind'."

"That's very true," said Morris.

Robert just remembered something. "Hey, Morris, I just now realized that we never saw any of those flying dragons back on Sirius B. Didn't you say to us back in March that you had seen some there?"

"Yes, you're right. I did," Morris admitted. "That's strange we didn't see any, either. The best I can say is that they exist in another plane of existence or in the astral world."

"Oh, okay," said Robert. "That would explain why we didn't actually see any."

"Why didn't any of them contact you while we were there?" Andrew asked Morris.

"That's a good question," he answered. "I don't really know. Maybe we were so busy doing other things, that they didn't have any use to contact us."

"Could be," said Andrew.

"Well, where do we want to go next?" Steven asked the others.

"How about the Pleiades?" Robert suggested.

"Yeah, that sounds like a good idea," Steven approved.

"Didn't you tell us, Morris, that it's heavily forested there?" James asked.

"Yes, I did, and the trees are sort of Palm-like and don't have branches until way up each tree."

"That's what I thought," said James.

"How much food do we have?" Paul asked everyone.

Everyone checked in his pack, and they determined that they had around a four-day supply left.

"I reckon we'd be better off starting our trip to the Pleiades with a full supply of food," James suggested. "Tell you what, I'll go down to Devonport and purchase enough food to stock us with a full supply again. Does anyone want anything special or unusual?"

No one could think of anything.

"Have you got enough Australian money with you?" Robert asked.

James pulled out his wallet. "Forty dollars."

"Here, I've got some left," Robert offered, and he handed him a 20 dollar note.

The others also handed James some leftover Australian cash. Morris checked, using his crystal ball, to be sure that all was clear at the location in Tasmania. It was, and James transported himself away, to return within an hour.

Meanwhile, the others waited while dawn arrived. Crickets could be heard everywhere, and many varieties of birds made their calls. The sky was hazy, and there were a few clouds here and there.

"I'm just curious, Robert," Chris asked, "what time is it in Tasmania?"

Robert looked at his watch, thought for a few seconds, and said, "It's 7 p.m. there."

"Good," said Chris. "The stores will be open there."

"What do you think we want to do in the Pleiades?" Andrew asked the others.

"Well, I know I want to have a good look through the forest," said Robert.

"I have a feeling that it will have a lot to offer us," Morris predicted.

"How do you mean?" Chris asked him.

"I have no idea how," Morris explained, "but my feeling is that there is a lot we may learn there."

"Well, as soon as James returns, we'll take off and find out," said William.

"Oh," Robert brought up, suddenly remembering something, "I think it might be a good idea if I go down to the step office building and call the telephone station on the Pleiades and tell them we're coming. We didn't do that for Vega. The Vegans, as we all noticed, were not so hospitable as the Sirians. I don't know if not having called Vega prior to our arrival made a difference or not."

"I wouldn't have thought so," said Morris.

"I'll go on down there and call the Pleiades, anyway," said Robert. "I'll be back in half an hour." With that, he walked to the building at the foot of the woods and made the phone call. The party on the other end of the line was pleased to hear that they were coming and made preparations to receive them. Robert was happy to find this out and was glad he'd called them.

He returned to the top of the knob where the others were still waiting. James arrived with a bunch of food 10 minutes later, and they divided up the supplies and packed them away into their backpacks. By the time this was done, it was 6:30 a.m.

"Is everyone ready?" Morris checked.

All answered yes.

"Here is the visual image of the telephone station on the Pleiades, in case any of you have forgotten." Morris transmitted the image. After he made sure that everyone knew what it looked like, they transported themselves away.

14 The Trip to the Pleiades

As they made their arrival, rematerializing as the pink glow and whirring wind faded away, a young female was standing and waiting for them. She was, no doubt, a human being, and she appeared to be the same age as they were. She stood around 5½ feet tall and had lighter colored hair. To their surprise, she was dressed in normal Earth-type clothing.

"Hello there," she called out to them. "You all must be the group from Earth."

"That we are," Morris verified.

"That's good," she said. "Welcome to the Pleiades. We're glad you're here, and you're welcome to spend as much time here as you like."

"Thank you," said Paul.

They looked around them. The telephone station had been placed right in the middle of a lush, prehistoric looking forest with trees that they had never seen before. Many of them were huge, and they recognized the foliage way in the tops of each tree, just like Morris had shown them in his visual image transmission to them. Their appearance was truly incredible, as their trunks had a checkered or cross-hatched appearance, and their fern-like foliage created a dense canopy that caused the entire forest floor to be completely shaded. The ground was covered with various types of ferns and mosses, and the smell of the forest was dominated by the scent of moisture and of these mosses.

Various types of unfamiliar birds made their calls, and most of them were perched high up in the canopy. Here and there, a bird would swoop down and fly under the canopy to another tree. Various insects, some of them fairly large, flew through the air, making their buzzing sounds with their wings. The largest ones appeared like dragon flies, and they were half a meter long. None of the insects appeared threatening, however.

Inhabiting the forest floor were various types of salamanders, lizards, and frogs, all very similar to the types they were familiar with back on Earth. Other four-legged reptiles scurried across the ground from one tree to another, and some of them were as large as a domestic cat.

They gazed up into the canopy and could barely see the light of this planet's home star shining through. It appeared to be in the middle of the sky, and the temperature was cool with a feeling of moisture in the air.

"We have quite an abundance of life here, don't we?" the young woman finally said, having given them a couple of minutes to look around and orient themselves.

"You know," said James, "according to books I've seen that speculate on what Earth was like in prehistoric times, this place could well resemble what Earth looked like, say, 100 million years ago."

"Yes, that could very well be," she agreed. "I believe that life started on this planet around that many years later than life on Earth did. So, that would make sense. Further, our moist and mild climate is very suitable for reptilian life and lush trees like these here."

"What are the names of these trees?" Robert asked her.

"Well, these ones you see here are the dominant trees on our world. They grow in all parts of it, except for the north and south pole areas. We have our own name for them in our native Pleiadean language, but in your language, English, they would best be referred to as Fern-Palms."

"That's a very fitting name for them," James told her. "Down in Tasmania, Australia, where I come from, we have Fern Trees like these, but these here are much larger."

"Yes, I know what you're talking about," she said. "They are the closest comparison to these Fern-Palms here, and on Earth the Fern Trees you talk about are remnants of prehistoric times."

"That is true," said James, impressed with her knowledge. "Have you been there?"

"Yes, I have," she answered. "I've been there several times and have walked through Earth's forests."

"Is that right?" James asked in an enthusiastic tone. "But how?"

"Oh, we humans here can teleport ourselves around," she explained, "just like the humans on Sirius B can do."

"Anyway," she continued, "my name is Suzanne, and I would best be titled what you would call in your language, a princess."

"You're joking!" James declared. "You mean there's royalty here?"

"Oh yes," Suzanne told him. "We've operated on a system of royalty for thousands of years, and that influence has been handed down to your planet Earth, only we don't take it so seriously."

"Nor do the Earthlings anymore," James added.

"Oh, they still do in some places," she insisted.

"Oh, yeah," James realized. "I'd say you're right when you consider the whole of Earth. I was thinking of England and the British Commonwealth countries."

"Yes, now that's true for those countries," Suzanne agreed. "Their royalty subjects are only figureheads now."

"Where are your guards?" William asked.

"Oh, we don't have guards," she answered, laughing.

"But how do you keep safe and protected?" he further asked.

"We don't need to worry about that here," she explained. "Everyone here is perfectly safe, and everyone respects everyone else. There is no crime nor any intentional wrongdoing."

"That's great!" Steven remarked. "But then what good is having royalty if there is no law and order to maintain?"

"That's a good one!" she said, laughing. "Coming from Earth's point of view, I can see why you thought that. Our royalty, here on Aleyone, which is the name of our planet, by the way, doesn't serve the purpose of maintaining law and order. Our purpose here is to offer advice concerning peace, love, and friendship to those who need it. Our royalty doesn't operate on a system of fear but on one of love, and we're sorry that Earth doesn't see it in quite as good a context as we do here."

"That's interesting," Morris commented, "because I've heard that Earth's present culture is operating on the Pleiadean influence from 6,000 years ago. Most of it operates on the basis of fear and control, which is used to enforce law and order."

"When our ancestors introduced that culture on Earth 6,000 years ago," she explained, "we introduced it with all good intentions. Our base was in what you now call the Middle East. Unfortunately, the culture we introduced then has changed and evolved into what it is today. Anyway, don't despair. Things will drastically improve fairly soon when people start waking up on their subconscious levels."

"Interesting explanation," said Morris. "I'll ponder that."

"You know," Suzanne realized, "I haven't even found out your names yet."

"Oh, yeah," said James. "Sorry about that. My name is James West-field. I'm from Devonport, Tasmania, Australia."

"I'm Robert Joslin, and I'm from near Murfreesboro, Tennessee in the United States."

"I'm Morris England, and I'm also from near Murfreesboro, Tennessee, but I live just on the other side of that town."

The rest of them introduced themselves and told her where they were from.

"I'm very pleased to meet you all," she gladly told them, "and I'm sure you'll have a wonderful time touring our planet Aleyone."

Both Robert and Morris suddenly realized that they wanted to ask her more about the Pleiades star system, but they were momentarily side-tracked by Suzanne's next comment to James.

"You know, James," she said in a flirtatious affectionate way, "you're cute. You really have a sparkle about you."

James blushed to a nice hue of red in his face and couldn't respond. He turned away in slight embarrassment.

"Ah, James, looks like you got one there," Robert teased.

"Looks like the *love bug* has bitten you," Chris added, sort of lunging toward him as he spoke the words, *love bug.*

"Cut it out!" James angrily yelled at them. Both Chris and Robert jumped back in surprise.

Suzanne stood back and laughed heartily at the whole scene.

Morris stepped in and spoke to James. "James, Chris and Robert were just having a little fun. They were only teasing. They didn't mean any harm."

"Well, I don't want it!" he angrily declared.

"Look, James," Morris pointed out, "this is a perfect example of what I was saying to you when we were at Lake Windermere right after Chris and Richard Bell disappeared."

"What is?" James wanted to know.

"You can't take a joke," Morris reminded him.

"Yeah really, James," Chris added. "Lighten up!"

"Oh, I'll think about it," said James.

"Good! You just do that!" Robert angrily insisted.

Suzanne looked at them and had another series of laughter. When she finally calmed down, she said, "It's just like any Earthling, getting angry and worked up over petty issues. I said that to James to test out your trueness of friendship."

"Oh, you did?" Chris asked.

"Yes, and it answers my question too," she told them. "Once a fellow starts to fall for a woman, more often than not, he throws out his other friendships, usually over stuff like you all just did. Anyway, maybe you'll be better attuned to yourselves by the time you finish your visit here, and maybe you won't become overwhelmed by that instinct to flare up and bite some friend's head off."

"That's a good point," Andrew commented.

Morris now remembered to ask his question. "Suzanne, tell us more about the Pleiades star system. How many stars are there, altogether?"

"Well, there are seven main parts to the Pleiades Cluster," she informed everyone. "Five of them are single star systems: Pleione, Electra, Taygate, Merope, and Mato, and two of them are binary star systems: Aleyone and Atlas. This star system is Aleyone, and our planet, also called Aleyone, is the only planet with life on it in this system. In fact, this is the only planet with life on it in the entire Pleiades Cluster."

"That's surprising," Paul remarked. "Why is that?"

"Most of the Pleiades is quite new," she answered. "It's only 60 million years old, and somehow, this planet miraculously survived. Our binary star system, Aleyone, was caught up in the gravitational field of the new Pleiades Cluster when it first formed. Also, one of the stars of the Atlas binary star system is an old star. It was a bit of a jolt to our planet and star system, but we managed to survive it almost unharmed."

"Wait a minute," said Morris. "Let me get this straight. The Pleiades Cluster as a whole is only 60 million years old while, during its formation, it caught an older binary star system, this one?"

"That's right," she said, "and it also caught the planets of these two older stars."

"How could anything have survived that?" Morris wanted to know. "It seems like the unimaginable stellar event that occurred then, would certainly have blown this planet's future life away."

"It would have if the sentient species residing here at that time had not intervened," she answered.

"Oh, is that right?" Morris asked.

"Yes, according to the history we've been told," she explained, "the sentient species who appeared, as we would call it, humanoid, were and still are very advanced. They presently reside here on a higher vibratory level. What they did at the time, 60 million years ago, was to raise the entire planet to a higher vibratory level. They kept it there for several thousand years, and for that time, everything was totally unaffected by and protected from that unimaginable stellar event that would otherwise have ruined everything.

"When the system's formation had stabilized, they cleared the debris, using force fields, out of the way of our planet's path of revolution around Aleyone One, our star. Once this was done, they lowered our planet back down to the normal vibratory level of the physical 3-D universe, and we've been surviving ever since."

"That was good thinking on their part," said Steven.

"Actually, it was brilliant," Morris added. "They must be an extraordinary race."

"Oh, they are," she agreed. "We learn a lot from them. We only see them in our dreams, and we communicate with them telepathically."

"Oh really?" Andrew responded.

"Yes, and they have a lot to teach us. They have a lot to offer. Because of them, we Pleiadean humans even communicate telepathically with the trees."

"Is that so?" Morris asked with surprise. "I just dreamed a few nights ago, back on Vega, that I was telepathically communicating with a Eucalyptus tree."

"You see," she continued, "telepathically communicating on the dream level makes it easier."

"I'd say I agree with you," said Morris.

"Might I add," she said, "that I can tell that you, Morris, are the most attuned one out of your group."

"You got that right," Paul agreed. "We wouldn't be here, or on any other star systems for that matter, if it hadn't been for Morris' abilities."

"I can see that," she said. "Anyway, come on and let's take a walk through the forest. I'll show you around as we continue to talk."

She completely forgot to take them over to the telephone station to introduce them to the operator. Instead, she led them along a footpath that climbed uphill and put them on higher ground where the forest canopy was partially open.

They now had a look at the sky and realized that it was a greenish-blue, almost a turquoise color. Above them, they could see two suns, one larger and the other one more distant and fainter.

"I take it that the closer one is Aleyone One," said Paul, "and the further one is Aleyone Two?"

"That's correct," she answered. "I know it must seem strange to you, but living on a world in a binary star system is quite nice. At certain times of the year when our planet is between the two stars, much closer to Aleyone One, of course, it never gets dark. Our nights are dimmer, but we still receive enough light from Aleyone Two to enjoy the nights as if they were day."

"Must be nice," William commented.

"Yes, it's really great," she agreed. "It's too bad that Earth doesn't have the same setup."

"I know," said Robert. "It would be nice to have daylight all the way around the clock."

"By the way," Steven asked, "how long are your days here, and how many days are there to your year?"

"We have days that are 26 Earth hours long, and it takes 360 Earth days or 332 of our days for our planet Aleyone to revolve around Aleyone One."

"That's great!" Andrew exclaimed. "We won't have *any* problem getting used to this place."

"Finally, a planet that has nearly the same day-night hours as Earth!" declared Robert.

"Oh, another thing," Suzanne added, "Aleyone Two, the more distant one, is actually a bright giant star while our Aleyone One is a normal hot white star."

"It must be further to Aleyone Two than we thought," said Andrew.

"Aleyone Two is half a light year away, that is, Earth light years," she explained. "Aleyone One is very similar to your sun and is around 150 million kilometers away from here."

"That distance is pretty close to what it is for our sun at home," Andrew told her.

"Yes," Suzanne continued, "and our planet is also pretty close to the same size as Earth."

"Are these Fern-Palms the only species of tree here on Aleyone?" James asked, changing the subject.

"In this whole region, that's true," she answered. "These trees are very unique and special. This is the only planet in the whole galaxy, or possibly the universe, with trees like these, and these trees also serve a special purpose."

"What's that?" Steven asked.

"Their canopy gives us great shade," she continued, "and they therefore serve a great purpose in blocking or at least filtering out the harmful rays of direct starlight from Aleyone One and, in part, from Aleyone Two as well."

"So," Steven commented, "I assume that the telephone station got installed down the hill in a thicker part of the forest to give you that much more shade?"

"That's right," Suzanne answered. "There's another reason also. We humans on this planet, most of us anyway, are very sensitive to and attuned to energy fields, and these Fern-Palms emit great energy in a very positive way. In fact, they serve to filter out or block negative energy fields from all over the universe, a protection we don't get unless we are here in the forest."

"How does the forest do that?" Andrew asked, seemingly puzzled by this last statement from her.

"These trees are highly intelligent," she replied. "What they do by joint effort is to weave an energy vortex above the canopy, thereby creating a protective shield. Positive energies are allowed to pass through while negative energies are reflected and turned away back into space."

"Wait. How is that possible?" Robert asked her.

She thought for a few seconds. "You've got me on that one. I'm not sure how."

Morris was thinking and started to answer. "Energy fields carry vibrations, and positive and negative fields would have different vibrational frequencies. Let's see. How can it work?" he quietly asked himself.

Steven picked up the rest of the answer, saying, "Back in science, we studied waves and constructive and destructive interference. Waves of the same frequency come together and cause constructive interference, but that's only if they are in the same phase. Otherwise, they cancel each other out. Waves of different frequencies pass through each other. No, that won't explain how the energy fields do it. Gee!"

"Maybe," Andrew speculated, "the energy field's woven vortex consists of varying frequencies that are 180 degrees out of phase with all different negative energy frequencies, and they cancel them all out. No," he corrected himself, "that's too complicated. There's got to be another way." He pondered.

She paused and appeared to meditate for 15 seconds. "The trees have just given me an answer. The energy vortex they create transmits positive energies and love. How that works on a technical level, I don't know. There's something else I was going to answer for you."

James repeated his question to remind her. "Are these Fern-Palms the only species of tree here on Aleyone?"

"Oh, yeah. That was what I was going to tell you about," she recalled. "They are for this region and continent, and this continent is the largest, by far, of them all. On the other side of Aleyone, there is a fairly large sea or ocean. Within it are small continents or large islands. On some of those islands, grow other trees, many of them having been planted there by the sentient species, the ones I was saying that live on a higher vibratory level."

"Yeah right," said James, speaking for everyone and implying for her to continue.

"This sentient humanoid species has lived here on Aleyone for over 100 million years, and they collected many prehistoric Earth plants and trees and brought them here. For one thing, they knew a lot about stars and comets and other stellar bodies, and they knew that Earth would be struck by a large meteor, an event that actually happened 65 million years ago. So, they set out to collect and preserve as many species as possible, knowing that most or all of them would be wiped out. They brought them here and planted them on various islands in the ocean.

"Then, only 5 million years later, they discovered that their own planet this one, was in jeopardy. They still lived in the physical 3-D vibratory level then and were panicked as to what to do. They checked around and were overjoyed to discover other vibratory levels. Immediately, they set out to raise the whole planet to a higher level to protect it. After all, they had a treasure of living trees and plants to protect, many of which became extinct on Earth."

"Well, I'm glad they succeeded in protecting them," said Robert.

"Yes, we're glad too," Suzanne agreed. "Maybe you all can see some of these forests before you leave to go back to Earth."

"I would *love* to!" James declared.

"Anyway, what would you all like to do for your stay on Aleyone?" she asked them.

"Well, we definitely want to do some hiking for a few days," said Robert.

"I'd like to have a look at one of the cities, if there are any," said Andrew.

"There are great places to go hiking," she informed them, "and there is also one city. The city is not too far from here, and it's on one of our major rivers and is built on top of a natural clearing on a bank up from that river. Our technology center is there, and we are in close communication with the higher sentient humanoids for technological advice and other help in general."

"Oh really?" Andrew responded, as something seemingly dawned on him. "Robert, do you remember when Virginia at the stone hut on Lopeia told me that we knew each other in the Pleiades and that we were working on an engineering project or something like that?"

"Yes, I do," Robert recalled. "I guess that was here, then. We were probably two of those higher vibratory level humanoids. What do you think?"

"I guess we were," said Andrew. "I wonder what we were working on?"

"You got me," Robert admitted. "I know I don't remember."

"Me neither," said Andrew.

"Tell you what," Suzanne offered. "Why don't you all come and stay with me and my family overnight. Like I said, we're the royal family, and I'm sure you'll enjoy meeting the others in my family. We're not formal and dazzling like the royal families on Earth. After all, we help and advise others, and we don't want to impose sovereignty over anyone."

"I like that type of royalty," Andrew commented, laughing a little.

"Me too," Paul agreed.

"Just follow me," she offered. "It's only a few kilometers away."

She led the way as they walked back down the hill into the thick forest of Fern-Palms, passing near the telephone station and continuing through the shaded forest on mostly flat terrain along a dirt footpath.

"You mean there's no road from the city to the telephone station?" William asked.

"We don't have roads here," she answered. "All travel is done by foot or by teleportation or by spacecraft on occasion. Roads are very destructive to the land and the forest, and a footpath is small enough to go around any tree."

"What about all your technology at the technology center in the city?" Chris asked.

"Oh, it's a great one," she boasted. "Great things are made there, but automobiles are not one of them."

"Then what do they make there?" Andrew wanted to know.

"They make things like spacecrafts and other technological equipment for intergalactic trade," Suzanne answered.

"How do they make spacecrafts?" Robert asked.

"Actually, they grow them," she replied.

"Grow them?!" Robert exclaimed. "How?"

"You know how back on Earth that they grow silicon computer chips?" she asked.

"Yes," said Robert.

"Well, it's the same sort of way but on a much larger scale," she informed them. "They manifest energy into matter by certain thought processes from an etheric level."

"Certain thought processes from an etheric level," Steven repeated. "Huh! That is interesting." He pondered the idea as the rest of them also did.

"Actually," she continued, "they make nearly everything by manifesting energy into matter."

"Oh really?" said Andrew.

"That saves having to mine natural resources," Morris commented.

"Yes, that's correct," Suzanne agreed. "We like our planet to be as pristine and untouched as possible."

"That's very wise," Morris told her.

"I agree," she said. "Mining natural resources and minerals depletes the supply in only a few hundred years for a planet like yours with several billion people. Why go to all of the extensive trouble of mining when it's much easier to just manifest what you need directly out of energy?"

"Sounds good to me," William commented.

"Why doesn't Earth use the method of manifesting matter out of energy?" Robert asked.

"They actually know how, believe it or not," Suzanne explained, "but the problem is economic gridlock. Jobs for the miners of all the various raw materials on Earth have to be maintained. We Pleiadeans have made several visits to the top scientists and officials of Earth, but they won't initiate this method of manufacturing because they're afraid that the changeover will put too many people out of work."

"Yes, you're right about that, Suzanne," said Morris. "It's a really tight gridlock that Earth and its economy have gotten themselves into. I don't know if they'll ever overcome it."

"I think Earth will sometime, Morris," Robert predicted.

"But not until all of the natural resources are completely used up first," William pointed out.

"They'll have to change then, won't they!" Morris remarked.

"Anyway," she told them, "we, here on Aleyone, had enough foresight to preserve our planet and not tear it up like people on Earth are doing."

"When will they ever learn on Earth?" Chris asked everyone.

"Good question, Chris," said Robert.

They had walked through the deep forest quite a ways and were nearly to her parents' place by the river. They emerged from the forest into a partially open field dotted with younger Fern-Palms and green grass, and they now had an excellent view of the river down the hill from them, several hundred meters away. The greenish-blue, almost turquoise sky was spectacular with the appearance of puffy clouds that were slightly tinged with green. Other clouds were darker and were mostly gray in color.

On the other side of the river sat the city, a kilometer away. Some of it was underground, she told them, but most of it was above ground. Many of the buildings looked really modern with intricate geometrical designs. Very few were rectangular or cubical. Nearly every structure had plenty of windows to let in the natural light of Aleyone One.

It was becoming late afternoon, and Suzanne's family lived exclusively on this side of the river, overlooking it and the city beyond it.

"Let's go to my parents' house now," she offered. "It's to the left through this field. We'll go see the city tomorrow."

They followed her for another half a kilometer and suddenly came into view of a large, gray stone house nestled just inside the edge of the forest. The limbs and foliage of the tall Fern-Palms nearly created a perfect canopy well above the top of the house's roof. The house appeared to be three stories high and had plenty of windows to afford them views of their surroundings.

"This is an outstanding place you all have!" William commented.

"Absolutely fantastic!" Steven remarked.

"I'll say!" Paul agreed.

"I must say we do like it here," Suzanne agreed. "It looks very welcoming and attractive, and that's what we as the royal family want. People who come visit us feel relaxed and at ease here."

"It's like you said, Suzanne," Morris stated. "You all don't want to place a feeling of sovereignty over others."

"That's true," she agreed.

"I reckon you all have done very well," James remarked.

"Thank you, cute one," she remarked, slightly smiling.

"There she goes again, James," said Chris.

"Go after her, James," William urged. "She wants you."

James almost lost his temper, but he remembered what Morris had told him and squelched his anger, doing his best to take the teasing.

"Well done, James," Suzanne commended him. "You're doing better than I thought you would."

James made no comment, not yet knowing how to handle her flirting.

They reached the gate to the yard which surrounded the exposed side of the house, entered, and walked up to the front door. The whole house wasn't much different from a typical stone mansion on Earth. Even the door was normal with a proper doorknob. A middle-aged woman came to the door at the same moment that Suzanne and her eight new friends reached it. She opened the door and greeted them, speaking in an unrecognizable language.

"No, Mom, these eight are from Earth," Suzanne told her mother in English, "and their Earth language is English."

"Oh, right!" she corrected herself. "Sorry, that was our native Aleyone language that I was speaking. I rarely speak in English. The operator at the telephone station rang and said you were coming, and my spouse must have sent Suzanne, as I was over at the city until half an hour ago.

"Please come in and make yourselves at home," she offered. "I'm very pleased to have all of you as guests here. My name is Carya, as it would best be known in your language. My spouse's English name is Michael, and we have a son a couple of years younger than Suzanne named Harvey. Both of them are taking a short walk in the forest and will return soon."

Suzanne introduced Robert and his friends, starting with James, needless to say. The other seven could sense that she had an underlying attraction to James, but they weren't really jealous, even though they had been teasing him. Carya welcomed them inside and offered them glasses of water to drink. They became seated on some couches in a large open room.

"I just thought I'd mention," Morris brought up, "that you speak English very well. One would never know you speak it very little."

"Thank you very much, Morris," said Carya. "As you may already know, we people, here on Aleyone, are fully conscious beings, and as a result, languages are very easy. We know many since we are somewhat involved with intergalactic trade."

"Oh, I see," said Morris. "So is Tom, the galactic salesman from Sirius B. Do you know him?"

"Oh yes," Carya answered, "we know him very well. That's one reason the telephone station is near here, only a few kilometers into the woods."

"I'm just curious," Andrew inquired, "why is the telephone station way back in the middle of a forest instead of in the middle of the city across the river?"

"We chose for the station to be deep in the forest," Carya explained, "because if it had been placed in the middle of Towdenmore, there would have been too much interference."

"Towdenmore," said Morris. "Is that the name of your city?"

"Yes," she answered. "Didn't Suzanne tell you?"

"No, she never did," Morris answered. "That name really sounds familiar. I don't know why. Oh well, never mind."

"Maybe you heard it in one of your dreams," Chris suggested.

"Probably so," said Morris.

"Also," Carya continued, "since they make all sorts of equipment for intergalactic trade . . . Well, they grow some of it, actually . . . there would have been too much interference from the energies they use, and the result would have been a lot of static and humming on the telephone."

"That would be true," Andrew realized.

"I would imagine so," Steven agreed.

"You said the operator rang here and said that we were coming?" Robert asked.

"Yes, they did," Carya answered. "We had them run an extra extension to our house. The line is just under the ground surface and runs through the forest directly from here to the station."

"So, when calls come for you all, they are switched directly to here?" Andrew asked.

"Yes, by the operator," she said.

At that moment, the phone rang. "Ah, there's a call for me now. Probably someone I know on Earth." She got up to answer it.

Robert followed her into the kitchen where she went to answer the call. He was curious to see the phone. Sure enough, there was the desk phone on the counter top, a black Western Electric model with a rotary dial. He was quite surprised to see that it still had his parents' telephone number typed on the piece of paper in the center of the dial! No one had bothered to remove it after the duplication process where 120 of them had been duplicated in the Joslin's barnyard.

He walked back to the others saying, "My parents' phone number is still on that phone!"

"No kidding!" Steven remarked.

"Is that right?" William responded.

"Yes. The piece of paper is still on that dial," Robert told them.

The door opened, and in walked Michael with his son Harvey. He noticed everyone and said, "Well, hello there! You must be the group from Earth. My name is Michael, and this is my son Harvey."

They introduced themselves. Both of them stood around 6 feet tall, had light brown hair, and looked like ordinary Earthlings. They were even dressed in ordinary Earth clothing, such as normal pants and a casual shirt. In fact, all four of them were dressed in Earth-type clothing.

"Michael, I was wondering," Andrew asked, "how is it that all of you are dressed in Earth clothing?"

"Believe it or not," he answered, "we like Earth's wide variety of clothing and styles. We teleport ourselves there several times a year and purchase clothing and other practical items as well. Earth is a great place to visit, and we have a ball every time we go there. No one ever suspects that we're aliens, either."

"I'd say not in that normal attire," Andrew stated.

They laughed a little, and Harvey asked them, "So, tell me, how did the eight of you get involved with Tom from Sirius B and also into all this travelling?"

"Morris," said Robert, "would you like to do the telling?"

"Sure," he said. "Everyone sit back, and I'll start at the beginning. It all started with this amazing dream that I had back in March. Actually, Robert also had some of the same dream. Anyway . . ."

For the next 20 minutes, Morris related the whole story about how they built the galactic communications device, the deal with Tom, the crystal ball, the gift of transport Tom gave them, the visual images, and the places they had travelled.

". . . Like I said, we've already been to Sirius B and Vega, and now we are here to travel, learn, and have new experiences."

"Wow!" Harvey exclaimed. "You fellows have been around!"

Carya was now seated on the couch, having finished talking on the phone in the kitchen. "That's really nice," she commented. "I'm going to return to the kitchen to prepare a meal for all of us." She got up from the couch, and Suzanne went with her to help. The kitchen was a side room adjoining their large living room.

"What do you do as king, here on Aleyone?" Robert asked Michael.

"Well, I guess, according to Earth's culture, I would be titled a king, but we don't operate on a law and order scheme where I actually rule."

"Yes, that's what Suzanne was telling us," said Robert.

"Right. Well good," said Michael. "What I actually do is to help people gain a better understanding of themselves by various methods. I am here to talk to them or to help them, and I advise them when necessary."

"How do you have time for all that?" Paul asked.

"Actually, a very small percentage of Aleyone's population needs guidance from me. Most already instinctively know their path to follow, and those few who are confused receive my help."

"Even still," Paul insisted, "you'd still be swamped by people, it seems. I mean, this planet probably has a few hundred million people, at least, doesn't it?"

"No, Paul, actually it doesn't," Michael corrected him. "Our planet Aleyone has around 90,000 people."

"You're kidding!" Paul exclaimed. "That's all?"

"No way!" Steven remarked at the same time.

"I know that seems impossible to believe, coming from Earth," Michael realized, "but keep in mind that Towdenmore is the only city on our entire planet. It's all we need. Everything is made in one location. We don't have to ship and receive goods to and from all over the planet. Most of all, by keeping our population small, we are able to keep our planet in pristine condition. Mind you, there are a few of us spread out across our planet, and there are a few small communities as outposts, but basically, we have decided to leave the rest of our planet in the hands of nature without any interference or destruction from us."

"That's a good way to do it," said Morris.

"Must be nice," Chris remarked.

"I wish Earth could have done the same," Robert commented.

"It would have been nice," said Michael. "People on Earth have no real sense of importance of population control, and it's sad because the Earth doesn't belong to them to overrun and destroy. We value our planet Aleyone, and we would never do anything to harm it in any way. After all, the planet supports us, and we would die without its support."

"I fully agree with you," said Morris. "When will Earthlings ever learn?"

"They'll learn when they become fully conscious beings like we are," Michael answered.

After a few more minutes, Carya and Suzanne called to the others, informing them that the meal was ready. All of them walked into the kitchen where she had several large pots full of various mixtures of fruits and vegetables. After they filled their plates, they returned to where they had been sitting and began to eat.

"This is really tasty," Paul told Carya.

"It's all natural: fruits and vegetables, no salt, no sugar."

Paul was very surprised at that. "Is that right?"

"That's the truth," Carya confirmed.

"Where do you grow your food?" William asked.

"Some of it is grown in large indoor greenhouses," she replied, "and much of it is grown in large fields on the other side of the city."

"Why don't you just manifest it?" Robert asked.

"When it comes to food, that's not always a good idea," Carya explained. "It's not quite right to do that to the food because it would feel abused by us. We don't want to abuse our ability to manifest matter out of energy. Inorganic matter is fine, but organic matter has a mind of its own, and we humans need to respect that."

"I guess I do see your point about food," Robert admitted.

"Tell us more about your work, Michael," Morris requested.

"Well, I will add that I am a healer in addition to advising people."

"Oh really?" Morris asked.

"That's right," said Michael. "Most of the healing I do is through the use of crystals."

"Is that right?!" Paul asked with surprise. "But I thought crystals were just rocks."

"No, they are actually living and thinking beings," Michael insisted.

"Paul," Morris brought up, "what do you think my crystal ball is, just a glass ball with cracks?"

"Well, yeah, Morris," Paul agreed. "Of course . . . Well, you know . . . It's just a glass ball with cracks."

"It's more than that, Paul," Morris informed him. "My crystal ball is made out of natural quartz and was artificially crafted by man into a round ball from a large, geometrically shaped quartz crystal. That glow that my crystal ball emanates comes from within itself. It's really powerful and emits energy and white light. You remember what Virginia told me at the stone hut, don't you?"

"Oh, yeah," Paul recalled. "I forgot about all the stuff that your crystal ball does."

"Really, Paul," Morris went on, "crystals are living beings even though we may not be aware of it. In a way, crystals are what they aren't, if that makes any sense."

"Further," Michael added, "crystals grow themselves, usually inside various sizes of geodes. They are not formed during extreme heat within but actually grow at normal temperatures. Crystals do a lot more than you would realize. Come on, I'll take you all into my healing room."

They set down their plates with their unfinished meals and followed Michael down a hallway. Harvey came along with them. They turned left at the end of the hall and climbed a stone spiral stairway to the second floor. He led them across the second floor hallway and into a room which had an examining table. Shelves full of various crystals, gems, and rocks lined the walls. In the back of the room was a large glass window, affording them a magnificent view of the Fern-Palm forest in the back of their house. The scene added a sense of calmness to the whole room.

"As you see," Michael announced, "I have a lot of crystals. Those on the shelves to the left are my healing crystals. The ones on the shelves to the right are crystals that I give to people who I treat so that they may go home and continue the healing process on their own. Anyway, it is my feeling that each of you needs a certain crystal or gem to take home with you."

"Are you saying you're going to give each one of us a crystal?" Morris asked.

"That's right, if all of you are willing," Michael replied.

"Well, sure," said William. "Thank you very much."

"Good," said Michael. "What I'm going to do is to match a crystal or gem to each one of you. Everyone stand in a row near the examining table and face me. I will receive your energies."

They did as he directed, and for each person, he extended his arm with the palm of his hand facing each one of them. Standing a couple of meters away, he proceeded to receive each person's energy, one at a time. At the same time, with his hand still facing the person, he carefully selected a certain crystal or gem from one of the shelves. As he compared the person's energy to that of the crystal or gem he selected, he would sometimes put it back and select a better one. One by one, he selected something and gave it to each appropriate person.

"Andrew, for you, I'm receiving a call for Amethyst." Michael placed his hand on a beautiful purple Amethyst crystal with several geometric points. They were flawless. "This is known as the stone of spirituality and contentment, and it controls temperament by imparting a soothing and calming influence while clearing away irritating and negative vibrations or energies. It also provides a sense of common sense, encourages flexibility in decision making, and guards against physical attacks. I bestow this Amethyst crystal upon you." He placed it in his hand.

"Wow!" Andrew exclaimed. "This is spectacular! Thank you very much."

"Steven," Michael immediately continued, "I'm receiving a need for green Malachite." He selected an opaque gem which had layers of various colors of green. It was crafted and rounded into the shape of an egg and had a perfect shape. "This gem will help you by creating unobstructed paths leading to your desired goals in life. It stimulates your intuition to select the right answers and to make correct decisions prior to your response and subsequent actions, and it also helps you take responsibility for your actions. Further, it represents fidelity in peace, love, and friendships and provides practicality and responsibility in making business transactions." He placed the green gem in Steven's hand. Steven felt a warm sensation go into his hand and travel up his arm to his head.

"Huh!" he exclaimed. "I felt a sensation go from my hand to my head!"

Michael smiled at his comment. "That's a sign that this gem was intended for you all along. It has found the right person and signalled to you that you were ready for it. It's yours."

He next selected one for William. "William, I'm choosing a nice blue, almost turquoise, smooth stone for you. This is called Angelite. It is excellent for balancing and aligning the physical body. Also, it is a sender and receiver of information and enhances telepathic communication. You may be able to initiate contact with other worldly beings. Wait!" he stopped himself. "I don't know why I said that. All of you already *are* communicating with other worldly beings, like us. It's almost as if I'm channeling when I select gems and crystals for people. Lastly, Angelite dispels any possible anger and renews one's ability to connect with universal knowledge."

"Thank you," said William. "You know, sometimes when I think I hear something or think I sense something, I will feel my ear sort of pull back."

"That's a start," said Michael.

"William," Robert informed him, "I also feel that same sensation with my ears, at times."

"Oh really?" William responded.

"For you, Chris," Michael continued, "I'm receiving a call for Hematite, the stone of the mind." He picked up a large and smooth pebble which was dark gray, almost silver in color. It was totally metallic and appeared to be composed of the element nickel. "This gem is good for helping you sort out ideas and philosophy in your mind. It keeps you mentally attuned and also assists you in manual dexterity. It will stimulate your desire for peace, self control, and inner happiness." He handed Chris the metallic pebble.

Chris looked at it in his hand and quite surprisingly commented, "Hey! Let's get crackin'!"

Michael gave him a brief and strange look and then continued. Chris' comment was a local expression for getting oneself busy, and Michael had never heard that one before.

"Paul, I'm receiving an order for a large one for you." He reached for a sky blue, translucent piece of Fluorite, and it was several times larger than what he had already given to the others. This piece was 15 centimeters across and was shaped nearly like a pyramid. "This fine crystal produces calm energy and stimulates clear and concise communicative skills. It will help you develop orderly sequential thoughts and is good for promoting orderly record keeping in business transactions which I sense you will be doing plenty of in the years to come. He placed the large blue crystal in both of Paul's hands.

Immediately, Paul felt a rush of energy through his whole body, and he nearly dropped the beautiful piece. Michael rushed over and helped Paul onto the examining table, placing the crystal off to the side for the moment. "Golly! What was that?!" Paul exclaimed.

"That," Michael replied, "was the crystal's strong signal to you to let you know that it is indeed a living being. It realized what you previously thought, that crystals were only rocks. The crystal's made its point, and you and it will be fine together from now on. Rest here a few minutes while I finish with the matching of crystals and gems for the others."

"Robert, I'm also receiving a call for Amethyst as I did for Andrew." He chose another flawless purple-colored crystal and took it from the shelf. "For you, I stress the crystal's importance of controlling temperament by imparting a soothing and calming influence while clearing out negative vibrations."

"Also, Robert," he continued, "you need a second crystal." He selected a greenish-colored cluster of square-shaped crystals or grains, speckled with Pyrite. "This is green Fluorite with specks of Pyrite. It diminishes mild emotional trauma in yourself. This particular crystal will give you joy, gentleness, and desensitization." He handed both crystals to Robert.

"Two crystals! What do you know about that!" Robert declared. "Thank you. Thank you very much." The appearance of both crystals intrigued him.

"You're welcome," said Michael, "However, you're not the only one to receive more than one, as you'll see."

"Morris," he continued, "in addition to the clear-colored crystal ball which Tom gave you, I'm receiving a call for a piece of purple and green Fluorite with a solid Pyrite base." He picked from a shelf a narrow, artificially cut piece around the size of a finger and handed it to him. "This one is excellent for protecting you against disease. It has an excellent defending quality in shielding you from negative energies. Also, it inspires universal concepts and knowledge.

"Further, I am choosing a green Fluorite crystal ball, slightly smaller than your clear-colored one. It will provide you desensitization as does the one I gave Robert. In addition to eliminating the negativity in your presence, I stress the importance that it calms any possible emotional trauma." He handed the green ball to Morris. Immediately, it glowed a color of forest green.

"Oh wow!" Morris shouted, as he received an emotional rush. "Thank you! I will admit that I do have some emotional trauma, so I believe this one will really help me. Thank you very much." He looked into the green ball. "Look at that! It's got so many sections and chambers in it, and look at the layers of green." Morris held it up to the light of the window to view it better. "Well, well, would you look at that! It's got a faint red line right around its equator! I'm overjoyed to have it." Morris was more excited by his crystals than any of the others.

"I can see that *that* crystal is definitely for you," Steven said to Morris.

"You got that right," Morris agreed. "Believe it or not, I feel as though I've had it all my life."

"That's a thought that the crystal is imparting to you," said Harvey.

"Lastly," Michael continued, "for you, James, I'm receiving a call for a cluster of gems. I sense that you will have a need for several in the years that come." As he faced the palm of his hand toward James, he placed his hand on several polished gems. "The most important one is this piece of Unakite." He handed James an opaque pebble which was randomly speckled with various colors of green and orange. "This one balances the heart and soul and the emotional body. It provides a gentle release of any conditions which have inhibited your spiritual and soul growth.

"Next is a piece of Rose Quartz." He handed him a light pink translucent pebble, slightly larger than the other gems he had selected. "This one emits a calming energy, and it provides the message that there is no need to act in haste, no matter what the situation is. I don't sense that you are hasty now, but I can see that when you enter the real work world on Earth that you will be acting with great haste to accomplish all of your tasks. This gem will bring calmness and clarity to the emotions and will restore your mind to tranquility after future chaotic and crisis situations.

"Next, here is a piece of Tiger Eye." He handed James a small black, nearly opaque pebble with gold-colored fibers running horizontally through it. "This one provides sharpness and grounding and helps in seeking clarity for times when you will have to deal intelligently with the scattered details of what must be accomplished. It will help you organize these scattered details into a pattern.

"Here's a special one," Michael went on. "It's from Venus in your solar system." He handed him a mostly black, geometrically cut, long narrow piece of stone, speckled with brown and blue spots. It was slightly translucent and appeared almost holographic. "This gem is called Petersite, and it stands for unconditional love and will prove very useful to you in the future.

"Lastly, I'm getting a call for Amethyst but not as a flawless crystal. What you need is a smooth pebble." He handed the last of the five pieces to James, and he just stared at the handful of gems, not knowing what to say.

"Five pieces, James!" Steven remarked in a teasing manner. "I'm jealous."

"Come off it, Steven!" James requested.

"He needs all of them," Michael explained to the others. "Each person is different. The goal here is to help each one of you."

"Yes, thank you very much from all of us," said Morris.

"All of you are very welcome," said Michael. "You are fine people and have great lives ahead of you. Each one of you will sooner or later realize the true value of the crystals and gems I have given you. Now, let's return to the living room, and we'll finish our meal."

They returned to the large living room downstairs and ate the rest of their now cold food, but they didn't mind the interruption at all, especially for a rare event of being given crystals and gems. They all visited a while longer after their meals and admired each other's crystals and gems. Night arrived, and Michael eventually showed them where to sleep for the night, telling them that he would come for them not long after dawn and that they would visit the city of Towdenmore across the river.

Everyone had a good night's rest and awoke, ready to visit Towdenmore today. Michael came into the room to wake them not long after the crack of dawn. They were looking forward to seeing what the city had to offer.

Carya had breakfast ready for everyone, and they had a seat on the couches and ate a hot porridge type of cereal followed by fresh fruit. When they had eaten their fill, Michael announced that it was time to leave. He,

Suzanne, and Harvey accompanied them while Carya stayed at the house to take care of things for the day. At Michael's suggestion, Robert and his friends took their newly acquired crystals with them.

They left the house and made their way down the grassy slopes, dotted with Fern-Palms, soon arriving at the river's edge. It was a fairly large river, 100 meters wide, and it's banks were lined with plenty of Fern-Palms of various sizes. Michael untied a large rowboat from his dock, and all eleven of them piled in. Needless to say, Suzanne took a seat right next to James. Michael and his son, Harvey, sat at the rear and did the rowing as they crossed this gentle flowing river, soon reaching the larger dock on the city's side.

He untied the boat as everyone stepped off, and he led them up a short footpath which accessed the city. When they reached the top of the bank, they were clear of the Fern-Palms and were met by brownish-colored buildings that had many windows. Almost none of the buildings were rectangular, as most of them had at least six sides with many unusual angles as seen from Earth's standpoint. Other buildings were rounded and dome-like, and they had windows mounted in their roofs.

Michael led the way as they walked down a street into the city center. There were no cars or trucks, but there were plenty of bicycles. People walked up and down the street as well. As they continued, they crossed intersections and saw side streets on either side of them. The whole place was filled with the same type of buildings.

"What are these buildings used for?" Chris asked Harvey.

"These are residences for the people of this city," he answered. "Some of them are houses, each for one family, and others are apartments or flats."

"Where is the manufacturing done?" Andrew inquired.

"That's further on," Michael replied. "It's on the other side of the city, furthest from the river, and the fields and orchards where the food is grown are beyond that."

"Why isn't your manufacturing done right by the river?" Andrew wanted to know.

"Since many of the items are manifested directly from energy instead of being mined," Michael explained, "we don't need the river's water for anything. Further, we have no need to be next to the river since we don't have any waste to discharge into it."

"There's no waste at all?" Robert asked in a surprised tone.

"That's right," Michael confirmed. "When items are manifested from energy, there's no waste."

"Are the bicycles made here?" Steven asked.

"Many of them are manifested here," Harvey answered, "but there are also a lot of them that were purchased by some of the residents when they made visits to Earth."

"Do you and Suzanne have bicycles?" Steven asked Harvey.

"Yes, we do. Tell you what, before you all go home, we'll go riding on some of the footpaths behind our house."

"Sounds great!" Steven enthusiastically remarked.

After walking for nearly half an hour, they arrived at the center of Towdenmore. They were now well above the river, as the streets gently sloped upwards away from the river.

"These buildings are generally the business offices," Suzanne told everyone. "Much of the planning and preparations for the items made for intergalactic trade takes place in these offices. The actual manufacturing takes place further on at the upper edge of Towdenmore."

"Would you like to walk inside one of these buildings and have a look?" Michael offered.

"Sure," said everyone.

They followed him into a three-story brown building and climbed some stairs to the top floor. As they walked down a hall, they looked at the offices on each side. In addition to the electric lights, every office had large windows to allow the natural light to enter. Each one was a little different. Most of the offices had desks with people working on projects and designing equipment. Every desk also had a rock or crystal on it, and they noticed various types as they looked into each office.

The most unusual thing was that every office had a large, tree-like plant, up to three meters tall, and every limb had clusters of Yucca-like leaves. The leaves were long and narrow and were spiked at their ends, and most of them pointed upwards.

"Michael," Robert asked, "are those Joshua Trees that are in each office?"

"Yes, they certainly are," he replied. "As you may already know, they are native to the southwest region of the United States on Earth."

"I thought that's what they were," said Robert. "What a surprise to see them here!"

"Come into this next office, everyone," Michael offered. "A lady from Earth teleports herself here for a few hours each week. She might just be here." He entered the office and called back to the others as they were entering. "We're in luck. She's here."

They all entered this office with brownish-colored carpet and turned left. A woman sat at a desk in the middle of the room. This desk was situated under a large Joshua Tree (*Yucca brevifolia*), three meters tall and full of branches with Yucca-like leaves. All of them stared at her with some amazement, as she looked so familiar.

"Virginia!" Steven suddenly burst out.

"Oh, yeah," Morris recalled, "the lady from the stone hut on Lopeia."

"How surprising to find you here!" Robert remarked.

"That's right," she told them. "You never know *where* you'll find me."

"I'd say," Paul agreed.

"You mean you come here to the Pleiades Cluster too?" Andrew asked.

"Oh, I go to a lot of places," Virginia admitted. "I visit many places and do work like I'm doing now, or I go to other places to relax and collect thoughts, like when you saw me at that stone hut on Lopeia."

"What do you do here?" Chris wanted to know.

"Here, I mainly help people on the dream level," she answered.

"Oh, really?!" Morris responded.

"Yes," she answered. "See, people come and visit me in their dreams, and I talk with them and sort of check up on them at the same time. This Joshua Tree really helps."

"Yes, I was wondering," Robert brought up, "what is the purpose of the Joshua Tree?"

"Well, you see, the Joshua Tree is a beautiful spiritual tree," Virginia explained.

"Let me guess," Morris suddenly said, "does it help you channel information?"

"I wouldn't say that so much as it's a clear place with no interference," she answered. "However, that is partly true. It's a great antenna, if you want to call it that, for tuning into the etheric knowledge."

"So, that's why every office has one," said Morris. "The office workers gain knowledge and ideas by the presence of the Joshua Trees."

"That's *exactly* it," she confirmed, "and they can also think more clearly since it blocks out any interference."

"Brilliant!" Morris declared.

"How are you fellows liking your summer travels so far?" Virginia asked.

"We're having a great time," Steven answered.

"We're so thankful to have the wonderful ability to transport ourselves at will to other planets and star systems," said Robert.

"I know," Virginia agreed. "It's a great gift. I consider it an honor."

"Oh, believe me," Robert assured her, "we do too."

"Yes, thanks to Tom, the galactic salesman," Paul added.

Robert took his newly acquired crystals out of his daypack and showed them to her. "Virginia, look at these crystals that Michael gave us." He handed them to her.

"Those are *great* crystals!" she remarked with enthusiasm. "That Amethyst one is especially good. It has all those tiny crystals near the base, and the base is nice and thin, not so rocky. Yes, you were ready for that one. It's yours. That green Fluorite one is also a great one. It will help keep you desensitized."

Paul showed her his large one. "Blue Fluorite!" she exclaimed. "That's the perfect one for you. Hold onto it, and you'll go far in life."

All of them showed her their crystals and enjoyed hearing her positive comments and praise toward them.

"Michael," Virginia told him, "you made excellent choices in selecting the appropriate crystals and gems for these fellows. They will be of great help to them."

"Thank you, Virginia," said Michael. "I'm glad I could help them out."

Suddenly, a person appeared in the room. Everyone could see through him, and his translucent appearance was quite surprising to them. "Ah, I've got another visitor on the dream level from Earth," Virginia announced. "Take care, everyone, and have a great summer." With that, she turned to her ghostly visitor and talked with him. Michael, Harvey, and Suzanne led everyone out of the room back into the hallway, leaving Virginia to her counseling.

"So, *that's* what people look like when they appear on the dream level," William remarked.

"They do for her, at least," said Morris.

"Let's go see the manufacturing," Andrew requested.

They walked out of the building back onto the street and continued walking slightly uphill and further away from the river. For 10 minutes, there were the usual business offices, and then they came into view of a group of large buildings, most of them rectangular and basic looking. Michael led them inside, and they saw all sorts of equipment being assembled by workers. Among the items were cabinets, appliances, utility equipment, machinery, electro-mechanical and electronic appliances, and more.

"This is what you would call an assembly line," Michael announced. "Our manifested objects are manually put together here, as it is easier and more accurate than manifesting these particular finished products directly from energy. Our workers only work a few hours a day, having the rest of the day to be with their families or to do their own things. None of them are overworked like people are back on Earth."

"Do they get paid for their work?" Paul wanted to know.

"We don't use money here, as such," Michael explained. "However, they are guaranteed a decent place to live and are given enough food and clothing to support themselves and their families."

"They don't look the least bit sullen," Chris commented, noticing how happily they went about their work.

"That's right," Suzanne agreed. "When people are not overworked and can live a good life other than their work, they do their work with love. They're not tired, and they don't grumble about it. These good vibrations that they put into their work are very important, as most of our intergalactic customers are very sensitive to that. If bad attitudes were put into our products, we would likely have them returned with notices of dissatisfaction from our customers. The product would just not feel right to them."

"That's really something," Steven commented. "I never thought of it that way before."

"So, it really doesn't pay to work too hard or overwork," said James.

"That's right, James," said Suzanne with a twinkle in her eye. "That way, you'll have more time to spend with people like me."

"You do have a bit of a crush on me, don't you!" James firmly declared.

"Yes, it's true. I do," she admitted, laughing a little.

"James, I wish we'd asked Virginia about the destiny between you two," said Robert.

"Yeah, I wish I'd thought of that," he said.

They walked among the rows of assembly lines, noting the items being made and waving to some of the workers. Many of them waved back. When they had seen enough of this area, they proceeded to the manifesting section of the factory.

They walked into a large room full of bays. Each bay was used to manifest or create a different raw material. Over cycles of 15 seconds, a pink glow would come into appearance along with the sound of whirring wind, and a sizeable lump of raw material would materialize as the pink glow faded. Then, levitation was used to lift the material out of the bay to be taken to another section of the factory. The cycle would then repeat.

"That's so similar to our transporting procedure!" Steven declared.

"Yes, it's nearly the same method," Michael agreed.

"Are you sure the objects aren't being transported or taken away from somewhere else physically?" William asked.

"Yes," Michael answered, "we're definitely sure. These manifested lumps of metal or other elements are 100 percent pure, absolutely no impurities at all, better than the natural universe can supply on its own. All we do is to feed certain energies into it, focusing the thoughts necessary for manifestation, and it happens, as you can see."

"Amazing!" Robert remarked.

"If you all have seen enough here," said Michael, "then let's go into the next room."

They did as he offered and saw more manifesting, only this time it wasn't just raw materials being created. There were many various objects being manifested, including nuts and bolts, hardware, simple tools, and other materials, such as sheet metal and plastics of various sizes and thicknesses. Even building materials, such as squared-shaped rocks, stones, and bricks, were being manifested. There was much more.

"Why are raw materials in lump form being manifested when you can do *this*?" Morris wanted to know.

"We need the raw materials for use in casting," Harvey explained.

"Can't the casted objects be manifested?" Morris further asked.

"They can be, and they are," Harvey admitted, "but some of our customers want the objects to be casted instead. They argue that they are stronger as far as metallurgical strength is concerned and that they seem a bit more realistic. Others aren't so picky, in which case, we manifest the objects they need.''

"Very interesting," Morris commented. "There are so many possibilities."

"In the next room," Suzanne announced, "is where complete, ready-to-trade items are entirely manifested." They followed her into the next room where they saw nearly the same items being manifested in bays, as they had earlier seen being manually assembled. "Before you say anything," she continued, "some of our customers prefer our products to be hand assembled while others don't mind totally manifested ones."

"Why would they care on this level?" Chris asked.

"It has to do with love and vibrations of that sort being put into the work," she explained. "These products carry neutral vibrations and are therefore preferred by some of our customers who don't wish to possess products with either positive or negative vibrations. They want the products to arrive *clean*."

Everyone looked around the place, walking among the rows of bays, watching the pink glow and hearing the whirring wind materialize the products out of seemingly nothing, and watching the objects being levitated off the platforms. It was really an interesting phenomenon to watch.

"Have you thought about manifesting humans themselves?" Andrew asked with a smile.

"The thought has crossed our minds," Michael admitted, "but that procedure is strictly forbidden by the Galactic Federation. Besides, even if we did so, we would, in actual fact, be transporting humans against their will from any possible planet that they would be inhabiting in this galaxy, to here. The same applies for any sort of living matter, and that even goes for crystals. Crystals are a rare, limited, and valuable material, and they have to be literally grown from seeds, if you know what I mean."

"I see your point," said Andrew. "I'm glad you all are so considerate."

"We do our best to be," said Michael. "Anyway, that is about all for what goes on in our factory. Come on out the back of this building with me, and I'll show you our orchards and fields where all of our food is grown."

He began to lead them out the door, but Morris was hesitant. He was thinking there was something he wanted to see or know about, but he wasn't sure what it was. Then, it dawned on him. "Michael, wait!" he called out. "Suzanne was telling us about how spacecrafts are made here. Can we see that procedure?"

Michael paused and finally said, "Okay. I don't see why not. Let's go and see it." He, Harvey, and Suzanne turned around and went back inside. "It's to the right in the next room further over. Normally we don't show anyone the process, but you all are unique, and I trust you." He led them through a door, and they entered.

The room was quite large and was full of square-shaped bays which were completely sealed and were transparent. Only a slight humming sound could be heard. As Michael led them through the area, they saw that the spacecrafts were in various stages of development. They were literally being grown from their bases up, and various types of silicon and metals were being used in the growing process.

"How in the world is this possible?" William asked.

"We feed energies into each bay such that conditions are just right for the growing process to occur," Michael explained. "Atom by atom, these crystalline spacecrafts are grown. The elements necessary for their construction are literally being transferred from the supplies of silicon and metal within each bay, and the process is far from instantaneous. The crystal assembly process takes place according to a certain etheric genetic code, if that makes any sense. That's the best way to explain it in English."

"I don't understand," said Paul.

"Crystals sort of have a mind of their own," Michael further explained. "They know what to do as far as how to grow themselves. In the cases here, the idea of creating or growing a spacecraft has been implanted within the mind of the crystal, and it grows itself accordingly."

"Wait," Morris asked, "isn't that a violation of the crystal's free will?"

"No, it isn't," Michael assured him. "We always begin by asking the base crystal if it would like to grow into a spacecraft, and we inform it of the benefits of doing so and the adventures it would experience by travelling throughout the galaxies. Yes, we've had some that didn't want to participate in this type of venture, and whenever they decline, we choose another base that wants to."

"What do you do with the base crystals that refuse?" Andrew asked.

"We ask them what they want to do and allow them to do just that," Michael replied.

"I'd say that's fair enough," Morris approved.

"Yes," Michael agreed, "we would never abuse, as we don't believe in abuse."

"That's great!" said Morris.

"Anyway," said Michael, "if everyone's seen enough of this, Harvey, Suzanne, and I will now take you all outside and show you where our food is grown."

Everyone agreed to it, and they walked outside. Many fields were full of different grasses and grains while other fields had various fruit trees and vegetables as well.

Also, there were various large domed buildings where more exotic herbs and foods were grown in more specialized conditions. The whole arrangement was extraordinary, and the eight of them were seriously impressed at how orderly everything was. Michael explained that all foods were organically grown and that they had no need for pesticides or herbicides since there were no destructive insects nor noxious weeds.

"This is really an excellent setup here," Robert commented.

"Yes, we are proud of it," Michael told them. "We hope the people of Earth will do the same one day."

"I'll agree with that," said Morris.

After everyone had seen enough of the impressive place, Michael led them around the right-hand side of the factory buildings. They followed a footpath through the forest bordering the city as they made their way back to the river. The forest floor was mostly open as they went up and down small rises. The majestic Fern-Palms towered above them, their tops reaching nearly 100 meters. The overall terrain descended slightly, and after nearly an hour's walk, they reached the river's edge.

They turned left and followed a footpath for 15 minutes along the riverbank, lined with Fern-Palms. They could see the edge of the city further up along the top of the bank. Finally, they reached the dock, and they rowed across to the other side of the river, after which all eleven of them returned to the royal family's large, gray stone house.

Michael led them around to the backside of the house, and they became seated at the benches and tables situated under the large Fern-Palms in their backyard. Carya came outside with a large platter of fruits, vegetables, and plenty of slices of homemade bread. It was well into the afternoon, and everyone was certainly hungry. As she greeted them, all of them helped themselves and thanked her very much.

She sat down with them and visited, and they told her what they had seen and done and how impressed they were with the entire city of Towdenmore.

"It's a really fine place," she said. "So, have you decided what to do with yourselves on Aleyone?"

Andrew looked at Robert and asked, "What are we going to do on this planet?"

"I haven't really thought about it," he answered. "Harvey, Suzanne, what do you suggest?"

They both looked at them and pondered.

Suddenly, they heard the phone ring inside the house. Michael got up, saying, "Excuse me just a minute." He walked into the house to answer the call.

Robert and his friends continued talking to Carya, Harvey, and Suzanne about what there was to see and do on Aleyone. She made some suggestions and told them about some of the other areas and islands on the planet.

Michael came out of the house and said, "It looks like you fellows may have plenty to do here after all. That was Tom from Sirius B. He has a proposition for you all and is going to teleport himself here any moment."

"Hmm . . ." said Morris. "I wonder what he's got in mind, now."

Sure enough, a few seconds later, Tom emerged from the Fern-Palm forest behind their house and walked into their backyard.

"How are you doing, Tom?" Michael asked.

"How's it going, Tom?" Robert asked, speaking for everyone.

"I'm doing great. How are you all?" Tom asked everyone.

"We're fine," Morris now answered. "We had some strange things happen on Vega. I'll tell you that."

"Oh, really?" Tom responded with surprise.

"Yeah, a whole city of Shakeilar disappeared on us," James told him.

"Oh yes, that'd be right," Tom agreed. "They don't want you all to know too much. You're not ready for that."

"That's what I thought," said Morris.

"So, *that's* why it disappeared on us," Steven remarked.

"Anyway," Tom announced to everyone, "I have a proposition for you."

"Oh really?" Robert asked. "What is that?"

"Do you remember when we spoke of planet Earth and how I said that the rest of my mission was to save it from destruction?" he asked them.

"Oh, yeah," Paul recalled, "Wasn't that on the day we first arrived on your planet?"

"That's right," he answered. "Anyway, I've been pondering it for several days now, and I believe I've figured out a way to save it."

"Oh wow!" Steven exclaimed. "How in the world are you going to do that?"

"It has to do with crystals, and it goes back to the times of Atlantis at a period approximately 15,000 years ago."

"My goodness!" Morris exclaimed. "This sounds interesting. Tell us all about it."

"Yes, we're all ears," Robert added.

"All right, I will tell the story according to Sirian legend."

Michael, Carya, and their children also listened as Tom paced back and forth in their backyard and began.

"Like I was saying, approximately 15,000 years ago, the Atlanteans were a flourishing and advanced race of people, living in an area which is now known as the Bermuda Triangle in the Atlantic Ocean. They used crystals for many things, including using them for powering their flying machines. Those particular crystals were around half a meter long, and they sat in the rear of these vehicles and received their power from large central crystals stationed throughout the land, sort of in the same configuration, as to location, as telephone repeater towers are today on Earth.

"They used crystals for healing people's ailments, energy treatments, storing information, communication, and many other things. Some crystals were kept just for their beauty to be admired while other crystals served better, more useful purposes.

"Now, keep in mind that the Atlanteans had intergalactic trade, up until the time that their civilization was destroyed when they sank. We Sirians were in close communication with them via telepathy, as all Atlanteans were fully conscious, that is, before the genetic experiments began.

"To get to the point, there was one crystal which was very unique. It was a perfect specimen, grown by one of the earlier advanced human civilizations on Earth, and they existed in what is now Antarctica prior to the Ice Age. This was over 100,000 years ago. That civilization left Earth when the Ice Age arrived, and somewhere during the early history of Atlantis, some of them returned and presented this special crystal to the Atlanteans to ensure their well-being."

"What did this crystal look like?" Morris asked.

"Hold on, Morris," Tom kindly said. "I'm getting to that. This special crystal was basically greenish-blue, almost turquoise in color, and the colors varied in bands or layers throughout it. It was actually grown in the shape of a large egg and was around 25 centimeters from end to end. It was quite a spectacle of beauty, according to Sirian legend. Within that crystal was a central core matrix which was the shape of a pyramid, and it was of an orangish-yellow color. It is believed that no matter what position the crystal was in, the pyramid always pointed upwards."

"Oh, come on!" Steven insisted. "No way!"

"Actually, it's possible," Tom explained, "if the pyramid is perfectly geometrical and sits in a perfectly spherical chamber within the crystal itself. If the pyramid is weighted properly, then it will always right itself in an upward position, no matter what position the crystal housing it is in."

"Yeah, but won't the pyramid get caught up on the chamber walls?" Andrew asked.

"Actually, it won't since the chamber walls are perfectly smooth and hard," Tom answered.

"How could they have made such an exotic crystal?" Robert wanted to know.

"That pre-Ice Age advanced civilization fed the exact formulas of thoughts and energies into the chamber where they grew it. It was quite a complicated process, as they had to grow it in two parts, the pyramid, and then the greenish-blue egg to envelope it. They had to ensure that the central chamber was a perfect sphere, and they grew the walls thicker on the right and left than in the middle, so that it would take the shape of an egg. They grew it so precisely that it didn't need to be artificially cut, smoothed, or polished to give it the perfect appearance of an egg. Evidently, they were very advanced in mathematics to have achieved such a feat, because crystals tend to grow in geometric angles and points, as in pyramids."

"So, growing the pyramid was no problem," William commented.

"That's true," Tom agreed. "It was probably made of Citrine. The difficult part was the greenish-blue Fluorite egg to surround it."

"That really sounds like a work of art!" Steven remarked.

"You're not kidding," Paul agreed.

"To continue," Tom went on, "this greenish-blue crystal served the purpose of being a peace keeper in Atlantis. As it transmitted its positive vibrations throughout the land, everyone was influenced to have a sense of preservation and caring for the planet on which they lived. They were attuned to their natural surroundings in those days and were too sensible to exploit natural resources which they would have used up entirely in a couple thousand years. They lived a life which they knew they could maintain indefinitely, generation after generation, and they never needed to mine natural resources to fill their needs.

"Then, somewhere around 15,000 years ago, some alien culture, and we have never been able to determine who they were, arrived and stole the crystal from Atlantis. As they were returning to their world, they realized their wrongdoing, but they were too ashamed or afraid to return it, facing certain punishment. So, they got rid of it by stopping on another alien world and hiding it. It's been my increasing feeling that the planet on which that crystal is hiding is this one, Aleyone."

"On this planet?" Michael and Carya both asked.

"Yes," Tom insisted. "I feel pretty certain that it's hidden somewhere on this planet."

"To think we may have had such a wonderful item here on Aleyone for 15,000 years," Harvey commented.

"I wonder if it could be found," Suzanne added.

"Where do you think it might be on our planet, Tom?" Michael asked.

"If the thieves were who we think they were, then my best guess is that they could have buried it deep within a forest, possibly on one of the islands out at sea, or it could have been hidden way up high in some mountains somewhere."

"Good gracious!" Michael exclaimed. "That's an amazingly large area! I'm not sure it's ever going to be found."

"Oh, I'm sure there's a way to find it," Tom insisted. "We'll just have to be creative and invent some ways to help us locate it. Anyway, I meant to say earlier, would the eight of you be interested in pursuing this quest for this large, greenish-blue, exotic crystal?"

They thought for a moment, and Andrew spoke first. "I think I'd like to. It would give us a sense of adventure and give us a chance to see more of Aleyone as well. What do you think, everyone? Do we want to go for it?"

"Tom," Paul asked, "how do we know, for sure, that it's even on this planet? I mean, we may be wasting our efforts over nothing."

"To answer your question, Paul, I feel very certain that it's hiding somewhere on this planet. I'd say the chances are 99 percent that it is here on Aleyone. Like Andrew just said, this will give you a sense of adventure, and it will be like a treasure hunt for all of you. If that crystal can be found and then returned to Earth, I believe your world Earth will soon become a much better place. You fellows, being residents there, will be rewarded by the positive results offered by the crystal far more than I can personally offer."

Robert and his friends thought about it.

"Yeah, sure!" Steven spoke.

"Yes, come on. Let's go for it," William urged everyone.

Finally, everyone else answered with their approval to Tom's request.

"I really appreciate this," Tom told them, "but your planet Earth will appreciate it more than I ever can. I wish you the best of luck in your quest. Once found, this crystal needs to be returned to Earth and placed in a safe, exotic, and inaccessible location where it will ground itself and go to work in altering Earth's fate for the better."

"Are you coming with us, Tom?" Morris asked.

"I have other things I have to work on, even though this mission is a priority of mine. In addition to normal routine business transactions back on Sirius B, I will be conducting more research through contacts in hopes of narrowing down the wide range of possibilities of the whereabouts of this exotic crystal. So, I regret that I will not actually be accompanying you eight on your quest."

Michael stepped in and offered, "Quite possibly, Harvey and Suzanne might want to accompany you eight in this quest. What do you think?" He looked at his son and daughter as he spoke.

They thought for a moment. "Yes, certainly!" Suzanne enthusiastically answered. "I'd be glad to accompany them throughout this quest."

"Me too," Harvey also answered. "I'd love to be a part of this treasure hunt."

"Okay, it looks like the plans are on go," Tom remarked. "Again, best of luck in your quest. If you have any questions, please contact me."

"Oh wait, Tom," Robert requested.

"Yes, Robert?" he said.

"Aren't you going to tell us what happened to Atlantis and the rest of Earth after the exotic crystal was stolen?"

"Oh yes, that's right," said Tom. "Sorry about that. Yes, anyway, once the crystal was stolen, the Atlanteans were suddenly without the positive vibrations of that crystal. They lost their sense of preservation, and they made a turn for the worse. Greed and control overcame them. They conducted many experiments in genetics. They placed implants in the brains of many of their people to squelch emotions. It's quite a story.

"Finally, they became so bad that they abused the crystals they still had. They were using their large crystals to direct energy rays through the Earth and toward other cultures to subdue them. That was their fatal last move, and their last project was a disaster. Those energy rays they transmitted through the Earth were very upsetting to the natural balance of the world itself, and the result was major earthquakes. Lands buckled and actually shifted the weight of the mantle around to different areas, causing some lands, like At-lantis, to sink and other lands to rise. As a result, Atlantis was no more."

"Wow!" Paul remarked. "They went right on down, didn't they!"

"Yes," Tom agreed, "they did, and it was sad that they went all into the mind. They lost their equilibrium between the physical, mental, spiritual, and emotional aspects, and when that happened, the results were not very good."

"So, they went all into their minds, did they?" Morris commented.

"That's right," Tom verified. "Once the Atlanteans became so un-balanced, it was good that they got wiped out, and it made way for newer, better-balanced societies and cultures. They've done fairly well without the exotic crystal, but I've recently been picking up strong feelings that it's time for the crystal, if found, to be returned to Earth in hopes of waking up socie-ty in a positive manner for the good of all."

"If it's all *that* important, Tom," said Robert, "we'll do all we can to find it."

"Anyway, fellows," said Tom, "I must go now. This is your treasure hunt. Use your intuitions. Listen to your dreams. Be original and creative. If you do succeed in finding it, let me know, and we'll discuss where it needs to be placed on Earth. Again, all the best in this quest. I'll let you know if I come up with any more leads." With that said, he instantly and silently dis-appeared.

All of them were left wondering how to go about this complicated task.

"Where do we start?" William asked everyone. "How do we find this thing?"

"I'm not sure," said Morris.

"Maybe you'll have a special *dream* tonight," Chris suggested.

"Could be," Morris calmly agreed.

"Are there any legends or stories here on Aleyone about this exotic crystal?" Paul asked Michael.

He thought for a moment. "I don't believe there are. Carya, Harvey, Suzanne, have you heard any stories?"

The three of them pondered for a few seconds and replied that they hadn't either.

Andrew was thinking and suddenly asked Michael, "Do you think that any of your crystals, seeing that they are actually living as you told us, would *know* about this exotic crystal and possibly its whereabouts on this planet?"

"Yes, that may actually be true," he responded. "It's also possible that those crystals I gave each one of you may prove very helpful and guiding in your quest."

"Morris, I think that's where you'd be most useful," said Robert.

"Yeah, your crystal ball glowed for you back in that Eucalyptus forest on Vega," Chris added.

"If you like," Michael offered, "stay with us overnight tonight, and I'll send Harvey and Suzanne with you all tomorrow. Meanwhile, I'll familiarize you with the layout of our planet, and maybe we can determine the most likely places that this exotic crystal may be hiding."

"Steven," Harvey asked, "would you like to go bicycle riding with me on the paths back behind our house?"

"Yeah, sure!" he enthusiastically responded.

"All right, let's go," he said.

They immediately walked to a shelter next to the house and took out two bicycles and went riding for the remainder of the afternoon.

"James, do you want to take a walk with me through the forest?" Suzanne offered.

He felt a rush of excitement and anxiety at the same time, and he was unsuccessful in squelching his feelings for her. "Oh . . . Yes, all right, but no funny stuff," he replied.

"Oh, don't worry," she assured him. "I was only teasing earlier." She could detect through her own intuitions that the love bug was taking hold on him. "Come on, let's go. I'll tell you more about the trees."

The two of them took a three-hour tour of the large, continuous forest, and they had a wonderful time. She knew a lot about the trees of the area and told him a lot about them and their history. James became used to her and took a strong liking to her as well.

The other six remained, and Michael and Carya offered them inside. He showed them maps of different areas of Aleyone, and they discussed possible places to search.

"We are on the largest continent of Aleyone," Michael informed them, placing his finger on the appropriate area on one of the maps, "and we are around 1,000 kilometers from the nearest sea. Our latitude is approximately 40 degrees north, and we are 500 meters above sea level."

Morris looked at some of the islands of the sea in the southern hemisphere and was especially drawn to one that was the size of California. He pointed to it and showed the others.

"Tell us more about this island," he asked Michael.

"That island is one of the most beautiful ones on Aleyone. It has many prehistoric trees and plants that were brought here from Earth just over 65 million years ago. It's a mountainous place, most of it heavily forested, and there are many streams and waterfalls. It has a lot to offer, and I believe you would thoroughly enjoy the place."

"Yeah, let's go there," Andrew urged the others.

"How do we get there from here?" William wanted to know.

"There are no roads to get there," Michael answered, "but I've been there before. I'll transmit the visual image to all of you tomorrow morning."

"Oh, okay," said William.

"So, I assume we'll just transport ourselves there?" Robert asked.

"Right," said Michael. "That's how any of us go there also, except by teleportation, which is nearly the same as your method. By the way, why didn't Tom just go ahead and grant you the gift of teleportation instead of that ridiculous transport procedure using the pink glow and whirring wind?"

"Hmm . . ." said Chris. "We never gave that any thought."

"It could be that the transport procedure was easier for us, being from Earth, to get used to," Morris answered.

"I'm sure there was some good reason," said Chris.

"Anyway, it works for us," Andrew pointed out, "and that's all that matters."

"Fair enough," Michael admitted. "I was just curious."

They continued looking at maps and discussed other possible areas to visit while on Aleyone. He also took them to the healing room again and showed them more crystals, explaining what each type of crystal does.

Later on, Robert separated from the others and took a walk through the forest by himself, making sure not to go so far as to become lost, but that didn't matter since the gift of transport was at hand. He just needed the time to think to himself for a while.

Evening arrived. Harvey and Steven returned, dusty and dirty from their ride. Both of them went inside the house to shower and clean up. Suzanne and James also returned from a wonderful walk in the forest.

Carya fixed another fine supper of fruits and vegetables with bread on the side. They visited during the evening and eventually turned in for the night. All of them were eagerly looking forward to visiting the large island in the southern seas.

The next morning was a cloudy, overcast day. Michael said that it was building up to a rain, as there was no dew on the ground. Carya served breakfast to everyone, and they ate well, knowing that they would need it for their adventure.

They returned to the room where they had been sleeping and packed everything, including their newly acquired crystals, into their backpacks. They still had 10 days of food left, as they had not eaten any of their own food since arriving on Aleyone. Harvey and Suzanne were simultaneously packing their backpacks since they, too, were going on the adventure.

When they brought out their packs and gathered in the living room, Michael transmitted the visual image of the large island to them. They all thanked Michael and Carya for their kind hospitality and said goodbye for the time being, knowing that they might possibly return for more help or advice concerning the location of the exotic crystal. They all walked into the backyard.

"Don't concentrate or think too hard about finding the exotic crystal," Michael told them. "It's my feeling that you'll find it when the time is right.

Pay attention to clues, relax, and just enjoy the place. Like I said, the island has a lot to offer."

"Thanks again," said Robert.

"Bye for now," he and Carya both said.

Harvey and Suzanne teleported themselves away, and the eight of them proceeded to transport themselves away, and they all arrived on a light-colored sandy beach by the ocean. Large waves were breaking onto the shore. The upper edge of the beach immediately gave way to a thick, pre-historic-looking forest.

"Yeah mates, this looks just like a prehistoric forest of Earth," James commented.

"Yes, that's what I was saying to you yesterday," Suzanne agreed.

"This forest looks impenetrable," William remarked. "How in the world are we ever going to get through it?"

"I don't know," said Robert.

"I believe it will become much easier once we move further into it," Morris speculated.

"Well, let's get started," Steven suggested.

"We may as well," said Andrew.

"I hope we ever find this exotic crystal," said Chris.

They entered the edge of the forest of prehistoric-looking trees. There was quite a variety of trees and plants. Many of them had fern-like leaves, but there were others that looked more like Palms and others like Cycads. Some of the trunks had ringed or layered bark while others had a diamond-shaped checkered or crosshatched appearance. Others, still, had more normal-looking bark from an Earth standpoint. Some trees were very primitive and had limbs with no leaves while others had whorls of branches on which there were whorls of flat leaves.

The going proved quite difficult for the next two hours. Plenty of wet, slippery logs blocked the way, at times, and the tall fern plants presented a real problem as far as passibility was concerned. Plenty of insects, some of them half a meter in length, flew here and there, and there were also various types of birds. Large mosses, up to half a meter thick, covered the more open areas of the forest floor as they advanced deeper, climbing slightly uphill all the while.

Most of them were grumbling about the difficulty in traversing this area. At one time or another during this two-hour struggle, every one of them had slipped and fallen at least once, and all of them were dirty and muddy. This was not their idea of fun.

"I'm telling you what," William brought up. "If it weren't for our quest for that exotic crystal, I'd have turned back in the first 10 minutes."

"I don't know if it's worth all this," said James.

"Now James," Suzanne pointed out, "if Harvey and I are tough enough to endure this, then I know you can."

"Yeah, you're right, Suzanne," he agreed. "Let's keep going."

Finally, after an additional half hour of struggling, they were through the worst of it. Now further inland, they were in a slightly drier type of forest, and the forest floor was considerably less cluttered. What a relief it was to all of them to now be free of the rigorous wet forest that they had just endured. They didn't miss it, either. Luckily, none of them had been injured.

Soon, they crossed a stream winding its way gently between the exotic looking trees. Immediately, they set down their packs and proceeded to clean themselves up, as they were really filthy. Afterwards, they decided to rest by the stream.

"Let's dig into our packs and eat some lunch," said Paul. "I'm starved."

"Good idea," Robert agreed.

All of them now realized how hungry they were after their morning struggle.

"I hope we don't have any more of *that!*" Chris declared. "If the going gets that tough again, I'm out of here."

"I believe that's the worst we're going to have," Suzanne assured them. "Now that we're further inland, the forest floors won't be so cluttered."

"Thank goodness for that," Robert declared.

They ate a good lunch and continued resting with their backs against different trees by the stream. Birds and insects of various types flew through the air, and their sounds could be heard everywhere. Lizards, salamanders, and other fast reptiles scurried across the ground.

"What types of trees are these?" Morris asked Harvey and Suzanne.

"Most or all of the trees on this island have been brought here from Earth, originally," Harvey answered. "Many of them were brought here before 65 million years ago, and I believe a lot were brought even longer ago than that, back when life really began flourishing here on Aleyone. Life started here around 400 million years ago, while on Earth, that was 500 million years ago.

"To answer your question, the trees you see that don't have leaves, as such, are called Lepidodendrons. As you see, they have that diamond-shaped checkered bark. The trees you see with whorls of branches and leaves are called Calamites. Their bark looks ringed or layered. There are other types here as well, but I don't know much more than that.

"There is one other type of tree that I know about, and I don't see any here. We'll see some of them later on, I'm sure, since they grow at higher altitudes. They are called Archaeopteris, and they have whorls of flat and webbed, fan-shaped leaves on their branches. They more closely resemble an Earth-type tree than these you see around here. I believe the Archaeopteris trees used to live on Earth 350 million years ago and that they were the forerunners of the gymnosperms and the conifers presently there. I'll point them out when we see some later on."

"That last one sounds very interesting," James commented. "How tall do they grow?"

"They reach up to 30 meters," Harvey answered.

"That's pretty tall," said Robert, "close to 100 feet in our terms. Still, that's small, compared to the Fern-Palms back where you live."

"That's true," Harvey agreed.

They finished lunch and continued walking through the forest. Most of the land was fairly flat, but at times, there were hills to climb over, and there were gullies to cross with streams flowing through them. Most of the gullies were loaded with ferns, as well as Fern Trees, similar to the ones in Australia.

In other areas, there were natural meadows which were grassy and were interspersed with various types of trees. Hills and small cliffs surrounded some of these meadows, and the color of their exposed rocks was a mixture of mostly brown and a little bit of red.

For the rest of the day, they continued inland, exploring more of the large island. The terrain alternated between forest and partially open meadows, and they were glad the weather was so nice and sunny. The rich greenish-blue sky had only a few small clouds in selected areas near the horizon, and only a slight breeze blew.

When Aleyone One was about to touch the horizon, everyone decided to stop for the night. They found a small stream flowing through the middle of a mostly open meadow. Various types of trees lined its banks.

They set up their tents and proceeded to cook supper. It had been a long day, and they wondered how many days it might take them to find the exotic crystal that Tom had told them about.

After everyone ate supper, Robert walked up and down the stream, looking at some of the trees. He especially noticed that some of the trees closely resembled a Ginkgo, except that the leaves were narrower. He returned to the others, wondering if they were indeed the Archaeopteris trees that Harvey had mentioned.

"Harvey," Robert called out as he approached everyone.

"Yes?"

"Are those Ginkgo-like trees the Archaeopteris trees you were telling us about?" He pointed at some of them.

"No, those are actually Ginkgoes but with a narrower leaf," he answered. "They used to grow on Earth, back when the Ginkgoes flourished there. We haven't seen any Archaeopteris trees yet, and I'll let you know when we do, but you *are* close. They actually do resemble the Ginkgoes."

"I sort of thought so," said Robert.

"I wonder how many days it will take us to find the crystal," Chris said to the others.

"It may take as much as a week," Morris predicted.

"It could be that we are meant to experience a certain amount of time here on this island before we actually locate it," Paul commented.

"I don't agree that destiny has anything to do with it," said Robert. "We'll find it when we find it. It could be tomorrow, next week, or possibly never. I don't think anything is predetermined."

"I disagree, Robert," said Morris. "If things are meant to happen, then they will."

"It's all how we look at it," Chris brought up. "Even though we are all friends, we are all different from each other in some ways."

"I think the future is what we make of it," Steven stated.

They continued discussing destiny, predetermination, the future, and other subjects. Harvey and Suzanne also had their input, telling them that life had the free will to do whatever was desired. Finally, it became dark, and the more distant Aleyone Two was also out of sight.

"Oh wow!" Andrew exclaimed. "Look at the stars. They really stand out clearly here."

Harvey and Suzanne pointed out the other six nearby stars of the Pleiades Cluster. They were the brightest ones in the sky and were only a few light years away.

Tiredness set in, and all 10 of them crawled into their tents in the meadow by the stream.

Four days passed. They had continued penetrating deeper into the large island, looking and listening for clues to help them locate the crystal. Morris had been using his original crystal ball from Tom, as well as his newly acquired green Fluorite crystal ball with chambers, to see if they would signal any clues. Nothing had happened yet.

They had climbed slowly higher in altitude and had left the thicker, more lush forests behind. The terrain had become more mountainous, and the meadows were now larger and more alpine looking. Various sizes of lakes dotted the scenery, and there were groves of trees in more protected areas.

Mountains stood all around them, and snow covered their highest peaks which were quite jagged in places. Plenty of streams and waterfalls flowed down their rocky slopes, and their sounds, along with the calls of birds, filled the air.

Upon first arriving, they noticed the trees to look more coniferous in appearance. At a glance, they looked like Baldcypress trees, and their bark was very similar as well. The difference was that the leaves were not needle-like. Instead, they grew in whorls around the branches. Sure enough, Harvey informed them that they had reached the groves of Archaeopteris trees, and they were now high enough that they grew in pure stands. The altitude was approximately 1,600 meters, and some of the mountains towered well above that.

For the past four days, the weather had been mostly good, although they did experience a violent thunder and lightning storm on their second day, and it poured for an hour. They had taken shelter under the trees the best that they could.

At this higher altitude, the sky was a darker green compared to the lighter, almost turquoise color back at sea level. They noticed that the air was thinner as well.

According to their watches, it was Wednesday, June 26, and they were halfway through their food supply, but that didn't bother them. All of them knew that when necessary, they could transport themselves to Tasmania to resupply. The last four days, aside from the rainstorm, had been fun and adventuresome for everyone, and the eight of them were glad that Harvey and Suzanne had accompanied and guided them.

It was becoming late afternoon, and they decided to look for an appropriate place to camp. The groves of Archaeopteris trees situated throughout the alpine meadows looked very inviting, especially a grove to their left in a protected area at the bottom of a steep, exposed mountain slope. They crossed the open, grassy meadow and soon reached it.

"This looks like a great spot to camp," Andrew told the others upon reaching the grove.

"I agree," said Robert. "Let's set up camp underneath the trees. They'll give us shelter and shade."

"Good idea," Steven approved.

The 10 of them walked into the grove which was approximately 1½ hectares in size. A stream ran through the middle of the grove, and as they walked further in, they saw that the stream originated from a most attractive looking spring. They looked into its still water and noticed that the sides were lined with white quartz rocks which sparkled as they reflected the few rays of Aleyone One that managed to pass through the trees and limbs. They were actually appalled that a spring could be so beautiful.

"Let's set up camp near this spring," Morris suggested.

"Yes, I'm for that," Paul agreed.

Around 30 meters from the water's edge, they set up their tents and then filled their water jugs. With a few hours of daylight left, some of them went out exploring the hillsides and meadows.

Nearer to sunset, after everyone had returned from running around and exploring, they cooked and ate supper. Harvey and Suzanne had brought dried fruits and vegetables along with several types of dried bread and grains.

The forest floor of this grove of Archaeopteris trees was mostly open with no undergrowth, except for saplings and seedlings of the same type of tree. Not even any ferns grew in this area.

As Robert was sitting with the others after supper, he suddenly heard a slight ringing in his ear which was normal from time to time. However, this time, he thought he heard thoughts or words formulating in his mind.

Oh my goodness! he thought. *I believe I'm hearing telepathic communication!* He listened with his mind as the faint, high-pitched ringing in his ears continued. The others were talking, but he tuned them out. Morris noticed Robert's actions, however, and quietly called everyone to silence.

Robert heard the following:

'I don't know about you, but look at all those people that have camped under us.'

'Don't worry. I don't believe they'll bother us. They look like nice people. Let's welcome them.'

Harvey and Suzanne, having the regular ability to communicate telepathically, joined in and telepathically said, 'This group of eight fellows with the two of us is visiting from planet Earth. All of us have come for reasons of good.'

"Oh, well that's good,' one of the voices communicated. 'We haven't seen your kind, humans, for many years. Welcome to our grove. We call it Crystal Spring.'

'Thank you,' Harvey communicated. 'We're glad to be here, and we admire your unique and majestic appearance.'

'That's a very kind comment,' the voice replied, 'and we are pleased that you appreciate our kind.'

Robert finally realized that the two telepathic voices were coming from two Archaeopteris trees, some of the largest ones in the grove.

'Tell your group of eight,' one of the trees went on, 'that our kind used to grow on their planet, Earth, over 300 million years ago.'

'Yes, I have already informed them, four days ago,' Harvey communicated.

None of Robert's seven friends could detect any communication, not even Morris. However, both Harvey and Suzanne were remaining still and were in a slightly meditative state.

'We have a request for you,' one of the trees communicated. 'We have some of our kind that have volunteered too close to us, and they are invading our space. We're glad you're here, and we'd like you to pull them up for us, as we are incapable.'

Robert couldn't believe what he had heard within his mind, and he just about laughed out loud. The tree's request sidetracked him and caused him to lose telepathic contact. He heard no more. Harvey and Suzanne carried on communicating as follows:

'I have a better idea,' Suzanne stepped in and communicated. 'Why don't we see if the eight of our kind from Earth would like to gently dig up your seedling kind invading your space and take them to plant elsewhere?'

One of the trees communicated to the other, 'What do you think?'

'That sounds like an excellent idea,' the other one approved. 'In fact, why don't we bestow each one of them with a seedling of our kind. After all, we have at least 10 of them we'd like to get out from under us.'

'Excellent idea,' the tree communicated in a praising manner. 'They could take them back to Earth, couldn't they.'

'Yes,' they both communicated to Harvey and Suzanne, 'we welcome your offer and would greatly appreciate you and your Earthly friends taking these invading seedling kind of ours with you.'

'We'll be glad to,' Suzanne communicated. 'So, you don't mind if they take these seedling kind of yours back to Earth with them?'

'Not at all,' one of the trees assured her. 'We would like that, as our kind has been absent from Earth for so long. We welcome the opportunity.'

'Not a problem,' Harvey communicated. 'All of us are here on a quest to find an exotic, egg-shaped, green Fluorite crystal which has an orange-colored pyramid inside it. It is a large crystal. Have you ever heard of such a crystal as I have mentioned?'

'No,' one of the trees answered, 'but if you like, we can check around with our kind in other groves and also with our cousins, the other trees in other areas, and find out.'

'Oh really?' Harvey and Suzanne both responded.

'Yes,' the same tree assured them. 'Tell our kind everything you know about the crystal.'

Robert and the other seven watched as Harvey and Suzanne continued the silent meditation for another 10 minutes, communicating to the trees the complete details about the exotic crystal and the story Tom had told them. Of course, at the time, the eight of them had no idea what they were communicating about. Robert had earlier lost telepathic contact, and the eight of them didn't say a single word, for fear of interrupting Harvey and Suzanne. They related the whole story later.

"The trees told us they are going to check around and see if any of them has ever heard of such a crystal," Suzanne explained to them 15 minutes later.

"That's great," said Paul.

"I agree," said Robert. "You know, I'm just beside myself that I actually tuned in and telepathically heard some of that conversation!"

"I know," Chris agreed. "Why didn't the rest of us hear it?"

"What happened to you, Morris?" Andrew asked him. "Didn't you hear it?"

"No, I didn't, unfortunately," he admitted, "but I believe the message may not have been intended for me so much as for you, Robert. I believe that you, well, all of us, for that matter, are developing faster than we realize."

"I would believe it after that," Robert agreed.

"Anyway, the message was intended more for you than for the rest of us," Morris concluded.

"Could be," said Robert.

"Maybe the Archaeopteris trees will be able to tell us where this exotic crystal is," Andrew said with confidence. "We'll find it, do what's necessary to transport it to Earth, and go on to something else."

"I don't know if it will be that easy," said Paul.

"We'll see," said Chris.

"Hey, everybody," William announced. "I've got something to tell you."

"Yes, what is it?" Robert asked.

"Right about the time you began to listen to the telepathic messages, I remember feeling my right ear pull back."

"Really?" Robert asked.

"Yes," said William, "and it could be that I almost tuned into what you, Harvey, and Suzanne heard."

"Wait," said Morris, "didn't that stone . . . It was Angelite, wasn't it?"

"Right," William answered.

"Didn't Michael say that Angelite enhances telepathic communication?"

"Yes, he did!" William recalled. "Oh, yeah, and he also said that I would be able to initiate contact with other worldly beings."

"So the key word is *other*," Paul suddenly pointed out, "other, as in, the trees . . ."

". . . of other worlds," Steven added.

"You may be onto something," William told them.

"I think pretty soon you're going to be able to communicate telepathically," Suzanne predicted. "Just concentrate and relax at the same time, and let your thoughts flow freely."

"I'll let you know if anything happens," he told her.

Darkness arrived, and the clear sky offered excellent views of the stars and constellations. They walked out of the grove into the meadow to observe them, later returned to their campsite, crawled into their tents, and went to sleep. The sound of waterfalls and distant mountain streams filled the air.

By the time morning arrived, and it was a cold morning, Harvey and Suzanne had already found out the information they needed from the Archaeopteris trees. The trees had checked with their same kind in other groves throughout the mountains and had indeed found out that a few of them remembered seeing such a crystal. Through combined telepathic communication among themselves, they had come to the conclusion that it was further up in the mountains.

"But where, exactly?" Andrew asked.

"They don't exactly know," Harvey informed everyone. "That was the best they could do in answering. That narrows down our search quite a bit. We know it's in this vicinity somewhere."

"Yeah, that's good to know, at least," said Chris.

"Last night, I was thinking about the exotic crystal," Robert brought up, "and suddenly, the words, *land line-connect*, came to me for no apparent reason."

"I wonder what that's supposed to mean," Andrew commented.

"Hmm . . . I don't know," said Morris.

"I don't either," said Robert.

"I wonder if it's some sort of riddle," Chris suggested.

"I say let's get with it and comb the hillsides," Paul urged everyone.

"Be patient, Paul," Robert insisted. "Let's do it in a more orderly manner, and we may have it found sooner than later."

"I think the chances are good that it's underground after 15,000 years," James pointed out.

"I don't doubt it," William agreed.

"Yes, but it might be up on a ledge or a cliff somewhere up there," Steven suggested.

"If that's true, it might not be buried," said Morris.

"What do you think?" Robert asked Harvey and Suzanne.

"I think the crystals bestowed upon you will come in very useful," Suzanne told them.

Paul suddenly struck upon an idea. "Robert!"

"Yes, Paul?"

"What was that phrase that came to you earlier? Was it *land line-connect*?"

"Yes, that's right."

"Steven, why did you suggest that it might be on a ledge or a cliff?" Paul asked.

"I don't know. It's just a thought that came to me."

"Well, there you are," Paul offered.

"You mean *land line-connect* refers to a ledge or cliff?" Robert asked, puzzled.

"Well, yeah," Paul insisted. "I mean, you've got the horizontal and vertical surfaces meeting each other at the edge of any cliff, and that edge would be like a *land line*. Therefore, the horizontal and vertical surfaces *connect* at the *land line*."

"Hmm . . ." said Robert, pondering what Paul had pointed out. "You know, I believe you've got it, Paul."

"I think you're right on the mark," Morris added.

"Good thinking, Paul," Andrew praised.

"Yeah, I believe you've solved the riddle," said Chris.

"Okay, everyone," Harvey announced, "with that new information brought out into the open, I believe that the first places that need to be searched are the cliffs and ledges."

"I believe you're right, Paul," Suzanne told him. "That's the most likely place that a thief would have hidden a stolen item. It's inaccessible, and people usually wouldn't bother to go there, let alone, search there."

"I agree," said Andrew. "It's up out of the way, unlikely to be found. I'll bet 99 percent that it's been hidden on some ledge."

"All right, everyone," Harvey suggested, "how about let's divide up into groups of two and search the ledges and cliffs in the vicinity. Remember, it could be buried, as some of the ledges carry enough soil to grow trees. Use your crystals. If anything strange happens, or if they suddenly glow or send out a surge of energy, pay close attention. Use your own intuitions. All of us will meet back here at the end of the day."

"Let's all go in different directions and see what we turn up," Suzanne added. "The beautiful sunny weather is on our side. James, would you like to come with me?"

"Suzanne, I knew you'd ask him," Robert remarked.

"Yes, of course," she admitted, laughing. "He's my cutie, aren't you, James?"

"I'm telling you what, James," William insisted. "You better go after her. I mean she *wants* you!"

"Hey, knock it off, William!" James ordered. "Come on, Suzanne. Let's leave them to their teasing." He took her hand, and they walked out of the grove and made their way up the rocky slopes of the mountain.

The others separated into groups of two as follows: Harvey and Steven, Morris and Paul, Chris and William, and Robert and Andrew.

They combed the slopes of the mountain, checking every cliff and ledge in sight. Several times through the day, they found that there was no conventional physical way, short of ropes and climbing gear, to access many of the high cliffs and ledges. They were simply inaccessible, and their gift of transport came in very useful, as they transported themselves to each site and checked each ledge with the greatest of ease.

Many of the ledges were very attractive, and several of them had Archaeopteris trees growing on them, some of them full size. There were clumps of grass and other plantlife, including mosses. The ledges, being isolated, were very unique, and it was like each one of them was a separate ecosystem. Water usually seeped onto their surfaces from above, and the moss-covered dirt remained wet.

"This whole mountain range takes on a different perspective when you see it from one of these isolated ledges, doesn't it," Andrew pointed out.

"Yes, you're right. It does," Robert agreed.

"Have you had anything strange happen from your crystal?" Andrew asked.

"Nothing yet."

"Me neither," said Andrew.

"There's another ledge further up," Robert pointed out. "Let's go search up there."

Both of them transported themselves 50 meters vertically to the next ledge directly above them. This ledge was around 5 meters wide and 100 meters long and was situated on a huge vertical cliff at least 200 meters above the ground at its base.

"Whew!" Andrew exclaimed. "We're way on up here, now!"

"I'll say!" Robert agreed. "It must be another 100 meters to the top of this entire cliff."

"And that's not even the summit of the mountain," Andrew added.

"Well, let's see if we turn up anything on this one."

Suddenly, they were startled by a whirring sound. Robert and Andrew quickly turned around to see what it was. Immediately, they were relieved when they saw a pink glow. Morris and Paul both materialized.

"Well, I will say!" Robert declared.

"Oh, hey Robert and Andrew!" Paul exclaimed. "How are you all?"

"Hello there," Morris added.

"How's it going?" Andrew asked them. "We didn't know you were in the area."

Our search paths must have converged," said Morris. "Seeing how we've met like this, I have a strong feeling that we're getting very close to possibly finding it." He pulled out his two crystals and felt them. "My green one feels downright hot! Here, feel of it." He handed it to Robert.

"Good gracious!" Robert exclaimed, handing it back to him. "I can hardly hold it. *You* couldn't have been that hot. That sort of heat was generated from within the crystal, itself."

"Tell you what," Andrew suggested. "Let's comb this area very well."

All four of them proceeded to meticulously search the entire ledge for any signs of the exotic crystal. There was a fair amount of soil on this particular ledge, more than on most of them, and various sizes of Archaeopteris trees grew along its entire length.

Sure enough, as Andrew scanned the ground's surface with his Amethyst crystal, he suddenly felt a surge of energy run up his left arm. He was two meters away from a group of four large Archaeopteris trees.

"Hey!" he shouted. "I think I've got it!"

Morris, Paul, and Robert rushed over to him to see for themselves. Robert's Amethyst crystal also gave the same sort of energy surge. Paul's blue Fluorite crystal glowed the most dazzling blue imaginable.

"Ouch!" Morris yelled. He immediately dropped his green Fluorite crystal ball like a hot potato.

"What happened, Morris?" Robert asked.

"My green crystal ball is burning up!" he exclaimed. "I had to drop it!"

"Let's get to it and dig!" Paul urged everyone.

All four of them scooped the moist rich dirt away with their hands as they dug a hole. It was fairly easy to dig through, and in minutes, they were nearly half a meter below the surface. Suddenly, they ran into a smooth solid surface.

"I think we found it!" Andrew exclaimed.

Sure enough, as they pushed the dirt aside, they revealed the top of the smooth, green translucent crystal. What a sight it was to behold, and they had only revealed a portion of it, as it was still imbedded in the ground. Already, it was glowing, signalling to them how glad it was to have been found after 15,000 years.

"Hurry!" Robert impatiently urged them. "Let's get it out of there!"

They fast and furiously dug around the edge of this large, egg-shaped crystal. It was 25 centimeters from end to end and was perfectly smooth, just as Tom had said. Finally, they had removed the dirt from all sides, and Andrew lifted the gem out of the ground. It weighed around 20 kilograms. They brushed and wiped the wet dirt off of it as best as they could. Excitement ran through all of them. They just couldn't believe they had actually found it. How elated the four of them were to have succeeded!

Suddenly, Morris heard a ringing in his ears. "Wait!" he called out. "I hear something."

Immediately, the other three stopped what they were doing and gave Morris their undivided attention.

"I'm hearing some phrase over and over," he informed them. "It keeps saying, '*Land line-connect*: Timpanogos. *Land line-connect*: Timpanogos.'"

"Well, we know what *land line-connect* means," Andrew pointed out, "but what in the world is Timpanogos?"

Morris kept hearing the voice in his head. "Here, it's telling me more. It's now saying, '*Land line-connect*: Timpanogos. Place it there.'"

"Oh!" Robert realized. "It's like a place!"

"Where is Timpanogos?" Paul asked them.

"Is that some place on Earth?" Andrew wanted to know.

"I haven't heard of it," said Robert. "What about you, Morris? Do you know?"

"No, but I guess we're going to need to find out," he told them. "Obviously, this exotic crystal needs to be placed there, and therefore, I assume it's some place on Earth."

"It seems to me," Robert suggested, "that the place on Earth that it wants to be placed bears close resemblance to this sight here."

"Yes, this is a really attractive and beautiful spot," Andrew commented. "Look at the great view around us."

Being high up on the ledge, they were well above the surrounding scenery. Several meadows, dotted with lakes, were visible, both near and far. Beyond a nearby and lower range of jagged peaks was the meadow where they were camping. Way into the distance, they could see the seemingly endless forest stretching to the horizon. They were far enough inland that the sea was not visible.

It was now early afternoon, and they pondered what to do next.

"Let's return to our campsite and wait for the others," Paul suggested.

"Wait, let's fill this hole back up first," Robert reminded them.

"Oh, yeah," Paul realized.

The four of them raked the dirt back into the large hole, quickly filling it up. They placed the layer of moss back on its top, restoring it to the way they had found it. Andrew picked up the exotic crystal and carefully placed it in his pack. Next, Morris picked up his now cool, green crystal ball, and the four of them transported themselves directly to the grove of Archaeopteris trees where they were camping.

None of the six others had returned, and they knew they wouldn't be back until evening. Andrew took the crystal out of his daypack, and they went to the stream and proceeded to wash any remaining dirt from it. What a dazzling appearance it had once it was clean! It had every feature that Tom said it would, and they were beside themselves as they admired its main feature: the orangish-yellow pyramid within it which kept an upright position no matter which way they turned the crystal. Also, like Tom had said, the crystal had bands or layers of various colors of green, some of them almost turquoise. As the light of Aleyone One struck its surface, the pyramid glowed vividly within its veil of green Fluorite.

"Wow!" Morris exclaimed. "I'm tingling all over!"

"That crystal is beyond belief!" Robert calmly declared.

"Cleaning it up really made it stand out," said Paul.

"I'll say!" Andrew agreed.

"Anyway, I'm going out to explore some more," Robert informed the others. "Do you all want to come?"

"Yes, let's go," said Andrew.

"I'm coming too," Morris announced.

"I'll stay here and rest," Paul told them. "I don't want *anything* to happen to the treasure we've just found."

"I assure you, Paul, there's no one going to steal it up here," said Robert. "However, if you want to stay, then stay. The rest of us are going exploring."

The three of them left the grove and went walking and running across the meadows, visiting different Archaeopteris groves and lakes. They went climbing on the rocks and ledges in the vicinity. After several hours, they returned. Paul had taken a nap in his tent, having been exhausted after the rigorous activity from the past five days.

Harvey and Steven returned an hour before sunset, telling them that they had not found anything. Chris and William arrived a few minutes later. Paul immediately went inside his tent, and weren't they surprised when he emerged with the exotic green crystal! Steven's mouth dropped open as he stared at its dazzling appearance.

"Huh!" he exclaimed. "I'm not believing my eyes! That's incredible!"

Harvey was not nearly so surprised, having been more used to crystals.

"Where did you find it?" William wanted to know.

"It was way up on a ledge, 200 meters above the ground," Robert told him.

They related the whole story, telling them about how their crystals signalled to them when they were over the exact location and how they had dug for it. Also, they told them that Morris had received a telepathic message about where the crystal needed to placed on Earth.

"Have any of you heard of the name Timpanogos?" Robert asked them. "That's the name that Morris kept hearing."

"That sounds a heap familiar," William answered. "Let's see . . . Oh, yeah. I know what it is and where it is."

"Really?!" Robert responded with surprise.

"Yes, it's a mountain," William informed them, "and if I remember correctly, I believe it's in Utah. We can check the road atlas when we return home to Earth."

"That's great, William!" Paul exclaimed. "I guess that solves our problem."

"Wait," Andrew suddenly announced. "None of us have ever been to Utah. How are we going to get there?"

"Well, if worse comes to worse," Chris pointed out, "we can always drive there."

"I've got a better idea," Paul suggested. "Let's look it up at the library back at home. Maybe we'll find some pictures. Then we can transport ourselves there."

"Good idea, Paul," Robert approved. "That sounds like a good plan."

Sunset would be in less than an hour, and they decided to cook and eat supper. Suzanne and James had not yet returned, and they wondered what had happened to them. They hoped they would return soon. Two more hours passed, and it was now dark.

"Where are James and Suzanne?" Robert asked the others.

Harvey decided to answer. "I think you all have noticed that she is a little flirtatious, at times. I have a feeling, a strong feeling, that those two have gone off somewhere to . . . you know . . . make out, as you call it in English, I believe."

"Oh my goodness!" Robert remarked.

"I just *knew* he'd go after her," William declared.

"Yeah, she's got him now," Chris added.

"I could see that those two lovebirds were going to go after each other," Paul said with a smile.

"You don't think that James and Suzanne are going to stay out all night and . . . sleep together, do you?" Robert asked Harvey.

"I don't know," he replied in a straightforward manner. "Quite honestly, it wouldn't surprise me if they did."

"Well, I will say!" Andrew declared.

"I'm telling you what," William added. "There *ain't no way* I'm sleeping with a woman, unless we get married!"

"Yeah, well that's *your* viewpoint, William!" Morris firmly told him. "I don't see anything wrong with it."

"You're kidding, Morris!" Paul exclaimed. "Well, I sure do!"

The discussion escalated into an argument, and all of them expressed their strong opinions on the morals of sleeping with women. Harvey stood back and watched, as it was quite intriguing to him to watch Earthlings having an argument over such an issue. Finally, he'd had enough.

"Hey! That's enough!" he shouted. Everyone instantly became silent. "I can see that all of you have strong opinions on that issue, but there is no need to get angry at each other over it."

"Yeah, you're right," Andrew admitted. "What do we care. Let James and Suzanne do what they want."

At that moment, they heard footsteps approaching from the hillside behind them. The sound became louder and closer, and they could tell that whatever it was, it had entered the grove and was coming toward them. With apprehension, they shined their flashlights in that direction.

"Oh, it's just James and Suzanne," said Robert, relieved.

"How are you going, mates?" James asked everyone.

"Fine," Paul answered. "We were just about to send out a search party for you."

"Yeah, we were worried about you two," Chris added.

"Oh, we're fine," Suzanne assured them. "We just decided to search as long as we could."

"James, look what I found," Andrew casually announced. He shined his flashlight directly onto the exotic crystal.

"Oh, right!" James shouted. "You found it, mate!"

"Yeah, it was way up on a ledge on a tall cliff," Andrew began, and he told the whole story to James and Suzanne while the others also listened.

"Well, I guess tomorrow we'll transport ourselves back to your place," William said to Harvey and Suzanne, "and then back to Earth to deliver this crystal to its new home."

"And let's not forget to take the Archaeopteris seedlings with us in the morning," Harvey reminded them.

"Right, I'll make sure we don't forget," Robert assured him.

They made further plans for the next day and decided to go to sleep for the night.

The next morning was cold again, and there was a light frost on the ground in the meadow beyond the grove. Steam rose from the white quartz crystal spring near them. After eating breakfast and taking down their tents, Harvey and Suzanne pointed out which Archaeopteris seedlings needed to be removed.

Carefully, they dug out 10 seedlings. Robert had brought a garden trowel with him, and it proved very useful. The two large trees above them telepathically gave their thanks to everyone, even though only Harvey and Suzanne heard it. All of them carefully packed the seedlings into their backpacks.

Andrew decided to carry the exotic crystal in his backpack, and he noticed the added weight. They said farewell to this beautiful grove and to the crystal spring and walked out into the meadow.

From there, they proceeded to transport themselves away, back to Michael and Carya's house across the river from Towdenmore. They made their arrival in their backyard. Michael, who was inside the house at the time, no doubt, heard the sound of the whirring wind, and he came outside to greet them. Carya soon followed.

"How are you all doing?" he asked them.

All of them were glad to see one another, and Andrew related their adventures. After several minutes of story telling, he opened his backpack and revealed the exotic crystal. Both Michael and Carya's mouths dropped open in surprise. Michael walked over to the pack and carefully picked up the heavy gem, not believing what he was seeing.

"Even though I'm used to crystals," he pointed out, "this crystal is far more exotic and spectacular than I ever thought possible!" He walked over to a nearby table and carefully placed the crystal on top of it. Then he placed his hands upon it and meditated.

"What's it telling you?" Robert asked.

"It's saying, 'Land line-connect: Timpanogos. Place it there,' and it's saying it repeatedly."

"That's the same message I got!" Morris enthusiastically shouted.

Michael continued to meditate while keeping both hands on the crystal. "It's now giving me a visual image of a beautiful mountain. The sky is deep blue, so I know it's not Aleyone. Yes, it's just given me verification that the scene is of Mt. Timpanogos."

"Oh, brilliant!" Morris exclaimed. "Now, all you have to do is transmit the scene to us, and we can go there. We didn't know how we were going to get there, as none of us have ever been to Utah."

"Oh, I see," said Michael, still concentrating on the crystal. "All right, everyone, here's the scene."

He transmitted the scene, and everyone saw a steep mountainside that looked like a stack of layered rock. Nearer the top, they could see several rock ledges at different levels within the tall vertical cliff. Fir trees and other plants were perched on those ledges, and they quickly realized that one of those ledges would become the new home for this exotic crystal.

In the foreground of the scene, there were several lakes. Snow covered the ground in selected areas, and there were patches of Fir trees interspersed throughout this large meadow.

"Yes, that looks like the perfect spot for it," Andrew commented.

"I agree," said Paul.

"Let's go there right away," James impatiently urged everyone.

"Wait, James," said Robert. "Let's not act on the spur of the moment. Let's get our plans straight first."

"Oh, and Michael," Robert continued, "do you think that our taking this beautiful green crystal back to Earth and away from Aleyone is going to have any negative repercussions on this planet?"

"None at all," he assured everyone. "Humans have done very well here on Aleyone for hundreds of thousands of years, and that's far longer than this crystal has been hiding here. Your Earth needs it returned. It was intended for Earth in the first place. As you see, it has requested a specific spot, Timpanogos, to be its new home, so it's ready to be transferred there."

"Good, that makes me feel a lot better," said Robert, "because I only want the best for your planet Aleyone."

"Thank you, and don't worry," Michael reassured him. "All of us have achieved full sentience here on Aleyone. Now, it's time for the Earthlings. They need the help of the crystal more than any other civilization in the galaxy."

"I'll agree with that," Morris commented.

"Oh, yeah," Robert suddenly realized. "Michael, we need to call Tom and tell him we've found the exotic crystal. Can I use your phone?"

"Certainly," he consented. "It's in the kitchen."

"Thanks," said Robert. He walked into the house to make the call. Meanwhile, the others discussed Earth, Mt. Timpanogos, and where on that mountain to possibly place the crystal. Robert entered the kitchen and picked up the handset of the phone. The dial tone came through but sounded more distant, originating from the Joslin's step office, 363 light years away. He dialled 274-7015 to reach the telephone station on Sirius B. The call went through, and he heard the ringing over the line.

"click ...BBBBBB...BBBBBB...BBBBBB...BBBBBB... Sirius B," answered a female voice.

"Yes, this is Robert Joslin. I'm calling from planet Aleyone in the Pleiades. Is Tom around?"

"Hold the line, and I'll send for him."

Robert waited 30 seconds.

"Hello, Robert," said Tom. "How are things going?"

"Great, Tom. We found the exotic crystal, and it looks just like you said."

"Have you?! Wonderful!" he declared. "That's great! Where did you find it?"

"We found it up on a high ledge on a cliff," Robert told him, and he related the whole story of their trek on the large island in the south sea, the mountains, the Archaeopteris trees, the clues, and exactly how they found it. "Also, Tom, we've been getting a strong message to place it on a mountain called Timpanogos."

"Yes, that name does sound familiar," said Tom. "If that's the message you've been receiving, then that's the place for the crystal to be taken."

"Okay, we're going to transport ourselves there today and place it on an inaccessible ledge on a cliff."

"Excellent idea," Tom approved. "It won't be stolen that way. I'm so overjoyed that you fellows have found it. Now there's hope for Earth after all."

"We're glad to be a part of it," said Robert.

"Oh, and Robert," Tom continued, changing the subject, "the Galactic Federation and I have decided that starting in September, we are going to upgrade the galactic communications device such that Chris and Richard's thousand-line step office will be the main galactic switching station while the one at your place in the woods will remain as the direct link to Earth's telephone network."

"We'll be back in school by then," Robert told him. "So, our summer travels will be finished."

"Anyway, those are the plans," said Tom. "Like I said earlier, we're not going to clutter your woods with a whole bunch of towers, but I think we may want to add four more towers, all facing the Garnet Star, as direct links to Chris and Richard's thousand-line step office."

"Yeah, I don't see any problem with that," Robert consented. "We already have six. So, with four more, that will be a total of 10. Yeah, that's okay with me, but let's not increase that anymore, after that."

"Fair enough, Robert. Anyway, thanks again for finding that exotic crystal. Your planet Earth will greatly benefit by its being returned there."

"We're glad to do it, especially since it will help out Earth," said Robert.

"Have a great rest of the summer travelling to different places, and feel free to come and visit me on Sirius B."

"Thank you, Tom. I guess we may see you later this summer, or we'll all talk in September, for sure."

"Right. Bye for now."

"Bye."

-click-

Robert hung up and then decided to make two more phone calls, and no, he didn't feel obliged to go ask Michael's permission. After all, the calls didn't cost any money! He phoned his parents and let them know that all of them were doing fine, and he briefly related all of the stories and adventures. Lastly, he asked them to tell the other parents that their next stop was Utah and that they were going to do some hiking in the mountains.

After he finished talking to his parents, he decided to check on Mr. Mayfield. He dialled 274-7010, the number assigned to Chris and Richard's thousand-line step office at their Earth museum. He heard the somewhat distant ringing over the line.

"click...pop...CHRRRR...CHRRRR...CHRRRR... Hello?" answered a female voice.

"May I speak to Chris or Richard Bell? This is Robert Joslin."

"Oh, right! Yes, I'm their mother. Hold the line, and I'll go fetch them."

Half a minute later, both Chris and Richard came on the line.

"Hello, Robert. How are you?" Chris spoke.

"I'm just fine. How are you all, and how is Mr. Mayfield?"

"We're both fine," Chris answered, "and Mr. Mayfield is really enjoying the place. He's explored a lot and has done some fishing as well."

"Where are you now?" Richard asked.

"We're all on planet Aleyone in the Pleiades Cluster," Robert informed them.

"Really? Tell us all about it," Chris requested.

For the next several minutes, Robert briefly related everything that they had done.

"That's really something!" Richard declared. "So, you're taking the crystal back to Earth with you?"

"That's right," Robert confirmed.

"When are you all coming to visit us and our planet?" Chris asked.

"Probably pretty soon, or some time in July, anyway," Robert answered. "I'm not sure, exactly. We may return here to explore some more first. This is a really peaceful and scenic planet."

"We'll look forward to your visit," said Chris. "Give us a ring when you know something about when you're coming."

"Will do," Robert agreed.

"Okay, all the best till then," said Richard.

"Same to you," said Robert.

"Okay, bye."

"Bye."

-click-

Robert hung up and returned to the others.

"My! You were on the phone a good while, weren't you?" James remarked.

"Yes," Robert admitted. "Tom and I had a lot to talk about. He said that he and the Galactic Federation decided that they'd like to upgrade the galactic communications device, starting in September."

"Really?" Steven responded.

"Yes, and they want to add four more towers to our step office in the woods," Robert informed them.

"You're going to have all kinds of clutter in your woods, aren't you, Robert?" William teased.

"Not if I have anything to do with it," Robert firmly stated. "I told him that once we reach 10 towers, that would be enough. He said fair enough."

"That's good," said Andrew. "After all, won't the main switching station be at Chris and Richard's Earth museum?"

"That's right," Robert answered.

"Are we ready to go?" James asked everyone.

"Yes, I believe so," said Robert.

"Harvey and Suzanne, do you want to come with us?" Steven offered.

"We'd love to," Harvey answered, "but we feel like the choosing and placing of the exotic crystal is totally in your hands."

"Tell you what," Suzanne offered. "Once you finish placing it on Mt. Timpanogos, feel free to return here. We'll be glad to join you for more adventures, here on Aleyone."

"Thank you very much," said Morris. "We may actually return, then. What do you say, everyone? Do we want to return here right away?"

"Sure," most of them said.

"James, I'm *sure* you want to return," Chris teased.

"Oh yes, of course," James replied with a smile, going along with the teasing.

"Well done, James," Suzanne told him.

"Yeah, you didn't even get mad this time," Robert added. "That's good."

"Not a problem, at all," he assured everyone.

Andrew retrieved the exotic crystal from the table and placed it inside his backpack.

They said farewell to each other, and the eight of them said that they would probably return sometime in the next couple of days. With those plans made, they transported themselves to the high alpine meadows on the east side of Mt. Timpanogos in Utah.

Epilogue

They arrived next to a grove of Fir trees at the edge of the grassy meadow. There was a lake nearby. It was the evening of Thursday, June 27, 1985, and it would not be much longer before sunset. The walls and cliffs of the mountain range to their west blocked the sun's rays, and the whole meadow was completely shaded as a result.

"My goodness!" Paul remarked. "It looks like it won't be long before dark, and we haven't been up very long today."

"I know," Chris agreed. "It still feels like morning to me."

"Well, let's set up camp," said William, "seeing it's soon going to be dark."

Immediately, they walked across the meadow and chose a nice spot by a lake that was next to a grove of Fir trees. The higher reaches of the mountain range were nearby, and lots of snow sat on its slopes. From the edge of this meadow, they could see far into the valley beyond them. In the distance were more mountains. They began to unpack their packs to set up camp.

Robert opened his pack and saw his Archaeopteris seedling.

"Oh, yeah!" Robert suddenly called out. "The Archaeopteris seedlings, everyone. We need to decide what to do with them."

"Right now?" Andrew asked.

"Yes," Robert insisted. "They need to be planted as soon as possible."

"What did Harvey and Suzanne do with theirs?" Morris asked.

"I don't know," Robert replied. "I guess they still have them."

"Maybe they planted them in their backyard," James speculated.

"Anyway, we have eight of them among us, right?" Robert checked.

All of them dug through their backpacks and carefully took out their seedlings. Every one of them was still intact. They placed them on the ground together.

"Who among us wants one?" Robert asked them.

"I know I do," James spoke up.

"Me too," said William.

"And, of course, I do," said Robert.

No one else spoke.

"What about the rest of you?" Robert asked with some concern. "We've got a total of eight, one for each of us."

"Robert, I just don't think my parents would be interested in having one," Steven told him.

"My parents just don't have time to take care of trees, seeing how busy they are," Paul informed him.

"Same here," Chris added.

"Robert, I don't have a good feeling about planting one in my yard," said Morris, "but I do have an idea. For those of us who, for one reason or another, don't want to plant them in our yards in Tennessee, let's plant our seedlings on the same ledge that we place the exotic crystal."

"That'll work," Paul approved.

"That's a good idea," Robert also approved. "Thank you, Morris. Okay then, it looks like we'll place five of these Archaeopteris seedlings with the crystal on one of those ledges further up the mountain. I believe I'm going to take mine home and plant it, right now." He picked out one of the seedlings.

"I'll go home too, Robert," William announced. "My father and mother both know the whole truth, anyway." He chose one of the seedlings.

"Take mine and plant it at your place, Robert," James offered. He picked one out. "I want our two Archaeopteris trees to grow by each other and keep each other company. Besides, they can represent our lifelong friendship."

Robert was astounded at his kindness. "Well, thank you very much, James. That's very kind of you. We are all good friends, here, and I hope that continues for all of us throughout our entire lifetimes."

"Tell you what," James offered. "I'll come with you, Robert, and we'll pick out a good spot in your yard."

"Go ahead and finish setting up camp," Robert told the others. "James, William, and I will return by dark." They transported themselves away, each one with a seedling.

The others remaining set up their tents and took it easy by the lake. Darkness arrived, and James, Robert, and William returned and informed the others that they had successfully planted three of the eight seedlings. The night was quite cold.

A frost sat on the ground the next morning, and the sky was entirely clear. When the sun broke the horizon, its light reflected and created a dazzling appearance on the ground as well as on the surrounding mountain slopes and cliffs. The bright snow really stood out.

They ate breakfast, packed up, and proceeded to hike further up the mountain slopes. It wasn't long before they found the main trail that led up to the summit of Mt. Timpanogos, and they followed it as it gently ascended and wound its way through a mostly open meadow full of various alpine flowers and boulders. Parts of it were still covered in snow.

There was a tall mountain range on their right, and it was only a subrange, as Mt. Timpanogos was more to their left. As they climbed through a mostly snow-covered gully, they crested and entered a large basin directly ahead of them. The main feature was a large glacier which ran from near the summit of the range and terminated in a medium-size lake directly ahead of them.

The horizontal layers of sedimentary rock, both limestone and sandstone, were clearly visible, and they made up the entire mountain range which towered above them. Much of the range consisted of sheer cliffs, and on the cliffs to their left, there were several ledges or shelves at different levels, most of them containing Fir trees. They looked entirely inaccessible. Nothing short of a highly technical climb, using ropes and climbing gear, would have allowed them access by conventional means. However, with their gift of transport, they knew it would be a piece of cake.

They walked through the basin and left the trail, after which they climbed the mostly snow-covered slopes to reach the bottom of the enormous cliff. When they were close enough to have a clear view of the ledges, they chose the most inaccessible one which was at least 200 meters above them. Together, they transported themselves and safely arrived on this narrow ledge.

"Whew-wee!" William shouted as he looked down. "I sure wouldn't want to fall off this one!"

"Yeah, no kidding!" Paul agreed.

The shelf or ledge was around 150 meters long, and its widest point along the entire length was seven meters. The rest of it was narrower. Clumps of Fir trees, some of them full size, grew in selected areas on this ledge, as they also did on other ledges in the vicinity. Shrubs, grasses, and moss grew on the soil which, in places, was several feet thick.

All eight of them walked up and down the length of this ledge, looking for the best possible spot to place the exotic crystal. Morris used his green Fluorite crystal ball to help him, hoping for it to glow at the appropriate time. It never did.

"My crystal won't glow or do anything," Morris informed the others.

"I believe the decision is entirely up to us," said Robert. "Let's use our decision-making abilities and choose a spot."

After walking up and down the ledge several times, they finally chose out a spot near a clump of Fir trees. The soil was at least two feet thick and was rich and moist. Water trickled down from above, and the location was very similar, geographically, to the spot on Aleyone where they had found the exotic crystal. The view of the partially snow-covered basin below was spectacular, and they could see far into the distance. The highest mountains of Utah, the High Uintas, sat to the east on the horizon.

"I believe this is a good spot," Andrew mentioned to the others.

"Yes, I like it too," Robert agreed.

"I say let's plant the seedlings first," James suggested.

"Good idea," Chris agreed.

Using a garden trowel, they dug five holes in the soft, rich soil and planted the five seedlings in two rows: two in the front near the edge, and three in the rear near the cliff's wall behind them.

Next, Andrew withdrew the large and exotic egg-shaped green crystal from his backpack and personally placed it on the soil in the middle of the five, newly planted Archaeopteris seedlings. To their absolute surprise, the crystal suddenly glowed a forest green, and the image of the orange pyramid within it glowed the most unusual orangish-yellow color imaginable. They stared at it in amazement as the crystal further proceeded to project a rainbow of colors around it. The illusion it created around itself twirled and pulsated for 20 seconds. After the incredible performance, its glow subsided, and the crystal resumed its normal state again.

"That was incredible!" Steven remarked.

"How in the world could that have been possible?" William asked everyone.

"You got me on that one," Paul admitted.

"I believe the crystal is in the right spot," Andrew declared with confidence.

"Yeah, that's an understatement," said James.

"I think that's the crystal's sign of thanks to us for bringing it to Earth," Morris told them.

"I agree," said Chris. "Let's hope things improve, now that this crystal is in place."

"Who knows," William speculated, "maybe the United States and the Soviet Union will stop being enemies and become friends."

"Huh! That'll be the day," Paul remarked.

"My mouth will drop open if *that* ever happens," Steven added.

"I think the miracle may actually occur, now that this crystal is in place," Robert predicted.

"You might be right," Chris agreed.

"I'll have to see that one to believe it," said James.

"Well, what do we want to do now?" Robert asked everyone.

"Let's go up Mt. Timpanogos," James eagerly suggested.

Everyone liked his idea. They took one last look at the crystal and at the five Archaeopteris seedlings and then proceeded to transport themselves off of the ledge. Seconds later, they returned to the lakeside at the bottom of the glacier in the basin.

They rejoined the trail and climbed uphill for a short while, soon arriving at a stone hut. All of them set their backpacks inside the shelter, ate some lunch, and then continued to the summit with daypacks.

As they followed the trail, they passed through a large level meadow. Next, they veered to the left and approached the foot of a massive cliff on whose top sat the summit of Mt. Timpanogos. At first, it was very rocky, and then they entered a snowfield which ran for over a mile, veering slowly to the right at the base of the curved cliff.

Finally, they left the snowfield and followed the trail as it switchbacked up the steep slope to the top of the jagged rocky ridge at a saddle. When they reached the ridge, they had excellent views of the huge valley beyond them to the west. At the base of the mountain sat the cities of Provo and Orem, and beyond that was a large lake with mountains further in the distance. To the northwest, they could just barely see Salt Lake.

They followed the trail as it kept along the ridge, mostly ascending, quite steeply at times. The wind blew fiercely, and it was cold. In 30 minutes, they reached the summit at 11,750 feet. There was an open metal shelter on top, and from it, they admired the views they had far and wide.

The ridge of Mt. Timpanogos stretched out from them, both to the north and the south. To the east, they could see even more than they had seen from the ledge where they had been this morning. They were on top of it all, and no land anywhere appeared to be higher.

After half an hour of resting, they started back down, reaching the saddle in half an hour. Once they began descending the steep slope on the trail's switchbacks, they were relieved to be out of the cold blowing wind. They continued for the next hour as they carefully made their way across the snowfield again.

To the north, they saw a dark cloud mass approaching, and plenty of thunder accompanied it as well. By the time they reached the lower end of the snowfield, the storm was very close, and they moved along as fast as they could, hoping to reach the stone hut before the storm.

As they ran across the open meadow, the downpour began, and even though they were only a couple hundred yards from the hut, they became drenched. Thunder and lightning bolted here and there, quite close at times. They reached the hut and immediately entered, glad to be out of the rain.

"I'm telling you what!" William declared. "I'm glad we didn't climb that mountain any later."

"Me too," James agreed.

"Greg and Eric sure have missed out on our adventures," Chris brought up.

"Yes, they certainly have," Morris agreed. "I don't guess it was meant to be."

"Probably not," said Andrew, "but I'm glad the eight of us could do all we've done."

The storm passed over in half an hour, and when the skies cleared above them they went outside to look at the scenery. It was now late afternoon. When they looked to the southeast, the direction the storm had moved, they couldn't believe what they saw. As the sunlight reflected off of the dark clouds, it created a double complete rainbow, the fainter one being above the main one. What a spectacular sight it was to behold! All of them were appalled.

"That is really a special gift!" William declared.

"I'll say," Robert agreed.

"It's as if the crystal is giving us one last sign of thanks," said Andrew.

". . . and is promising a better future for planet Earth," Morris concluded.

"Well, we still have two entire months left," Robert brought up. "Do we want to return to Aleyone or do something else?"

"Let's return to Aleyone," said James.

"Yeah, of course *you* do, James," Chris teased. "I know why *you* want to return."

"Chris, you'll never live that down, will you!" James remarked.

Suddenly Morris detected a slight ringing in his ears. "Hey, everyone! Quiet!" he called out. "I'm hearing some sort of message."

Everyone became silent.

"It's strange," Morris continued, "but I think it's something to do with that exotic crystal, where it came from. Yes, I'm hearing it! Antarctica! Something about . . ."

—TO BE CONTINUED—

Appendix:
Technical Description of Characters

8 Main Characters:

Chanford, Chris:
   species: human being, Earth type
   race or color: irrelevant
   height: 5′ 10″
   hair: brown, straight, medium
     length (ears partly covered)
   eyes: brown
   appearance: slender and strong
     with somewhat rounded face,

England, Morris:
   species: human being, Earth type
   race or color: irrelevant
   height: 5′ 8″
   hair: dark brown, mostly straight,
     shorter length (ears exposed)
   eyes: brown
   appearance: strong and stocky with
     long, rounded face,

Johns, William:
   species: human being, Earth type
   race or color: irrelevant
   height: marginal 6 feet
   hair: black, longish, parted in the
     middle (ears covered)
   eyes: brown
   appearance: slender and strong
     with somewhat rounded face,

Joslin, Robert:
   species: human being, Earth type
   race or color: irrelevant
   height: 5′ 10″
   hair: medium brown, slightly curly,
     shorter length
   eyes: green-brown
   appearance: slender and strong
     with somewhat long, narrow
     face,

Price, Steven:
   species: human being, Earth type
   race or color: irrelevant
   height: 5′ 10″
   hair: light brown, straight, medium
     length
   eyes: blue
   appearance: slender and strong
     with somewhat rounded face,

Tremain, Andrew:
   species: human being, Earth type
   race or color: irrelevant
   height: 5′ 9″
   hair: black, straight, medium
     length,
   eyes: brown
   appearance: slender and strong
     with somewhat narrow but
     rounded face,

Westfield, James:
   species: human being, Earth type
   race or color: irrelevant
   height: 5′ 10″
   hair: brown, straight, medium
     length
   eyes: brown
   appearance: slender and strong
     with somewhat rounded face,

Wilson, Paul:
   species: human being, Earth type
   race or color: irrelevant
   height: 5′ 10″
   hair: very light brown, somewhat
     wavy, longer length
   eyes: brown
   appearance: slender and strong
     with somewhat narrow face but
     higher cheekbones.

Other Characters:

Archaeopteris:
  species: tree, Pleiadean type (prehistoric to Earth)
  race or color: progymnosperm (forerunner to the conifers), mostly green
  height: to 30 meters
  leaves: Ginkgo-like, arranged in whorls around the branches
  appearance: like a Baldcypress, at a glance, but a broadleaf tree,
Bell, Chris:
  species: human being, from Garnet Star
  race or color: irrelevant
  height: 6' 1"
  hair: brown, fairly short
  eyes: brown
  appearance: tall and slender, squarish face, dressed in Earth-type clothing,
Bell, Richard:
  species: human being, from Garnet Star
  race or color: irrelevant
  height: 6' 2"
  hair: brown, medium length
  yes: green-brown
  appearance: tall and slender, squarish face, dressed in Earth-type clothing,
Carya:
  species: human being, Pleiadean type
  race or color: irrelevant
  height: 5' 6"
  hair: brown, straight, longer length
  eyes: brown
  appearance: slender and attractive, somewhat longer face, dressed in Earth-type clothing,

Caymar:
  species: human being, Sirian type
  race or color: irrelevant
  height: 6 feet
  hair: dark brown, medium length
  eyes: brown
  appearance: tall and slender, appearing to be in his 20's, somewhat longer face,
Crystal Ball:
  species: crystal, silicon type, naturally grown on Earth
  race or color: Natural Clear Quartz
  size (diameter): 7 centimeters
  appearance: artificially crafted into a round ball from geometrically shaped clear quartz, contains internal cracks,
Exotic Crystal:
  species: crystal, silicon type, artificially grown on Earth over 100,000 years ago
  race or color: Green Fluorite and Citrine (orange)
  length (end to end): 25 centimeters
  appearance: egg-shaped, greenish-blue appearing in various shades or bands throughout, contains pyramid within,
Forvueweb, Mrs.:
  species: human being, Earth type
  race or color: irrelevant
  height: 5' 5"
  hair: gray and gathered around head
  eyes: hazel (blue-gray)
  appearance: stocky, round faced, older looking,
Harvey:
  species: human being, Pleiadean type
  race or color: irrelevant
  height: 6 feet
  hair: light brown, shorter length
  eyes: green-brown
  appearance: slender and strong, dressed in Earth-type clothing,

Ingra:
  species: human being, Vegan type
  race or color: irrelevant
  height: 5' 10"
  hair: brown, longer length
  eyes: brown
  appearance: slender, mid 50's,
    wears a white robe,
Mayfield, Gordon:
  species: human being, Earth type
  race or color: irrelevant
  height: 6 feet
  hair: grayish, wiry but straight,
    short
  eyes: blue
  appearance: slender, stocky (strong
    as an ox), stocky face,
Michael:
  species: human being, Pleiadean
    type
  race or color: irrelevant
  height: 6 feet
  hair: light brown, shorter length
  eyes: blue-brown
  appearance: slender and strong,
    dressed in Earth-type clothing,
Nelson, Greg:
  species: human being, Earth type
  race or color: irrelevant
  height: 6' 1"
  hair: brown, straight and somewhat
    thin, medium length
  eyes: blue
  appearance: slender and strong,
    squarish face with high cheek-
    bones,
Peters, Mark:
  species: human being, Earth type
  race or color: irrelevant
  height: 5' 8"
  hair: dark brown, shorter length,
    slightly curly
  eyes: brown
  appearance: slender, almost wiry,
    strong,

Smotherman, Eric:
  species: human being, Earth type
  race or color: irrelevant
  height: 5' 10"
  hair: light brown, curly, medium
    length
  eyes: blue
  appearance: slender and strong
    with rounded face,
Suzanne:
  species: human being, Pleiadean
    type
  race or color: irrelevant
  height: 5' 6"
  hair: lighter colored, almost gold-
    en, longer length
  eyes: blue
  appearance: slender, attractive,
    rounded face, dressed in Earth-
    type clothing,
Tom:
  species: human being, Sirian type
  race or color: irrelevant
  height: 6' 4"
  hair: nearly black, mostly straight,
    longer length
  eyes: brown
  appearance: tall and slender,
    almost boyish with somewhat
    longer face; wears a white robe,
Vance, Michael:
  species: human being, Earth type
  race or color: irrelevant
  height: 5' 11"
  hair: black, curly, fairly short
  eyes: green-brown
  appearance: slender with somewhat
    narrow face,
Virginia:
  species: human being, Earth type
  race or color: irrelevant
  height: 5' 5"
  hair: lighter colored, almost gold-
    en, longer length
  eyes: blue-brown
  appearance: stocky but still slender,
    rounded face.

Acknowledgments & Credits

I wish to give thanks to the following people for their help and/or ideas:

—Dr. Glenn Turner for spending time explaining to me about the evolution of trees on Earth, showing me various books, and loaning me others,

—The real Morris England of the story for speculative data and ideas on various star systems, letters, and conversations,

—Mr. William Goodlett for talking with me by telephone, discussing his experiences and ideas, sending me a list of books to read, and for sending me two 90-minute cassette tapes detailing his experiences, (William Goodlett passed away in January 1996. He was 87.)

—Mr. Arthur Ebbets for putting me in contact with William Goodlett,

—The real Virginia of the story for her conversations, ideas, and speculation in general,

—My aunt Joan Pelot Rice for phoning a man in California for speculative galactic data,

—Mr. Vanzant for having a discussion with one of his classes about dolphins, whales, and their intelligence in comparison to humans,

—Riverdale High School library for allowing me to check out a novel which contributed ideas,

—Mr. Lamar Ray for taking me on a tour of the Abbeville, Georgia step-by-step telephone exchange in January 1995 and for explaining to me how it works, (Abbeville was converted to digital May 14, 1995.)

—Mr. Ray Crawford and Mr. Ray Wilson of Alpha Equipment Company, Crossville, Tennessee, for showing me around the warehouse and explaining to me exactly how a step-by-step telephone exchange works,

—MR. and MRS. CHARLES SMITH for the use of their computer and printer to type in my entire novel, a most generous thing, indeed,

—LOUISE POWELL "SAM" ALEXANDER for her generosity in scanning in all of my illustrations and storing them on disks, as well as printing them out on her laser printer in half-tone format,

—Andrew Tramell for his help and technical assistance as I typed in my novel on the computer, and for a preliminary printout,

—Paul Smith, Elaine S. Smith, and Mark Bailey for their help and advice as I used the computer,

—Eric Fagerburg for his technical assistance along the way,

—Jason Daniel Fisher for his fine illustrations used throughout the text of my novel, as well as drawing the color front cover,

—Donald R. Bachler and Greg Nicholson for their time and effort in being contributing artists,

—Corky Dunagan for his ideas and conversations about crystals,

—Martin A. Enticknap for the use of the words and concepts of: Danetar, Delikadove, Dolphs, and Shakeilar via his novel EXODUS, Book One of the Dolph/in Saga, 1990-95, (His science fiction-fantasy novel is an excellent story about the history of the origin of the dolphins and whales, their previous home planet, and how they arrived on Earth. EXODUS, Book One of the Dolph/in Saga has yet to be published at this time, 1996, but once it is, I recommend reading it.)

—[For those who wish to read EXODUS, Book One of the Dolph/in Saga, I am requesting that you write or phone Orion House in London, England and urge them to publish his novel. They have a copy of his manuscript.]

    Caroline Oakley
    Orion House
    5 Upper St. Martin's Lane   ph. 011-44-171-240-3444
    London, England WC2H 9EA
    <u>Great Britain</u>

—Dr. Mark Semon, a physics professor, for checking my accuracy in technical descriptions of transport and of galactic communication through the use of gravity waves,

—My immediate family for their support, suggestions, and ideas and for helping me to think of a title, something I didn't do until I had written half of this story,

—Friends and relatives for their support and ideas,

—Richard Courtney, Harold McAlindon, and Kay McGhee of Eggman Publishing Company in Nashville, Tennessee for taking on the project of publishing my novel,

—Donna Paz for her consultation and suggestions pertaining to my cover design,

—Becky Menn-Hamblin and Laurelyn Douglas for their steps in editing and proofreading my novel,

—Kevin Kearney for converting my computer files from Lotus Ami Pro to Word Perfect to make them easier for the typesetter to read them in,

—Thomas P. Seigenthaler Public Relations for their assistance in marketing and public relations,

—Guy R. Dotson, Jr., Kevin Kearney, and Sandra Y. Taylor for their advice and consultation,

—Eric Kampmann of Mid Point Trade Book Company.

Copies of the novel: MISSION OF THE GALACTIC SALESMAN may be ordered directly from:

Armstrong Valley Publishing Co.
P.O. Box 1275
Murfreesboro, TN 37133
Ph: 615-895-5445
FAX: 615-893-2688

Please send me:	quantity	amount
MISSION OF THE GALACTIC SALESMAN @$14.95	_____	$_____
Plus 8¼% sales tax (Tennessee residents only)		$_____
Plus shipping and handling for one book (surface rates: $2.50 within U.S.A., $4.00 foreign)		$_____
Plus shipping and handling for each additional book ($1.50 within U.S.A., $2.50 foreign)	_____	$_____
Please remit funds in U.S. Dollars	Total enclosed	$_____

Discounts:
      10 to 99 books: 10% off
      100 or more books: 20% off

Books make great gifts for your friends and relatives.

Send order to:

Name _____

Address _____

City _____ State _____ postal code _____

phone number (optional) _____

A query for the reader:
    If you are someone who astral travels to other star systems and are also very interested in trees and shrubs, knowing and having paid special attention to details such as specific species types, and also knowing which specific star systems you've travelled to, I would like to talk to you about which trees grow where and how they compare to Earth's trees and shrubs, whether the same or different. This is a subject of interest I am researching. Please contact me at the above listed Armstrong Valley Publishing Company. *Robert L. Sanders, Jr.*

ORDER FORM

Use this form to order additional copies of
MISSION OF THE GALACTIC SALESMAN
for your friends or family members.

Name: _____

Address: _____

City: _____ St:____ Zip: _____

Daytime phone: (_____)_____

If gift, message that you would like enclosed: _____

_____

_____

If gift, ship to:

Name _____

Address: _____

City: _____ St:____ Zip: _____

Quantity: _____ x $14.95 = $_____

TN residents add 8.25% sales tax: $_____

Shipping & Handling for <u>one book</u>

(surface rates: $2.50 within U.S.A., $4.00 foreign) $_____

Shipping & Handling for <u>each additional book</u>

($1.50 within U.S.A., $2.50 foreign) Qty: _____ x _____ = $_____

Please remit funds in U.S. dollars   Total: $_____

Volume discounts available. See previous page.

Please return form and payment to: **Armstrong Valley Publishing Co.**
P.O. Box 1275
Murfreesboro, TN 37133
Ph: 615-895-5445
FAX: 615-893-2688

Thank You!
Your order will be shipped within 3-6 weeks from receipt